How to access the supplemental online student resource

We are pleased to provide access to an online student resource that supplements your textbook, *Leisure Services Management*. This resource offers sample documents and forms used by practicing managers, case studies, Web links, a competency scorecard, and more.

Accessing the online student resource is easy! Simply follow these steps:

1. Using your Web browser, go to the **Leisure Services Management** product Web site at **www.HumanKinetics.com/ LeisureServicesManagement**.

2. Click on the **View Student Resources** button on the right side of the home page.

3. Click on the please register now link. You will create your personal profile and password at this time.

4. Write your e-mail and password down for future reference. Keep it in a safe place.

5. Once you are registered, enter the key code exactly as it is printed at the right, including all hyphens. Click **Submit**

6. Once the key code has been submitted, you will see a welcome screen. Click the **Continue** button to open your online student resource.

7. After you enter the key code the first time, you will not need to use it again to access the resource. In the future, simply log in using your e-mail and the password you created.

For technical support, send an e-mail to:
support@hkusa.com . . . . U.S. and international customers
info@hkcanada.com . . . . Canadian customers
academic@hkeurope.com . . . . European customers
keycodesupport@hkaustralia.com . . . . Australian customers

HUMAN KINETICS
The Information Leader in Physical Activity

Product: Leisure Services Management online student resource

Key code: HURD-62U3PU63-0736069224

This unique code allows you access to the online student resource

Access is provided if you have purchased a new book. Once submitted, the code may not be entered for any other user.

Leisure Services Management

Amy R. Hurd ❙ Robert J. Barcelona ❙ John T. Meldrum

Human Kinetics

Library of Congress Cataloging-in-Publication Data

Hurd, Amy R.
  Leisure services management / Amy R. Hurd, Robert J. Barcelona, John T. Meldrum.
    p. cm.
  Includes bibliographical references and index.
  ISBN-13: 978-0-7360-6922-9 (hard cover)
  ISBN-10: 0-7360-6922-4 (hard cover)
  1. Recreation--Management. 2. Public relations. I. Barcelona, Robert J., 1970- II. Meldrum,
John T. III. Title.
  GV181.5H87 2008
  790.06'9--dc22

                            2008009100

ISBN-10: 0-7360-6922-4
ISBN-13: 978-0-7360-6922-9

The Web addresses cited in this text were current as of May 2008, unless otherwise noted.

Acquisitions Editor: Gayle Kassing, PhD; **Developmental Editor:** Ray Vallese; **Special Projects Editor:** Anne Cole; **Assistant Editors:** Derek Campbell and Anne Rumery; **Copyeditor:** Alisha Jeddeloh; **Proofreader:** Anne Rogers; **Indexer:** Betty Frizzell; **Permission Managers:** Carly Breeding and Martha Gullo; **Graphic Designer:** Bob Reuther; **Graphic Artist:** Denise Lowry; **Cover Designer:** Bob Reuther; **Photographer (cover):** © Human Kinetics and © Photodisc (top left); **Photographer (interior):** © Human Kinetics, unless otherwise specified; see page xi for a full list of photo credits; **Photo Asset Manager:** Laura Fitch; **Photo Office Assistant:** Jason Allen; **Visual Production Assistant:** Joyce Brumfield; **Art Manager:** Kelly Hendren; **Associate Art Manager:** Alan L. Wilborn; **Illustrators:** Jennifer Gibas and Joanne Brummett; **Printer:** Sheridan Books

Chapter 4: Legal Foundations for Managers written by John O. Spengler, JD, PhD.

We thank the Springer Cultural Center in Champaign, Illinois, and Durst Cycle in Urbana, Illinois, for assistance in providing the locations for the photo shoot for this book.

Printed in the United States of America   10   9   8   7   6   5   4   3   2   1

Human Kinetics
Web site: www.HumanKinetics.com

United States: Human Kinetics, P.O. Box 5076, Champaign, IL 61825-5076
800-747-4457
e-mail: humank@hkusa.com

Canada: Human Kinetics, 475 Devonshire Road Unit 100, Windsor, ON N8Y 2L5
800-465-7301 (in Canada only)
e-mail: info@hkcanada.com

Europe: Human Kinetics, 107 Bradford Road, Stanningley, Leeds LS28 6AT, United Kingdom
+44 (0) 113 255 5665
e-mail: hk@hkeurope.com

Australia: Human Kinetics, 57A Price Avenue, Lower Mitcham, South Australia 5062
08 8372 0999
e-mail: info@hkaustralia.com

New Zealand: Human Kinetics, Division of Sports Distributors NZ Ltd., P.O. Box 300 226 Albany, North Shore City, Auckland
0064 9 448 1207
e-mail: info@humankinetics.co.nz

Contents

Preface

The leisure services profession is vast and ever changing, and it requires managers who are equipped to meet its challenges. The purpose of *Leisure Services Management* is to prepare students to be those managers. Whether students plan to pursue a career in commercial recreation, work in a public agency, or be part of the nonprofit sector, they all will need management skills to be successful. The authors have worked to make each chapter a journey through management that requires students to step into the manager's shoes and explore modern concerns in leisure services.

By the end of the book, it is our desire that students will understand what a manager does and how this work affects the agency, customer, and profession. Hopefully, students will feel better prepared to accept the challenges they will face as managers and have some foresight into what to expect in their first job.

Scope of the Text

The content of *Leisure Services Management* is competency driven. Research has determined what knowledge, skills, and abilities entry-level practitioners need in order to be successful, and the text presents these competencies in such a way that an effective manager can emerge. The book is aimed at junior and senior undergraduates who have some experience in the field. It is our hope that students will read each chapter and apply their own experiences to the discussion to better understand management in this dynamic profession.

The book begins by building a foundation of what management is and where it has been historically and conceptually. It then moves to the framework of organizations from structure to planning to coordinating resources. The remainder of the text focuses on specific skill areas that managers need, such as marketing, financial management, human resources management, technology, communication, and evaluation.

Features and Benefits

Leisure Services Management has several beneficial features:

▶ This text centers on making students better managers. A main component to that is the competency scorecard (see page 9), which details competencies needed for entry-level professionals. In addition to the scorecard highlighting competencies, students can use the scorecard to measure their own skills and experience.

▶ Each chapter starts with learning outcomes to guide the reader and illustrate the central themes and competencies of that chapter.

▶ Throughout the book there are snapshots of professionals in the field. These sections, called "A Day in the Life," come from current professionals who were students themselves not too long ago.

▶ To ensure that students understand the main concepts of each chapter, review questions are provided. These questions require students to analyze and apply the content.

▶ A running glossary is provided throughout the text as a quick reference to terms used in the chapters.

▶ A concerted effort is made to provide examples from the public, nonprofit, and commercial sectors. Sometimes these examples illustrate differences in sectors or further reiterate a point made in a particular section.

▶ This textbook features numerous examples and discussion about parks and recreation in Canada and the United States, providing a multinational perspective on management.

Leisure Services Management also includes three appendixes that outline how the authors believe the book addresses professional standards.

▶ The National Recreation and Park Association (NRPA) Council on Accreditation has standards that university-accredited programs must follow. Accredited programs meet or exceed established criteria to demonstrate educational quality. The accreditation standards addressed by the chapters are outlined in appendix A.

▶ The Commission for Accreditation of Park and Recreation Agencies (CAPRA) administers a voluntary program of accreditation to entities that manage park and recreation systems. The CAPRA standards addressed by the chapters are outlined in appendix B.

▶ Becoming a certified park and recreation professional (CPRP) is one source of credentialing for this profession. The CPRP examination is one of the primary requirements for certification, and appendix C outlines the study guide topics addressed in the chapters.

The text also comes with an online student resource. This resource includes:

▶ an electronic version of the competency scorecard on page 9, allowing students to print a copy to fill in,

▶ an overview of the key concepts covered by each chapter,

▶ links to relevant Web sites where students can find further discussion of chapter content,

▶ case studies presenting situations that students may encounter as leisure services managers, and

▶ more than a hundred real policies, organizational charts, budgets, and other documents provided by leisure and recreation agencies to illustrate how students will use similar tools in their first job.

A reminder at the end of each chapter directs students to take advantage of the resources offered by this online ancillary.

Acknowledgments

A textbook is quite an undertaking and one that is challenging, frustrating, rewarding, and time consuming. Because of this, it is important that we thank Illinois State University, the University of New Hampshire, and the University of Victoria. Administration and fellow faculty were always supportive, and our students played an instrumental part in allowing us to test material and case studies on them—jokingly serving as our guinea pigs.

This text would not have come about without the tireless efforts of the Human Kinetics staff. They were a terrific group to work with and we appreciate them immensely: Gayle Kassing, Ray Vallese, Derek Campbell, Carly Breeding, Bob Reuther, Denise Lowry, and many others.

In addition, it is imperative to acknowledge the researchers in the field who have impacted management. For Bob and me, Dr. Dan McLean would be at the top of the list. Dan gave us our foundation in management as graduate students at Indiana University and sparked competency research in parks and recreation.

Although we are bound to leave someone out, we want to show our appreciation to the following people for making management in this field a part of their scholarly agenda: Joe Bannon, John Crompton, Chris Edginton, Gary Ellis, Alan Graefe, Mark Havitz, Dennis Howard, Susan Hudson, Richard Kraus, Sam Lankford, Ron McCarville, Bill McKinney, Larry Neal, Ellen O'Sullivan, Robert Rossman, Betty VanDerSmissen, and Peter Witt. Your influence is immeasurable.

Thanks to the practitioners in the field who allow us to stay "grounded" in practice by allowing us access to their organizations for research and student development opportunities, and pro-viding their expertise and thoughts on real-world applications of management scholarship.

All three of us must thank our families and friends. I don't think any of us thought this one book would impact so many people before even one copy was printed. I am most indebted to my family and support system, Dr. Deb Garrahy, and my parents Mike Hurd and Linda Downhour. You gave a lot of much-needed patience, love, and support throughout this process. I would also like to thank Dr. Alberto Delgado for his assistance on some fiscal management aspects of the book and Dr. Sandra Little Groves, who gave me the best advice: just get it on paper; you have great editors to clean it up!

—Amy

* * *

I would like to thank my wife (Heather-Dale Barcelona) and children (Madeline and Nathan) for their patience and support during the textbook writing and editing process.

Thank you to my colleagues in the department of recreation management and policy at the University of New Hampshire for their encouragement and flexibility during the writing process. Special thanks to Dr. Janet Sable for providing me with the time, space, and resources to contribute to this book, and to Dr. Ann Morgan for her willingness to answer my questions about federal, state, and provincial nondiscrimination legislation.

—Bob

* * *

I would like to express my deepest appreciation and thanks to Mary for her love, support, and humor; to J.P. and Cameron for continuing to put a smile on my face and helping me keep my priorities straight; and to my mom for her unquestioning love and support. I would also like to acknowledge my dad, a true gentleman who taught me by example that it is important always to acknowledge the efforts and contributions of those people in our lives who often go unrecognized.

—John

Credits

Photo on page xii by Eyewire.

All "A Day in the Life" photos are courtesy of the respective contributors.

Photos on pages 12, 84, and 164 © Brand X Pictures.

Photos on pages 18, 29, 38, 44, 49, 67, 128, 232, and 274 © Photodisc.

Photo on page 23 by AP Photo/Ford Archives.

Photo on page 45 courtesy of Cameron Meldrum.

Photos on pages 54, 122, 199, 318, and 331 © Amy Hurd.

Photos on pages 58, 215, and 266 © AP Images.

Photo on page 80 (top) © Realistic Reflections/Getty Images.

Photo on page 106 © AP Images/Francois Mori.

Photo on page 119 © AP Images/M Spencer Green.

Photos on pages 138, 158, 284, 304, and 342 © Bananastock.

Photo on page 146 courtesy of the Saint Paul Parks and Recreation Division.

Photo on page 194 © Tim Boyle/Getty Images News/Getty Images.

Photo on page 204 © AP Images/Daniel Ochoa de Otza.

Photo on page 220 © AP Images/Steamboat Pilot & Today, Matt Stensland.

Photo on page 244 © AP Images/The Journal Record, Jennifer Pitts.

Photo on page 262 © Getty Images/DAJ.

Photo on page 279 © 1999 PhotoDisc, Inc.

Photo on page 293 courtesy of Seattle Parks & Recreation.

Photo on page 296 courtesy of Kevin Laven.

Photo on page 338 © PhotoDisc/Getty Images.

Photo on page 357 courtesy of Deb Garrahy.

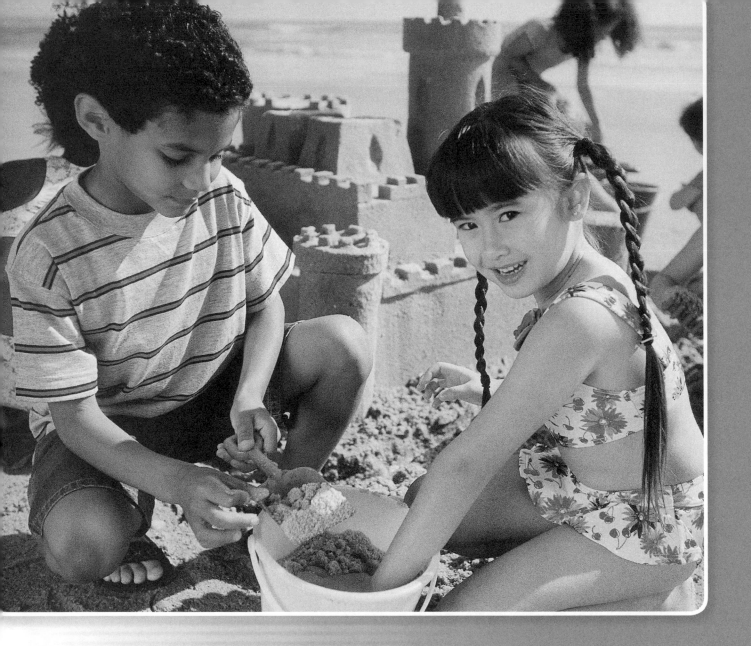

KEY WORDS

competencies, characteristics

COMPETENCY CHECK

Take another look at table 1.3 (page 9) to see how you assessed this related competency.

3. Possess knowledge of management principles.

CHAPTER 1

The Competent Leisure Services Manager

1. Define *management*.
2. Understand the model for effective performance.
3. Understand competency-based management.
4. Describe competencies needed by entry-level park and recreation managers.

The greatest part of working in college athletics is that a new and unpredictable challenge always awaits. My job primarily involves six key aspects within event management and game operations: planning, preparing, implementing, monitoring, reacting, and problem solving. The most vital part of my job relates to the problem-solving component, which is making good decisions and choices for the well-being of the department. The purpose of my position is to communicate and coordinate with our game day staff. Many issues come up with games and events, including weather-related issues where we have to plan to evacuate 10,000 patrons efficiently from the stadium in case of lightning, finding NCAA Division I basketball officials within an hour's notice, or dealing with irate fans or upset patrons. The best part of working in athletics is being a part of the team. Each and every day, you feel valued and know you had a little part in creating a winning competitive environment. At the end of each event, it is my purpose to make sure that we functioned effectively as a staff and that our customers left with an enjoyable experience at Redbird Athletics.

Tracie Brown
Director of Events and Game Operations
Illinois State Athletics
Normal, Illinois

The park and recreation profession is often misunderstood by the general public. As professionals in this field, you will most likely hear questions such as the following:

▶ "What do you do in the winter?"
▶ "They pay people to do that?"
▶ "That's a real major?"
▶ "How did you learn about that profession?"

People may not realize that this is a profession, but they know leisure when they see it. They recognize it when they enjoy their vacation at Amelia Island Plantation in Florida, when their child takes swim lessons, or when they visit a national park. People understand what leisure is, but they do not understand what goes into being successful in the field. Among other things, success will result from a proper education and from experience that includes leadership, programming, and management. At this point in the academic career of a student majoring in parks and recreation, leadership and programming classes have probably been completed and the next step is management.

What Is Management?

Management is the critical centerpiece of any agency regardless of whether it is a public park and recreation department, a facility on a military base, a nonprofit agency such as the Boys and Girls Club, or a commercial agency such as Hilton Head Resort. Management is the driving force that ensures tasks get done correctly.

Management has been defined in a number of ways because it is a broad area and an integral part of all

Coordination and integration of resources
• Human
• Financial
• Physical
• Technological

→ Efficient and effective achievement of goals and objectives.

Figure 1.1 Management defined.

organizations. For the purpose of this text, *management* is defined as the process of coordinating and integrating resources in order to effectively and efficiently achieve organizational goals and objectives (figure 1.1). These resources include human, financial, physical, and information and technology resources, and they are discussed in detail throughout the text.

Given this definition of management, logic tells us that managers are people who manage—they motivate others to get things done. Imagine a company that has no managers. No one is organizing the tasks to be done and no one is accountable to anyone else in the organization. The result is chaos, which does not lead to success. Thus, managers are a necessity in any organization.

Universality of Management

Before going any further, it is important to talk about the universality of management. Students have many different interests in the field of parks and recreation. They may be interested in tourism, sport, arts, therapeutic recreation, military recreation, fitness, outdoor education, or public parks and recreation. This text does not focus on any one of these areas; given the nature of management, such specification is not necessary. Management has a universality that makes it applicable to all fields: All managers have to coordinate and integrate their resources. The difference lies in what those resources are. National parks have park rangers, hotels have sales staff, and Boy and Girl Scouts have troop leaders. These human resources all have different jobs, but there is still a need to coordinate them.

Multisector Perspective

In addition to creating effective managers, this book examines management from the perspective of the public, nonprofit, and commercial sectors in both the United States and Canada. It looks at the similarities and differences among various jobs in the recreation field. Examples are provided that cover outdoor recreation; municipal, state, and provincial recreation; the hospitality industry; sport; arts; and special events. Throughout the text, the term *parks and recreation* is used to cover the gamut of the profession from tourism and therapeutic recreation to military recreation and public parks. Many times the sector will not matter in terms of management, but when it does, it will be brought to the forefront. The chapters that follow are meant to provide a well-rounded glimpse of management in the profession, not just management in public, nonprofit, or commercial recreation alone.

Stepping Into a Manager's Shoes

Over the following chapters, you will put yourself in the shoes of a manager. You will explore many aspects of management, including human resources management, marketing management, planning, and technology. You will be given exercises, case studies, and scenarios drawn from real situations in the field to help you start to think like a manager. By the end of this book, it is our hope that you will understand what being a manager is about and have the skills to work in an entry-level position in this field.

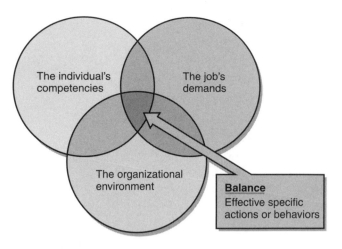

Figure 1.2 Model for effective performance.

Adapted, by permission, from R.E. Boyatzis, 1982, *The competent manager: A model for effective performance* (New York, NY: John Wiley & Sons, Inc.), 13.

competencies—Skills, knowledge, and characteristics needed to be successful in a job.

Being an Effective Manager

Being an effective manager means meeting the goals, objectives, and expectations of the agency you work in. Although effectiveness is discussed in chapter 3, the model of effectiveness is discussed here to show you where this text is headed and what you can expect to learn.

To be an effective manager, there are three components to consider. Effectiveness results when there is a balance between a person's competencies, the job demands, and the organizational environment (figure 1.2) (Boyatzis, 1982).

First, individual **competencies** are skills, knowledge, and characteristics that a person needs to be successful in a job. In the model of effectiveness, individual competencies encompass not only what people do on the job but what they are capable of doing as well. In order for an agency to be effective, the staff has to be highly skilled. Later in the chapter, you will learn what competencies are needed to be successful as an entry-level manager in the field. These competencies are the foundation for this text. Individual skill will also be built in the areas of marketing (chapter 8), human resources management (chapters 10 and 11), finance and budgeting (chapters 12 and 13), and evaluation (chapter 14), among others. These chapters focus on skills in technical areas that you can bring to that first job.

The second component of effectiveness is job demands. Job demands are the functions of management—planning, organizing, leading, and controlling—that are discussed throughout the text. Such demands include tasks performed, roles of the manager, and the manager's function within the organization. The job functions aspect of effectiveness will be learned through topics such as theory and current issues in management and leadership (chapter 2), the roles and functions of managers (chapter 3), legal concerns and risk management in recreation (chapter 4), and the role of technology in the profession (chapter 7). These factors compose the culture and structure that an organization needs in order to be effective.

Finally, the organizational environment includes the climate and culture of the organization. It can include structure of the organization (chapter 5); policies, procedures, and coordination of resources (chapter 6); and communication methods (chapter 9). A manager is only effective when the three components are balanced. An incompetent manager, an organization with poor organizational structure and policies, or a misalignment of job demands will not be effective. Only when all three are aligned and working properly will effectiveness occur.

As you can see, each chapter in *Leisure Services Management* is a building block to becoming an effective manager. By the end of this book, you should have a solid understanding of the dimensions of management and how the skills you have learned can be applied in the field.

Competency-Based Management

Many textbooks on management are divided into sections based on the functions of management—planning, organizing, leading, and controlling. Because it is the intention of this text to help create a successful manager, a competency-based approach to effective management is ingrained throughout the chapters more so than a typical function of management approach.

The competency piece of the model for effective performance is the foundation of the text because competencies help build the other two pieces. In order to be successful in the dimension of job demands, a person must be skilled and able to meet the demands of the job. The organizational environment dimension of the model is a little more difficult to conceptualize because it represents the big picture, or the organization as a whole. For managers to be successful at the organizational level and not just the individual level, they need to acquire competence in areas that affect the entire organization, such as structure and communication. Because job demands and environment are so closely tied to competencies, there is a significant amount of discussion on competencies.

The competencies required for a successful leisure services manager are broad, as can be seen from the diversity of topics covered in this text. By no means are entry-level employees expected to be experts in all areas, but new managers must be proficient enough to make good decisions and be willing to ask the right questions of people who are experts in various areas.

Entry-Level Management Competencies

Academic preparation to become a leisure services professional develops a knowledge base leading to a set of skills that can be used in an entry-level position. The ultimate goal of a degree program is to get a job, but many students question whether they are skilled in the right areas to be competitive in the job market. We propose that there is a competency set that students should strive to attain in order to reach the goal of being hired in an entry-level position upon graduation. Each chapter focuses on different parts of this competency framework.

Before discussing the specific competencies required for entry-level managers, the term *competencies* needs to be defined. Competencies are skills, knowledge, characteristics, and abilities needed to be successful in the profession (figure 1.3).

Developing competencies for a broad profession such as parks and recreation is a difficult task. As you will see throughout this book, the different sectors have special challenges in terms of management, particularly structure and funding. However, research on competencies in the public sector (Hurd, 2005), recreational sport (Barcelona & Ross, 2004), commercial recreation (Hammersley & Tynon, 1998), park and recreation professional certification specifications, and the nonprofit sector has been used to create a competency model to guide the development of qualifications for

Skills	**Knowledge**
Physical or psychomotor aptitudes required to perform particular tasks and actions of a job	Understanding of information required for the position
Characteristics	**Abilities**
Distinguishing qualities, attributes, or traits	Aptitudes for a position, or what and how well a person is able to perform certain tasks or behaviors

Figure 1.3 Elements of competencies.

Table 1.1 Entry-Level Competencies

General competency categories	Specific competencies
Business acumen	Understand financial processes (i.e., purchasing, budget).
	Develop, monitor, and stay within a budget.
	Possess knowledge of management principles.
	Demonstrate basic knowledge of laws and legal matters affecting the field.
	Understand technology and how to use it.
Communications	Clearly communicate with staff, customers, and the public.
	Possess effective written and oral communication skills.
	Listen to staff and customers.
	Implement marketing techniques.
	Communicate the organization's values, vision, and mission.
Community relations	Know the community and its needs.
	Understand customer service practices.
	Have the ability to deal with the public.
	Develop partnerships with other organizations.
	Work with boards and elected officials.
Interpersonal skills	Be creative and innovative.
	Be flexible.
	Have patience.
	Be enthusiastic and have a positive attitude.
	Be open-minded.
	Deal with personality conflicts.
	Understand the concept of criticism and accept constructive criticism.
	Take initiative.
Management techniques	Use effective problem-solving and conflict-resolution skills.
	Make ethical decisions.
	Understand the hiring process.
	Supervise, discipline, and evaluate a diverse staff.
	Motivate employees.
	Have leadership skills and abilities.
	Be able to work in a team.
	Use effective organizational skills.
	Prioritize and manage multiple tasks.
	Demonstrate effective time-management skills.
	Conduct program evaluations.
	Schedule programs, leagues, and staff.
	Network within and outside the profession.
	Participate in policy formation, evaluation, and revision.
Planning and evaluation	Provide input on strategic, master, recreation, marketing, and technology plans.
	Conduct research and evaluation.
	Conduct needs assessments.

entry-level positions in the park and recreation field (table 1.1). The topics discussed in this text will help build these competencies and the competency portion of the model of effectiveness.

The competencies for entry-level park and recreation professionals can be categorized into six general categories, including business acumen, communications, community relations, interpersonal skills, management techniques, and planning and evaluation. Not every entry-level position in the field will require all of these competencies, but they are an excellent starting point for future professionals to gauge their strengths and weaknesses. Similar to a strategic plan for an organization, these competencies can serve as a scorecard for developing the skills to be a better manager and increasing your chances of being hired. Each chapter provides a snapshot of the competencies that can be met by acquiring the knowledge from that chapter.

Competency Use for Managers

Competencies are outlined here to create a picture of what you need to be able to do in order to get an entry-level position in the field. However, competencies are not just for students. They are for all levels of the organization and serve several functions for managers. The commercial and public sectors have used competencies for many years, although the public sector has lagged behind a bit. The entire park and recreation profession has fallen even further behind. The good news is that the profession is beginning to see the value of competency-driven organizations. Competency-based organizations determine the skills, knowledge, characteristics, and abilities needed for different jobs and then use them to increase efficiency and effectiveness.

There are four main uses of competencies in organizations (Hurd, 2005):

1. Competencies establish training and development benchmarks. Employees can use competencies to measure their own skills and address any deficiencies through training and development. Students can also use competencies while completing their final internships and preparing for an entry-level position. They can measure their own skills against needed competencies and then create a plan to fill in deficiencies during their internships.

2. Competencies establish hiring criteria. Although job descriptions are required for all jobs, they are usually broad. Competencies can be added to job descriptions to make them more specific or a separate list of desired competencies can be attached. These competencies ensure that new employees fully understand

Table 1.2   Competency-Based Interview Questions

Broad interview questions	Competency-driven interview questions
What experiences have you had in dealing with angry customers?	Give us an example of an issue brought to you by a disappointed customer. What was the issue and how did you solve it?
Describe your ability to work in a team.	Describe a project where you were required to work in a team. What did you bring to the team? What could you have done to be a better team member?
Evaluate your ability to deal with conflict.	Give an example of when you had to deal with conflict in a work environment. How did you handle it? What would you do differently the next time?

what is required of them. In addition, they ensure that the hiring committee is looking for the same competencies from each candidate by guiding interview questions. Competency-driven interview questions are more specific than broad questions about education and general experience (see table 1.2).

3. Competencies are used for evaluation. Developing competencies and using them for evaluation purposes is at the core of human resources management (Oss, 2004). Competencies set performance standards and expectations for employees that should be measured during performance appraisals.

4. Competencies form the basis of career advancement. Most professionals will want to move beyond being frontline managers to being middle- or top-level managers, and competencies can help direct this process. An entry-level professional is most likely to rely on the agency or a mentor to help with career development whereas a more experienced professional will move toward self-directed career development. Career development happens through training and setting career goals. Competencies can be used to set career goals by detailing what experiences are needed.

Although the uses of competencies discussed here focus on entry-level positions, competencies exist for CEOs, middle managers, and board members of leisure services organizations. As careers change and progress, so do the competencies needed to succeed.

Competency Scorecard

Throughout the text, references are made to the competency scorecard. This scorecard includes the competencies outlined in table 1.1 needed for entry-level professionals. Content is directed at enhancing knowledge in many of these areas. Remember that competencies are skills, knowledge, abilities, and characteristics that entry-level professionals need to be successful, and a single course in management cannot totally prepare students for their first job. If that were the case, you would not need the other courses required in the major! Furthermore, some of these competencies are **characteristics** and will come with experience. For example, the interpersonal skills of the competency framework include aspects that will either develop over time or are part of someone's personality; it is difficult to teach patience, enthusiasm, and initiative in the classroom. Many of these characteristics will develop further with experience in the profession.

Before beginning the journey through this textbook, let's develop a picture of where you are in terms of your own competence to become a manager in an entry-level position. Table 1.3 is a rating sheet listing all of the entry-level competencies. Rate yourself in terms of your skill, knowledge, ability, characteristics, and experience. You may feel you have knowledge in an area but have not had an opportunity to put it to work yet. In this case you may rate yourself lower on experience than competence. Rating all the competencies in this fashion can determine how current skills compare to those needed in entry-level positions. Many of you will not have any experience in most of these areas, which is understandable because you are still students. Do not forget that not all learning comes from the classroom. While you are building these competency areas in class, complement that learning through

characteristics—Distinguishing qualities, attitudes, personality factors, or mental traits needed to perform a job.

experiences in the field, such as working in an afterschool program, volunteering at special events, or shadowing a manager in a resort. Once you complete this management course and read the text, rate yourself again to see how you have improved, and do it a third time once you complete your final field experience. Then you will see how far you have come and how prepared you are to become a manager in this dynamic field.

Notice how the competencies in table 1.3 are numbered. These competencies are listed for each chapter using the same numbering. Thus, when you reach a specific chapter, you can see the competencies that will be covered and refer back to your own ratings to see what you need to learn in a specific area. This allows you to track your progress through your management course.

Table 1.3   Sample Competency Assessment

Competencies	SKILL, KNOWLEDGE, ABILITIES				EXPERIENCE		
	Excellent	Good	Fair	Poor	A lot	Some	None
1. Understand financial processes (i.e., purchasing, budget).	4	3	2	1	3	2	1
2. Develop, monitor, and stay within a budget.	4	3	2	1	3	2	1
3. Possess knowledge of management principles.	4	3	2	1	3	2	1
4. Demonstrate basic knowledge of laws and legal matters affecting the field.	4	3	2	1	3	2	1
5. Understand technology and how to use it.	4	3	2	1	3	2	1
6. Clearly communicate with staff, customers, and the public.	4	3	2	1	3	2	1
7. Possess effective written and oral communication skills.	4	3	2	1	3	2	1
8. Listen to staff and customers.	4	3	2	1	3	2	1
9. Implement marketing techniques.	4	3	2	1	3	2	1
10. Communicate the organization's values, vision, and mission.	4	3	2	1	3	2	1
11. Know the community and its needs.	4	3	2	1	3	2	1
12. Understand customer service practices.	4	3	2	1	3	2	1
13. Have the ability to deal with the public.	4	3	2	1	3	2	1
14. Develop partnerships with other organizations.	4	3	2	1	3	2	1
15. Work with boards and elected officials.	4	3	2	1	3	2	1
16. Be creative and innovative.	4	3	2	1	3	2	1
17. Be flexible.	4	3	2	1	3	2	1

CONTINUED

Table 1.3 Sample Competency Assessment (CONTINUED)

Competencies	SKILL, KNOWLEDGE, ABILITIES				EXPERIENCE		
	Excellent	Good	Fair	Poor	A lot	Some	None
18. Have patience.	4	3	2	1	3	2	1
19. Be enthusiastic and have a positive attitude.	4	3	2	1	3	2	1
20. Be open-minded.	4	3	2	1	3	2	1
21. Deal with personality conflicts.	4	3	2	1	3	2	1
22. Understand the concept of criticism and accept constructive criticism.	4	3	2	1	3	2	1
23. Take initiative.	4	3	2	1	3	2	1
24. Use effective problem-solving and conflict-resolution skills.	4	3	2	1	3	2	1
25. Make ethical decisions.	4	3	2	1	3	2	1
26. Understand the hiring process.	4	3	2	1	3	2	1
27. Supervise, discipline, and evaluate a diverse staff.	4	3	2	1	3	2	1
28. Motivate employees.	4	3	2	1	3	2	1
29. Have leadership skills and abilities.	4	3	2	1	3	2	1
30. Be able to work in a team.	4	3	2	1	3	2	1
31. Use effective organizational skills.	4	3	2	1	3	2	1
32. Prioritize and manage multiple tasks.	4	3	2	1	3	2	1
33. Demonstrate effective time-management skills.	4	3	2	1	3	2	1
34. Conduct program evaluations.	4	3	2	1	3	2	1
35. Schedule programs, leagues, and staff.	4	3	2	1	3	2	1
36. Network within and outside the profession.	4	3	2	1	3	2	1
37. Participate in policy formation, evaluation, and revision.	4	3	2	1	3	2	1
38. Provide input on strategic, master, recreation, marketing, and technology plans.	4	3	2	1	3	2	1
39. Conduct research and evaluation.	4	3	2	1	3	2	1
40. Conduct needs assessments.	4	3	2	1	3	2	1

From A. Hurd, R. Barcelona, and J. Meldrum, 2008, *Leisure services management* (Champaign, IL: Human Kinetics).

Conclusion

▶ Management is the process of coordinating and integrating resources in order to achieve organizational goals. Many different elements are required for the manager to be successful, and a driving force behind these elements is competencies. It is hoped that by the time students reach the end of this text, they will have stepped into the shoes of the manager to build an understanding of what a manager does and all the aspects that go into being effective and efficient.

REVIEW QUESTIONS

1. Define *management*.

2. Describe how competencies can be used in a competency-driven agency.

3. Give examples of competencies needed by entry-level professionals.

4. Describe the model of effectiveness for managers.

KEY WORDS

management, leadership, empirical, learning organizations, outcomes-based management, strategic management

COMPETENCY CHECK

Take another look at table 1.3 (page 9) to see how you assessed these related competencies.

3. Possess knowledge of management principles.

29. Have leadership skills and abilities.

30. Be able to work in a team.

CHAPTER 2

Foundations of Management

1. Compare and contrast leadership and management.
2. Identify the four generations of leadership theory and how they are used today.
3. Develop knowledge of how management theory has evolved since the Industrial Revolution.
4. Demonstrate an understanding of management issues and trends in the field.

A Day in the Life

Each Monday through Friday, most people wake up, get dressed in their business attire, and take the typical drive to work. I, however, wake up 10 minutes before I need to be in the office and stay in my pajamas until lunchtime. My office is located in my home, and I work virtually as a meeting planner for American Express Company. My typical day in the office usually consists of domestic and international conference calls and communication through e-mails to plan events worldwide.

When I'm not in the office, I'm on site helping to manage an event while continuing to plan for upcoming programs. Being a virtual employee in my profession means being flexible, self-motivated, and able to multitask. Quite frankly, I feel fortunate to work from home with the feeling of being self-employed without the stress of a daily commute.

Amy Tonyan
Meeting Planner
American Express Company, Corporate Meeting Solutions

The term *management* has many uses. Management can be a group of people who direct employees and resources in an organization, such as the arts and culture management team. Management can refer to the level in the organization that an employee falls within, such as middle or frontline management. It can also be the process of reaching organizational goals by working with others. Lastly, it can be a discipline with its own body of knowledge, principles, concepts, and theories (Dumler & Skinner, 2005). It is management as a discipline that sets the foundation for the other uses of management.

This chapter lays the groundwork of key concepts that are tied throughout the text, such as management, leadership, and trends for each of these areas. It also outlines a competency framework so students can see what competencies are needed in the field and thus may be successful in an entry-level position.

Leadership as a Discipline

Although the purpose of this text is to outline management principles, management cannot be addressed without discussing leadership. The topic of leadership could more than fill an entire textbook; it is as vast and deep as management. Because leadership and management are so interconnected, a brief discussion of leadership is warranted.

Few people are able to concisely differentiate between management and leadership. For our purposes, they are defined as follows:

management—Process of coordinating and integrating resources in order to effectively and efficiently achieve organizational goals and objectives.

leadership—Interpersonal influence over others aimed at achieving organizational goals, objectives, and strategies.

▶ **Management** is the process of coordinating and integrating resources in order to effectively and efficiently achieve organizational goals and objectives.

▶ **Leadership** is interpersonal influence over others that is aimed at achieving organizational goals, objectives, and strategies.

The main difference between the two is the interpersonal influence of leadership and the planning, organizing, leading, and controlling aspects of management. (These four aspects are the functions of management and are discussed in detail in the next chapter.) Both leadership and management are directed at achieving goals, but they require different processes to do so. People in administrative positions in an organization are often called *managers,* yet they are required to use both management and leadership skills. Management skills are more task oriented whereas leadership skills are more people oriented. A task orientation focuses on things that need to get done, such as budgeting, writing a news release, or screening job applications, whereas a people orientation focuses more on relationships with supervisors and coworkers. People can demonstrate both sets of skills and different degrees of management and leadership as the situation dictates. These two concepts are best understood by examining leadership and management theories as they have developed over time.

Leadership theories have evolved through four generations: trait theories, behavioral theories, contingency and situational theories, and modern theories.

Trait Theories

This group of theories posits that certain traits are inherent in leaders, and people who are born with these traits will be good leaders. The focus was originally on physical traits such as height or eye color and later moved to interpersonal characteristics such as being decisive, diplomatic, creative, and assertive (Stogdill, 1974). Research has discredited this theory over time, showing that situational factors dictate needed traits and skills more than any genetic traits or personality characteristics do. Furthermore, leadership as a learned process is not a part of the trait theories. According to trait theory, a person must be a born leader and cannot learn to be a leader.

Behavioral Theories

Behavioral theories focus on the behaviors leaders exhibit rather than the traits they possess. These theories claim that leadership is learned rather than inborn and that followers learn from leaders by watching what they do. There are many behavioral theories, but three popular examples include Lewin's Leadership Styles, the Ohio State studies, and the Leadership Grid.

Lewin's Leadership Styles

Kurt Lewin's work at the University of Iowa pioneered the notion of leadership behavior. His studies explored three broad leadership styles: autocratic leadership, democratic leadership, and laissez-faire leadership. Autocratic leadership reflects a leader who limits employee participation, dictates work methods, makes unilateral decisions, and centralizes authority. Democratic leaders, on the other hand, involve employees in making decisions, delegate authority, encourage participation in creating work methods and goals, and use a coaching style to provide employee feedback. The third style, laissez-faire leadership, reflects a hands-off leader who gives employees complete freedom to make decisions and determine work methods.

Lewin and his associates wondered if one behavioral style might be more effective than the others. From their studies of actual leader behavior, they concluded that a laissez-faire leader was not effective on any of the performance indicators of leadership (quantity and quality of work as well as group satisfaction) compared with the other two styles. When examining the quantity of work done, the studies suggested that democratic and autocratic leaders performed equally well. However, the quality of work completed and group satisfaction were higher in the democratic group. Lewin's work raised the idea that it may be important to differentiate between getting work done and focusing on employees. This dual nature of leader behavior is the central feature of the Ohio State studies.

Ohio State Studies

The Ohio State studies sought different dimensions of leader behavior and narrowed more than 1,000 behavioral dimensions to two main dimensions they called *initiating structure* and *consideration*. Initiating structure refers to focusing on the work; it is the degree to which leaders define and structure their role and the roles of employees in order to achieve organizational goals. Consideration, on the other hand, is the degree to which leaders develop mutual trust and workplace relationships based on respect for employees' ideas and feelings.

The Ohio State model suggests that a leader can fall into one of four quadrants. The leader who scores high in both consideration and initiating structure gets both high employee performance and satisfaction scores. However, high ratings on these dimensions are not always positive. For example, leaders who are high on initiating structure have shown higher rates of employee turnover, more grievances, higher absenteeism, and lower job satisfaction for employees undertaking routine tasks (e.g., staff members taking tickets or checking passes at a facility).

At around the same time, leadership studies at the University of Michigan found similar results. They came up with two dimensions as well: employee orientation and production orientation. Employee-oriented leaders take a personal interest in their employees, whereas production-oriented leaders are more focused on the technical approaches to getting the job done. Both the Michigan and Ohio State studies were instrumental in furthering our understanding of leadership, yet they still lacked the ability to take context, or setting, into account. Contingency leadership theories attempted to resolve this problem, as will be discussed later.

Leadership Grid

Built on the people and task orientation of the Ohio State studies, the management grid was first developed by Blake and Mouton (1964) and later revised and renamed the Leadership Grid by Blake and McCanse (1991). The grid (figure 2.1) shows varying degrees of people and task orientation with labels for each quadrant. Although this theory is considered a leadership theory, it has strong elements of management theory with the task variable. It combines leadership and management theory and measures a person's tendencies on both aspects, which is a more realistic assessment of what a manager does.

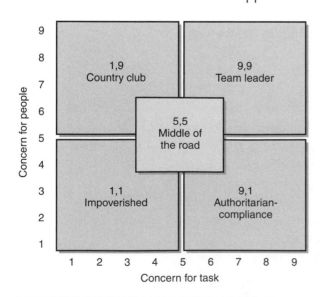

Figure 2.1 Leadership Grid.
Adapted with permission from Grid International, Inc.

The five different types of managers or leaders from the Leadership Grid include the following:

1. Impoverished management has little concern for people or task and tries to do as little as possible on the job. This person does not want to be held responsible for anything.

2. Country-club management is concerned with the leader's relationship with people and has little concern for task. This leader hopes that by building good relationships with people, productivity will result.

3. Authoritarian-compliance management focuses on arranging work environments and people to maximize productivity and minimize the human elements.

4. Middle-of-the-road management satisfactorily balances the needs of people and the need for production.

5. Team leaders rely on teamwork to get things done. They want employees to know that they are important, and they help employees achieve company goals. This is the ideal leader for most organizations.

This leadership theory has been widely used in research. It is a solid mix of management and leadership, as can be seen from the five dimensions.

Contingency and Situational Theories

After the behavior theories, it was clear that no single set of traits or leadership styles could adequately describe leadership effectiveness, so researchers began to look at context and how leadership changes as the situation changes. The result was a group of theories labeled as *contingency* and *situational theories*. These theories take into account the leader, the follower, and the situation. When a person's skills and the situation match, then that person will emerge as a leader in that situation. Situational theories indicate that different situations require different leaders, whereas contingency theories suggest that different situations require the leader's style to change rather than requiring the leader to change (Jordan, 2001).

Probably the most well-known situational theory is Hersey and Blanchard's tridimensional leader effectiveness model. They developed four leadership dimensions that change based on the situation—the leader assesses the situation and selects the best leadership style for that situation. The dimensions (task behavior and relationship behavior) are dictated by the direction given to staff in terms of tasks, processes, and patterns of organization, as well as how supportive the leader's relationship is with the staff in terms of being sensitive to their needs, listening to them and respecting their ideas, and establishing trust (Hersey, Blanchard, & Johnson, 2001). The following describes the four leadership dimensions:

▶ High relationship behavior/low task behavior: Highly supportive leader with followers who control how they do things; joint decision making, values harmony first, and will not risk relationships; appears to totally trust staff

▶ Low relationship behavior/low task behavior: Control is with the follower; no structure or socioemotional support; considerable delegation of tasks to staff

▶ High relationship behavior/high task behavior: High socioemotional support; often appears non-genuine in relationships; meets goals of organization and workers

▶ Low relationship behavior/high task behavior: Well-defined methods for completing tasks; directs, guides, and makes decisions; imposes processes on others

The relationship and task behaviors make the model two-dimensional, and adding the effectiveness dimension completes the tridimensional model. When a leader's style is appropriate for the situation based on the task and relationship behaviors exhibited, the leader is effective. When the leadership style is inappropriate for the situation, the leader is ineffective (Hersey et al., 2001).

Contingency theories look at how the situation changes a person's leadership style. Fiedler (1971) presented a contingency model asserting that group performance depends on the leader's style. This style is determined by (a) leader–member relations, or how well the leader is accepted, trusted, and respected by the followers; (b) task structure, or how well the goals and objectives of the task are defined; and (c) position power, or the leader's level of control over rewards and punishments. High or low levels of these factors create a favorable situation for leaders who are more task oriented, whereas relationship-oriented leaders work best when levels are more in the middle. Fiedler suggested that it is difficult for people to change their leadership style, so the situation needs to change rather than the style for the leader to be effective. Thus, people who consider themselves to be a good leader overall will not always be a good leader in all organizations. They have to be in the right situation where their strengths complement the organization.

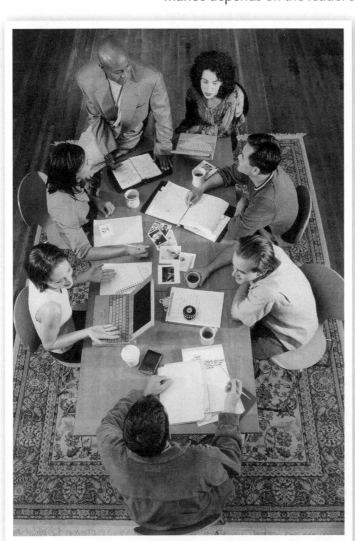

Modern leaders focus on their staff by motivating, rewarding, and challenging them to be better.

Modern Leadership Theories

Four current theories have received a great deal of attention and deserve mentioning. They include charismatic leadership, transactional leadership, transformational leadership, and Kouzes and Posner's leadership challenge (2002).

Charismatic Leadership

Charismatic leaders use personality and charm, or charisma, to draw followers to them. They speak and behave in ways that reach people's emotional levels and inspire them to act. Conger and Kanungo (1998) describe charismatic leaders as having a vision for where the organization is going, being able to articulate that vision, being sensitive to the environment and to the needs of the people in it, willing to take risks, and performing unconventional behaviors.

Transactional Leadership

Transactional leadership looks at the behaviors leaders use to influence their staff. Leadership is seen as a transaction between leaders and followers where followers are motivated to work by receiving rewards. Leaders use rewards to recognize quality work, and they use punishment to correct followers so that standards are met. Although it has received a great deal of attention, this theory of leadership pays little attention to the needs of workers, and some consider it to be more similar to management than leadership.

Transformational Leadership

Transformational leaders have a passion to achieve great things. They create a vision for the organization and get their followers to understand and accept this vision. Transformational leaders want their followers to succeed, and they work to motivate them to do so. These types of leaders build trust, work with integrity, and set an example for their staff. Transformational leadership was a forerunner to Kouzes and Posner's five practices of exemplary leadership.

Kouzes and Posner's Practices of Exemplary Leadership

Kouzes and Posner (2002) interviewed thousands of workers and managers to find out what characteristics were desirable in leaders. The interviewees responded that they wanted leaders to be honest, forward looking (have vision), competent, and inspiring. These are the same characteristics Kouzes and Posner found in 1987 and 1995, showing that even as business and the world have changed, people still look for the same characteristics in their leaders.

  Kouzes and Posner used the results of their interviews to develop five practices that exemplary leaders need to implement as part of their leadership abilities:

1. Model the way—Leaders and followers should work side by side, leaders should not ask followers to do things they themselves would not do, and leaders should set an example through their own behavior.
2. Inspire a shared vision—Leaders should have a vision for what could be, help followers understand and embrace that vision, and communicate their own passion and try to ignite that passion in their followers.
3. Challenge the process—Leaders should be risk takers, recognize good ideas and then challenge the system and the staff to get them done, and be innovative and creative.
4. Enable others to act—Leaders should empower their staff to accomplish tasks, goals, and objectives; they should build a team atmosphere; and they should foster collaboration among the team.
5. Encourage the heart—Leaders should recognize the skills, abilities, and accomplishments of their staff, and they should celebrate achievements.

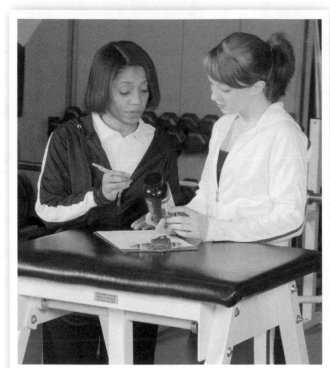

Good managers work with their staff to model good habits and set a positive example.

Summary of Leadership as a Discipline

The five practices of exemplary leadership define what leadership has become. It embraces the interpersonal elements that leaders use to achieve goals. However, without the management elements, an organization and its employees are unable to accomplish all that they should. It is leadership and management working together that makes effective employees, whether they are in upper-level, midlevel, or entry-level positions. The next section looks at the management elements of organizations by examining the history of management.

Management as a Discipline

When students hear the term *theory,* it is often accompanied by yawns, eye rolling, and disinterest. However, management theory and the historical aspects of management are the roots of management today. The history of management and its accompanying theory help explain how management works, help us predict behaviors, and allow us to see the big picture of management. You will find that although many of these management practices came into being during the Industrial Revolution, they still influence modern management today.

Management can be roughly categorized into four eras—the classic era, behavioral era, human relations era, and modern era. These eras are not a time line through the history of management but a continuum of management practices that have evolved within organizations.

Classic Era of Management

The classic era of management, occurring approximately from 1880 to the early 1930s, has also been labeled *traditional management* and *machine models.* The *machine models* label will become clear as these early theories are unveiled.

Traditional management styles were prompted by the Industrial Revolution and the resulting rapid economic growth. Although the Industrial Revolution began around 1810, its impact on management practices was not seen until the late 1800s. Work moved from agrarian to industrial, and people moved from working in their homes to working in factories. These jobs were low paying, had long hours, had poor working conditions, and resulted in less leisure time despite improvements in transportation. The result of this important time in history was a set of management theories and practices that established rational principles for making an organization more efficient.

The classic era can be subdivided into two approaches: the scientific management and general administrative approaches. Proponents of scientific management believed that there was one best way to complete tasks that resulted in efficiency. This approach focused more on individual workers, whereas the general administrative approach looked at the organization as a whole and good management practices. Scientific management is most defined by the work of Frederick Taylor and Frank and Lillian Gilbreth. General administrative approaches are reflected by Henri Fayol and Max Weber, among others.

Frederick Taylor

Arguably, Frederick Taylor started modern management with the publication of his instant bestseller, *The Principles of Scientific Management,* in 1911. Working in a Pennsylvania steel company, Taylor observed workers who were purposefully not working to their full potential, which he labeled *soldiering.* Many workers soldiered for fear of losing their jobs if productivity increased too much, since wages were not incentive based and there were no standardized methods of completing tasks.

Seeking to increase productivity, Taylor engaged in time and motion studies where workers performed tasks in different ways while he timed them on each method. From the results, he developed the most efficient means of performing tasks both with the motion of the workers and the time it took them to complete the task. Taylor ultimately arrived at four principles of scientific management:

1. Replace existing work methods with methods based on a scientific study of the tasks.
2. Scientifically select and train workers rather than passively leaving them to train themselves.
3. Cooperate with workers to ensure that they follow the scientifically developed methods.
4. Divide work and responsibility almost equally between managers and workers so that the managers apply scientific management principles to planning the work and the workers perform the tasks (NetMBA, 2007).

By 1908, Harvard Business School declared Taylor's approach the standard for modern management.

Frank and Lillian Gilbreth

Frank and Lillian Gilbreth (1916) were disciples of Taylor. Frank started out as a construction worker and Lillian as a psychologist. They studied work environments, especially in bricklaying, to eliminate wasted hand motions and body movements. They also looked at the design and use of tools in performing these tasks, and their research was the first to use motion-picture film to study these movements. Land was inexpensive at the time and most homes and business buildings were made of brick. The largest cost of building was labor, so by reducing wasted motions, labor costs substantially decreased.

Henri Fayol

Fayol (1949) was one of the first to deal with the administrative side of management; he looked at the entire organization, not just motions and methods. Fayol is most known for creating the five functions of managers and the 14 principles of management (see table 2.1). He posited that managers do five things (Jarvis, 2007):

1. Planning—Look at the future and develop plans to meet future challenges.

2. Organizing—Examine how employee duties will be planned and structured.

3. Commanding—Maintain activity among personnel in terms of motivation, communication, and use of power.

4. Coordinating—Bring together and harmonize efforts of people, ensuring proper direction and teamwork.

5. Controlling—Ensure that activity conforms with policy and practice; establish performance principles.

Although Fayol was prominent in the early 1900s, in looking at the definitions of management you will see that many of these same principles define management today.

Table 2.1 Fayol's 14 Principles of Management

In addition to the five functions of management, Fayol described 14 principles.

Principle	What the manager and employees do
1. Division of labor	Jobs are divided by specialization of tasks by employees.
2. Authority	Managers have the power to give orders.
3. Discipline	Employees must respect and follow the rules of the organization as directed by the manager.
4. Unity of command	Employees report to only one supervisor.
5. Unity of direction	All employees should move the organization toward common goals.
6. Subordination of individual interests	Personal interests are put aside for the good of the organization.
7. Remuneration	Fair pay is given for work done.
8. Centralization	Decision making is relegated to different levels of the organization.
9. Scalar chain	Employees must follow the chain of command from the lowest level to the CEO of the organization.
10. Order	People and things should be in the right place and in an orderly fashion.
11. Equity	Managers are to be kind and fair to employees.
12. Stability of personnel tenure	It should be a priority to retain quality employees.
13. Initiative	Managers should encourage employees to take initiative.
14. Esprit de corps	Managers should encourage harmony and unity within the organization.

Max Weber

Weber was a German sociologist who described an ideal organization that he called a *bureaucracy*. Bureaucracies are driven by clear rules, defined hierarchy, and impersonal relationships. Weber felt that a bureaucracy is a dominant institution because it is most efficient in terms of precision, speed, continuity, unity, and strict subordination (Dumler & Skinner, 2005). Bureaucracies have six key characteristics (Robbins, 1997):

1. Division of labor—Jobs are broken down into well-defined, routine tasks.
2. Authority hierarchy—Roles in the organization are positioned so that each lower job is supervised by a higher one.
3. Formal selection—All employees are selected based on qualifications, skills, training, education, or formal examination.
4. Formal rules and regulations—Formal rules and regulations are strictly relied upon to ensure uniformity and regulate the actions of employees.
5. Impersonality—Rules and regulations are applied to all employees uniformly so as to avoid the personal preferences of employees.
6. Career orientation—Managers are professional officials who work for a salary and pursue a career in the organization.

The term *bureaucracy* is often seen as being negative and associated with government, but careful examination shows that those same practices are used in many organizations that are nongovernmental.

Summary of the Classic Era

The classic era of management originated as a means to make management a scientific discipline of study. It is responsible for defining management and the role of managers, as well as improving efficiency and productivity. Many of the management functions found today in parks and recreation are derived from the classic era of management, including work simplification, production schedules, estimates of how much product can be made in a day, development of more efficient tools and products, and qualifications-based hiring practices. Many of these principles can be seen in chapter 5 when organizational structure and design are discussed.

The Industrial Revolution sparked a very systematic and rigid form of management, with some of these principles still found in management today.

The shortcoming of these theories is their oversimplification of management and jobs. The main criticism of this era is its lack of concern for the human element in management, including communication, conflict management, motivation, and interpersonal relations. The behavioral theories of management came next and addressed some of these shortcomings.

Behavioral Era of Management

The behavioral era came into being in the 1930s and 1940s. There was not any one defining moment such as the Industrial Revolution that shaped management at the time. However, there were some milestones that had a major impact on how management was perceived and carried out, including the Great Depression (1930s), the Fair Labor Standards Act establishing the 40-hour work week and banning child labor (1938), World War II (1939-1945), the introduction of the first computer (1944), the establishment of Wal-Mart (1945), passage of the Taft-Hartley Act restricting union practices (1947), and Peter Drucker becoming professor of management at New York University (1950), the first person to hold that title (Crainer, 2000).

The behavioral era of management focused on why people do things rather than how they do them. Psychology and sociology became important disciplines in management as theorists attempted to understand employee behavior. Although there are a number of behavioral management theorists, a few of the most influential at the time were Elton Mayo, Mary Parker Follett, and Chester Barnard.

Elton Mayo and the Hawthorne Studies

What began as a scientific management study at the Western Electric Hawthorne Works plant in Cicero, Illinois, became an important study that sparked the behavioral era of management (Mayo, 1933). Mayo's study initially focused on the impact of illumination levels on productivity in controlled and experimental groups. The lighting levels for the experimental group were manipulated whereas those for the control group did not change, and the results showed that the productivity of both groups increased regardless of the change in lighting levels. Only when the lighting dropped to the level of moonlight did productivity drop. These results led to additional experiments where small groups of workers were isolated and studied. Productivity increases in these groups were attributed to the workers liking the recognition and attention paid by the researchers. Mayo concluded several things:

- ▶ Financial incentives did not increase productivity; being singled out and given attention was far more motivating to the workers.
- ▶ Workers would work harder if they felt managers were concerned about their well-being.
- ▶ Work norms drove productivity by establishing standards for a fair day's work.
- ▶ The social environment, or informal organization, influenced productivity; relationships with bosses and coworkers made the work more palatable.

Mary Parker Follett

Mary Parker Follett was seen as a management prophet by Peter Drucker and as the mother of management by many others. Follett's work was groundbreaking in that she saw the organization as a group of people and not just as a means to production. She argued that managers should use their skill and knowledge to lead workers rather than rely on a strict line of authority. Furthermore, she suggested that workers should be given more responsibility and managers should receive training in management, which was unheard of at the time. Follett strongly influenced how managers approach decision making, motivation, leadership, teams, power, and authority today (Robbins, 1997). Follett's work was virtually ignored at the time, yet today her views on management are seen as cutting edge.

Chester Barnard

Barnard, once the president of the New Jersey Bell Telephone Company, believed that an organization is a behavioral system consisting of people with interacting social networks. He suggested that there are three functions of managers: to motivate personnel, to maintain effective communication with personnel, and to hire and retain quality personnel. In addition, the success of an organization is based on common goals, but to achieve these goals, the individual needs of employees must be met. Barnard focused on leadership, communication, and motivation.

Summary of the Behavioral Era

The behavioral era of management and the resulting human relations era have many commonalities. What began with an examination of behaviors led to an even more pronounced focus on human relations.

Human Relations Era of Management

Sparked by the Hawthorne studies, the human relations era was characterized by a people-oriented approach to management. Management scholars looked at the interaction of people and its impact on the organization. In this era, the ultimate goal within the organization was to enhance success by building appropriate relationships among employees (Certo, 2003). The human relations era occurred approximately from 1950 to 1980 and saw such historical influences as the employment of women reaching the highest point in history in 1951, the New York Stock Exchange prices reaching the highest point since 1929, IBM introducing the first business computer in 1955, the Civil Rights Act of 1964 making workplace discrimination illegal, and Apple introducing the first personal computer in 1977 (Crainer, 2000).

As with the other eras, there were a number of significant contributors, but the most recognized are Abraham Maslow, Douglas McGregor, Frederick Herzberg, and systems theory.

Abraham Maslow

Maslow was a humanist psychologist who developed what is known as Maslow's hierarchy of needs (figure 2.2). There are five needs that must be met according to their order on the hierarchy before the next level may be achieved. Once a need

empirical—Relying on observation or experimentation to verify or disprove an assumption of an issue.

is met, it no longer serves as a motivator for behaviors (Maslow, 1954). On the basis of this theory on motivation, countless managers reexamined their policies and practices to further aid people in reaching the self-actualization level in the hierarchy (Robbins, 1997). Although there is no **empirical** research to substantiate or discredit this theory, it is still respected and used in management today.

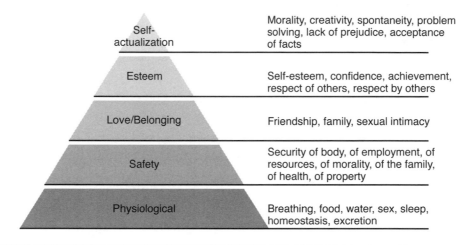

Figure 2.2   Maslow's hierarchy of needs.

Douglas McGregor

In *The Human Side of Enterprise* (1960), McGregor formulated two sets of assumptions about workers. He labeled these as theory X and theory Y (table 2.2).

These two theories appear to be polar opposites and difficult to attain. McGregor understood this and argued that people will be more productive if they are valued and given responsibility. He suggested that theory Y is the true nature of workers and should guide management practices.

Table 2.2   McGregor's Theory X and Theory Y

Theory X: Negative view of people	Theory Y: Positive view of people
People dislike work and have little ambition.	Work can be enjoyable and is as natural as rest and play.
People avoid responsibility.	People accept and seek responsibility.
People need to be closely supervised.	People can be self-directed.
People need to be controlled and threatened to get them to perform.	People want rewards that satisfy self-actualization.

Created from text in D. McGregor, 1960, *The human side of enterprise* (New York, NY: McGraw-Hill).

Frederick Herzberg

Wanting to find out what motivates employees, Herzberg developed the motivation-hygiene theory to explain employee attitudes and motivation (table 2.3). He found that there were satisfiers (motivators) and dissatisfiers (hygiene factors) that influenced feelings toward the work environment (Herzberg, Mausner, & Snyderman, 1959).

Table 2.3   Herzberg's Motivation-Hygiene Theory

Hygiene factors *Dissatisfiers*	Motivators
Can lead to dissatisfaction:	Lead to satisfaction:
Policies	Recognition
Working conditions	Growth on the job
Relationship with supervisors	Advancement
Supervision received on the job	Interesting work
Salary	Responsibility

Created from text in F. Herzberg, B. Mausner, and B.B. Snyderman, 1959, *The motivation to work* (New York, NY: Wiley).

Hygiene factors are environment related and do not provide satisfaction, but if they are absent, dissatisfaction occurs. In essence, hygiene factors will not motivate an employee, but without them, the employee is not happy. Motivation factors, on the other hand, focus on what people do at work, and these factors lead to motivated employees who will perform well for the organization. Motivation factors need to be present because they lead to satisfaction in the workplace.

Systems Theory

Systems theory began as a biological theory and has since been adapted into management and organizational theories. The premise of systems theory is that an organization is a system with interrelated parts, such as skilled people and departments. These individuals and groups rely on each other to get their job done. Not only is there a connection between internal parts, but there are external influences as well. For example, a special events management company is holding a major event that will attract 100,000 people to the community in a weekend. It will take a large number of employees in different departments working together to plan the event. In addition, a multitude of organizations outside of the agency are required, such as hotels, beverage distributors, security organizations, sanitation providers, and sponsors. Key to a systems approach is the idea of stability in the organization. The more stable the organization, the more effectively it will respond to problems. Stable and skilled staff working on this event will be better prepared to handle difficulties such as rain, sponsors pulling out, or entertainment acts canceling at the last minute.

Also within systems theory are the concepts of inputs, processes, and outputs. An organization has various inputs such as resources, time, money, and program ideas. These inputs go through processes such as program planning and event management, resulting in programs, trips, and other products (figure 2.3). A systems approach is an underlying premise of team-based organizations,

Figure 2.3   Systems theory example from the Fort Dix Morale, Welfare, and Recreation Program.

which is discussed in chapter 5. It also is a part of the outcomes-based management approach discussed later.

Summary of the Human Relations Era

Until the 1980s, management saw many transformations, from a scientific perspective in the classic era to the human relations era where the relations among and between workers and managers was studied. Many prominent principles in each era carried over into the modern era of management.

Modern Era of Management

The modern era of management has taken a slightly different twist since it began in the 1980s. Productivity in North America was falling and there was a growing distrust of major corporations and their commitment to their communities. However, the Japanese economy was flourishing at the time and expected to have the largest gross national product in the world by 2000 (Pascale & Athos, 1981). What resulted were Deming's theory of total quality management and a plethora of other management scholars presenting best practices.

Total Quality Management

W. Edwards Deming played an important role in the growth of the Japanese business market in the 1970s and 1980s, yet he was unknown in North America. Deming convinced the National Broadcasting Company (NBC) of his abilities and respect from the business world in Japan, and on June 26, 1980, NBC featured Deming in a broadcast titled *If Japan Can, Why Can't We?* This show changed the face of management in North America. Deming introduced total quality management (TQM) with the premise that managers must focus on quality from the customer perspective and make it the basis of everything the organization does. TQM had 14 points (Crainer, 2000):

1. Create constancy of purpose toward improving products and services.
2. Adopt a philosophy of improving products and services so it is ingrained in the company.
3. Reduce variation in products so that dependence on inspection is not needed. Fix defects before the product is made rather than finding them during inspection.
4. Work with only one supplier to minimize variation in supplies. This may mean not going with the cheapest items.
5. Improve constantly and forever.
6. Institute training on the job.
7. Institute leadership where managers lead rather than supervise.
8. Drive out fear so workers will ask questions and give input.
9. Break down barriers between departments so teams will improve productivity.
10. Eliminate slogans, exhortations, targets, and posters because they generate frustration and resentment.

11. Eliminate quotas because they encourage the delivery of lesser goods.

12. Remove barriers to pride of workmanship, including annual employee evaluations and rating systems.

13. Institute education and self-improvement.

14. The transformation to TQM is everyone's job and all employees should be involved in its implementation.

TQM is not without its critics; some perceive it as inflexible and unable to quickly adapt to change. However, many principles are still in use today. Many of the principles work in the service industry, but TQM is better suited for companies that manufacture goods. A service industry such as parks and recreation would find it difficult to embrace some TQM principles, such as eliminating variability in products.

Best Practices

TQM sparked a new wave of management scholars who looked to present ideas on best practices within management. The leader in this wave was Peter Drucker, who wrote 38 books and countless papers on management. His last book was published in 2005, the year he died at the age of 95. Not only did Drucker study commercial business, but he also worked with nonprofit groups, focusing on the specific needs of the sector. Drucker influenced many of the management practices that are considered the foundation of the field today.

Modern management has focused on reworking past theories and practices and includes such names as Mintzberg, Peters, Blanchard, Waterman, and Covey, in

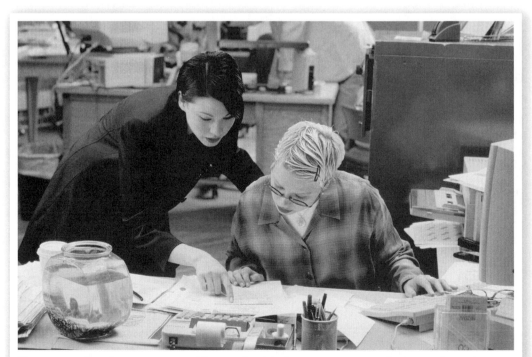

Over many decades, management has evolved to focus more on employees and creating a positive work environment.

addition to Deming and Drucker. Eight key best practices emerge from their writings that contribute to management today:

1. Organizations must be driven by clearly defined values.
2. Organizations must have a known vision for where they are headed.
3. Organizations should be customer driven.
4. Managers must recognize the contributions of employees to the organization.
5. Managers must foster collaboration among staff, encourage cooperation, and treat employees as valuable assets.
6. Organizations must continually train and invest in employees, who are their greatest asset.
7. Managers must give employees the freedom to take risks so they may learn from mistakes and foster innovation and change.
8. Organizations must create a culture of trust among all employees that precipitates honesty, integrity, and ethical behavior.

Summary of the Modern Era

The focus of this era can best be described as quality and best practices. This approach to management combines the three previous eras to depict how a manager should both manage and lead.

Summary of Management as a Discipline

Walk into any bookstore and you will find shelves of books on management practices. Managers today could read a book a week throughout their entire career and never scratch the surface of all the publications that are out there. The practices outlined by great management thinkers have come a long way since the days of the classic era. Some of the original practices are still evident in management today, but where the focus was once on productivity, it is now on people. The behavioral and human relations eras laid the groundwork for management today, which is people focused and where leadership becomes intertwined with management. As stated earlier, it is difficult to differentiate between management and leadership since they each hold principles of the other as their foundation. As these two areas have come closer together, a few management trends have emerged in parks and recreation that deserve mention.

Management Trends

The theoretical history of leadership and management demonstrates the interaction and progression of the disciplines. It explains behaviors and helps us understand the bigger picture of both management and leadership. This foundation has led to several current trends in management. Many of these trends are philosophies adopted by the public, nonprofit, and commercial sectors. The more popular ones right now include learning organizations, outcomes-based management, strategic management, and competency-based organizations.

Learning Organizations

Peter Senge developed the concept of **learning organizations,** which emphasizes continual learning in order to get better. In a learning organization, learning and education are encouraged among staff because increasing one person's competence strengthens the organization so that it is better able to respond to changes. Senge (2006) outlines five disciplines that are required for learning organizations:

1. Systems thinking
2. Personal mastery
3. Mental models
4. Shared vision
5. Team learning

> **learning organizations**—Agencies that instill the value of learning and education as means to developing individual staff members and the organization as a whole.

Systems Thinking

The most important discipline, systems thinking, stems from systems theory. In this theory, all the parts in a system are interdependent. Personal development means organizational development, and when one part of the system is weak, such as an employee, it weakens the entire organization. This idea of systems ties the other four disciplines together and makes them work so that the organization is stronger.

Personal Mastery

Workers must commit to personal mastery and have a personal vision for where they want to be and what they want to accomplish. Employees seek a special level of proficiency by committing to lifelong learning and developing the full potential of others and themselves.

Mental Models

Everyone has deeply ingrained images, assumptions, and generalizations of how things are in the world. These mental models influence our thinking and decision making, and many of them are subconsciously ingrained. In terms of management, mental models define what we can and cannot do. Learning organizations force people to scrutinize their mental models to see how the models impede progress. This scrutiny increases the capacity of workers to see beyond their mental models and think outside the box.

Shared Vision

The organization must have a unified vision for where it is going and how it is going to get there. People thrive on lofty goals and dedicate themselves to improving their intellectual capacity to help reach those goals.

Team Learning

Workers must have positive group interaction involving open dialogue and skillful discussion. The members of the team learn from each other, and the intelligence of the team is superior to the intelligence of its individual members.

Many organizations today are learning organizations. They dedicate money to staff for workshops, conferences, and classes toward advanced degrees. For managers who have completed a degree in parks and recreation, this is just the first step in the learning process. Good managers will develop their intellectual abilities throughout their careers.

Outcomes-Based Management

Many of the management and leadership theories that have been discussed thus far were developed in the commercial sector and most likely with big businesses. However, **outcomes-based management** has strong roots in the nonprofit and public sectors. It is particularly strong in parks and recreation.

outcomes-based management—A management philosophy in which the agency carefully plans and sets priorities with the purpose of realizing quality results rather than quantified results.

The purpose of outcomes-based management is to uncover what programs and services actually mean to users. It moves away from counting the number of people served, the number of programs offered, and the number of units sold to identifying how people benefit from the programs. The United Way has been a front-runner in developing outcomes-based management. Their model (figure 2.4) has four elements: inputs, activities, outputs, and outcomes (United Way of America, 1996).

Inputs are the resources dedicated to the program such as staff, money, volunteers, and facilities. Activities are the result of the inputs, and in recreation they include programs or products. Outputs are the volume of activities. In this field, we have a tendency to count the number of programs offered per season, the number of memberships sold, or the number of people in the facility each hour. Up to this point, the model looks like systems theory. However, outcomes-based management goes one step further by adding the outcomes variable. Outcomes are the benefits people receive from participation in the program or purchasing the product. Out-

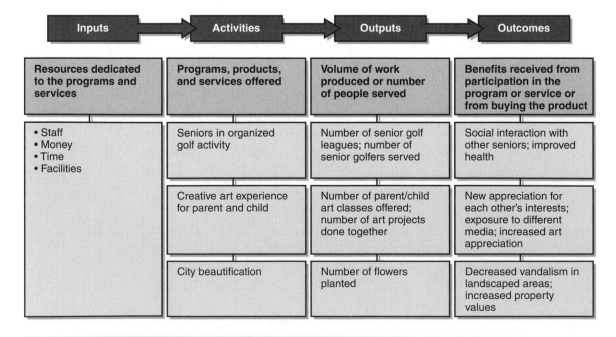

Inputs	Activities	Outputs	Outcomes
Resources dedicated to the programs and services	Programs, products, and services offered	Volume of work produced or number of people served	Benefits received from participation in the program or service or from buying the product
• Staff • Money • Time • Facilities	Seniors in organized golf activity	Number of senior golf leagues; number of senior golfers served	Social interaction with other seniors; improved health
	Creative art experience for parent and child	Number of parent/child art classes offered; number of art projects done together	New appreciation for each other's interests; exposure to different media; increased art appreciation
	City beautification	Number of flowers planted	Decreased vandalism in landscaped areas; increased property values

Figure 2.4   **Performance outcome model.**

Adapted from: *Measuring Program Outcomes: A Practical Approach* (1996). Used by permission, United Way of America.

comes can be "related to behavior, skills, knowledge, attitudes, values, condition, or other attributes" (United Way of America, 1996, p. 2).

In the early 1990s, the National Recreation and Park Association (NRPA) and the Canadian Parks and Recreation Association (CPRA) developed benefits programs to help agencies better position themselves so that the community can see what they get from programs rather than just the program itself. These benefits are actually outcomes. Many of the benefits efforts were marketing driven. They then moved to being management driven with the introduction of benefits-based management, which gave the field a clearer understanding of the management process and resulting outcomes. Benefits-based management is the same as outcomes-based management but designed for recreation, focusing on developing objectives to guide planning and programming in order to facilitate the desired benefits (Borrie & Roggenbuck, 1995). It integrates a benefits-based approach not only with marketing but also with all aspects of management, including values, vision, mission, goals, operations, and philosophy (Forest, 1999).

Benefits-based management, which was first tested by the Rocky Mountain Experiment Station of the U.S. Forest Service (Lee & Driver, 1992), is now used in countless cities, counties, and park districts across the United States. It has made its way back to the federal level with the U.S. Bureau of Land Management (BLM) releasing an instructional memorandum in January of 2006 directing the BLM to implement benefits-based management for all recreation and visitor services (Bureau of Land Management, 2007).

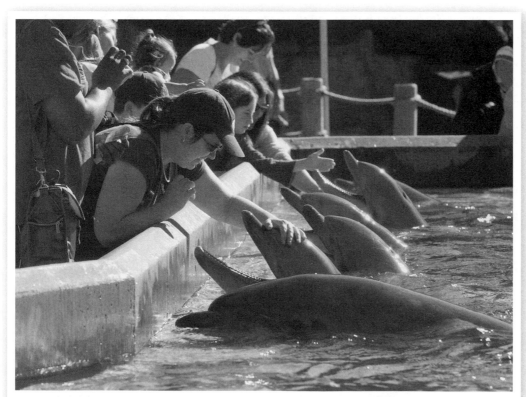

Visitors to San Diego's Sea World pet dolphins, a first-time experience for many of them. These experiences are the premise behind outcomes-based management.

Understanding the concept of benefits and outcomes seems logical, but what does it have to do with management? Outcomes can serve several management functions. First, they make agencies accountable for resources. Resource usage should tie directly to the outcomes received. A program that demands a large proportion of staff time should prove to be worth that expenditure in terms of what people get from the program. Second, outcomes demonstrate how organizations make a difference in the community by promoting the value of programs and services. This leads to increased public support, which is needed for such things as funding and capital projects. Third, having a clear understanding of outcomes often leads to more focused and productive staff (United Way of America, 1996). Finally, outcomes drive program decisions, such as when an organization expands programs that are delivering the outcomes it has deemed important according to its values, vision, mission, and goals.

Strategic Management and Leadership

strategic management—A management philosophy that assumes planning improves performance by setting strategies that the staff tries to achieve to strengthen the overall organization.

Strategic management and leadership is based on the concept of strategic planning. Strategic planning guides the staff of an organization in envisioning its future and then developing an outline of what they need to do in order to become that organization over a certain time frame (e.g., 5 years). Strategic planning requires agencies to follow several steps, including the following. (These steps are further explained in chapter 7.)

1. Develop and clarify values, vision, mission, goals, and objectives.
2. Complete a performance analysis to determine what the organization does right.
3. Complete a SWOT (strengths, weaknesses, opportunities, threats) analysis.
4. Identify strategic issues and strategies.
5. Approve and implement the plan.
6. Monitor, review, and update the plan.

The main premise of strategic management and leadership is that planning improves performance. It shows the organization what its strengths are and matches those strengths with customer needs. The developed strategies help the organization get stronger and better able to compete in the market, and they ensure that all staff members are headed in the same direction.

Strategic management and leadership have been embraced by managers. Many park and recreation agencies are committed to regularly creating strategic plans, and a number of educational sessions on strategic planning are offered each year at professional conferences. Twenty years ago agencies created strategic plans because they were good public relations tools or they were needed to apply for grants. However, these plans were rarely implemented. Today, strategic plans are highly valued and seen as a must in the field. It is not unusual for agencies to refer to their strategic plan as a scorecard where they track what strategies and actions have been implemented and make decisions based on the plan. Managers plan, organize, and direct employees to make decisions and achieve goals and objectives set by the strategic plan. Leaders use their interpersonal influence over their staff to achieve the same organizational goals, objectives, and strategies.

Competency-Based Organizations

Chapter 1 outlined the uses of competencies. However, they are also worth mentioning here as a modern management trend. Agencies are beginning to understand the need for competencies. For example, the Community Association of The Woodlands in Texas uses competencies as part of their internship program by outlining what interns will learn and experience during their 12- to 16-week endeavor.

The California Park and Recreation Society (CPRS) is on the cutting edge of strategic planning and competency development. Their VIP (vision, insight, and planning) action plan provides a statewide strategic planning framework (figure 2.5). This framework includes the following:

▶ Values, vision, and mission for the park and recreation profession

▶ Key trends that affect parks and recreation, including the changing California economy; demographic, social, and cultural trends; and political and legislative trends, to name just a few

▶ Core competencies that park and recreation professionals need, including business acumen, communications and marketing, planning and evaluation, community relations, and leadership and management

▶ Strategies and performance measures to reposition parks and recreation as an important player in building strong communities

The VIP action plan asserts that the profession needs people who are willing to develop their skills in order to be proactive and successful in the field.

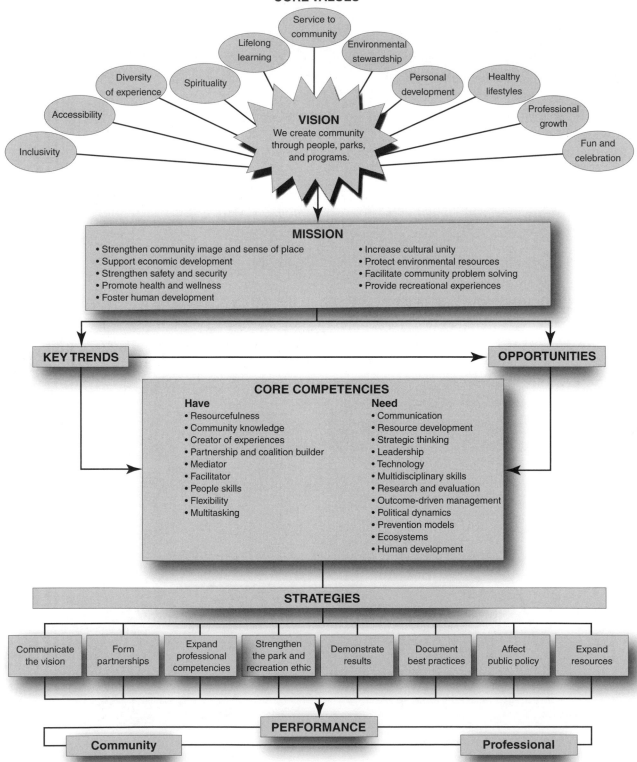

Strategic Planning Framework for Parks and Recreation

CORE VALUES

Service to community

Lifelong learning

Environmental stewardship

Diversity of experience

Spirituality

Personal development

Healthy lifestyles

Accessibility

Professional growth

Inclusivity

VISION
We create community through people, parks, and programs.

Fun and celebration

MISSION

- Strengthen community image and sense of place
- Support economic development
- Strengthen safety and security
- Promote health and wellness
- Foster human development
- Increase cultural unity
- Protect environmental resources
- Facilitate community problem solving
- Provide recreational experiences

KEY TRENDS

OPPORTUNITIES

CORE COMPETENCIES

Have
- Resourcefulness
- Community knowledge
- Creator of experiences
- Partnership and coalition builder
- Mediator
- Facilitator
- People skills
- Flexibility
- Multitasking

Need
- Communication
- Resource development
- Strategic thinking
- Leadership
- Technology
- Multidisciplinary skills
- Research and evaluation
- Outcome-driven management
- Political dynamics
- Prevention models
- Ecosystems
- Human development

STRATEGIES

| Communicate the vision | Form partnerships | Expand professional competencies | Strengthen the park and recreation ethic | Demonstrate results | Document best practices | Affect public policy | Expand resources |

PERFORMANCE

Community

Professional

Figure 2.5 VIP action plan.

Reprinted courtesy of the California Park & Recreation Society.

Conclusion

▶ This chapter covered the history of leadership and management, showed how they are similar and different, and ended with key management philosophies in the park and recreation profession. It is an evolving field that will require managers to continue learning throughout their career. Parks and recreation has its own body of research on management and leadership, which can be found in journals such as the *Journal of Park and Recreation Administration*. With the exception of textbooks, most books view management as a blanket approach to doing business, and many focus on big business. However, the principles can be applied in all professions because we all manage the same set of assets—people, facilities, finances, and programs and services. Managers must continue to hone their management skills and leadership styles to remain effective in the workplace. Complacent managers who do things the same way throughout their entire career are doing a disservice to themselves, their employees, and their agency. Managers need to have a solid grasp of the past and the present to grow and develop into what is needed in the future.

REVIEW QUESTIONS

1. Compare and contrast leadership and management.

2. Describe the four eras of leadership theory and how they are used today.

3. Describe the four categories of management theory. Which theories are still in use today?

4. Which management theories sound the most similar to leadership?

5. Which leadership theories sound the most similar to management?

6. Can an organization be both a learning organization and implement strategic management? Why or why not?

7. Select two management trends and discuss their importance to the field.

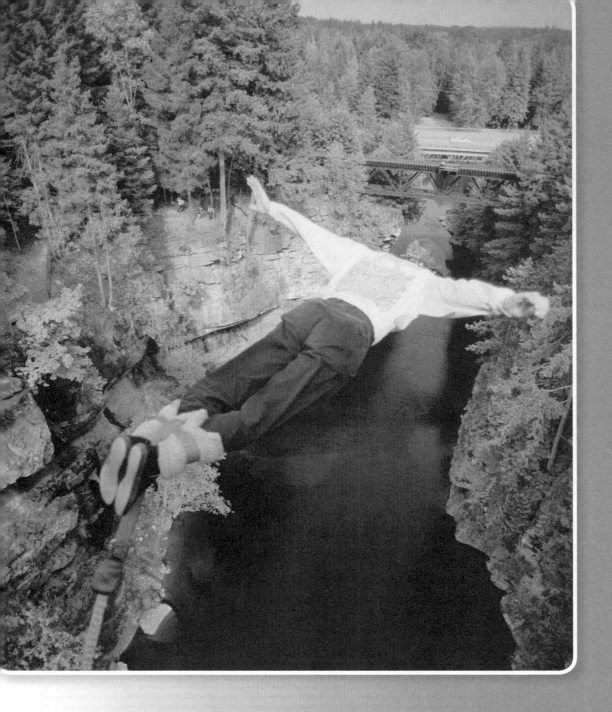

KEY WORDS

responsibility, authority, resources, mentorship, management drivers, values, shared values, vision, mission, goals, objectives, efficiency, effectiveness

COMPETENCY CHECK

Take another look at table 1.3 (page 9) to see how you assessed this related competency.

10. Communicate the organization's values, vision, and mission.

CHAPTER 3

Leisure Services Managers

LEARNING OUTCOMES

1. Understand the interrelationship between the levels and functions of managers.
2. Demonstrate knowledge of the four main resources within an organization.
3. Describe how managers experience career progression.
4. Compare and contrast values, vision, and mission statements.
5. Formulate goals and objectives.
6. Differentiate between efficiency and effectiveness.

A typical day before an event is actually anything but typical. My day usually starts out with compiling my to-do list, organizing a supply list, and of course checking the weather, because most of my events are outdoors. I strive to have a detailed timeline in place for the day before an event to make sure everything runs smoothly. Once I fill the van with supplies, I proceed to the venue and set up the fencing for tomorrow's event. The day quickly gets away from me as I work on my event tasks because the weather has not held off and it is raining; I cannot set up for the event the day before as I would have liked.

Instead I must return indoors and finish working on the remaining tasks I have for tomorrow's event, including printing evaluations, volunteer job descriptions, sponsorship signage, and additional event signage. Due to the rain I will need to get up extra early tomorrow to get the event set up. I have learned as a community events specialist that you need to be flexible, cool under pressure, and confident in your decision-making skills.

Sarah Nix
Community Events Specialist
City of Bloomington, IN, Parks and Recreation
Bloomington, Indiana

Chapter 2 outlined a foundation and historical perspective of management, allowing you to see where management and leadership started and where they are today. Now that we've established the big picture of management, it is time to look at the details, the nuts and bolts of daily management activity. Discussion in this chapter focuses on what a manager does, different levels of management within an organization, management resources, what drives management, and organizational efficiency and effectiveness. Together these things represent the total manager and give a picture of what to expect as a manager.

Levels and Functions of Managers

A soon-to-be graduate probably wants to know what managers do and where they are in the organization. Regardless of whether the manager works in a resort, a city park and recreation agency, or a nonprofit organization, the functions and levels of management are similar. The two are tightly connected, with the level of management dictating many functions.

Levels of Management

responsibility—Designated area of the organization that an employee is in charge of.

authority—The right to exercise influence, give directives, or make certain decisions within an organization.

Managers are found throughout an organization with varying levels of responsibility and authority. A discussion of what managers do cannot happen without understanding what these two terms mean. **Responsibility** refers to the aspects of the organization that the manager is in charge of, such as arts, sales, sport, or the Midwest region. **Authority,** on the other hand, is the power that comes with the position a manager occupies in the organizational chart (Hersey, Blanchard, & Johnson, 2001). Authority is given to managers who oversee employees or certain areas of the organization. Both responsibility and authority change as managers change levels in the organization.

Managers can be classified into three levels (figure 3.1). The base of any organization is its frontline managers or direct service providers. Managers at this level are responsible for such things as teaching aerobics or dance classes, preparing ball diamonds for play, or leading activities at a resort. Frontline managers usually do not supervise other employees and can be either full- or part-time employees. These jobs are usually considered entry-level positions and are most plentiful in an organization.

The next level in the organization consists of middle managers, who supervise the frontline managers. Middle managers are often considered department heads, such as director of sales, cultural arts manager, or coordinator of interpretive programs. They have responsibility and authority over a particular area in the organization.

At the top of the organization are the top managers—the chief executive officers (CEOs), presidents, and vice presidents. They make up a small group of senior executives responsible for managing the entire organization. They supervise the middle managers and have ultimate responsibility for all aspects of the organization from finance and facilities to planning and marketing.

Figure 3.1   Levels of management.

Adapted from R.V. Russell, 2004, *Leadership in recreation*, 3rd ed. (New York, NY: McGraw-Hill), 32, by permission of The McGraw-Hill Companies.

As a manager moves up the levels of management, the number of positions decreases; there are only one or two people within an organization at the top level of management. Also, as a manager moves up through the three levels, responsibility and authority will increase, with the top-level manager having the most responsibility and authority.

Functions of Management

At each level in the organization the manager has specific functions and, similar to varying responsibilities, these functions change as the manager moves up in the organization. There are two schools of thought on the functions of a manager. The first approach is the conceptual, human relations, and technical functions of managers. The second approach includes the functions of planning, organizing, leading, and controlling.

Conceptual, Human Relations, and Technical Approach

The conceptual, human relations, and technical functions of managers are most often examined in connection with the three levels of the organization. Technical functions are those things done by the manager in order to accomplish tasks and complete procedures, and they are predominantly a function of frontline managers. Going back to the competencies discussed in chapter 1, technical functions require competencies such as conducting program evaluations, developing budgets, and implementing marketing techniques. When comparing the levels of management and their functions, the frontline managers are most likely to use technical skills, followed by middle managers and then top managers. Thus, the technical skills are stressed during undergraduate and graduate education to prepare future managers for entry-level positions.

Human relations functions deal with internal customers (i.e., employees) and external customers (i.e., participants and visitors). Human relations competencies include the ability to deal with the public, to work in a team, and to deal with personality conflicts. Human relations functions are used extensively by all levels of management, with no one level performing this function more than others. However, the ways in which these functions manifest themselves at each level may be quite different. For example, a CEO may use human relations skills to work with potential donors, the board, or CEOs of other organizations, whereas the frontline manager is most likely to use human relations skills with participants by leading activities, teaching fitness classes, or registering participants.

The last function of management is the conceptual function. This is the big-picture function where managers view the organization as a whole and make decisions based on how they will affect everyone in the organization. The top-level manager has a much larger conceptual function than the middle or frontline manager. As far as entry-level competencies go, conceptual skills are limited, other than problem-solving skills. However, several CEO competencies demonstrate conceptual functions, including the ability to create a vision or direction for the agency and to make effective long-range plans (Hurd & McLean, 2004).

Table 3.1 depicts a sample of competencies needed at the three organizational levels, categorized by function. It is clear that competencies change as the level of the manager changes within each function. Although these functions are universal to management in all fields, seeing them in the context of parks and recreation can aid in understanding what a manager actually does in this setting.

Planning, Organizing, Leading, and Controlling Approach

The planning, organizing, leading, and controlling approach was first introduced by Henri Fayol, the same person who introduced the 14 principles of management discussed in chapter 2. Despite the development of management theory, this concept has remained a prominent school of thought regarding what a manager does.

The planning function involves establishing goals and objectives, as well as strategies for achieving them (Dumler & Skinner, 2005). The planning function sets a course of action for the organization through short-term and long-term goals. Short-term goals should be accomplished within a year whereas long-term goals are designed to be achieved within 5 to 10 years (goals and objectives are discussed later in this chapter). The planning function of management can take on many forms, including planning staff goals and objectives, long-range strategic planning that drives agency operations over a longer time frame, marketing planning, and master planning for land and facility acquisition and development. Planning is more fully addressed in chapter 7.

The organizing function results from the planning function. It takes the plans and assigns them to the proper staff to carry out. In other words, organizing is the mechanism that puts plans into action (Certo, 2003). This includes setting up an

Table 3.1 Function and Competency Comparison

Function	Frontline managers	Middle managers	Top managers
Conceptual	—	—	Understand organizational dynamics.
	—	—	Possess knowledge of business and administrative principles.
	—	Possess knowledge of organizational goals.	Set goals and objectives.
	—	Possess working knowledge of agency mission.	Operate according to agency mission.
	—	Have the ability to plan.	Make effective long-range plans.
	Possess general knowledge of the park and recreation profession.	Possess knowledge of all jobs within their area of responsibility.	Possess comprehensive knowledge of the park and recreation profession.
Human resources	—	—	Work effectively with a board or elected officials.
	—	—	Establish positive public relations.
	—	Develop staff.	—
	—	Understand personality styles.	—
	—	Be a good mediator or negotiator.	Be an effective facilitator.
	—	Build partnerships and collaborations within the community.	Build partnerships and collaborations within the community.
	Possess effective written and oral communication skills.	Possess effective written and oral communication skills.	Possess effective written and oral communication skills.
	Possess good listening skills.	Possess good listening skills.	Possess good listening skills.
Technical	Develop and stay within a budget.	Possess budgeting and financial management skills.	Possess sound overall financial management skills.
	Understand the hiring process.	Possess knowledge of effective and legal hiring practices.	Understand personnel law.
	Program activities and events.	Possess knowledge of programming skills.	—
	Conduct program evaluations.	Conduct program evaluations.	—
	—	Manage contracts.	Manage contracts and projects.
	—	Solicit donations and raise funds.	Raise funds.
	Schedule programs, leagues, and staff.	—	—

appropriate structure of employees within the organization, as well as hiring and training staff so they can do the necessary tasks to accomplish goals and objectives. The organizing function of a manager in parks and recreation is quite prominent. Programs, events, and staff and volunteers must all be organized. A major portion of a manager's job in this profession is planning and organizing.

The leading function involves influencing staff to carry out the assigned tasks. This function is obviously staff focused because of the need to respect staff, to motivate staff to achieve established goals, to be honest and ethical with staff, and to be an overall good leader.

The controlling function is the evaluation part of management where performance is measured. Managers establish performance standards and use these standards as benchmarks for achievement. The manager's role with this function is to address how employees can improve as well as how the organization as a whole can improve. The controlling function includes program evaluations, employee evaluations, monthly sales reports, event and program implementation results, and so on.

An instructor demonstrates leadership and management skills as he teaches dog sledding.

Summary of Functions of Management

Two schools of thought on the functions of management have been presented. Technical skills are present within all four functions (i.e., planning budgets, hiring staff), the human relations functions are closely aligned with the leading function, and conceptual skills are most prevalent within planning and controlling. The two approaches to functions of management share many similarities; the major difference lies not in what the manager does, but in how it is labeled.

Resources to Manage

There has been much discussion on the history, competencies, levels, and functions of managers, but nothing has outlined what resources managers actually manage. Resources can come in many different forms. For our purposes, **resources** are the financial, physical, technological, and human assets that organizations need for the production of goods or services.

Financial resources (discussed in detail in chapters 12 and 13) drive many of the decisions managers make. Budget restrictions, available capital, and monthly sales numbers affect what things managers do and how they do them. For example, managers are responsible for determining how money will be spent throughout the year, what programs or events can be planned, and what equipment can be purchased. Financial management may also mean deciding where to cut a budget, how to

resources—Financial, physical, technological, and human assets that organizations need for the production of goods or services.

deal with unanticipated decreases in revenue throughout the year, or simply how to allocate resources. Few agencies have unlimited financial resources, so taking care of them is a large part of management. The higher the level of the manager in the organization, the more responsibility the manager will have for financial resources.

Physical resources are those things that people can see and associate with the agency. They may include a high-end resort, a roller coaster at an amusement park, an ice rink, or a store. In addition to large facilities and amenities such as these, physical resources also include equipment, such as mowers, water fountains, treadmills, and banquet tables.

Technological resources aid in the creation of products or the provision of services. Technology is changing so rapidly that it is difficult to keep up with. For many agencies this is often due to the limitations of financial resources. Larger agencies may have a staff member or department dedicated to technology, whether it is a registration system, computer-aided design (CAD) used for parks and facilities, or Web-based evaluation systems. Years ago, managers spent little time on this resource, but today's managers need to manage technological resources—and rely heavily on technology to do so.

The last, and arguably most important, resource is people. Chapter 2 discussed in detail how employees are used in organizations. They are the impetus behind production, and they require a great deal of time from managers. Employees need to be trained, motivated, and evaluated. They also need to be allowed to take risks and be innovative. It is

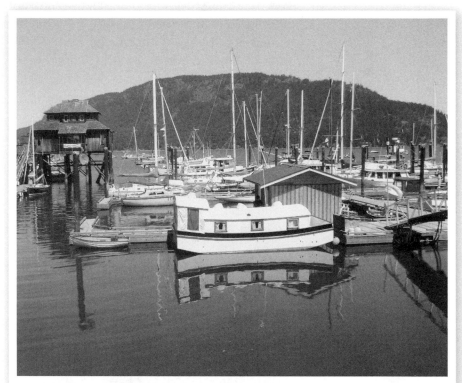

Cowichan Bay in British Columbia requires the management of resources such as a budget, staff, the waterfront, and the marina.

people who are the focus of almost all park and recreation agencies.

Managers have a lot on their plates. They have to manage people, finances, and technology. They have different responsibilities and parameters of authority. They serve a variety of functions from technical to conceptual and they are responsible for planning, organizing, leading, and controlling various parts of the organization. Although all levels of managers are discussed throughout this text, this does not mean that a new graduate with little experience will be expected to be a top-level manager right away. Most will start as frontline managers and work their way up to the desired level where increased responsibility and authority will be bestowed upon them.

Career Progression of Managers

People who are new to the field and equipped with a degree in parks and recreation will most likely find themselves in a frontline management position. However, many frontline managers aspire to middle management and possibly top management. This career progression starts by gaining experience in the field and building competencies needed for the next level. Functions change from level to level, but it is necessary to gain an understanding of how competencies change as well so that managers can put their career progression into perspective. Table 3.1 demonstrates competencies of frontline, middle, and top managers grouped by function.

Several competencies will be important throughout a manager's career regardless of level, such as public speaking and written and oral communication skills. However, there are far more differences than similarities in the competencies needed by managers at different levels. These differences are not drastic; they are subtle increases in the skills, knowledge, and abilities required for increased responsibility and authority. When considering career progression, look at the conceptual competencies of knowledge of the profession (table 3.1). Competence moves from a general knowledge of the field for frontline or entry-level employees, to knowledge of a specific area such as sport for middle managers, to comprehensive knowledge of the profession for top managers. Within the technical functions, a steady progression of all three levels can be seen in hiring competencies. For example, a manager moves from understanding the process to knowledge of effective and legal hiring practices to understanding personnel law.

Although a manager's job and competency requirements change, this does not mean the knowledge and skills learned as a frontline manager can be forgotten. It is more accurate to assume that some of the competencies are not used as much but still serve as foundational knowledge needed for supervising other staff. Take

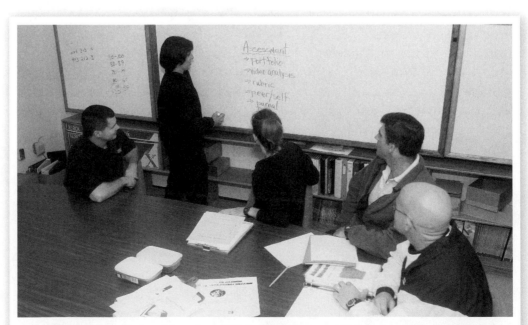

A good manager enhances his or her skills by attending a workshop, seminar, or other kind of professional development.

programming, for example. Both frontline and middle managers have programming skills listed as a competency, but the top-level manager does not. This is because both frontline and middle managers are responsible for planning programs. Furthermore, middle-level managers are most likely supervising people who are running the programs. Although top-level managers are probably not programming at all, they supervise people who program or oversee programmers. The CEO, however, makes decisions every day that require program knowledge, such as how much space is needed for youth and adult soccer fields and what sorts of programs could operate on each field size. This example illustrates the relationship between levels and technical, human relations, and conceptual skills.

Career progression is an ongoing concern for managers. Everyone will approach it differently, but there are several common practices. First, professionals will gain experience in different areas of the organization. They might begin as a student through internships and summer jobs. Positioning yourself for career progression means gaining as much experience as possible. Once in the field, experience is gained through daily tasks and taking on added responsibilities.

Second, **mentorship** has helped many managers move up within the profession. Mentors guide their mentees in making good career choices, advising them on what additional responsibilities to take on and how to network with others in the profession. Mentors can be within the same agency or in a different one.

Finally, career progression happens with education. Just because the degree is in hand does not mean that education stops. Many middle- and top-management positions require master's degrees and several years of experience. In addition, education is not just gained through universities. It is also obtained through state and national conferences, workshops, and professional development seminars. The park and recreation profession has a number of professional certifications that require more education and are highly respected in the hiring process (table 3.2).

Although career progression may seem like a simple concept, it takes a lot of planning to achieve the desired goals and level in the profession.

mentorship—Professional relationship established between a more experienced employee (mentor) and a less experienced employee (mentee) designed to guide career development.

Table 3.2   Select Certification Opportunities in the Field

Certification	Web site
Aquatics Facility Operator (AFO)	www.nrpa.org/content/default.aspx?documentId=5633
Certified Heritage Interpreter	www.interpnet.com/certification/index.shtml
Certified Interpretive Manager	www.interpnet.com/certification/index.shtml
Certified Interpretive Planner	www.interpnet.com/certification/index.shtml
Certified Meeting Professional (CMP)	www.conventionindustry.org/cmp
Certified Park and Recreation Professional (CPRP)	www.nrpa.org/content/default.aspx?documentId=551
Certified Playground Inspector	www.nrpa.org/content/default.aspx?documentId=5137
Certified Special Events Professional (CSEP)	www.ises.com/CSEP
Certified Therapeutic Recreation Specialist	www.nctrc.org
Leave No Trace Master Educator	www.weainfo.org/en/cms/?145

Management Drivers

Thus far this chapter has focused on what managers do and what functions they play in the organization. Several underlying premises require further discussion. Roles and functions define what a manager does, but the organization's values, vision, mission, goals, and objectives drive the roles and functions of the manager. These **management drivers,** as we will call them, guide how managers make decisions, solve problems, allocate resources, and train staff. They also help people become more efficient and effective managers and improve the overall organization.

Values

Values underline the agency's reason for existing. They are the principles, qualities, and beliefs regarding the organization. Values have the greatest influence in an organization when they are shared by the staff. These **shared values** are embraced by all staff from the top managers to those on the front line. Organizational values are the underlying principles that drive decision making, corporate culture, and priorities. They are formed by merging three value systems—member values, leader values, and societal values (McLean, Bannon, & Gray, 1999).

Member values come from the staff. Many people are drawn to companies because their own values match those of the company. Research has shown that when employee and company values match, employee loyalty, creativity, quality and accuracy of communication, and integrity of decision making increase (Kouzes & Posner, 2002). For example, take Patagonia, a company that manufactures clothing and accessories for outdoor recreation adventures from surfing to alpine climbing to fly fishing. The company demonstrates its commitment to the environment by reducing pollution during manufacturing, contributing a percentage of sales to grassroots environmental groups, and using organic materials when possible. Because of these values, Patagonia is looking for staff with similar values. Patagonia's job announcements state, "We're especially interested in people who share our love of the outdoors, our passion for quality and our desire to make a difference" (Patagonia, 2007a).

Leader values come from top managers. Leaders have their own values that guide organizational values. The impact of leader values within an organization will change with each company. Some will subtly influence organizational values whereas others will be a driving force, as is the case with Ben and Jerry's ice cream. Ben Cohen and Jerry Greenfield started their ice cream shop in 1978 in Burlington, Vermont. Their personal values are the impetus behind the company values, which include peace, environmentalism, and social responsibility (Ben & Jerry's Homemade Ice Cream, 2007).

Societal values come from the community, customer, and society in general. They influence agencies, especially public agencies that have a responsibility to their community. This is not to say that pockets of vocal constituents with particular values could influence the value system of an entire organization, however. Societal values are adopted based on the good of the entire community, not just a select few. For example, societal values have changed the way food is prepared in New York City. As of July 2008, all restaurants must eliminate trans fat from their food (Jones & Hellmich,

2006). This change resulted from the national obesity epidemic and concern over growing rates of heart disease. Changes in how people value health will affect organizational policy, decisions, and operations for years to come.

With values coming from three perspectives, an organization must bring all of these perspectives together to form shared values. Shared values drive the entire organization and are supported by the staff, owners, and customers, not just upper management. Shared values make sure everyone in the organization is operating from the same perspective regarding customer service, working relationships with peers, and the reasons the organization is in business. Furthermore, shared values result in more ethical behavior among employees, reduced stress and tension on the job, increased pride in the company, and increased understanding of job expectations (Kouzes & Posner, 2002). Having shared values thus results in a more successful organization.

Here are a few examples of values statements.

Societal values affect many different industries, including restaurants, fitness facilities, and environmental organizations.

The Madison (Wisconsin) Park System believes that our success is based on the following values:

- We strive to provide outstanding public services.
- We encourage public participation through outreach and community relations.
- We celebrate ethnic diversity.
- We use professional and equitable standards when planning, preserving, and maintaining our resources to reflect community and neighborhood heritage, needs, and changing interests.
- We recognize the contributions that a professional staff makes to our success. We believe in career development, ongoing training, participation in our decision-making processes, and recognition for accomplishments.
- We are committed to public and employee safety.
- We accept our roles as stewards of our natural environment.
- We recognize the contributions that volunteers make to our success.
- We believe in demonstrating fiscal responsibility.
- We recognize the added benefits of interagency and community partnerships.

www.ci.madison.wi.us/parks/aboutPark.html

Every member of the Arlington Convention and Visitors Bureau team believes in and practices these core values every day to the benefit of our partners and our clients.

- Honor relationships.
- Work with integrity.
- Be consistent and fair.
- Always yield to cooperation.
- Always seek collaboration.
- Practice and prize initiative.
- Extend and share expertise.

www.arlington.org/cvb.php

Vision

In a study involving more than 75,000 managers on six continents, it was determined that honesty is the most important characteristic workers want in their leaders. The second most important characteristic is forward thinking—having a vision (Kouzes & Posner, 2002). Kouzes and Posner defined **vision** as "an ideal and unique image of the future for the common good" (p. 125). Similar to values, a vision must be shared among the workers in an organization. This shared vision is derived from the organizational values and depicts what the company will look like in 5 to 20 years. Having a shared vision requires the entire staff to work together to see what the company can be. Good vision statements should be realistic and achievable, as well as optimistic and ambitious. To get a better idea of what vision statements are, here are a few examples.

vision—Realistic and desirable view of where an organization will be in the future.

KABOOM! (NONPROFIT ORGANIZATION FOR BUILDING PLAYGROUNDS)

Our vision is a great place to play within walking distance of every child in America (www.kaboom.org/AboutUs/WhatIsKaBOOM/OurVisionandMission/tabid/108/Default.aspx).

OKLAHOMA CITY ZOO

The Oklahoma City Zoological Park and Botanical Garden will be one of the world's premier zoological institutions, providing visitors and the community with exemplary recreational and educational opportunities (www.okczoo.com/abou.htm).

HARRAH'S ENTERTAINMENT (CASINO AND HOTEL)

Each of our brands will be the overwhelming first choice for casino entertainment of its targeted customers (www.harrahs.com/harrahs-corporate/careers-mission-vision.html).

Managers play a major role in the development and achievement of the vision. They should not create the vision on their own; instead, they are responsible for bringing staff together as a group to develop an idea of where the organization will be in the future. They work with staff to look at the past of the organization, assess where it is today, and create a vision for where it will be in the future. Although the manager facilitates creation of the vision, the staff has a major role in its creation. This involvement reinforces staff commitment to achieving what they create, making this a shared vision. A shared vision results in significantly higher job satisfaction for workers, who are more motivated, committed to the organization, and productive (Kouzes & Posner, 2002).

Mission

mission—Statement of purpose for an organization that describes who the customers are, what services are provided, and how the services are delivered.

A **mission** is a more detailed extension of the values and vision of an organization. Specifically, a mission statement addresses who the customers are, what services the organization provides, and how services are provided (McLean et al., 1999). Mission statements are much more readily publicized than values and vision statements even though they are no more important to the organization than the other two. Overall, a mission statement is a concise purpose statement reflecting what the company does. Here are a few examples.

BOISE STATE UNIVERSITY CAMPUS RECREATION

Campus Recreation enriches the university community by providing diverse recreational and leadership opportunities that foster personal growth and lifelong healthy habits (http://rec.boisestate.edu/mission).

CONNECTICUT DEPARTMENT OF ENVIRONMENTAL PROTECTION

The department provides for the conservation and management of statewide recreation lands and resources through the acquisition of open space and the management of resources to meet the outdoor recreation needs of the public (http://dep.state.ct.us/rec/mission.htm).

U.S. ARMY GARRISON–DETROIT ARSENAL

The U.S. Army Garrison–Detroit Arsenal provides base support, housing, morale, welfare, recreation, religious programs, and continuing education to a joint military community, residing on Selfridge and in the surrounding communities. The Garrison promotes readiness, health, and retention through quality of life programs (www.selfridgemwr.com/home/mission.htm).

Values, vision, and mission function together and are tightly entwined. Think of them as an inverted pyramid (figure 3.2) to see how they work together to drive the day-to-day operations of managers. The values are the overarching premise of the organization and are general guiding principles resulting in a more specific vision, leading to the most specific of the three, the mission.

Figure 3.2 Values, vision, and mission.

Goals

Sometimes the terms *goals* and *objectives* are used interchangeably when in fact they are distinct. **Goals** are broad statements of intended actions. They outline what an agency wishes to accomplish, which helps move the organization in the desired direction to fulfill its mission and achieve its vision. Here are some examples of goals.

goals—Broad statements of intent set by organizations to guide actions.

The City of Dubuque (Iowa) has the following as some of its goals.

- To provide a safe park and recreation system that continues to meet the community's needs for useable and accessible parks and open space
- To offer a variety of affordable and accessible spectator and participatory events and experiences for people of all ages
- To coordinate the implementation of the recreation, entertainment, culture, and education planning component of the Riverfront Plan with other public and private organizations.

www.cityofdubuque.org/index.cfm?pageid=673

The Bedford (Massachusetts) Conservation Commission developed nine goals from its 1996 10-year open space and recreation survey of community needs.

- Goal 1: Preserve Bedford's small-town image.
- Goal 2: Protect valuable water resources and unique wildlife habitat areas.
- Goal 3: Protect aquifer recharge areas for existing and future water supply.
- Goal 4: Develop and promote a public awareness program for Bedford's conservation and recreation areas.
- Goal 5: Preserve and protect historic and cultural properties and sites.
- Goal 6: Preserve large tracts of undeveloped land.
- Goal 7: Improve access and trail linkages to conservation, recreation, and other land uses.
- Goal 8: Enhance the quality and variety of passive and active recreational opportunities for all age groups and abilities.
- Goal 9: Increase the town's responsiveness to protecting environmentally sensitive and culturally significant properties.

www.town.bedford.ma.us/conservation/open_space.html#anchor.osrp.goals

Goals can be either short term, achievable in a year or less; intermediate term, achievable in 1 to 5 years; or long term, achievable in 5 to 7 years. Agencies set short-, intermediate-, and long-term goals to drive decision making and carry out planning functions. They set goals for marketing, productivity, and the use of financial resources.

Although the focus has been organizational goals thus far, goals are infused throughout the organization right down to individual employees. For example, each department may have its own goals. Furthermore, employees may have annual, semiannual, or biannual goals for themselves. Often these goals are used as performance measures during employee evaluations.

Participation in organizational goal setting is a must. Staff members need to feel they have a role in determining the direction of the organization. This increases their commitment to achieving the goals. Also, the people responsible for achieving the goals know the ins and outs of the area better than upper management would. Additionally, organizations should set goals because much research has indicated that when people set goals, they outperform those who do not set goals (Locke, 1968). In addition, when difficult goals are set and accepted, a higher level of performance results.

Objectives

In order to achieve goals, it is necessary to establish objectives. **Objectives** are measurable steps to achieving goals. In essence, goals are what an agency wants to accomplish and objectives are how the staff is going to accomplish them.

SMART Objectives

Few organizations develop well-written objectives. A well-written objective should be SMART—specific, measurable, achievable, realistic, and time-related (Drucker, 1954). Objectives are far more difficult to write than goals because of the need to make them SMART. Let's use the following objective for a convention and visitors' bureau to demonstrate the SMART acronym.

Objective: The sales and marketing staff is responsible for bringing three new conferences to the Binghamton Convention Center by the end of 2009.

SPECIFIC

Objectives should clearly state what is to be accomplished. They should be detailed, focused, and concrete as to what is to be achieved. For the sample objective, there is no doubt what is to be achieved. The sales staff knows they need to find three new clients and get their conferences scheduled at the convention center.

MEASURABLE

Objectives should be written so that they can be assessed as to whether or not they are achieved. The specification of three conferences makes this objective measurable. A manager should be able to answer yes or no as to whether or not three conferences were booked and thus the objective was achieved.

ACHIEVABLE

If objectives are not achievable in the near future, staff will not stay motivated to complete them. For example, if the convention center did not have space for three more conferences until 2011, this objective would not be achievable. Or, if the date to fulfill this objective is set 4 years into the future, it is too far away to keep staff committed to it, again making it unachievable. Objectives are regularly reviewed either semiannually or annually to update progress, add new objectives, and change objectives that are not achievable.

REALISTIC

A good objective must be realistically attainable; the organization needs to have the appropriate resources such as staff and budget. Assume the sales and marketing department consists of two people who have a lot of responsibility and who are short-staffed. A few more conferences might be realistic, but if the objective was changed to 20 new conferences, two people realistically could not accomplish it. Although this example is exaggerated to illustrate a point, it shows why staff at all levels should be involved in setting goals and objectives—they have intimate knowledge of what objectives are realistic.

TIME-RELATED

In order to know if the agency is on target to achieve the goals, the objectives must be time-related, meaning there is an established time frame or deadline, such as a

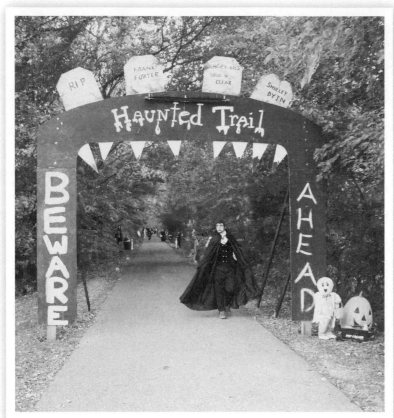

Any large-scale special event requires solid goals and objectives that will ultimately guide the planning process.

year, a month, a specific date, or a season, that indicates when the objective will be achieved. This is where many objectives fall short. The objectives may follow SMART in everything but the component that makes the objective time-related—the deadline. This is not to say that the deadline cannot be changed. It is not always possible to predict when an objective can be achieved. For example, assume an agency evaluates its employees based on employee- and manager-determined objectives each year. During the employee evaluation meeting, progress on objectives is discussed. If an objective was scheduled to be completed by the evaluation meeting and it was not, the objective can be carried over to the next evaluation with a new deadline (if feasible) and a discussion can be held to ascertain why the objective was not met.

Three Types of Management Objectives

Following the SMART method of writing objectives will provide a solid framework of work to be accomplished over a certain length of time. However, managers should not only be concerned with how objectives are written, they should be concerned with the type of objectives they are writing as well. There are three types of management objectives: process, impact, and outcome objectives (March of Dimes, 2007).

Process objectives hold agencies accountable for what and how they accomplish things. These objectives could pertain to staff or customers. For example, a process objective could be the following.

> The maintenance staff will review park mowing schedules with recommendations for changes by January 2009.

This objective is designed to examine the current process and to make suggestions for improving it.

Impact objectives focus on changes in attitudes, knowledge, perceptions, and other behaviors, such as the following objective for the marketing department of the Parks and Recreation Department of the fictional city of York.

> The marketing department will develop a promotional campaign to position recreation as a contributor to physical and mental health in this community by the end of 2010.

Outcome objectives focus on the end result of an action. As mentioned in the discussion of outcomes-based management in chapter 2, outcomes can be skill, knowledge, attitude, value, and condition oriented (United Way of America, 1996). To help clarify the distinction between impact and outcomes objectives, consider the following outcome objective. Now that the marketing staff has started their campaign to reposition parks and recreation as a viable source of wellness, as outlined in the impact objective, the next objective is outcome based.

The City of York Parks and Recreation Department will strive to become a Fitness City USA award finalist by the end of 2010 based on its services and reputation as contributing to the health and wellness of its citizens.

Goals and objectives have been a common topic of study in beginning leadership and programming courses as well as in more advanced evaluation and management courses. The need to work with goals and objectives will also be a mainstay throughout a manager's career.

Efficiency and Effectiveness

New organizations open every day, from restaurants to fitness centers to outdoor recreation equipment stores. Some close within a few months whereas others thrive for years. What makes organizations successful? There are many answers to this question, but one key is whether an organization is efficient and effective. The most important goal of this book is to teach you to be an efficient and effective manager, which will lead to an organization that has a much better chance of succeeding. Since these two terms will be used throughout, it is important to understand what they mean.

Efficiency is concerned with minimizing the amount of resources that an organization wastes. An efficient organization does not waste resources such as money, people, or technology. All of these resources cost money, and quality organizations do not waste resources. Examples of wasted resources include keeping lifeguards on the clock and paying them to do nothing when the pool is closed due to inclement weather or buying 20 more staff uniforms than are actually needed.

Effectiveness refers to how capable an organization is of achieving its goals and objectives. An agency might strive to increase membership by 20 percent, to sell 20 percent more units each quarter, or to operate at 85 percent of room capacity each month. The degree to which the organization meets these goals and objectives is a measure of its effectiveness.

Efficiency and effectiveness are measured in numerous ways and from many perspectives. Customers measure them through participation in programs, facility use, and product purchases. The community as a whole can evaluate efficiency and effectiveness by passing referenda and valuing the quality of life that results from agency products and services. Internally, organizations can measure efficiency and effectiveness by looking at how monetary and human resources are used in relation to quality of products and services or how well the organization is meeting the needs of the community.

Do not assume that all organizations that have been in business for years are both efficient and effective. Efficiency and effectiveness can be measured on a continuum from efficient to inefficient and effective to ineffective (figure 3.3). Organizations can have varying levels of each, and these levels can change over time. So, how can organizations remain both efficient and effective? That question will be answered throughout this book by providing insight into how to be a better manager. For

efficiency—Minimizing the waste of human, financial, technological, and physical resources.

effectiveness—Capability of an organization to achieve its goals and objectives.

example, managers must be efficient and effective employees themselves. Most park and recreation agencies have limited resources, and employees are expected to be as efficient as possible while still providing quality services. Managers are also responsible for measuring the efficiency and effectiveness of employees through employee evaluation and continual feedback on performance (chapter 10), having sound financial management processes (chapters 12 and 13), and evaluating the effectiveness of programs and services (chapter 14). All of these and more contribute to the efficiency and effectiveness of organizations.

Figure 3.3 Efficiency versus effectiveness.

Conclusion

▶ Regardless of what level you are as a manager and what agency you work for, several things will hold true. First, efficiency and effectiveness will always be a vital part of success in an agency. Second, managers will be driven by values, vision, and mission statements so that they know where the company is headed and how they are going to get there. Finally, a manager can always count on having goals and objectives that guide the agency, the department, and the individual employee. All of these things working together form what managers do, why they do it, and how they get it done.

REVIEW QUESTIONS

1. Discuss the three levels of management and give an example of each.

2. How do the three levels of management relate to the technical, human relations, and conceptual functions of managers?

3. Differentiate among the planning, organizing, leading, and controlling functions of management.

4. Define *responsibility* and *authority*. How do they change as a person moves up the three levels of management?

5. Give examples of the four types of resources a manager must deal with in the workplace.

6. How do competencies change in terms of career progression and the functions of management?

7. Define *values, vision,* and *mission.* How do they each drive management?

8. Differentiate between goals and objectives, and then write an objective that follows the SMART acronym.

9. Discuss efficiency and effectiveness. Give examples from your own experience of good and poor efficiency and effectiveness.

10. Describe how managers experience career progression in terms of competencies needed from entry-level through top-level managers.

Check out the online student resource at www.HumanKinetics.com/LeisureServicesManagement for additional material, including sample documents, case studies, Web links, and more.

KEY WORDS

common law, torts, negligence, invitee, licensee, assumption of risk, comparative negligence, statute of limitations, waivers, sovereign immunity, tort immunity statutes, battery, assault, defamation, false imprisonment, contract, gross negligence, Good Samaritan statutes, eminent domain, due process

COMPETENCY CHECK

Take another look at table 1.3 (page 9) to see how you assessed this related competency.

4. Demonstrate basic knowledge of laws and legal matters affecting the field.

CHAPTER 4

Legal Foundations for Managers

My job is to solve problems. A person comes to me and explains an issue that needs to be resolved. She was too cold on her last camping trip, she gets blisters from her boots, or she needs a new way to transport her bike on road trips. We discuss these issues and come up with solutions that best fit the needs of the customers. Whether that is finding a warmer sleeping bag, showing her how to adjust her boot laces so they fit better, or explaining the dif-

ferences between hitch-mount and roof-mount bicycle racks, a proper solution can be found. Risk management plays a big part in the decision-making process when it comes to particular pieces of equipment such as climbing rope and bicycle helmets. If a customer isn't going to use the equipment properly or for its intended uses, I won't sell it to them.

Jill Fogleman
Sales Associate
REI (outdoor gear store)
St. Louis, Missouri

A basic understanding of legal concerns is crucial for students who will soon be working in the leisure services industry. Whole courses are devoted to legal concerns and risk management. Even some of the subtopics of this chapter, such as negligence and contract law, are given semester-long coverage in law schools, business schools, and other curricula. Therefore it is not the purpose of this chapter to provide a complete understanding of legal concerns or to provide legal advice. The intent of this chapter is to introduce legal concepts and applications to prepare you for further study or on-the-job learning.

It would be rare indeed if you did not encounter a situation in your career or personal life that required your involvement in litigation to some extent. You might merely work for an agency or business that is involved in a lawsuit, or you might be a direct part of a lawsuit in your capacity as an employee or manager. If this happens, an understanding of legal implications may empower you to better handle the legal process and the subsequent decisions that you will make with the aid of your attorney.

common law—Rules of action derived from judicial decisions.

The Canadian legal system and the U.S. legal system share a common ancestry, one that began when they were part of the British Empire. The legal systems of both countries are primarily based upon English **common law**, a system that deals with legal relationships and liabilities of individuals and organizations. In both countries, cases are decided in courts of law with judicial decisions made by judges or juries. Published cases may set precedent for future judicial decisions, which means Canadian courts can use previous Canadian case law to help shape future law and U.S. courts can use previous U.S. case law. Both countries also have statutory law, or laws created by their legislatures. The United States has both state and federal statutory law, and Canada has statutory law for each province in addition to federal law. Although Canadian case law does not have precedent-setting value in U.S. courts and vice versa, cases might still be used as a secondary source of information by the courts. This chapter focuses on legal issues from the Canadian and U.S. perspectives. Understand that there are many similarities and differences between the two legal systems, and this chapter focuses more on the U.S. system. However, the terminology in both countries is very similar.

This chapter addresses major legal topics in the context of specializations within the field of leisure services. The chapter first introduces current trends, then provides an overview of relevant legal terms and concepts, and finally provides an overview of legal issues and risk management principles with unique applications for managers.

Current Legal Issues and Trends

The importance of understanding legal issues and risk management in leisure services management is unique to each student. A few students may wish to pursue future legal studies by choosing law as a profession. For this group, understanding legal issues is the first small step in a long journey of learning. For the majority of students, the importance of this study will not be as great, but it may still become important in future career endeavors. A few students may wish to be risk managers for their organization, with the specific job of managing risk, improving safety, and limiting the liability of the organization. Others will be involved in risk management and reducing the risk of liability through their roles as managers and leaders in various organizations. Some may even begin as interns where they are asked to help draft waivers before final review by upper management and legal counsel or when they notice hazards that could lead to legal liability. And for those who become personally involved in a lawsuit, a basic understanding of legal issues might bring empowerment to better handle the litigation process.

Regardless of your specialization in the field, the possibility of a lawsuit is ever present. You can likely imagine the many situations in leisure services where injury and subsequent lawsuits can occur. For example, in natural resources management, lawsuits have resulted from the following categories of potential harm:

▶ Water features such as fast-moving rivers and streams, lakes, and ocean currents
▶ Encounters between humans and carnivorous animals such as bears, cougars, and alligators
▶ Scenic overlooks and high cliffs
▶ Search-and-rescue operations

In the area of hospitality and tourism, litigation has arisen from the following categories of events:

▶ The serving of alcohol
▶ Swimming and diving in hotel pools
▶ Hotel security
▶ Cruise ships and ports of call
▶ Travel and tour planning

In the area of recreational sport, the following categories encompass litigated areas:

▶ Facilities such as basketball courts and fitness centers
▶ Supervision of sport activities
▶ Equipment

In municipal recreation, areas of concern for litigation include the following:

▶ Youth supervision
▶ Lightning preparedness
▶ Facilities and equipment
▶ Playground safety

In the nonprofit sector, litigated areas include the following:

▶ Protection of lakes and streams
▶ Protection of endangered species
▶ Fighting for roadless areas in national parks and other federally managed land

In therapeutic recreation, important legal issues include the following:

▶ Employment of people with disabilities
▶ Inclusion and safety in sport
▶ Communication regarding participant disabilities

It is clear to most anyone that there are a lot of lawsuits in the United States, and a lot of lawyers. Go to any town or city and look in the phone book, and you will see that the section for attorneys is usually large. Why are there so many lawsuits? Some people suggest that it is the result of the number of attorneys, and hence competition and advertising drive demand. Others think that the reason lies in the lottery mentality of many who see the big-dollar verdicts and want a piece of the pie for themselves. Still others speculate that the driving force is a change in societal values that has shifted the focus of responsibility from self to others. The reason for the amount of litigation may be a combination of these and other factors, but whatever the cause, leisure services managers must be prepared for a possible lawsuit.

The most common type of lawsuit that a leisure services manager might face is a negligence lawsuit. Recreational pursuits often involve some element of physical risk from competitive and recreational sport to rock climbing to swimming and diving. When personal injury is involved and someone seeks money for the injury, and there was no intent to injure, the type of lawsuit that often results is a negligence lawsuit.

Negligence is a concept that every leisure services manager needs to understand. The cases in this area of law are often interesting and arouse emotion, such as lawsuits against fast-food chains for claims that fast food made the plaintiffs overweight or obese, or the famous case of the woman who sued McDonald's after she spilled hot coffee in her lap. Cases in the field of recreation also are often interesting and engage emotion. We know about many of these cases from the media or from published legal decisions. There are tens of thousands of recreation-related published cases. The majority of cases, however, never go to trial and never result in published decisions. These cases are settled by the attorneys and their clients.

Given the large number of legal cases and the perception that many suits do not have merit, several states and the U.S. government have attempted to reduce the number of lawsuits. They have gone about this through a process known as *tort reform,* which involves passing legislation to reduce the incentives for bringing lawsuits and to increase the difficulty in bringing them in the first place. Even with tort reform, however, the best practice for managers is to keep informed and develop a basic understanding of legal concerns as they pertain to managing leisure services.

Overview of Key Legal Concepts

A basic understanding of key legal concepts is important for the leisure services manager. Knowledge of the basics is the first step toward becoming empowered and understanding the rationale behind preventive risk management and safety measures. An introduction to **torts,** contracts, and legislation relevant to leisure services management is a good place to start.

> **torts**—Civil wrongs or injuries that may result in monetary damages.

Negligence

The duties owed by leisure services organizations to the public are governed by common-law tort rules. Torts are often governed by state law, meaning that the interpretation of state laws determines the outcome of a case. As mentioned, **negligence** represents the most likely type of lawsuit a leisure services manager might face when someone is injured on the property of the organization. Negligent conduct occurs when a defendant fails to meet the standard of care for the protection of others and as a result someone is harmed.

> **negligence**—Unintentional tort that results in personal injury.

Four Elements of Negligence

In order to pursue a negligence cause of action, one must prove the existence of four elements. These elements are duty, breach of duty, causation, and damages.

Duty   The first element, duty, is a special relationship established inherently, voluntarily, or statutorily between a service provider and participant. Managers of leisure services typically owe a duty to provide a reasonably safe environment and keep participants from an unreasonable risk of harm. Establishing the standard of care (the duty or responsibility of the plaintiff) is critical to whether a case is won or lost. Following is a list of factors that a court might consider when determining whether the standard of care was met. Often, a combination of factors determines whether the standard of care was met.

- ▶ *Case precedent:* Courts will look to the outcomes of previous cases to determine the standard of care.
- ▶ *Rules and regulations:* The standard of care might be written in a rule put forth by a regulatory agency (e.g., pool safety standards regarding the proper number of lifeguards for a pool of a given size).
- ▶ *State and federal laws:* Legislation may mandate a certain act. For example, in some states, fitness centers, high schools, and park and recreation agencies are required to have automated external defibrillators (AEDs) on the premises.

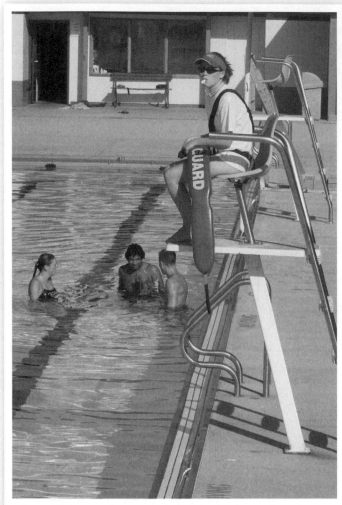

Lifeguards have a duty to patrons to provide a safe swimming environment and adhere to a standard of care.

▶ *Community practice or industry standard:* The standard of care might be influenced by what others in the industry or community are doing. For example, do other playgrounds in the city or state adhere to certain guidelines?

▶ *Federal regulatory agencies:* The Consumer Product Safety Commission (CPSC) has guidelines for playground safety that are often used by courts in determining whether the standard of care was met for playgrounds.

▶ *Professional associations:* Position statements are often published by organizations such as the National Collegiate Athletic Association (NCAA), the American College of Sports Medicine (ACSM), and the National Athletic Trainers' Association (NATA) that provide guidelines on subjects as diverse as lightning safety and equipment safety. These guidelines might be used by the courts in determining the standard of care.

▶ *Agency manuals:* The policy and procedure manuals of organizations might be used in determining whether they met their own standards.

▶ *Expert opinion:* The opinions of experts from various fields might be used to help a court determine the standard of care.

The legal obligation, or duty, of leisure services managers might further be influenced by the legal category under which a user of their facilities falls. In general, the law recognizes three categories of users: invitees, licensees, and trespassers. Invitees are afforded the greatest legal protection, followed by licensees and trespassers. For a legal discussion on negligence, tort law, and categories of users, see Keeton (1984).

An **invitee** is someone who enters the property of another for a business purpose. Invitees often pay a fee, such as a visitor to a state park or someone who pays money to enter a recreation facility or participate in a program. A **licensee,** on the other hand, is a guest who does not benefit the landowner economically (Restatement of the Law of Torts, 1965). Depending on the jurisdiction, the responsibility of the leisure services manager to a licensee might be to remove or warn of any hidden dangers that are known to personnel; to keep the property, facilities, and equipment in reasonably safe repair; and to protect visitors from reasonably foreseeable dangers (Kaiser, 1986). Finally, a trespasser is someone who enters the property of another without permission. However, managers may still owe a duty of care to this person, the nature of which depends on the circumstances.

invitee—Person who is invited onto another's property with the consent of the landowner and who often pays a fee.

licensee—Invited guest, or one who enters the property of another without paying a fee.

Breach of Duty   The second element, the breach of duty, or the act causing damage, may be either a commission (something you did) or an omission (something you did not do but should have). Failure to properly supervise young children at soccer practice is an example of omission, whereas removing warning signs from a lake-front swimming area is an example of commission.

Causation   The third element to be proved is that there is a connection between the injury and the breach of duty. Causation is the crucial link between the act and the damages.

Damages   Finally, damages are simply the injury received. In order to pursue a negligence claim, the plaintiff must show that some physical, emotional, or economic harm resulted from the act.

Defenses to Negligence

Defenses to negligence claims emanate from three sources of law: common law, contract law, and statutory law. **Assumption of risk** is a legal theory that falls under the common-law category. Under this theory, plaintiffs may not recover for damages if they were injured as a result of a risk inherent to the activity and they voluntarily exposed themselves to a danger that was known and understood. Some courts recognize that three elements must exist for an assumption of risk defense to shield the defendant from liability:

1. The risk must be inherent to the activity.
2. The plaintiff must voluntarily consent to participate in the activity.
3. The plaintiff must have knowledge, understanding, or appreciation of the risks involved in the activity.

> **assumption of risk—** Defense to negligence recognized by some jurisdictions when three elements are met: The risk is inherent to the activity, the plaintiff voluntarily consented to participate in the activity, and the plaintiff had knowledge, understanding, or appreciation of the risk.

Assumption of risk is an effort to shift the responsibility for the injury back to the plaintiff. Note that the interpretation of this doctrine varies from state to state. The interpretation in this section is but one example. To learn more about assumption of risk, see *Prosser and Keeton on the law of torts* (Keeton, 1984).

Providers of leisure services must ensure that patrons know of the risks inherent in an activity. They can tell patrons about the risks either verbally, such as in a short presentation before a rafting trip, for example, or in written form, such as on a warning sign or in a document that lists the risks. Often a waiver will contain language that warns of the risks in an activity. When risks are told or written, the assumption of risk that might protect the service provider is termed *express assumption of risk*.

Another way that participants might be held to have knowledge of risk is through their background, experience, or common knowledge. A skilled climber, for example, might be held to assume the risks in climbing, just as an experienced athlete might be held to assume the risks inherent to a particular sport. When knowledge of the risk comes from a person's background, experience, or common knowledge, the assumption of risk that might be raised as a defense is termed *implied assumption of risk*.

Finally, certain risks that are deemed to be inherent to certain activities are written in state laws. For example, in some states, a collision with a tree would be a risk assumed by a snow skier. It would not be feasible to remove all trees bordering a ski slope. Trees are part of the experience and an inherent risk in skiing.

Another method by which defendants might seek to protect themselves by shifting responsibility is the **comparative negligence** defense. With this defense, a plaintiff might be entitled to only that part of the final judgment for damages for which the court determines the defendant to be responsible. For example, where a defendant is found 60 percent responsible, the plaintiff is found 40 percent responsible, and the total verdict is for $100,000, the plaintiff would only recover $60,000, the proportional amount by which the defendant was found responsible. This type of defense is called *pure comparative negligence*. Other forms of comparative negligence might proportion damages only if the plaintiff is less than 50 percent at fault.

In addition to these defenses, there is a maximum amount of time that a plaintiff can wait before bringing a lawsuit. This is called the **statute of limitations.** As an example, if the plaintiff brings a lawsuit after 5 years and the statute of limitations is 4 years, then the defendant will be protected from the lawsuit.

Defenses to negligence claims also exist in contract law. Waivers, informed consent forms, and facility lease and equipment rental agreements can all be defenses in contract law. There are many types of **waivers,** but the common denominator is exculpatory language protecting the service provider from ordinary negligence. A well-written waiver releasing a leisure services provider from liability for ordinary negligence while participating in an activity can be enough to protect an organization from liability for a negligence claim. One caveat with defenses in contract law is that the parties involved must be of legal age in order for the contract to be legally enforceable. Defenses in contract law are not effective when the plaintiff is a minor (under the age of 18 or 21, depending on the state).

Another type of legal protection comes from legislation. Defenses to negligence in statutory law encompass those acts established by a legislative body at the state or federal levels. Historically, governmental immunity provided protection from liability to municipalities (e.g., cities and towns), which included park and recreation departments. As a result of governmental immunity (sometimes referred to as **sovereign immunity**), it was difficult for plaintiffs to make claims of liability against public agencies. In 1946, the U.S. Congress passed the Federal Tort Claims Act, which replaced governmental immunity and allowed the government to be held liable for certain negligent acts. State legislatures also enacted their own tort claim acts to enable people to file negligence claims against public entities at the state level.

Because of this movement to abrogate governmental immunity, there has been an increase in the number of statutory defenses to negligence for public, private, and nonprofit entities. These include **tort immunity statutes,** such as recreational user statutes and sport safety statutes that require a higher level of negligence for liability to be found, and caps on damages for negligence claims.

Recreational user statutes are legislative acts established in all states for the purpose of protecting landowners from liability if they permit the public to use their property at no cost for recreational activities. Since the inception of recreational user statutes in the mid-1960s, the statutes have been interpreted in a variety of ways at the state level and have evolved to protect both private and public landowners.

---

comparative negligence—Defense to negligence whereby some degree of fault and subsequent monetary damages are shifted away from the defendant. In a pure comparative negligence jurisdiction, defendants are only liable for the proportion of fault attributed to them.

statute of limitations—Amount of time in which a lawsuit can be brought.

waivers—Contracts, often also termed *releases*, that form an agreement designed to protect a potential defendant from liability.

sovereign immunity—Protection from liability provided under statutory law for government entities.

tort immunity statutes—Laws created by legislatures most commonly designed to protect public and private entities from liability.

Sport safety statutes exist in most states to limit the liability of certain commercial leisure enterprises. The theme of these laws is to shift responsibility to participants for risks that they voluntarily assume. The most common types of sport safety statutes provide legislative protection for snow skiing, roller skating, and equestrian activities. In addition, the list of protected activities has expanded to include limitations on liability for activities as diverse as hang gliding, snowmobiling, and white-water boating. Additionally, some states have enacted statutory provisions that provide blanket protection to all sport and recreational activities.

Intentional Torts

As mentioned previously, the most common type of lawsuit in recreational settings is negligence, since most managers and staff do not intend to act in such a way that will bring harm to others. In some cases, however, intentional acts are committed that result in harm to participants. Leisure services is a unique field that places unique stressors on people in the profession. Event managers, for example, often work extremely long hours. Sport participants (and parents of youth sport participants) can become hostile toward coaches and referees. Physical and emotional fatigue can take its toll on even the most well-intentioned people. Therefore, it is important to be aware of the types of intentional torts that can affect the leisure services profession. Situations that might result in intentional torts include

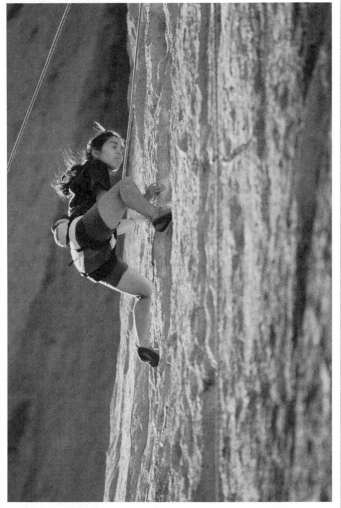

A climber assumes the risk for an activity such as this because it is considered to be inherent to the activity.

making verbal threats, unwanted touching, spreading rumors, employees dealing with abusive patrons by taking matters into their own hands, and holding people against their will. The categories of intentional torts that these acts encompass are battery, assault, defamation (libel and slander), and false imprisonment.

Battery and Assault

The law often makes a technical distinction between assault and battery that differs from common perceptions of the two. The distinction is that battery involves the touching of another whereas assault involves the threat of that touching. **Battery** is generally defined as the touching of another that is intentional, harmful or offensive, unprivileged, and unpermitted. The intentional aspect refers to the intent to make contact with another, either directly or indirectly (e.g., throwing a baseball at someone). The touch can be either harmful, meaning that the victim does not have to be bruised or physically hurt, or it can be offensive, such as an act associated

battery—Intentional tort involving the harmful or offensive touching of another.

with sexual harassment. Harmful touching is common in sport but often there is no liability because it is permitted (or consented to) as part of the game. Examples of situations where battery might come up include referees getting into fights with college intramural players or a counselor touching a camper inappropriately. Rules regarding appropriate touching, methods of discipline, and referees not taking matters into their own hands are put in place to avoid situations that might lead to battery and subsequent lawsuits against the organization.

assault—Intentional tort involving the threat of harmful or offensive touching of another.

Assault is closely associated with battery but differs in that assault is the threat of battery. An organization might be held liable for the acts of an employee who threatens to touch someone in a harmful or offensive way. Again, staff instruction on not taking matters into their own hands by threatening another person is important. Waiting for the proper authority to handle a heated situation is often the best measure to take.

Defamation

defamation—False and defamatory statement made in the presence of a third party. Defamation may be either spoken (slander) or written (libel).

Most people have heard about the intentional tort of **defamation.** Gossip in the workplace; media outlets that write harmful, untrue things about certain people to increase sales; untrue negative remarks that are made without knowing that they were overheard; and negative untrue evaluations of work performance can all lead to defamation under the right circumstances. *Defamation* is an umbrella term for two specific types of defamation: libel and slander. Slander represents the verbal form of defamation and libel represents the written form. In defamation lawsuits, plaintiffs have been injured as a result of something written or spoken about them that was untrue, harmful, and made public.

The law uses certain terms to describe that which is harmful and made public. The term used for harm is *defamatory*. Therefore, one element of defamation is making a statement that is defamatory. The term used to describe a statement that is made public is *published to a third party*. This means that a third person, someone other than the person making the statement and the person affected by the statement, has heard what was said.

The rules for defamation differ for public figures and ordinary citizens. Public figures generally have less protection against statements about them that are untrue and negative. Also, certain categories of defamatory statements are potentially more libelous, including statements about someone's moral character (e.g., falsely calling someone a child molester), a person's chastity (e.g., sexual promiscuity), and specific diseases, as well as statements that affect a person's occupation and profession.

To avoid defamation, managers must discourage gossip in the workplace, back up performance evaluations with objective factual information, and not say anything if they are unsure of the truth in a given situation.

False Imprisonment

false imprisonment—Intentional, wrongful confinement of another.

Another intentional tort that leisure services providers should be aware of is the tort of **false imprisonment.** The word *imprisonment* brings to mind prison bars or being locked in a room. However, confinement does not necessarily have to occur. Depending on the court and jurisdiction, people may be imprisoned merely if they believe that they cannot leave a certain location (e.g., a child is told by an adult to stay in one place for an unreasonable amount of time or a person cannot leave an area without fear of being harmed). False imprisonment may arise from seemingly innocent situations. Children might be held against their will as punishment without the supervisor realizing the error in keeping them from leaving a certain area for an unreasonable amount of time, or an innocent person might be held because a manager believed that the person had stolen an item from the organization.

Because of the potential for false imprisonment claims, the leisure services manager should be extremely careful in making decisions that could result in people being held against their will. Managers of commercial establishments must consider the reasonableness of their actions. For example, did the manager have reasonable suspicion to detain the person, was the person detained for a reasonable amount of time, was the use and amount of force reasonable, and was the person brought back from a reasonable distance outside the business? These are all concerns that the leisure services professional should consider and discuss with legal counsel before acting.

Contracts

A **contract** is an agreement between people that is enforceable by law if certain conditions are met. Contracts are usually agreements of exchange for tangible items such as money for food or beverages. However, the leisure services industry often has intangible forms of exchange such as an agreement where participants pay money (a tangible item) for an experience such as white-water rafting (an intangible item). The field may also have agreements (contracts) where neither item is tangible. For example, participants may sign a waiver (a contract) where they give up the right to prevail in a lawsuit if they are injured in exchange for the right to participate in the activity.

Contracts in the leisure services profession are common. For example, in hospitality, the hotel or resort might have contracts with food and beverage providers, linen services, and security companies, as well as employment contracts with hotel and resort employees. With guests, the hotel might have contracts related to lodging, food and beverage, and the provision of hotel services. In tourism, contracts exist for travel package agreements, agreements with cruise lines, and air and ground transportation. Parks and public lands contract with concessionaires who run hotels or restaurants on public land. Public and private recreation providers often require waivers from participants. In sport, player and coaches' contracts are common agreements. You can probably think of many more examples.

To have a valid and enforceable contract that will bind the parties to an agreement, you must have a valid offer and acceptance. As such, a contract is an exchange. It is an agreement to offer a product, service, or experience that requires acceptance of the terms of that offer. Two important concepts form the basis for an enforceable contract: fairness and the ability of the person or organization to understand the terms of the contract. Factors that influence the ability to understand the language of a contract come from several sources, including the characteristics of the person agreeing to the terms of the contract and the way the contract is written.

What factors might make it difficult for someone to understand the terms of a contract? One that probably comes first to mind is the age of the person. Contracts

contract—Agreement that is enforceable by law if certain conditions are met.

signed by a minor (a person under the age of either 18 or 21, depending on the state) are unenforceable. The law uses the term *capacity* to describe the ability to understand. A person under the state-mandated legal age of majority does not have the capacity to enter into a contract. Another issue related to capacity is the mental status of the person agreeing to the terms of a contract. Mental status can be influenced by health status, disability, alcohol, or drugs. Therefore, when contracting for products or using waivers, it is important for managers to understand the mental state and age of the person signing the contract.

A second issue that relates to the ability to understand a contract is how the contract is written. For example, a contract written in confusing language with a lot of legalese may be difficult for the average person to understand. A waiver is an example of a contract where the language is crucial. For instance, another term for waiver is *exculpatory agreement*. It would be better to use the word *waiver* than the term *exculpatory agreement* since many would not understand the meaning of the latter term. Additionally, the size and type of font should be easy to read and understand.

The fairness of the contract is another overriding principle that governs the enforceability of contracts. The term *equal bargaining power* is often used in determining whether a contract was fair. This term means that one party should not be overwhelmed or unduly intimidated by the status and power of the other party. For example, governments and some large organizations have far superior bargaining power. Situations might arise where one party has no choice but to accept the terms of a contract given the power of the other party. In these cases, unequal bargaining power might be brought up as an argument for voiding a contract.

It is often said that a waiver is not worth the paper it is written on; however, this blanket pronouncement is false. As with any contract, a waiver may be binding (valid) if it meets the necessary contractual requirements. Courts will uphold waivers and make them binding on both parties if the requisite contractual elements are met.

Another issue of fairness involves whether a party has voluntarily entered into a contract. Contracts may be deemed unenforceable if one side is forced or tricked into signing. Managers should be aware of situations where people may feel they have lost their choice in entering a contract. An example might be where people participating in a dangerous outdoor climbing experience are given the waiver halfway through the activity. There would be no choice except to sign the waiver and continue under the guidance of experienced climbers or else try to make it back to safety on their own.

When dealing with contracts, managers should be aware of the bargaining power of both parties, the characteristics of the person signing the contract, and the language of the contract. All of these considerations should be taken into account and discussed with a competent attorney when contracts are drafted and administered.

Legislation

Legislation, or federal and state laws enacted by the legislature, greatly influences leisure services management. In some cases immunity, or protection from liability, is provided by state and federal laws. As mentioned previously, recreational user statutes protect both public lands and private landowners who lease their property for recreational pursuits. This protection is provided by an increase in the standard by which these entities are judged in negligence suits. The standard rises from ordinary negligence to a higher level often termed *willful and wanton behavior,* or **gross negligence.** The interpretation of these terms is subjective and depends on the circumstances of individual cases.

Another type of law provides some protection for commercial recreation. For example, some sport organizations (e.g., skiing operations, skating rinks, equestrian activity providers) are protected from liability when someone is injured due to an inherent risk in participation. Examples of injuries from inherent risks protected by statute include when someone hits a tree on a ski slope or when a horse is spooked and the rider is injured. The reasoning behind these laws is to protect an industry that provides economic support for the affected region.

Other types of legislation include liability protection for organizations that have AEDs, commonly used in such recreational places as fitness centers, golf courses, and stadiums. In addition, legislation provides protection for those who come to the aid of someone in need (e.g., a hotel guest providing cardiopulmonary resuscitation [CPR] to a stranger on the property) and do not owe some preexisting duty (e.g., a swimmer doesn't owe the same duty that the lifeguard owes to pool patrons). These laws are commonly known as **Good Samaritan statutes.**

In addition to providing protection from liability, some laws mandate certain actions by leisure services providers. For example, certain states have enacted legislation that mandates the placement of AEDs and their use by trained responders in fitness centers. Others have mandated AEDs in city parks, and still others require that high school athletic departments have AEDs.

Other types of legislation that are designed to protect include dram shop laws, which were created to protect people who suffer as a result of the illegal sale of alcohol. These laws should be known and understood by managers, particularly those in the restaurant and hotel industry. Dram shop laws impose liability on those who sell alcohol to a minor or to someone who is visibly intoxicated and then injures another person, usually by way of an automobile accident.

Another form of legislation relevant to leisure services is enabling legislation. Enabling legislation is either state or federal law that gives certain officials the authority to enforce

gross negligence— Higher level of negligence (subjectively determined) where a defendant has demonstrated a high degree of carelessness.

Good Samaritan statutes—Laws that limit liability for laypersons who provide assistance (often medical) to someone in need.

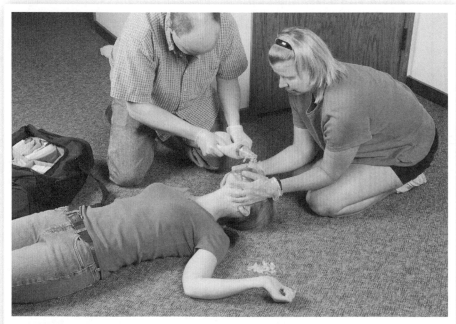

Good Samaritan statutes protect people who administer first aid or use AEDs in recreation places.

the law. Enabling legislation is often connected to the creation of parks and public lands. Federal land such as a national park, for example, will have enabling legislation. This legislation is an act of the U.S. Congress that creates the park and authorizes actions to set the park up. Examples of federal enabling legislation include the following:

▶ The Wilderness Act of 1964 mandates that federal land management agencies identify public lands suitable for wilderness designation and provide guidelines for their classification and management.

▶ The National Park Service Organic Act of 1916 established the national park system on the principle of conservation.

▶ The National Environmental Policy Act (NEPA) of 1969 requires environmental impact statements for significant changes contemplated by the National Park Service (NPS) in the management of its lands.

Another important type of legislation involves volunteer immunity. Volunteers for government and nonprofit entities are often protected from liability through state legislation and federal law. It is important for managers to know whether their state has a volunteer immunity law and, if so, what that law covers. Protection might not be available under certain conditions. For example, volunteers might not be protected from liability if, in the act giving rise to the lawsuit, they committed a criminal act, a sexual act, or an act of discrimination, or if they were under the influence of alcohol or a drug. Another common exception to the protections afforded by legislation is where the volunteer committed an act that rose above ordinary negligence to one categorized at a higher level, such as recklessness, gross negligence, or willful and wanton misconduct. Further, for the protections to apply, the volunteer must have been acting within the scope of employment when the incident occurred.

In addition to state laws, the leisure services manager should understand, with the advice and assistance of competent legal counsel, the Volunteer Protection Act of 1997. This federal law offers additional provisions that might influence the liability protections afforded to volunteers. Volunteers are often vital to the functioning of a leisure services organization; therefore, knowing the laws that offer protection for them is an important management function.

Applications to Leisure Services Management

There are several areas where legal concepts show their application to management. The two broad subject areas where this occurs are risk management, which has application to tort law, and employment law, which has clear practical implications for management. Both will be discussed in this and the following section in the context of managing leisure services.

Risk Management

In our litigious society, the leisure services professional must take measures to reduce the likelihood of injury to participants. This is the central motivation behind learning about legal concerns. Taking a proactive stance and dealing with potentially harmful situations before someone is injured is the key to an effective risk management program. A risk management plan is the process of assessing risk and taking actions to reduce or eliminate that risk. A variety of models, plans, or approaches can be taken to manage risk in leisure settings. For the sake of simplicity, however, a four-step process has been outlined that provides a starting point for dealing with risk. The four elements of this process are identification, evaluation, treatment, and implementation (Hronek & Spengler, 2007).

Identification

The first step of the four-step model is risk identification. This involves identifying both general categories of hazards and specific hazards within those categories. For example, a common general hazard is indoor and outdoor play areas. Specific hazards include uneven turf on playing fields, glass doors or windows in gyms, slippery surfaces, baseball and softball fixed bases, low fences, and inadequate protective equipment. Another key category is hotel and motel premises. Specific hazards might include lighting in parking lots, keys and locks, and hotel access points. Additional general areas relevant to leisure services management include child protection, lightning, heat-related illness, sport-related trauma, and travel to games and sporting events.

Hazards may not always be obvious. Sometimes trained inspectors are brought in from the outside to look at a facility or program with a fresh perspective. For example, the NRPA conducts a certification program for playground safety that equips people with the knowledge to identify certain hazards on playgrounds. (See www.nrpa.org/content/default.aspx?documentId=5129 for information on the NRPA playground safety certification course.)

From a liability perspective, the concept of foreseeability is important to risk identification. If a risk is foreseeable, there is a greater probability of liability should someone be injured as a result of that risk. A risk might be foreseeable if it involves places or situations where injuries have occurred in the past, places of high risk or danger, or situations where people do not understand a particular risk.

Evaluation

The second step in the model is risk evaluation. Once a risk has been identified, the manager must evaluate the frequency and severity of the identified risk. This procedure will enable managers to prioritize risks and attend to them in a timely manner. For example, risks that rate as low in both frequency and severity would be attended to after risks with either a high frequency or high severity rating.

Evaluating risks is a tricky process that involves thought and experience. Managers must be aware of potential hazards and understand their potential for harm. For example, consider a newly hired city park and recreation manager who finds that one of the parks contains a metal slide that has no shade and faces in a southerly direction. In the summer, the playground gets extremely hot. The metal slide can heat to very high temperatures, potentially resulting in a serious burn to an unsuspecting child. The leisure services manager must be able to recognize this risk and understand that the heated slide could result in serious injury.

Treatment

Once a hazard has been identified and evaluated, the third step is risk treatment. In this step, the manager decides whether to act on the perceived risk. This model provides four basic options, each of which represents a different approach to eliminating or reducing the risk. To understand the actions each option calls for, consider the following situation: During a heavy rain, the gym roof develops a leak that drips water directly on the sideline of a basketball court. Intramural basketball games are played on this court.

The first option is avoidance. This means eliminating or avoiding the risk by discontinuing the activity. The manager must cancel all games on the court until the leak is stopped.

The second option is reduction. This option, the most common type of action, involves reducing both the frequency and severity of incidents through some type of hands-on remediation. Under the scenario provided, this option would allow the games to be played but would require intramural staff to mop up the water as needed to ensure that the floor remains dry.

The third option is to transfer liability, which involves shifting the risk to another person or organization, often by contract. This option would transfer the responsibility of cleaning the water off the court (and potentially liability for injury resulting from the water) from the intramural staff to the building staff or another responsible party.

The fourth and final option is retaining the risk. This means the organization recognizes the risk but is willing to pay the potential cost. In this option, the intramural staff would feel that the water did not pose a serious threat because it was on the sideline as opposed to being on the court playing surface. Under this option, nothing would be done to clean up the water and the games would continue.

Implementation

The fourth step in the risk management process is risk implementation, or the means by which a recreation professional deals with a risk. Actions concerning risk come to fruition through the timely application of policies and procedures. A policy is a written rule governing the conduct of agency activities and programs, whereas a procedure is a written statement regarding employee actions in given circumstances. Information relevant to forming risk management policies and procedures is available from professional associations and regulatory agencies, and it is often available online. See Spengler, Connaughton, and Pittman (2006) for Web links and resources for developing risk management plans.

An effective risk management plan that is communicated to staff and properly carried out can help an organization reduce the probability of injury to its patrons and the subsequent liability that often results. Additionally, plans must be regularly practiced, evaluated, and updated. Practicing the plan will

Routine inspections of playgrounds ensure that equipment is safe and stays in good working order.

assist in working out any flaws. Announced and unannounced practice is necessary and should be conducted at least annually or more often if there are changes in staff. Documentation of the rehearsal should be carefully retained. Many administrators use standardized forms or videotape as evidence that the rehearsal was performed.

Eminent Domain and Legislative Takings

Under certain circumstances, the government has the authority to take land from private citizens for legitimate purposes of public use. A common example is where land is taken from private landowners in order to make road improvements or to run utilities such as water, gas, or power lines. Land could also be taken by the government to build a school or a public park. The legal term for this is **eminent domain.** Under eminent domain, land can be taken immediately through a legislative taking, which occurs when the government passes legislation granting the authority to take land from private landowners for a public use. Under both eminent domain and legislative takings, the private landowner is entitled to fair compensation for the property.

eminent domain—The taking of private land for a public purpose.

An example of a legislative taking occurred in the late 1980s when a large land developer bought land adjacent to Manassas National Battlefield Park outside of Washington, DC, metropolis (Spengler & Siehl, 1988). Although the park is dedicated to U.S. history and those who lost their lives in battle, it also provides a place for quiet hikes, picnics, and solitude. The developer had plans to build a large shopping complex with attendant roads, hotels, restaurants, and ancillary services. These plans created an uproar among local residents, advocates of historic preservation, and concerned citizens and interest groups from outside the immediate area. Congressional hearings were held on the topic and arguments were made from both sides. Antidevelopment interests argued that a shopping mall and the accompanying noise, traffic, and lights would destroy the aesthetic qualities of the park and its use for solitude and reflection.

It was also brought to light through little-known Civil War documents that significant fighting had taken place on the land in question. Court-martial proceedings had been brought against a Civil War commander who had been instructed to send his troops into enemy fire. He had disobeyed commands to save his troops but later was tried for not obeying orders. Since a court-martial proceeding had been initiated, a public record of the proceedings was kept. Maps were drawn up for the trial to show troop movements and positions. These maps gave evidence of troop activity on the parcel of land that the developer wished to build on.

Eventually, with these facts and with public sentiment leaning toward preserving the land in its natural state, the federal government passed legislation to preserve the land by taking it from the developer and adding it to the park. The developer was compensated for the land that was taken.

Legal Issues in Employment

It is important for leisure services managers to understand legal concerns associated with employment. The remainder of this chapter addresses a number of issues relevant to employment. It would be wise to supplement your knowledge of employment law with a thorough reading of the literature on this topic. Important employment issues with legal implications that will be covered here include

▶ discrimination based on race, color, national origin, gender, or religion;
▶ affirmative action;
▶ sexual harassment;
▶ disabilities;
▶ discrimination based on age;
▶ employee safety and health; and
▶ due process.

Additional discussion of employment laws in the United States (table 4.1) and Canada can be found in chapter 10.

Table 4.1   Summary of U.S. Employment Laws

Employment laws (federal)	Protected classes	Purpose
Title VII of the Civil Rights Act of 1964	Race, color, and national origin Gender Religion	Prevent discrimination
Age Discrimination in Employment Act (ADEA)	Age (40 yrs or older)	Prevent discrimination
Americans with Disabilities Act of 1990 (ADA)	Persons with disabilities	Prevent discrimination
Occupational Health and Safety Act (OSHA)	Employees	Employee health and safety

Employment Discrimination: Race, Color, National Origin, Gender, and Religion

The first three categories of classes are offered protection from discrimination under the Civil Rights Act. Title VII of the Civil Rights Act and its amendments apply to governmental agencies, federal government employees, labor unions, and companies with 15 or more employees.

This law governs race, color, national origin, gender, and religion. Hiring decisions must therefore be made with respect to Title VII. As such, you should also know about the Equal Employment Opportunity Commission (EEOC), the governmental agency that monitors compliance with Title VII. If qualified applicants feel they have been discriminated against in the hiring process, they would first file a claim with the EEOC. The EEOC would then decide whether to investigate the claim and take action. If they decide not to take action, the applicant may bring a lawsuit directly against the manager and the organization.

Discrimination claims can be brought on the basis of either intentional or unintentional acts of the employer. Unintentional discrimination is termed *disparate impact discrimination*. This is where the employer's workforce does not mirror the percentage of people in protected classes in the local labor market. Decisions about hiring, promotion, and retention must be based solely on job-related qualifications and cannot reflect discriminatory practices. This is the basic requirement of Title VII.

If employees or prospective employees felt that they were being unintentionally discriminated against, their claim would rest on disparate impact discrimination. This might happen where an organization hired a disproportionate number of people from outside a protected class. A potential defense to this claim would be the business necessity defense. This defense arises where an organization requires as a condition of employment that applicants be able to meet certain criteria essential to the job that has an unintentional discriminatory effect on a certain protected class. For example, a fitness club might require personal trainers to be able to lift a heavy amount of weight to be able to adequately

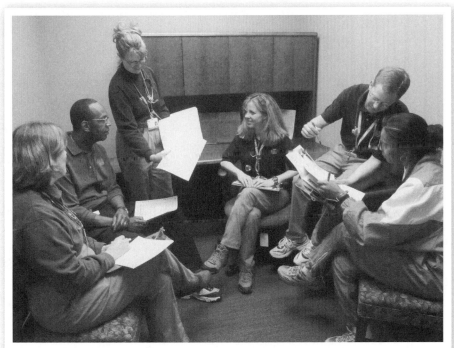

Can you think of any examples of bona fide occupational qualifications that might apply to the field of therapeutic recreation?

spot clients. This might unintentionally discriminate against elderly job applicants (see the section on age discrimination on page 80). If the club could prove that a definite connection exists between job performance and the strength requirement, then the club would likely succeed in the business necessity defense.

If applicants feel that they have been intentionally discriminated against, they have to prove three things: They have to show that they are a member of the protected class (e.g., by race, color, or national origin), that they are qualified for the job, and that the job remained open or was offered to someone not in the protected class. This type of intentional discrimination is termed *disparate treatment discrimination*. If a case for disparate treatment discrimination can be shown, then the organization has the burden of proof in defending its actions. One type of defense is the bona fide occupational qualification (BFOQ) defense. This defense arises when a particular trait is necessary for a particular job. Race, color, and national origin are never considered BFOQs. Gender, however, might be considered a valid BFOQ, such as when only female fitness instructors are hired to work in an all-female fitness club.

Affirmative Action and Equal Employment Opportunity

Affirmative action is a proactive process whereby employers take specific hiring and promotion actions to seek out, hire, and promote qualified individuals in protected groups. It is designed to reduce or eliminate discriminatory practices in hiring, promotion, and retention of employees by providing increased employment opportunities to people in protected classes and ensuring equal opportunity in employment. Although not a requirement under Title VII (and not recognized in some states), you should understand and be aware of affirmative action requirements when advertising and writing descriptions and applications for job positions. Sample affirmative action statements are provided here.

Your organization **actively seeks and encourages nominations of and applications from people who are members of underrepresented groups.**

Your organization **is an equal provider of services and an equal opportunity employer under the Civil Rights Act of 1964 and American with Disabilities Act of 1990. We actively seek candidates from diverse backgrounds.**

Your organization **is an equal opportunity and affirmative action employer. Women, minorities, veterans, and people with disabilities are strongly encouraged to apply.**

Managers should understand affirmative action requirements when advertising and writing descriptions and applications for job positions. They should seek guidance on affirmative action statements regarding women, minorities, and other protected groups, as well as the provision of advertisements in publications, online sources, and venues specific to protected groups.

Sexual Harassment

Sexual harassment is an employment issue that is critical from both an ethical and legal standpoint. Guidance on sexual harassment comes primarily from the EEOC and the Supreme Court. Additionally, many organizations and municipalities have attorneys on staff who communicate to management the important points regarding sexual harassment. Leisure services managers should educate themselves about sexual harassment from a valid and reliable source as a first order of business.

Basic points regarding sexual harassment derived from EEOC guidelines and the courts are as follows. Sexual harassment

- ▶ is unwelcome sexual advances,
- ▶ is not desired by the employee (victim),
- ▶ is conduct that creates a hostile or abusive work environment, and
- ▶ can arise from either verbal or physical conduct.

Sexual harassment therefore is conduct that is sexual in nature and can occur between any combination of genders. It is also conduct that is not consensual between both parties, meaning that one party does not want or agree to the sexual conduct. Physical conduct may first come to mind, but verbal conduct can amount to sexual harassment under certain conditions as well. The determination of a hostile and abusive work environment is the central issue in many sexual harassment claims. In general, it means that someone finds the sexual conduct so offensive or intimidating that it negatively affects job performance.

In a lawsuit for sexual harassment, the facts of the case are reviewed in light of these legal considerations. The key for the leisure services manager is to avoid lawsuits in the first place. This means having policies and procedures for managing sexual harassment claims in place and promoting a work environment where all employees are treated with dignity and respect and where everyone knows that sexual harassment will not be tolerated. Managers should also take every sexual harassment claim seriously and initiate the proper agency protocol for handling the situation, such as notifying the proper people in the chain of command and following the proper procedures for interviewing both the victim and the accused. If your organization does not provide guidance on sexual harassment, a competent outside source should be consulted. The proper handling of sexual harassment claims is not only the right thing to do, it is also important for protecting both the manager and the organization from liability.

Disabilities

The passage of the Americans with Disabilities Act (ADA) of 1990 greatly affected the leisure services industry. The intent of the ADA was to make places of public accommodation accessible to people with disabilities (e.g., providing full and equal access). People with disabilities must not only be able to physically access certain places, they must be allowed to participate and freely enjoy those places as well. Places of public accommodation are common in the leisure services industry and include most of the venues operated and managed by leisure services professionals. Title III of the ADA specifically addresses public accommodations. It states that travel services are public accommodations, including hotels, restaurants, bars, museums, amusement parks, theaters, and state and national parks.

One aspect of the ADA involves building codes and regulations. In the hospitality setting, certain places of lodging are considered places of public accommodation and therefore must be accessible to people with disabilities. Factors that affect the public accommodation status of a place of lodging include the number of rooms and whether the owner lives on the premises. Places of lodging deemed to be places of public accommodation must meet certain accessibility requirements. General categories include wheelchair accessibility and accessibility for people with visual and hearing impairments. Specific accommodations that are required under certain conditions include roll-in showers, elevators, telecommunication devices for people who are hearing impaired (TDD), Braille and raised-letter signage for people who are visually impaired, and closed-captioned decoders on televisions, as well as removal of barriers to access (e.g., installing ramps, widening doorways, installing grab bars in the toilet area, making curb cuts, and installing raised toilet seats).

Barrier removal, however, may be cost prohibitive and not readily achievable, particularly for historic structures. Therefore, the ADA makes an exception for buildings designated as historic under national, state, or local law where barrier removal would destroy the historical significance of the building. For further information, see the U.S. Department of Justice online publication of ADA standards for accessible design at www.usdoj.gov/crt/ada/reg3a.html#Anchor-44591.

Another important employment concern for leisure services professionals is the hiring and retention of people with disabilities. Employers are obligated to make a reasonable effort to accommodate the workplace needs of an employee with disabilities. The legal term *reasonable accommodation* applies to situations where an employer finds work responsibilities and environments that place employees with disabilities in a position to be successful in performing their job functions.

The ADA has an impact on accessibility to recreation places, programs, and events.

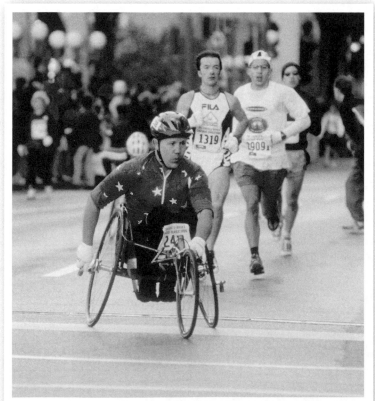

People with and without disabilities can compete in sports together rather than separately. In these cases, managers examine risks and adapt programs if needed.

A final area of mention is the ADA in the sport context. It is not uncommon for people with disabilities to coach, referee, or play with participants without disabilities. In places of public accommodation, a leisure services manager such as the director of intramural sport, for example, may have to make a decision as to whether to hire a person using a wheelchair as an intramural basketball referee. Concerns over the safety of participants (e.g., someone colliding with the wheelchair) must be weighed in light of the participation and accessibility requirements of the ADA. A person with a disability cannot be discriminated against. Also, blanket requirements such as the decision to never allow wheelchairs on a basketball court under any conditions cannot be made. Decisions must be made case by case based on objective criteria such as the skill and abilities of the person with disabilities and the facility and equipment design. Both legal and ethical considerations arise in these situations, which again underscores the importance of understanding both the language and implications of the ADA.

Age Discrimination

Leisure services managers need to be aware of the federal law governing age discrimination. Enacted in 1967, the applicable law is the Age Discrimination in Employment Act (ADEA). This law prohibits employment discrimination on the basis of age for people at least 40 years old. It applies to businesses that have 20 or more employees and whose activities influence interstate commerce. If a qualified applicant is 40 years of age or older, you must ensure that there is no implication of discrimination in the hiring process, as well as in promotion and termination.

Due Process

A difficult issue for leisure services managers is how to handle firing employees who have not fulfilled their job expectations, have violated agency policy, or have behaved in an unacceptable manner. Employees who are fired from public agencies are afforded protections under the U.S. Constitution called **due process.**

There are two types of due process—substantive due process and procedural due process. Substantive due process holds that the Constitution protects basic substantive rights such as freedom of speech and religion and the right to property. Procedural due process, on the other hand, influences how the government can lawfully go about taking away a person's freedom or property. Procedural due process, therefore, is the type of due process that is relevant to termination procedures. Public employees are afforded the right to due process before termination. This means that the employee has the constitutional right to be heard before being terminated, usually in a hearing before agency administrators.

The underlying principle behind due process is that employees deserve to have their side of the story heard before the government takes away one of their constitutional rights. The constitutional right at issue is a citizen's property right. The U.S. Constitution guarantees citizens the right to life, liberty, and property, and the right to property includes those things that we can touch and see, such as land, equipment, and even athletic scholarships under certain conditions. However, the courts have determined that a less tangible property right also exists—the right of employment. Since employment is considered a property right, public employees have the right to due process under the law.

Managers of public leisure services, therefore, should have a plan in place for termination procedures in the event that an employee is removed from an agency. Concerns such as the time allotted for termination proceedings and the manner in which employees are allowed to state their case must be considered.

> **due process**—Constitutional protections offered employees; includes both procedural and substantive due process.

Employee Health

Managers owe a duty to their employees to provide a reasonably safe work environment. Aside from this legal duty, there is also an ethical duty to protect those under their care. The U.S. government has taken this a step further by passing legislation that provides for the safety of employees. The most common and arguably most important law providing for the safety of employees is the Occupational Health and Safety Act. This federal law, enacted in 1970, established the Occupational Safety and Health Administration (OSHA), a federal regulatory agency with oversight responsibilities for safety and health in the work environment. There are many health hazards that employees might face in the work environment, including exposure to dangerous chemicals, airborne hazards, and dangerous equipment or facilities.

In leisure services management, a hazard for those who might be required to perform CPR is blood-borne pathogens (BBPs). BBPs are microorganisms in human blood that can cause disease. The BBPs of major concern include the hepatitis B virus (HBV) and the human immunodeficiency virus (HIV). A single exposure incident could result in infection, subsequent illness, and in some cases death (Spengler et al., 2006).

OSHA has created standards for BBPs. The basic components of these standards are as follows:

1. Employers are responsible for identifying job classifications that entail occupational exposure to BBPs (lifeguards, coaches, athletic trainers, and so on).

2. Employers must help to minimize employee exposure to BBPs through proper planning, education, and record keeping.
3. Employers are required to establish a written exposure control plan (ECP) that lists the tasks, procedures, and job classifications with which occupational exposure may occur.
4. The employer must also provide appropriate personal protective equipment, such as gloves and face masks, at no cost to employees.
5. The employer must offer voluntary HBV vaccinations at no cost to all employees with occupational exposure.

Leisure services managers should have a good understanding of OSHA regulations and their implications. This information can be obtained from various sources and should be implemented in consultation with qualified legal professionals. You can obtain a brochure and fact sheets about BBPs by writing OSHA Publications, 200 Constitution Avenue, NW, Room N3101, Washington, DC 20210, or by calling 202-219-8148. A videotape may be obtained through the National Audiovisual Center by calling 301-763-1896.

Conclusion

▶ As you can see from this chapter, a large part of management in the leisure services industry involves legal issues and a closely related concept, the management of risk. Often the steps needed to prevent or greatly reduce the chance of lawsuits are simple. Understanding key legal and safety concerns is a great place to start. Further coursework and on-the-job training likely lie ahead for you. It is hoped that this chapter has sparked your interest in increasing your knowledge of legal issues, with the ultimate goal of managing risk in order to provide a safe, enjoyable, and tolerant environment for both employees and patrons. Keep in mind that there are many resources available to help with legal issues. In addition to those already listed in this chapter, both the NRPA Law Review column in *Parks and Recreation Magazine* and the *Journal of Physical Education, Recreation and Dance* Law Review column are good sources of legal and risk management information for practitioners.

REVIEW QUESTIONS

1. Explain why an understanding of legal issues is important to leisure services professionals.

2. Describe the concept of negligence and its relevance to leisure services management.

3. Describe how and why intentional torts might occur when managing leisure programs and services.

4. Apply the risk management process to a hypothetical situation in your area of specialization.

5. Choose at least one statutory law and explain its relevance to leisure services management.

6. Describe the legal protections that would be most applicable to your area of specialization.

7. Describe the key federal employment laws discussed in this chapter and their relevance to leisure services managers.

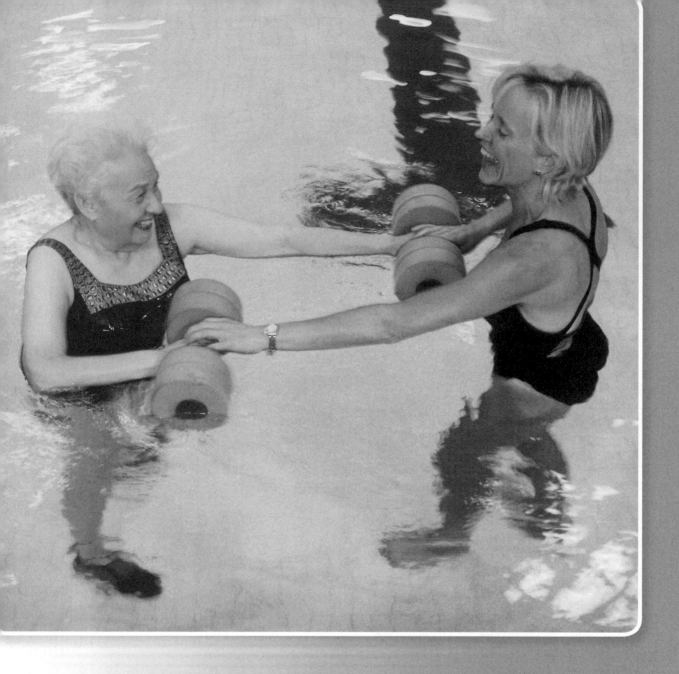

KEY WORDS

public sector, municipal organizations, nonprofit sector, voluntary sector, commercial sector, unlimited liability, limited liability, C corporation, shareholders, organizational structure, organizational design, simple structure, unity of command, organizational culture, boards, self-perpetuating board, quorum, closed sessions

COMPETENCY CHECK

Take another look at table 1.3 (page 9) to see how you assessed this related competency.

15. Work with boards and elected officials.

Organizational Structure

1. Compare and contrast the public, nonprofit, and commercial sectors.
2. Identify different types of organizations within each sector.
3. Evaluate the interrelationship between organizational structure and design.
4. Gain an understanding of the three types of boards, their roles and responsibilities, and their organizational structure.

Owning a personal training company from home is interesting. When at my desk, I am going over any new e-mails and sorting through which have priority. I get back to the e-mails that have priority and then move on to my checklist of things to do. Often that list will consist of phone calls I need to make. The administration side of the business includes the paying of trainers, drawing up and sending out invoices, and so on. When planning, I think about

marketing, networking, and communicating with the trainers or clients. In the evenings, it seems that I work on the more creative side of owning my own business. I work on programs or update my Web page. I must also end the night by replying to all e-mails and phone calls that I received that day. I really enjoy the challenge that I have with my business.

Petra MacDougall
Owner, administrator, and trainer
Inertia Personal Training and Rehab
Victoria, British Columbia

Whether starting a new agency or entering an established one, its foundation is the organizational structure, or how the interrelated components of the agency are constructed in order for it to function. The organizational structure is first influenced by whether the agency is in the public, nonprofit, or commercial sector and then by what type of agency it is within that sector, such as a federal agency, voluntary organization, or S corporation. These structural elements drive the configuration of the board, whether it is an independent, semi-independent, or advisory board; the board has its own organizational structure and design.

All of these complex factors form the skeleton of the organization, which greatly influences how managers communicate, how efficient and effective they are, and how they make decisions. Many aspects of organizational structure are well established and ingrained in day-to-day operations. Managers need a thorough understanding of these aspects because they can be changed to improve the organization. This chapter presents the three sectors that park and recreation managers may work in (public, nonprofit, and commercial), as well as organizational topics such as the organization of jobs, work environments, governing boards, and organizational culture.

Three Sectors

Park and recreation agencies can be found in the public sector, the nonprofit or voluntary sector, and the commercial sector. Each has unique characteristics in terms of governance, financial resources, and organization.

Public Sector

public sector—Organizations formed through legislation at the municipal, state/provincial, and federal levels dedicated to providing services to citizens at these levels.

Recreation agencies in the **public sector** are formed through legislation at the local, state or provincial, and federal levels. Recreation and park-oriented programs, services, and facilities are run by governmental agencies for citizens of the community, state, or country. These agencies receive money from taxes, such as property and sales taxes, to operate. This is one of the unique features of the public sector. A closer look at the three levels of public recreation (local, state or provincial, and federal) is needed to get a better understanding of how these organizations are formed and managed.

Local Park and Recreation Agencies

Local park and recreation agencies, also called **municipal organizations,** can be found in cities, townships, counties, and boroughs. They are operated through municipal government, county government, and special districts. In Canada, municipalities offer recreation, parks, sport, and culture through commissions, boards, and civic departments (Searle & Brayley, 2000). Both the United States and Canada have local recreation agencies that are funded largely through property taxes. Some of these agencies have special laws that regulate how they are established and special structural concerns that are an important part of management. Krause and Curtis (2000) identified several of the laws that affect the formation of local park and recreation agencies, including special recreation and park laws, special district laws, enabling laws, home rule legislation, and manager–council and mayor–council structures.

municipal organizations—Administrative entities at the local level, such as a city, county, or town governed by a mayor, city manager, or council.

Special Recreation and Park Laws   Special recreation and park laws were enacted to empower cities and towns to establish park and recreation agencies. The laws gave these agencies authority to tax, float bonds, and administer themselves. Under these laws, county and municipal agencies provide services for their designated areas. Not all counties have a county department; instead, they rely on the city park and recreation agency to provide services. When a county has both a separate county and city park and recreation department, differences in the two emerge in that county agencies usually provide services for a more rural area whereas the city agency predominantly provides services within the city limits. In addition, county agencies often have slightly different services. They may oversee regional parks and facilities, special facilities, and programs that are more conducive to rural areas, such as outdoor recreation.

Special District Laws   The United States has special districts that are independent governing bodies with a clearly defined geographic area, their own taxing authority, and their own administration and power. The number and types of special districts vary by state. Nine states have more than 1,000 special districts, including Illinois (2,920), California (2,797), Texas (2,266), and Pennsylvania (2,006). Almost 20

An example of a special district is the Western DuPage Special Recreation Association (WDSRA), which provides recreation opportunities for people with disabilities. It is a cooperative entity among nine park districts in the western suburbs of Chicago, and the board of directors consists of a staff person from each park district. The WDSRA provides programs at member districts' facilities, and it also provides assistance to each district when people with disabilities want to participate in programs through their home district rather than the WDSRA.

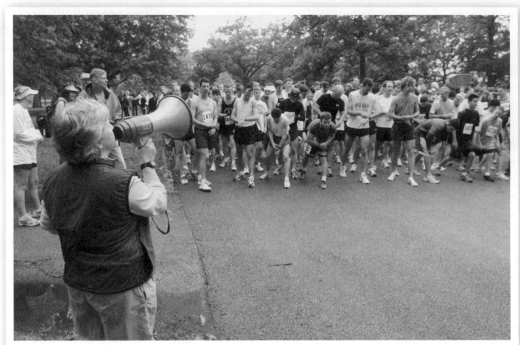

Special event planning as a profession has grown in the public and commercial sectors in particular.

percent of the 31,555 special districts in the United States perform functions related to natural resources, including soil and water conservation and flood control (U.S. Bureau of the Census, 1997). In Canada, the park district system does not exist. Parks and recreation are only administered within the municipality.

Enabling Laws   Enabling laws are enacted by the state or province to enable local governments to acquire, develop, and maintain recreation areas, including parks, programs, and facilities. These laws set parameters for the types of governments that may operate park and recreation agencies, fiscal practices, types of governing boards, and operational authority. Enabling laws are permissive rather than mandatory since the local government is not required to establish a recreation agency (Krause & Curtis, 2000).

Home Rule Legislation   Home rule legislation allows local governments to control issues at the local level without the interference of state government, and it shifts decision making from the state to local level. Home rule municipalities have greater control over zoning regulations, greater flexibility in using new funding sources, and reduced regulation from state mandates.

Strong Mayor–Council or City Manager–Council   Local legislation establishes the structure for municipal parks and recreation. Municipalities that are not considered special districts typically have one of two types of structures, either a strong mayor–council or a city manager–council. With a strong mayor–council form of government, the elected mayor has administrative control over the municipality. In many respects, mayors operate as CEO of the city. They have the power to hire and fire department heads, make decisions, and prepare and present budgets. The council acts as the legislative body for the city and works with the mayor. Strong mayor–councils can be found in such cities as New York City, Los Angeles, and Chicago, but the strong mayor–council is not found in Canada.

The city manager–council form of government, on the other hand, hires a professional city manager to serve as the CEO of the city. In Canada, the municipalities call this person the chief administrative officer (CAO). This person works with the council and has the authority and responsibilities of the mayor in the strong mayor–council form of government. The city manager–council form often also has an elected mayor, who presides over the council meetings, serves as a spokesperson for the community, and assists the council in decision making and policy setting. The mayor does not have as much authority for overall operation of the city as in the strong mayor–council structure; instead, this role is left to the city manager. City manager–council forms of government can be found in counties and cities including Charlotte, North Carolina; Clark County (Las Vegas), Nevada; and Winnipeg, Manitoba.

State or Provincial Park and Recreation Agencies

The next level of public agencies is state or provincial parks and recreation. Most state park and recreation agencies in the United States focus on outdoor recreation, resources management, arts, and tourism. All 50 states have state park systems with varying park lands and acreage (table 5.1). Legal authority for the development of state park and recreation areas comes from the Tenth Amendment of the U.S. Constitution. This amendment gives states all the powers that the constitution does not give to the federal government or take away from the states. The amendment is also referred to as the *states rights amendment* (McLean, Hurd, & Brattain Rogers, 2008). State legislation has established such departments as fish and wildlife, state forests, tourism bureaus, and arts commissions.

In Canada, the provinces have ministries or departments that oversee recreation. At this level, the ministries serve more as coordinators of programs and providers of information and financial resources than direct service providers (Hensley, Markham-Starr, Montague, & Hodgkinson, 2006). For example, in Ontario the

Table 5.1   Sample State Park Amenities

State	Number of park areas	Acres of recreation area (hectares)	Acres of natural areas (hectares)*	Miles of state trails (kilometers)**
Alaska	48	2,990,641 (1,210,270)	49,320 (19,959)	16 (25.7)
California	84	1,129,498 (457,092)	71,036 (28,747)	2,320 (3,734)
New Jersey	50	336,306 (136,098)	7,111 (2,878)	167 (269)
New York	172	317,215 (128,372)	26,528 (10,736)	3,431 (5,522)
Pennsylvania	106	280,099 (113,352)	1,638 (663)	1,274 (2,050)
Texas	80	522,567 (211,475)	77,759 (31,468)	93 (150)

* Colorado has the most acreage of natural areas with 191,356 acres (77,439 hectares).

** Idaho has the most state trails, with 8,604 miles (13,847 kilometers).

Adapted, by permission, from D.D. McLean, 2006, *2005 annual information exchange* (Raleigh, NC: The National Association of State Park Directors), 8-9.

Ministry of Tourism was established to provide tourism and recreation experiences for travelers to Ontario. The ministry contributes to planning and education, and it gives financial assistance to agencies that make tourism services available (www.tourism.gov.on.ca). In Saskatchewan, the Department of Culture, Youth, and Recreation focuses on the cultural, artistic, recreational, and social life of people in Saskatchewan through partnerships and legislative initiatives (www.cyr. gov.sk.ca).

Federal Park and Recreation Agencies

The highest level of public park and recreation agencies is the federal level. The primary functions of federal park and recreation agencies entail management of outdoor resources, conservation, preservation, open-space development, resource reclamation, advisory and financial assistance, and research and technical assistance (McLean et al., 2008). Authority for the two types of agencies—natural resources management and welfare of people—is not specifically outlined in the U.S. Constitution. However, it is provided under "broad authority of the general welfare (Art. I, sec. 8, cl. 1), commerce (Art. IV), and property (Art I, sec. 8, cl. 13) clauses" (Moiseichik & Bodey, 2005, p. 31). This legislation has granted the establishment of such federal agencies as the National Park Service (NPS), U.S. Forest Service, Bureau of Land Management, and Tennessee Valley Authority, just to name a few.

The federal government in Canada has responsibility over various arts, culture, sport, and fitness programs. Although parks and recreation is not specifically outlined in the constitution of Canada, the constitution has a section giving the government the power to act on behalf of the citizens, and it is felt that recreation is in the best interest of Canadians (Searle & Brayley, 2000). Searle and Brayley outline several important Canadian federal programs relating to parks and recreation, including the following:

▶ Health Canada—Designed to focus on fitness and active living, Health Canada directs policy, provides leadership, establishes partnerships between the federal government and private sector, provides information to the people, and encourages active living.

▶ Canadian Heritage—This department has two main charges in relation to recreation, including Sport Canada and Parks Canada. Sport Canada supports national and international sport competitions and Canadian athletes. Parks Canada is responsible for national historic sites, the national park system, and natural resources, among others.

▶ Industry Canada—This arm of the federal government promotes tourism, tourism research, and tourism development.

Nonprofit Sector

The **nonprofit sector,** called the **voluntary sector** in Canada, is extensive both in the number of agencies in existence in North America and the scope of services they provide. Nonprofit organizations provide services that meet a need in the

nonprofit sector—The U.S. term for a sector with nongovernmental and noncommercial organizations that are formally constituted for the public benefit.

voluntary sector—The Canadian term for a sector with nongovernmental and noncommercial organizations that are formally constituted for the public benefit.

community, including public services; thus, they are also called *quasi-public* and *semipublic*. The Canadian voluntary sector is so called because of its heavy reliance on volunteers and Canada's strong commitment as a nation to volunteerism. More than 45 percent of Canadians volunteer annually (Statistics Canada, 2006) and give an average of 149 hours per year (Hall et al., 1998), compared to 27 percent of the population in the United States, who average 50 hours per year (U.S. Bureau of Labor Statistics, 2006). Examples of nonprofit organizations include the United Way, Red Cross, and Metropolitan Museum of Art. Nonprofit agencies rely on fund-raising, grants, and program fees for sustenance.

The nonprofit sector is far more broad than many people realize. In the United States under the Internal Revenue Code there are more than 20 types of nonprofit organizations. The most common are 501(c)(3) organizations that are religious, charitable, or educational and exist for public benefit. These organizations are exempt from paying taxes, can apply for government and foundation grants, and can receive tax-deductible donations.

In addition to 501(c)(3) organizations, nonprofits can organize under the following:

▶ 501(c)(4): Civic leagues, social welfare organizations, and local associations of employees

▶ 501(c)(6): Business leagues, chambers of commerce, real estate boards, and boards of trade

▶ 501(c)(7): Social clubs organized for recreation and other purposes for the benefit of their members

There are several differences among these types of nonprofit organizations. For example, 501(c)(3) organizations are prohibited from any political activity whereas the other three can participate in political activity but are taxed on it (Form 1023 Help, 2007).

Because the 501(c)(3) is by far the most common recreation-related nonprofit organization, it is the focus of this section. Nonprofit organizations can organize as a coalition, an unincorporated trust, or a corporation. The nonprofit corporation is most common because it protects board members from personal liability based on the actions of the agency.

Establishing a nonprofit organization is a relatively straightforward process, yet it takes a considerable amount of time to complete the overwhelming amount of paperwork. To become a nonprofit organization, articles of incorporation must be developed. The articles of incorporation outline such things as the name and purpose of the organization, duration of its planned existence, office location, people and board members involved, and regulatory authorities to be followed (i.e., state and federal). They also outline how to change the articles of incorporation and how to dissolve the organization.

In addition to the articles of incorporation, bylaws must be written. Bylaws describe how the organization will be administered and operated; the authority, decision-making power, and responsibility of the board and staff; and the creation of the board, election of members, and procedures that will be followed.

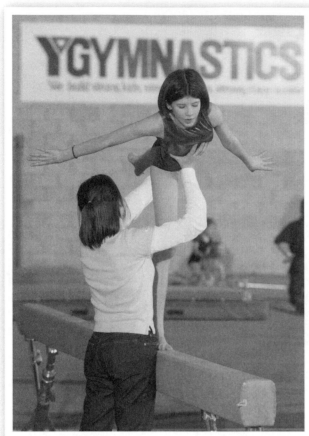

The YMCA is just one example of a nonprofit or voluntary organization found in both the United States and Canada.

The last major step in forming a nonprofit organization is to apply for tax-exempt status. The tax-exempt status for a 501(c)(3) means the organization is exempt from federal tax, sales tax, and real property tax, and donations made to the organization are tax deductible. Furthermore, a large majority of government and foundation grants are only given to 501(c)(3) organizations, so this status is vital to many organizations.

Although the name might suggest otherwise, nonprofit organizations can make a profit. If a profit is made, it is reinvested in the organization rather than distributed to staff or board members. A portion of the organization may make a profit on products or services that are not substantially related to the mission outlined in the articles of incorporation. If this happens, the organization must pay what is called *unrelated business income taxes*.

Recreation-related nonprofit organizations include Scouts Canada, Girl Guides, the YMCA and YWCA, and 4H. Many public park and recreation agencies are also starting their own nonprofit organizations for fundraising purposes in the form of friends groups, trusts, and foundations. For public agencies, establishing a nonprofit agency allows donations to be tax deductible. It also allows the public agency to apply for grants that are only available to 501(c)(3) organizations. Examples of public agencies with nonprofit organizations include the San Francisco Parks Trust, which raises money and partners with the San Francisco Recreation and Park Department (www.sfpt.org), and the Friends of Recreation Montgomery County, which seeks funding from the commercial sector for the Montgomery County Department of Recreation in Maryland (www.montgomerycountymd.gov/rectmpl.asp?url=/content/rec/for.asp).

Commercial Sector

commercial sector—
Sector with legally recognized businesses established for the purpose of generating a profit.

The **commercial sector** consists of profit-motivated businesses, and the drive to make a profit sets it apart from the public and nonprofit sectors. These businesses can be categorized into three types—sole proprietorships, partnerships, and corporations. Each has its advantages and disadvantages.

Sole Proprietorships

Sole proprietorships are unincorporated businesses that have only one owner. This owner is totally responsible for the business without reliance on partners or shareholders. The business and the owner are not separate in terms of financial responsibility, liability, and closure of the business upon death of the owner. Because of this lack of separation, if a business fails financially, then the personal assets of the owner can be taken to pay debts. Sole proprietorships are simple to start and dissolve and do not require extensive paperwork. However, there are state and local regulations such as zoning ordinances, licenses, and building codes to consider. Sole proprietorships are also exempt from corporate taxes since the owner includes the profits from the business on personal income taxes. A disadvantage of the sole proprietorship is the limited managerial experience that comes with only one owner. It is also difficult to raise capital since shares cannot be sold and there are no partners to contribute.

Advantages:

▶ Total control over decision making

▶ Revenues taxed only once

▶ Great flexibility

▶ Easy to form

▶ All profits retained by owner

▶ Less concern about confidentiality

▶ Easy to sell

▶ Fewer government restrictions

Disadvantages:

▶ Limited managerial experience

▶ Unlimited personal liability

▶ Lasts only as long as the owner lives

▶ Limited access to capital funds

Reprinted, by permission, from G. Fried, S. Shapiro, and T.D. DeSchriver, 2007, *Sport finance*, 2nd ed. (Champaign, IL: Human Kinetics), 57.

Partnerships

When two or more entities form a business, it is called a *partnership*. Partnerships can either be general or limited. Both types of partnerships are relatively simple to form and have state and local regulations similar to those for sole proprietorships. If the partners share equally in the profits, liability, and management of the business, it is considered a general partnership. There is **unlimited liability** in this business structure as well, meaning that the owners are personally held liable for any debt or legal problems with the business and they can lose an unlimited amount of money.

In limited partnerships, one or more of the partners is limited in that the partner did not invest as much capital in the business, does not have as much responsibility, or does not share equally in the profits. Limited partners have **limited liability** in that they are only responsible up to the amount of their investment. Limited partners also are not actively involved in the management of the business. If they do assume that role, they must become a general partner and assume unlimited liability.

Advantages:

▶ Some control over decision making

▶ Revenues taxed only once

unlimited liability— When business owners are personally responsible for any debt or legal problems within the business and may lose an unlimited amount of money.

limited liability— A form of business in which business owners are only responsible for debts up to the amount of their investment.

- ▶ Great flexibility
- ▶ Easy to form
- ▶ All profits retained by owners
- ▶ Easy to sell
- ▶ Fewer government restrictions

Disadvantages:

- ▶ Limited managerial experience
- ▶ Joint personal liability
- ▶ Limited access to capital funds
- ▶ Lasts only as long as the partnership survives

Reprinted, by permission, from G. Fried, S. Shapiro, and T.D. DeSchriver, 2007, *Sport finance*, 2nd ed. (Champaign, IL: Human Kinetics), 58.

Corporations

C corporation—For-profit business that has been established as a separate legal and taxed entity from its owners (shareholders).

shareholders—Individuals or companies who own shares in a company and are considered an owner of that company.

When a business is formed as a corporation, also called a **C corporation,** it is seen as a fictional, legal person. This means the corporation has many of the same rights and responsibilities as a person does, such as the right to own, manage, and sell property; to sign binding contracts; to sue and be sued; and to pay taxes. Owners of corporations are called **shareholders** and have limited liability for debts and obligations up to the amount of their investment. Corporations are formed by special charter of the state, province, or federal government and exist after the death of an owner.

An advantage of a corporation is the ability to raise capital by selling stock or borrowing money using company assets as collateral. In addition, ownership transfer is easy; it simply involves buying and selling stock. Disadvantages of corporations are that they have a complex formation process, they face extensive government regulations, and they are double taxed in that the corporation itself is taxed as well as the shareholders who make a profit on the stock.

Advantages:

- ▶ Unlimited life of the corporation
- ▶ Liability limited to the extent of corporate assets
- ▶ Creditors not permitted to come after individual investors for payment beyond their equity investment
- ▶ Ownership interest easily transferable in the form of shares
- ▶ Ability to hire a broad base of talented managers
- ▶ Dividends paid to corporation are 70% tax free
- ▶ Vendors more willing to provide credit to a corporation versus a single owner
- ▶ Ability to issue publicly traded debt and equity

Disadvantages:

- ▶ Complex formation process

▶ Answer to shareholders who might have ulterior motives

▶ Sometimes onerous government regulations

▶ Double taxation

Reprinted, by permission, from G. Fried, S. Shapiro, and T.D. DeSchriver, 2007, *Sport finance*, 2nd ed. (Champaign, IL: Human Kinetics), 60-61.

S Corporations   The formation of S corporations is similar to that of C corporations. However, S corporations can avoid double taxation because the "income flows through the corporation to the shareholders, who pay taxes as personal income" (Fried, Shapiro, & DeSchriver, 2003, p. 60). Although S corporations are taxed as a sole proprietorship or partnership, they are also responsible for certain taxes on capital gains and some other income.

It may seem that the S corporation is more beneficial, but a C corporation would not want to seek S corporation status if it is not going to distribute all profits to the shareholders. Regardless of whether shareholders receive the income, they are taxed on it. For example, if an S corporation makes $2 million in profit in a given year and decides to give $1 million to the shareholders and reinvest the other $1 million in the company, the shareholders are still taxed on all $2 million of the profit rather than the $1 million they actually received.

Limited Liability Companies and Limited Liability Partnerships   Limited liability companies (LLCs) and limited liability partnerships (LLPs) are a mix of partnerships and corporations, and owners are called *members* rather than *partners* or *shareholders*. The primary benefit of the LLC or LLP is that it is taxed as a partnership but has the limited liability of a corporation. In addition, it is easier to form an LLC or LLP than a C or S corporation. A disadvantage of the LLC and LLP is that it dissolves when a member dies, goes bankrupt, or wants out of the business.

Organizational Structure, Design, and Culture

Once an organization is established as public, nonprofit, or commercial, attention turns to how the organization is structured in order to deliver the services outlined in its mission statement. Organizations are made of people and groups who are goal directed. In other words, the organization exists for a purpose and the roles and responsibilities assigned to each employee are done to deliberately achieve organizational goals. Organizational structure, design, and culture work together to define the grouping of jobs, division of responsibilities, levels of authority within the organization, and formal reporting procedures. As can be seen from the descriptions in the following sections, structure and design are the formal elements of the organization whereas culture is the more informal element.

Organizational Structure

Organizations have both formal and informal structures. Informal structures are the ways that people interact, communicate, and behave and are discussed in detail later in the chapter. Formal structures, on the other hand, are the controlled and well-defined part of management. Formal organizations are controlled by policies,

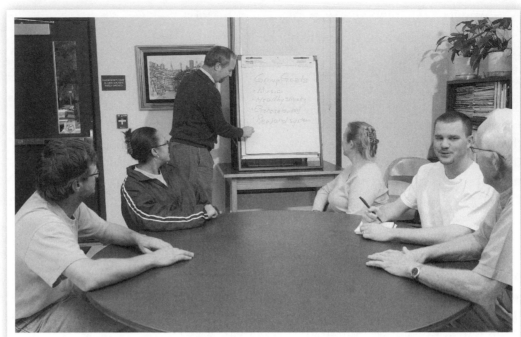

It is common for recreation managers to set and work toward common goals and objectives for the organization.

organizational structure—Process by which managers arrange and coordinate positions within an agency.

procedures, and organizational charts. A major element of formal organizations is **organizational structure.**

Organizational structure "defines how job tasks are formally divided, grouped and coordinated" (Robbins, 1997, p. 192). Robbins suggested that there are six elements to consider when creating an organizational structure: work specialization, departmentalization, chain of command, span of control, centralization, and formalization.

Work Specialization

Work specialization describes how narrow the focus of a job is. A highly specialized job requires a small variety of tasks or functions. An assembly line in a boat factory is a prime example of a highly specialized job; a person has one task to do in building the boat. People become quite skilled at their one task, but boredom and absenteeism are prevalent in jobs that are highly specialized.

In the park and recreation profession, managers take a broader approach to work specialization by hiring people with expertise in certain areas such as media relations, fund-raising, and sales. These people are considered specialists rather than generalists, although the work is not so specialized as to be monotonous.

Departmentalization

Once work specialization is determined, jobs must be departmentalized, or grouped according to function, product, geography, or customer. Departmentalization according to function groups similar jobs together. A resort may choose to have a landscape and maintenance division where groundskeepers and horticulturists are in the landscaping department and pool maintenance and carpenters are within the maintenance department. Departments may include arts, events, sports, sales, catering, membership, facilities, and so on.

Jobs also can be departmentalized based on products or services. For example, Nike has separate departments for different brands and products such as Nike Golf, Nike Brand, Jordan Brand, and Exeter Brands. Geography is another common departmentalization method. Jobs are grouped based on where customers are, or geographic regions. The NPS uses this method and has staff based in the various parks across the United States rather than in Washington, DC.

Finally, jobs can be departmentalized by customer. Customers may be departmentalized as retailers, wholesalers, or government clients; as corporate or individual customers; or by need. For example, the NRPA is departmentalized based on the needs of its members. The NRPA has 10 branches or sections such as leisure and aging, armed forces recreation, the National Therapeutic Recreation Society, and commercial recreation and tourism. However, the NRPA also uses geography as a means of departmentalization by having areas of concentration such as the Great Lakes region and the Pacific Northwest region.

Chain of Command

Chain of command has had a presence in organizational structures since the Industrial Revolution. It describes the line of authority, or who answers to whom in the organization. The organizational structure determines the direct supervisors of specific areas. In figure 5.1, the two recreation therapists are supervised by the program director. This is a direct chain of command.

Figure 5.1 Chain of command.

Span of Control

Span of control is the "number of people, units, and operations that a manager can control effectively and efficiently in a given period of time" (Chelladurai, 2001, p. 187). With a small span of control, a small number of employees report to a manager, whereas a large number of people report to a manager with a large span of control. Typically there is a smaller span of control at the top of the organization, with two to four people reporting directly to the CEO. The span of control increases further down the chart, and research on span of control indicates that seven is the optimum number a manager should supervise (Chelladurai, 2001). However, this number may vary depending on the type of work being done and the skill of the supervisor and employees.

Centralization

Organizational decision making is a key structural concern. Organizations can have varying degrees of centralization, which is the extent to which decision making is concentrated at one or a few points in the organization. In a centralized organization, top managers make all of the decisions. Although this brings consistency to decision making, it makes for a slow process because issues must move up through the chain of command. A completely centralized structure is most useful in a small company such as a sole proprietorship or partnership where the layers of management are limited.

With a decentralized organization, decision making occurs further down in the organization by managers who are closest to the situation. More than one person in the organization can make decisions. This form of organizational structure leads to faster decision making and allows for more input from employees. A large organization is more likely to function efficiently and effectively with a decentralized structure.

Formalization

The last element of structure to consider is formalization. Formalization is the level of standardization in a job. In a highly standardized job, an employee has little control over how, what, and when things need to get done. Little decision making is involved because policies and procedures are detailed. A less formalized structure gives employees freedom and allows for creativity, decision making, and control over work. In parks and recreation, an agency is most likely to be less formalized, with employees having structured jobs but the ability to make decisions about how to do those jobs. Keep in mind there is a difference between formalization and work specialization; work specialization focuses on how many different tasks a person performs whereas formalization focuses on the freedom of how, when, and where tasks are done.

Summary of Organizational Structure

Organizational structures vary from agency to agency regardless of the sector. Managers will need to consider how different structures influence the efficiency and effectiveness of production and program delivery. Look at the differences in how organizational structure can affect two managers.

- ▶ Manager 1: The organization is departmentalized geographically and has a wide span of control (six people), decentralized decision making, and lower levels of formalization.
- ▶ Manager 2: The organization is departmentalized by formalized functions and has a small span of control (three people) and centralized decision making.

Manager 1 supervises many employees, who have some control over how they do their jobs. Furthermore, this manager will be able to make decisions and include the employees in the decision-making process. Manager 2 only has a few employees to supervise and thus may spend more time interacting with them. Jobs are highly formalized without much freedom for how to do them, and the employees are in specialized areas such as arts or fitness. All decisions must go to the top of the organization. Manager 1 would most likely be present in a large organization whereas manager 2 is better suited for a smaller one.

Organizational Design

Once structure has been established, **organizational design** is considered. The design is shown in an organizational chart that illustrates how the different elements of the

organizational design— The means of arranging and incorporating organizational structure, which is typically depicted in the form of an organizational chart.

organizational structure are arranged and incorporated (Robbins, 1997). Designs change as people leave the organization and new people arrive, so an organization rarely retains the same design for very long. Adjustments are made as the need arises to make the organization more efficient and effective.

There are four types of designs: simple designs, bureaucracies, team-based designs, and matrix designs.

Simple Designs

A **simple structure,** also called *entrepreneurial startup,* is considered a flat organization (figure 5.2). Simple structures are characterized by a wide span of control, low degree of departmentalization, little formalization, and centralized decision making. These structures operate best in small agencies where the CEO has the decision-making power yet the employees have some freedom in how they get things done (Robbins, 1997). Although there is little formalization, tasks get done effectively because of centralized decision making. Many sole proprietorships and partnerships begin as simple structures and morph into other structures and designs as they grow.

> **simple structure—** Organizational design that is flat, or has few levels of authority. In simple structures, most people answer to the same supervisor.

Figure 5.2 Simple structure.

Bureaucracies

Bureaucracies were first introduced by Max Weber (see page 23 in chapter 2). They consist of highly formalized jobs that are guided by rules, regulations, and policies. This strong adherence to policies guides decision making and keeps decision making centralized. Most bureaucracies have a narrow span of control with jobs grouped by function. Because they are somewhat resistant to change, bureaucracies work best in stable environments that can be standardized. Bureaucracies often have a negative stigma, but they do have some positive aspects. Their strengths lie in the ability to perform standardized tasks efficiently and to function well with less talented employees due to the high level of standardization.

Bureaucracies still exist extensively in the park and recreation profession. Agencies make the bureaucracy work by reducing the level of specialization and decentralizing decision making to lower levels in the organization. These agencies are still guided by rules, regulations, and policies and have a functional division of labor, but they are not so structured as to make the organization rigid and unresponsive to change (figure 5.3).

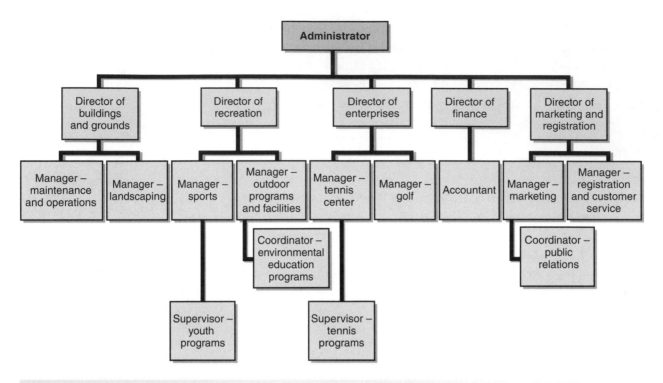

Figure 5.3 Bureaucracy.

Team-Based Designs

The term *team* is often misused in the workplace. It has become a popular management approach that many agencies adopt, yet they are merely renaming work groups without actually instituting teams. A group in the workplace is a collection of people working on a project who have their own responsibilities for a project, complete them individually, and come back to the group to share information on their progress. The group most likely has a designated leader who facilitates meetings and oversees project progress.

A team, on the other hand, has more interaction and interdependence. The team creates a synergy where the sum of the whole is greater than the sum of the individual parts. Work teams break down traditional barriers and department structures in the organization and move decision making to the team level. The team is given a project and members bring their individual skills together in such a way that innovation, creativity, and high performance result. Teams do not simply report what they have accomplished in meetings but use knowledge of each other to complete projects through discussion and active problem solving (figure 5.4).

The two most common types of teams are self-managed and problem-solving teams. Self-managed teams work together to perform a function or produce a product or service. The team has control over how tasks get done and are fully responsible for the quality and efficiency of the output. For example, an organization may have a marketing team that includes people in the areas of sponsorships, market research, media relations, public relations, and advertising. This self-managed team works together to market products and services for the agency.

Reading Organizational Charts

Organizational charts show the relationship of positions within the organization. Lines connect positions to show levels of authority. In figure 5.3, for example, the direct line between the director of recreation and the manager of sports shows that the director of recreation supervises the manager of sports, who supervises the supervisor of youth programs. Organizational charts also demonstrate different levels in the organization by title and by placement on the chart. Job titles should be consistent across levels, showing that the jobs at a particular level are relatively equal within the organization. For example, if an organization had four job classifications—director, manager, coordinator, and supervisor—there would be four horizontal levels on the chart. In figure 5.3 you can see that the directors are on the same level, followed by managers, then coordinators, and then supervisors. If an area does not have a coordinator position, as is the case with tennis, then the supervisor's position is dropped lower on the chart to be in line with other supervisors rather than directly under the manager at the coordinator level.

In addition to demonstrating different levels in the organization, the organizational chart demonstrates pay levels. Most organizations have set pay for each level on the chart. These levels are ranges where employees usually start when assuming a particular position.

Problem-solving teams, or task forces, come together with the purpose of solving a problem. Once this goal is achieved, they disband. An example of a problem-solving team is a team assigned the task of determining whether an indoor golf driving range is financially feasible for an organization.

Matrix Designs

The matrix structure brings together the concepts of teams and bureaucracies. It is a combination of both function and departmentalism where teams are created by

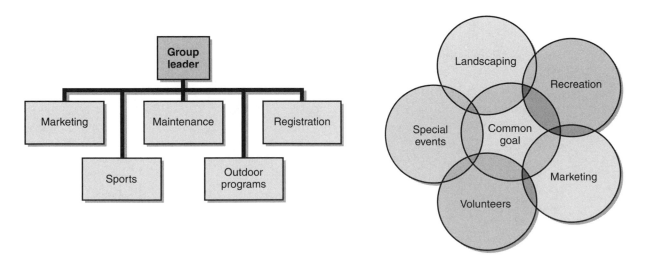

Figure 5.4 **Group structure (left) versus team structure (right).**

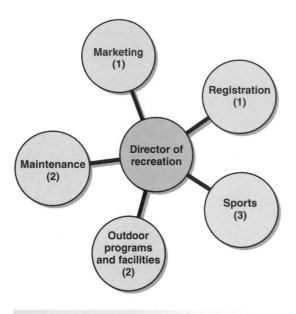

Figure 5.5 Matrix structure.

unity of command— When employees have only one identifiable supervisor.

organizational culture—Shared norms, values, and expectations that bind employees together and distinguish an agency from others.

bringing together select people from different departments for a specific function or problem. These are also called *cross-functional teams*. For example, the agency depicted in figure 5.3 is planning a triathlon for an anticipated 1,000 participants. The director of recreation decides to create a project team for this event with staff from different departments who have needed areas of expertise. Figure 5.5 demonstrates the 9 people who will be working on the triathlon, including 3 people from sports, 2 from outdoor programs and facilities (because the lake will be used for swimming), 2 from maintenance (because of the course setup), and 1 each from marketing and registration. For this event the project team members will answer to the director of recreation as well as to their original supervisor.

The matrix structure brings together expertise from different areas and can be highly efficient and effective; however, its weakness is that it breaks the **unity of command,** which asserts that each employee should have only one identifiable supervisor. Employees in a matrix structure have two supervisors during the project. Once the project is complete, the group disbands and unity of command is reestablished.

Matrix structures are used extensively in parks and recreation due to the nature of the business. Our products and services require knowledge of several areas that one person rarely possesses. Assembling people who have various knowledge areas for a project is an effective means of accomplishing a goal.

Organizational Culture

As previously mentioned, organizations have formal and informal elements. The formal aspects are structure and design, and the informal structure is the **organizational culture**—shared norms, values, beliefs, and expectations that bind employees together and distinguish the agency from others. In essence, organizational culture is the personality of the organization.

Schein (2004) describes three levels of organizational culture from very tangible to almost subconscious, including (1) artifacts, (2) espoused beliefs, and (3) underlying assumptions. Artifacts, the most tangible level, are things that may be seen and touched, as well as less tangible things such as the climate of the organization. Artifacts may include the look of the facilities and furnishings, the way the staff dresses, how the staff interacts with each other and the public, the language used, or how people address each other. A new manager coming into an organization can immediately get a feeling about the organization by observing these cultural indicators.

A new manager may also observe the next level of organizational culture. Espoused beliefs are those things that the staff has developed to show the outside world who the organization is, including slogans; values, vision, and mission statements; and credos. For example, Patagonia, a company that makes clothing and accessories for outdoor recreation, is known for its environmentally conscious behavior. A statement on their Web site demonstrates their professed culture:

> **Our definition of quality includes a mandate for building products and working with processes that cause the least harm to the environment. We evaluate raw materials, invest in innovative technologies, rigorously police our waste and use a portion of our sales to support groups working to make a real difference. We acknowledge that the wild world we love best is disappearing. That is why those of us who work here share a strong commitment to protecting undomesticated lands and waters. We believe in using business to inspire solutions to the environmental crisis,**

www.patagonia.com/web/us/patagonia.go?assetid=2329

Schein's (2004) third and most deeply ingrained level of organizational culture is underlying assumptions, which are the unwritten rules that guide behaviors. As new staff members come into the organization, they are socialized into the culture. Assumptions may include such things as expectations of team performance, risk taking, creativity, or competitiveness. New managers will often find it difficult to quickly gauge this level of organizational culture, but it will become more visible over time. It is difficult to change organizational culture because it is so deeply ingrained in employees. Although the formal structure of an organization can readily change on paper, certain elements of the informal culture will need special attention and time in order to change.

Summary of Organizational Structure, Design, and Culture

As you can see, organizations have extensive organizational structures, designs, and cultures, as well as formal and informal structures and expectations. These factors work together to make the organization what it is and how it operates.

Bringing together structure, design, and culture takes a great deal of time and consideration. The melding of these three aspects forms the roots of the organization. They dictate responsibility, the chain of command, the span of control, how specialized and formalized each job is, how jobs are grouped, and expected behavior. All three drive efficiency and effectiveness within an organization and require continual attention and monitoring so that improvements can be made.

Working With Boards

Once the organizational structure and design are determined, the manager has another major organizational factor to consider: boards. **Boards** are governing bodies within agencies. Many park and recreation agencies work with some form of board, and there are roughly 3.5 million boards in the United States (Pointer & Orlikoff, 2002), though not all are in park and recreation agencies. There are three types of boards—independent, semi-independent, and advisory—and they have several titles, such as trustees, commissions, councils, and directors. Each type of board has different powers, responsibilities, and authorities. Table 5.2 gives an overview of these differences and similarities.

boards—Governing bodies within organizations that can have authority ranging from setting policies to advising management.

Table 5.2 **Summary of Board Responsibilities and Authority**

	Independent board	Semi-independent board	Advisory board
SECTOR			
Commercial	✔	—	✔
Public	✔	✔	✔
Nonprofit	✔	—	✔
POSITION ATTAINMENT			
Elected members	✔	—	✔
Appointed members	—	✔	✔
AUTHORITY			
Set policy	✔	Limited	—
Ultimate financial responsibility	✔	—	—
Assess taxes	Some may (e.g., park district)	—	—
Hold property title	✔	—	—
Power	Full power	Dependent on independent board	Limited power to advise

Independent Boards

Independent boards can be found in all three sectors. These boards have the most responsibility and authority of the three types. In the public sector, recreation agencies that are independent taxing bodies, such as special districts, have independent boards. These boards, such as the Foothills Park and Recreation District board of directors in Colorado, are the only type of independent board that has the authority to assess taxes, and board members are elected by the general public.

In the nonprofit sector, boards such as the YMCA of Metropolitan Minneapolis are composed of members, whereas a board in the commercial sector, such as the Disney Corporation Board of Directors, is made up of shareholders who are elected by other shareholders. Because they are not public agencies, these boards do not have the ability to levy taxes.

An independent board has three core functions: policy formation, decision making, and oversight (Pointer & Orlikoff, 2002). All board responsibilities will fall within one of these core areas. Responsibilities include the following:

▶ Determining the values, vision, mission, goals, and objectives of the organization
▶ Selecting, evaluating, and replacing the CEO
▶ Providing advice to top management
▶ Approving and monitoring programs, services, and corporate actions
▶ Providing sound financial management

▶ Formulating and approving policies that guide the agency

▶ Ensuring the organization complies with laws and regulations

Independent board members also have fiduciary duties. Fiduciary duties require that board members do what is best for the organization, showing impartiality by acting in good faith and treating all stakeholders, members, and user groups equally and fairly. Fiduciary duties outline the obligations of board members to avoid conflicts of interest. For example, a conflict of interest would occur if a landscaping company owned by a board member were contracted to mow parks and install flower beds. Board members are required to act in the best interest of the agency and put their personal well-being aside.

In addition to these responsibilities, it is often expected that nonprofit board members will help raise funds for the organization. This is not the case with corporations and is only occasionally expected with boards in the public sector.

Semi-Independent Boards

Semi-independent boards exist in the public sector only. These boards are most often found within city government where a city council has the ultimate authority

Board Member Competencies

Competencies are the knowledge, skills, and abilities needed to be successful in a job. Research on public park and recreation boards has identified several competencies that board members need in order to be effective (Hurd, 2004). Table 5.3 shows a selected listing of these competencies.

Table 5.3   Board Member Competencies

Public sector	Nonprofit sector
Be willing to study issues before making decisions.	Have long-range and short-range planning skills.
Be willing to participate in committee and board meetings.	Have fiscal management skills.
Have the ability to make decisions.	Determine the mission, vision, goals, and objectives of the organization.
Be objective and fair.	Ensure efficient operation of the board.
Read and understand supplied information before board meetings.	Select the CEO.
Be prepared to give time to the board and agency.	Raise money.
Understand the role of the executive relative to the board.	Gain constituent support.
Be accountable to the public.	Select and orient new board members.
Understand the budgeting process.	Understand board functions.
Be supportive of staff.	Be able to problem solve.

over the park and recreation department but appoints a board to work directly with the department. For example, the city council of Bloomington, Indiana, has appointed a board of park commissioners to serve as the governing board. This board has many of the same powers and same fiduciary duties as an independent board, but it relies on an independent board (the city council) for the ultimate authority. A semi-independent board has the authority to direct policy formation, decision making, and oversight, yet budget approval and major policies may also require the approval of the independent board. Although this type of board has a great deal of control over an agency, it also has limitations, such as fiscal control lying with a higher board.

Advisory Boards

Of the three types of boards, the advisory board has the least amount of authority and responsibility. All three sectors have advisory boards; however, corporate entities use them a bit differently than public and nonprofit organizations do. Nonprofit and public agency advisory boards are established as links between the agency and the community. They have advisory responsibility and do not take on any policy or oversight duties. Members are a sounding board for problems and ideas, and the board serves as a means of citizen involvement. Advisory boards can be created to advise an entire agency, such as the National City Parks and Recreation Advisory Board in California and the Bellingham Parks and Recreation Advisory Board

Advisory boards serve as a liaison between the public and the agency to give support and advice on programming events, such as street music festivals, that are consistent with community goals.

in Washington. They can also advise particular areas, such as the Girl Scouts of Suncoast Council Teen Advisory Board or the Gulf Islands National Park Reserve of Canada Advisory Board.

Corporate organizations, on the other hand, have experts on their advisory boards rather than people who represent the general population. These experts are usually from other corporations, have specific areas of expertise, and receive a modest retainer fee for serving on the board. The advisory board commitment is short (1-2 years), and the board meets two to four times a year. The corporate advisory board reviews business plans, strategic plans, and special concerns and gives feedback to the company. As with public and nonprofit advisory boards, the corporate advisory board has no legal responsibility for the organization (Ward, 2000). The corporate world uses these boards more as consulting firms than advisory boards.

Board Structure

As with any organization, boards require structure. Board structure comes in the form of board qualifications and elections, board size, terms and term limits, board governance, and meetings.

Qualifications and Elections

Strong boards seek members with diverse expertise, demographics that reflect the constituents, and knowledge of and connections to the community. Expertise areas include marketing, finance, volunteer management, fund-raising, business planning, and so on. In the commercial and nonprofit sectors, the current board or a nominating subcommittee nominates potential candidates. Members or shareholders then vote on the slate of candidates to elect the members. Some organizations have a **self-perpetuating board** in which board members themselves vote for new members.

Boards in the public sector have slightly different ways of obtaining new members. The two predominant means of becoming a board member in a public agency are election and appointment. Park and recreation independent board members are elected by the community. For example, Illinois park districts are considered special districts. Rather than the board nominating potential members for the community to vote on, people choose to run, get signatures on a petition, and are then placed on the ballot. In this situation it is virtually impossible to control for expertise, demographic diversity, or community knowledge.

If boards in the public sector are appointed, usually by the city council, they may be political appointments that are made because of the connection between the new board member and the members of the city council. Appointments also may be made when the council interviews those who apply for the position and then chooses the candidate who best fits the board and the philosophy of the council.

self-perpetuating board—System where current board members elect new board members.

Size

Board size will vary from board to board and by sector. Public boards tend to consist of 5 to 15 people, with 5 to 7 being standard (Moiseichik & Bodey, 2005). Corporate boards average 10 people (Ward, 2000) and nonprofit boards average 17 people (Board Source, 2005). Nonprofit organizations tend to have larger boards because of fund-raising purposes—there is often an underlying expectation that members will donate money themselves or work to raise funds.

Small boards are advantageous in that they allow for more participation from board members. However, all of the work must be shared by the select few. Large boards, on the other hand, can share the responsibilities, but their numbers can inhibit participation and slow progress.

Terms and Limits

A term is the length of time that the board member serves without being reelected or reappointed. Rarely does a board member join a board for only a 1-year term; 2- to 4-year terms are more common. A short time on the board does not give members time to make a meaningful contribution because they are still learning about the organization, and longer terms prohibit new people and their ideas from influencing the board. Although there is much variance in term lengths among the three sectors, 64 percent of all boards in the Nonprofit Governance Index Report have 3-year terms (Board Source, 2005).

With term lengths come term limits. Term limits are the number of consecutive terms a person can serve on a board. Many organizations institute term limits so that one person does not get on the board for perpetuity and the board does not stay the same over a number of years. Term limits also allow new people to be involved. Two-term limits are standard, along with the ability to be off the board a year before coming back on. The board members should have a staggered rotation system where part of the board rotates off each year rather than having an entirely new board in a given year (table 5.4).

Board Governance

Boards operate according to their bylaws and policies and procedures manual. Bylaws are the formal rules governing the internal operations of the organization. They establish the size of the board, terms, term limits, board member rotation, officers, meeting procedures, quorum, proxies, board vacancies, dissolution of the agency, and so on (figure 5.6).

Table 5.4   Sample Board Rotation System

	Year on the board	Year off the board
Board member 1	January 1, 2008	December 31, 2010
Board member 2	January 1, 2008	December 31, 2010
Board member 3	January 1, 2009	December 31, 2011
Board member 4	January 1, 2009	December 31, 2011
Board member 5	January 1, 2010	December 31, 2012
Board member 6	January 1, 2010	December 31, 2012

This six-member board has 3-year terms and a rotation system where two people leave and two new people join the board each year. Assume there are four board members continuing from 2007 with two new members coming on the board in 2008.

ARTICLE II—BOARD OF DIRECTORS

Section 1

Board size and composition: The board shall be composed of nine members. There must be six members who represent each district in the region. The remaining three board members are considered at-large members and may come from any of the six districts, with no more than two people from any one district.

Section 2

The board of directors will meet quarterly at an agreed-upon time and place.

Section 3

Board elections: Board members will be elected annually by the members of the organization through a mail-in ballot.

Section 4

Terms: All board members shall serve 3-year terms but are eligible for reelection one time so as not to serve any more than two consecutive terms. Once the two consecutive terms are served, the member must remain off the board for 1 year before being reelected to the board. Board members will serve staggered terms so that three people rotate off the board each year.

Figure 5.6   **Sample section of bylaws.**

Just as the staff has policies, procedures, and operating manuals, so does the board. This manual is given to board members at the start of their term so they understand how the board operates and what its roles and responsibilities are. A board manual will contain some of the following items:

▶ Legal documents—bylaws, articles of incorporation, 501(c)(3) papers

▶ Organizational information—agency history; values, vision, and mission statements; goals and objectives; strategic plan; staff and board organizational charts; staff policies; program descriptions

▶ Board operations—ethics statement, conflict of interest statement, board attendance and expectations for committee participation, board member job descriptions, board evaluation procedures, professional development expectations

- ▶ Meeting procedures—board packets, agendas, minutes
- ▶ Financial information—policies, procedures, budget and financial reports and statements, previous and current budget

An important piece of information that must be included in the manual is the board's role in day-to-day operation of the organization. All too often boards overstep their jurisdiction and attempt to control more of the agency than they should. The role of a board is to advise management, not to run the agency. The only person who answers to the board of directors is the CEO. The remaining staff members either directly or indirectly report to the CEO. A well-designed policy manual can help alleviate some of these problems.

Both the bylaws and the operations manual can serve as an orientation for board members. All new board members should follow a structured orientation process and be assigned a current board member as a mentor. This will enable the new board member to become an active and contributing member more quickly. In addition to helping new board members, the bylaw and operations manual will guide the board in adhering to its roles and responsibilities, thus strengthening both the board and the agency.

Board Meetings

Board meetings are most likely to happen biweekly, monthly, or quarterly. They usually follow a standardized procedure that includes board packets, meeting announcements, agendas, and parliamentary procedures.

Board Packets   Most agencies send board members packets with detailed information before meetings. Such packets should be received a minimum of 1 week before the meeting. The packet includes minutes from previous meetings and any committee meetings that have occurred between board meetings, financial statements for review, study materials for issues to be discussed, and so on. Board members are expected to thoroughly review these materials so they are prepared to discuss the issues at hand and make sound decisions at the board meeting.

Meeting Announcements   Meeting announcements should be made to the community, members, and shareholders in advance. This is particularly important for public agencies in the United States because they are legally required to do so via an open meetings act. Although the details of the act vary from state to state, the act generally states that public agencies must notify the public that a meeting is to be held and that the public is invited to attend. A meeting is defined as a gathering of the majority of the **quorum** of board members who gather to discuss business pertaining to the agency. The size of the quorum is often 50 percent of the board members plus one, but it does not have to be; it can be a smaller or larger number of board members. The Open Meetings Act does not mean that all aspects of agency business are open to the public. State laws dictate which items are to be discussed in **closed sessions.** For example, personnel concerns such as personnel evaluations are discussed in closed sessions to protect the rights of employees.

quorum—Minimum number of board members needed to conduct official board business.

closed sessions—Board meetings that are not open for the public to attend. Closed sessions occur because of such things as personnel, litigation, or collective bargaining.

Agendas and Parliamentary Procedure   The meeting agenda is the roadmap that guides the business of the meeting. The agenda will often follow the rules in *Robert's Rules of Order,* also called *parliamentary procedure.* These rules delineate how meetings are started and ended and how votes are presented to the group, discussed, amended, and voted upon. A typical agenda looks something like this:

1. Call to order
2. Roll call of members present
3. Reading and approval of minutes
4. Officers' reports
5. Committee reports
6. Old business
7. New business
8. Announcements
9. Adjournment

Meeting Minutes   The board secretary or other designated officer is responsible for the minutes of the meeting. The minutes detail the date, time, and place of the meeting. They also include members present and absent, a summary of the discussion and deliberation, and any votes that were taken. The minutes serve as a record of the meetings and are usually saved for the life of the organization. For public agencies, the open meetings act requires minutes to be taken and made available to the public within a specified amount of time.

Summary of Board Structure

Board structure is just as complicated as agency structure. It requires time and attention in order for the board to function well. Boards have a tremendous amount of influence on organizations, especially independent and semi-independent boards that influence policy and financial decisions. A well-structured board that is able to conduct productive meetings is a true asset to an organization. It is in the best interest of managers to develop a positive working relationship with board members so that the staff and board are working together toward common goals rather than as two separate entities dividing the agency.

Form of Government and Organizational Structure and Design

Many aspects of an organization drive its structure, including the sector in which the agency exists, organizational culture, type of board, and strengths and weaknesses of staff. For example, a public agency that was established as a special district has an independent board. This gives the organization more freedom to adopt the structure that best fits its need. On the other hand, a public agency with a semi-independent board within a city system may have to follow a preestablished organizational structure that has set job titles such as coordinator, supervisor, or manager. These titles will most likely have comparable pay grades across the city. Furthermore, when developing its structure, the organization must consider the city council or a semi-independent board that answers to the city council.

A commercial agency will rely on advice from shareholders who examine the strengths and weaknesses of staff to determine organizational structure. The same can be said for nonprofit organizations, which also have an independent board that may or may not have valuable input on how jobs are structured and designed.

Finally, culture plays an important role in structuring an organization. Underlying assumptions and espoused beliefs and actions can drive an organization. Even when staff members say they want a change in the structure, it is often difficult to deviate from the norm because the people making the changes are the ones who have internalized the values, beliefs, and assumptions that have driven the organization for years.

Conclusion

▶ Given the sector, structure, design, and board concerns presented, it is easy to see that organizations are quite complex. The organizational structure and design can change as the agency's goals, objectives, and needs change. Since change is inevitable in any agency, managers need a solid understanding of structure, design, board responsibilities, and board meetings. In addition, state and federal legislation dictates such things as funding, profit distribution, and board meetings. A lack of knowledge in these areas can have a negative impact on the efficiency and effectiveness of the entire organization.

REVIEW QUESTIONS

1. Differentiate between strong mayor–council and city manager–council forms of municipal governments.

2. Outline how a manager might start a nonprofit organization.

3. Compare and contrast partnerships, sole proprietorships, and corporations.

4. Explain how organizational structure and design interrelate.

5. Describe organizational culture and its tangible and intangible elements.

6. What are the three types of boards, and how do they differ?

7. What items are contained in board bylaws?

8. What items are contained in board operating manuals?

9. What are open meeting acts?

Check out the online student resource at www.HumanKinetics.com/LeisureServicesManagement for additional material, including sample documents, case studies, Web links, and more.

KEY WORDS

functional resources, organizational resources, structural differentiation, structural integration, suboptimization, vertical coordination, human capital, policies, policy making, procedures, standard operating procedures, rules, standards, accountability, action planning, performance control, management by objectives (MBO), horizontal coordination, teams, task forces, synergy, intersectoral partnership, partnership, collaboration, alliance, administrative consolidation, joint programming (joint facility use), networks, partnership integration, joint venture, merger

COMPETENCY CHECK

Take another look at table 1.3 (page 9) to see how you assessed these related competencies.

14. Develop partnerships with other organizations.

37. Participate in policy formation, evaluation, and revision.

CHAPTER 6

Coordination of Resources, Programs, and Services

1. Understand the connection between various management functions (planning, organizing, leading, and controlling) and the coordination of agency resources, programs, and services.

2. Define the functions used for intra-agency coordination, including vertical and lateral coordination.

3. Provide examples of planning and control systems used to coordinate and control agency work processes, including performance control and action planning.

4. Define management roles for leisure services provision in the three sectors (public, nonprofit, commercial) and identify the opportunities for coordination both among and within sectors.

5. Identify the methods for coordinating interorganizational efforts, including both inter- and intrasector partnership strategies.

I run my own event management company, doing everything from organizing large and small fund-raising events to managing athletes and coaches attending major national multisport games. With contract work, there are days when life is slower and the day is more "normal." I often have a meeting of some sort each day, as I work with many different volunteer committees on projects. Day-to-day activities vary, whether it is writing reports, producing critical paths, balancing the finances, or proofing marketing materials. My work involves all aspects of an event; no task is too small.

Tami Tate
President
Triple T Consulting and Event Management, Ltd.
Victoria, British Columbia

---

functional resources—Personnel skills and knowledge.

organizational resources—Financial, physical, technological, and human assets that organizations need for the production of goods or services.

structural differentiation—Structural condition in complex organizations where many people and units must fulfill diverse roles.

The four major functions of management are planning, organizing, leading, and controlling. Together they provide the foundation for another important aspect of management—coordination. Coordination ability is one of the core competencies of organizations, and the capacity of an organization to coordinate **functional resources** (human assets) and **organizational resources** (physical, financial, and technological) has been linked to overall effectiveness and to competitive advantage (Jones, 2004). All four functions of management contribute to coordination ability. Successful coordination includes planning (setting goals), organizing (identifying and coordinating resources to achieve goals), leading (encouraging personnel to contribute to organizational success), and controlling (evaluating goals and developing processes to improve organizational performance).

To a large extent, coordination is a component of organizational structure (see chapter 5) and requires successful communication (see chapter 9). As organizations grow in size and scope, they become more complex. Complex organizations have higher degrees of **structural differentiation**—there are many people and units fulfilling diverse and varied organizational roles. The challenge for managers is to find an efficient and effective method for organizing and allocating work. This is accomplished primarily through organizational design (chapter 5). However, allocating work is just one piece of the puzzle; once it is allocated, it must be coordinated. Without coordination, an organization runs the risk of being disorganized, competing against itself, duplicating efforts, and squandering scarce resources. This chapter focuses on the process of coordination both from an intraorganizational and interorganizational perspective. Specifically, it examines methods for achieving organizational integration, as well as methods and best practices for coordinating interorganization collaborative efforts.

Internal Organizational Coordination

structural integration—Coordinating organizational tasks, roles, functions, and units so that they work together effectively.

The process of coordinating organizational tasks, roles, functions, and units so that they work together effectively is called **structural integration.** Creating a structure that clearly defines work roles is a necessary component of organizational design. However, structural differentiation alone cannot address coordination and control.

Coordination is necessary when the tasks of organizational units are highly interdependent. Specifically, coordination helps to

▶ achieve consistency for both staff and customers,

▶ ensure fairness and equity, and

▶ avoid duplication of efforts or unnecessary internal competition.

Consider the university campus recreation organization depicted in figure 6.1. The organization consists of six different functional units: sport clubs, instructional classes and programs, facilities, intramural sports, fitness and wellness, and outdoor adventures.

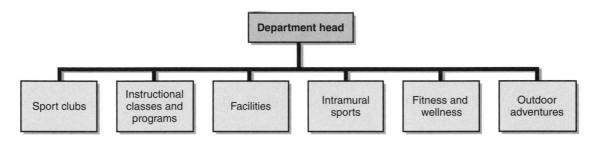

Figure 6.1 **University recreation organization.**

Each unit is responsible for a unique aspect of campus recreation programming, yet many of the units are functionally interdependent. For example, the intramural sport and sport club units rely on available and adequately prepared facilities to ensure that programs run effectively. Similarly, policy must be coordinated among units to ensure consistency. Suppose that access to the recreation center requires a valid student or member identification card. Eligibility for participation in an intramural basketball game would need to be limited to students or campus recreation members to ensure that participants would be able to access the facility.

Other policy areas such as program pricing and risk management require a coordinated effort to achieve consistency and fairness. For example, it might be unfair for intramural sport programs, which are typically male dominated, to be free of charge whereas group fitness classes, which tend to attract female participants, are offered for a fee. Finally, it is important that units do not compete against each other for participants and resources or unnecessarily duplicate efforts. If a department goal is to provide alternative late-night programming to discourage students from drinking or engaging in other risky behavior, it would not be wise to offer several competing late-night programs at the same times and on the same nights, especially if those programs attempt to attract the same participants.

Although certain courses of action might benefit a particular unit—such as allowing nonmembers to participate in intramural sport contests or charging fees for a kickboxing class—they might have a negative impact on the overall organizational effort. If the actions of individual units work against the mission of the organization, then inconsistency, inequity, and inefficiency are likely to occur. Ultimately, effective coordination helps to curtail this process of **suboptimization,** or emphasizing unit

suboptimization— Emphasis on achieving unit goals rather than focusing on the larger goals of an organization.

goals rather than the larger goals of the organization (Bolman & Deal, 2003). The central challenge for managers is to balance differentiation and integration so that both simple and complex organizations have the necessary systems to ensure effective coordination. Both too much and too little coordination lead to organizational inefficiency. For example, too much coordination wastes time and resources, and too little coordination leads to the problems discussed previously.

The structures that organizations use to coordinate internal efforts comprise two major areas: vertical coordination and horizontal coordination. Both vertical and horizontal coordination place high premiums on effective communication down, up, and across the organizational chart (see chapter 9).

Vertical Coordination

vertical coordination—Formal systems of control typified by hierarchies and authority; policies, rules and standards; and accountability systems.

Vertical coordination involves formal systems of control and is typified by use of the following:

▶ Organizational hierarchies and authority
▶ Policies, procedures, rules, and standards
▶ Accountability systems

Organizational Hierarchies and Authority

One of the principal methods for coordination and achieving integration involves structures of authority. Authority refers to power that is achieved through the position that a particular leader occupies in the organizational chart (Hersey, Blanchard, & Johnson, 2001). Coordination can be achieved by instituting a clear hierarchy of authority that leaves little room for unit or individual decision making that might work against overall organizational goals. In such organizations, leadership has the authority to act by making rules, allocating resources, controlling access to information, rewarding individual and team performance, and meting out punishment and discipline (George & Jones, 2002).

human capital—The knowledge, skills, and abilities possessed by individual employees.

One strength of hierarchical, authority-based organizations is their ability to achieve organizational integration. Recent management and organizational theory has raised the question as to whether such authority-based systems achieve integration at the expense of employees and whether **human capital**—the wealth of knowledge, skills, and abilities that individual employees possess—is wasted. Although authority might be granted by position, leadership is typically earned. In other words, employees matter. An organization might be able to achieve integration and coordination through draconian methods of command and control yet ultimately waste the potential that exists in individual employees.

At the same time, horizontally coordinated organizations, which are discussed later in the chapter, struggle with organizational integration and suboptimization, and therein lies a classic paradox. Gardner (1993) asks the question this way: "Should there be a high degree of structure . . . a clear hierarchy of authority with emphasis on detailed assignments and task specifications? Or should the relationship be more informal, less structured, with leaders making the goals clear and then letting (employees) help determine the way of proceeding?" (p. 25).

By strengthening the role of their supervisors, Southwest Airlines was able to increase organizational coordination without sacrificing employee empowerment.

A case study examining this paradox of coordination and control in the airline industry suggests that the answer might be a little bit of both (Gittell, 2000). By reorganizing management operations and strengthening the role of supervisors, Southwest Airlines was able to increase organizational coordination without sacrificing employee empowerment. Increasing the number of supervisors and decreasing management spans of control—the number of employees that each supervisor was responsible for—led to greater coordination among frontline employees. In the process, Southwest Airlines was committed to ensuring that the relationship between supervisor and employee was a cooperative one. Supervisors were present to ensure that goals and standards were upheld (i.e., on-time flight departures) by facilitating organizational learning among frontline staff. This was accomplished through troubleshooting problems and determining solutions in the context of Southwest's overall goals, such as what could be done better to ensure on-time flight departures. In this context, increased authority led to greater coordination and integration by providing frontline staff with the tools, resources, and support necessary to accomplish tasks.

Policies, Procedures, Rules, and Standards

Policies, procedures, rules, and standards limit discretion and guide organizational practice (Bolman & Deal, 2003). One method for limiting discretion and standardizing processes is to establish a clear set of guidelines that steer behavior. This is important because organizational situations often require a uniform and predictable response. It would be unfair to a customer, for example, if the same situation were handled differently depending on who happened to be handling the situation on any given day. For example, suppose a local YMCA has a policy that limits participation in an after-school art program to children over the age of 6. Parents who register their children in such a program would expect to be treated in the same manner, regardless of who was taking registrations. It would be unfair if one parent was allowed to register a child who was soon to be 6 years old but another parent in a similar situation was denied the same opportunity.

Similarly, it may be unfair for employees in the same organization to be treated differently based on who their direct supervisor happens to be. For example, suppose a large full-service resort has a family-leave policy that allows a non-child-bearing spouse to take up to 2 weeks off after the birth of a new child. An employee in one unit who makes a request to take time off under this policy should receive the same answer to this request as a new father in another unit in the same organization. In this case, coordination across units is important to achieve fairness and equity.

policies—Broad statements that flow from goals and objectives and provide direction.

Policies, procedures, rules, and standards are all mechanisms that organizations use to coordinate the actions of employees and units. **Policies** are broad statements that provide direction for an organization and flow from its goals and objectives. In the previous examples of the art program and the new parent, the organizations set policies to ensure predictability and to limit discretion in terms of how various cases are handled. Ideally, policy in both cases was set in accordance with the values, vision, mission, goals, and objectives of the organizations.

Policies can be both informal and formal. Informal policies are not put in a policy manual and given to staff as a directive but result from the day-to-day activities of the organization itself. Informal policies are derived from organizational culture where norms and customs emerge and guide behavior. An informal policy may be that all staff members work the major special events that the agency holds. This is more of an expectation than a directive and thus is considered an informal policy.

Formal policies are more structured and closely followed. They are written in a policy manual, approved by a governing board, and implemented as guidelines for behavior. Formal policies direct organizations in how to accomplish things such as hiring and accounting procedures. Policies can be established to prohibit behaviors as well. They may prohibit people under the age of 18 from renting boats or other equipment at a resort, or they may prohibit groups renting rooms at a hotel from using their own caterers for food and beverages. Finally, policies can regulate behaviors of staff and customers. For example, California State Parks (1999) has policies regulating the dress of its staff, among other things (figure 6.2).

policy making—Establishing policies by identifying critical issues and gathering information.

Policy making is the process of establishing policies and involves a number of people, including staff, the public, and the board. Policy making starts by identifying the need for policies. This identification may come from the strategic plan or from customer actions that require an organization to deal with a certain issue. Once the problem areas are identified, information is gathered. This information may include policies from other agencies; local, state, and federal laws that could affect the policy; and input from the community. Regardless of sector, the public can also be involved in the policy-making process. It probably is not feasible to involve the public in formulating smaller policies, but major changes in policies require input from constituents. This input gives the agency a different perspective, resulting in better policy making.

2301 Professional Appearance

The following are general rules concerning the use and wearing of any Departmental Uniform.

1. Uniforms shall be kept clean, have a well-pressed appearance, and shall fit properly at all times. Uniform clothing items with visible areas of disrepair including snags, holes, and tears and noticeable wear such as fraying, stains, and fading shall not be worn.

2. All uniform articles shall be neatly worn, fully buttoned, shirt tucked in, and sleeves not rolled up. Only the top button of the shirt may be left unbuttoned when the tie is not worn. Pocket flaps shall be buttoned at all times.

3. All hats/caps shall be worn with the front of the hat/cap to the front of the body. Hats/caps shall not be worn indoors except for presentations.

4. The authorized belt shall be worn through the belt loops.

Figure 6.2   California State Parks dress code.
Courtesy of California State Parks © 2002.

Once the issues are defined and information gathered, a policy is drafted, often by a small group of staff members. The policy draft is then discussed among the staff and the public if warranted. Changes are made after the staff and public review the policy, and this step is repeated as necessary until a final draft of the policy is developed. Then it goes to a policy-making board such as the board of directors or city council. Once approved, the policy is implemented and reviewed for effectiveness.

Procedures are specific actions or steps that help to carry out policy. Let's consider the YMCA's eligibility policy for the after-school art program discussed previously. Assume the policy states that the program is available for children who are 6 years old on the first day that the program begins. How do employees who are staffing the registration process determine a child's date of birth? Absent a procedure that details how the policy is to be carried out, this can be open to interpretation. One staff member might take a parent's word for the birth date, whereas another might request some form of official identification, such as a birth certificate. A procedure that specifically states the action to be taken in order to carry out the policy (i.e., verification of age by birth certificate or state-issued identification card) would be necessary in order to coordinate the actions of staff and to ensure consistency and fairness.

In more complex processes where specific actions are necessary, standard operating procedures may be used. **Standard operating procedures** are clear action guidelines that may not deviate. For example, in the case of an injury in an athletic

procedures—Specific action steps that help carry out policy.

standard operating procedures—Guidelines for performing an action that are absolute and cannot be deviated from.

contest, on-site staff must follow a specific set of guidelines and standard operating procedures to protect the safety of the participant and to minimize risk to the athletic organization.

rules—Statements that govern behavior, flow from policies and procedures, and spell out consequences.

Rules are developed to govern behavior. Whereas policies and procedures guide behavior, rules focus on governance and, in some cases, they spell out consequences. Rules generally flow from policies and procedures. For example, in the case of the YMCA's after-school art program, there is a specific eligibility policy that lists the age that a child must be to participate. Staff members must ask parents to produce an official identification document (birth certificate or state-issued identification) to verify a child's eligibility to register for the program. A program rule might state that failure to produce such a document would prevent the child from participating. In this case, the consequences are clear: no proof of identification, no participation. The more clarity and less ambiguity there is, the easier it is to coordinate actions among staff members and participants.

standards—Measures that help to gauge quality and determine when a particular goal has been met.

Finally, **standards** are measures that help to gauge quality and determine when a particular organizational goal has been accomplished (Bolman & Deal, 2003; Hersey et al., 2001). Standards are useful for ensuring that both services and staff are measuring up to the quality expected by the organization. Standards minimize variability because they clearly state the minimum requirements for performance. Programs, facilities, and staff can also be measured against a desired standard. One of the challenges in managing leisure services is their variable nature. It is difficult to standardize a leisure experience because many variables are outside the influence of management.

Consider snow skiing as an example. Each ski experience is likely to be somewhat different based on variables such as weather, crowd density, and snow conditions. However, service encounters between resort staff and customers, especially in posi-

This multisport athletic complex is managed by the local park and recreation department but is used and funded by a variety of leisure services organizations in the public, nonprofit, and commercial sectors through a partnership agreement.

tions with a lot of customer contact, can be standardized to minimize variability in customer service. Likewise, management can create standards for facility safety and cleanliness that clearly communicate expectations and coordinate maintenance efforts.

Accountability Systems

Famed management scholar Peter Drucker once stated, "What the business enterprise needs is a principle of management that will give full scope to individual strength and responsibility, and at the same time give common direction of vision and effort, establish team work, and harmonize the goals of the individual with the commonweal" (2001, p. 125). Drucker was talking about a system of accountability for both individual objectives and larger organizational goals.

There is no shortage of definitions for *accountability*. It has become a buzzword that defines management practice in all three institutional sectors (public, nonprofit, commercial). Definitions of **accountability** are varied, yet almost all refer to the responsibility of organizations or people for their actions, particularly the responsibility to explain or justify their decisions to stakeholders. Leisure services organizations have multiple stakeholders, including taxpayers (in the public sector), direct users, suppliers, and boards, among others. Leisure services managers are also accountable at multiple levels. They are accountable for their own performance, the performance of their unit, and their contribution to the overall goals of the organization.

Most accountability systems start with a set of goals that are clearly articulated and can be easily measured. The organization sets goals and objectives through the strategic planning process. Organizational goals and objectives are worked into unit, program, and performance goals and objectives for managers and employees.

Action Planning and Performance Control   Mintzberg (1979) specifies two types of planning and control systems: action planning and performance control.

Action planning involves the specific processes that are undertaken to achieve an objective that is not easily measured. For example, a municipal park and recreation department that is primarily taxpayer funded is accountable for the money that it spends on recreation supplies, equipment, and other expenditures. To cut down on overspending and waste (the objective, or outcome), a department might specify a process for bidding purchase requests (chapter 13) to three or more private vendors if the purchase is more than $500. The department would then compare the bids and contract with the lowest bidder for the purchase. As part of the action plan, the department specifies exactly how the bid process should be managed. In this way, the department is accountable to its taxpayers by spending money wisely, and it also promotes a level playing field for the business community by avoiding cronyism and other types of exclusivity in contracting. The key to action planning is specifying the objective and clearly articulating the steps for achieving the objective. This system tends to be most effective when the ultimate outcome is not easily measured (eliminating wasteful spending) but can be justified through specific staff or management activities (Bolman & Deal, 2003).

Performance control is less prescribed and tends to be used when objectives are easily measured, when there are multiple methods of achieving objectives, or when

accountability—The responsibility of organizations or individuals for their actions and to justify their decisions to stakeholders.

action planning—The specific processes that are undertaken to achieve organizational objectives that are not easily measured.

performance control—The methods that are used to achieve organizational objectives that are easily measured.

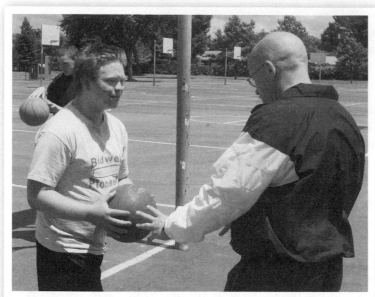

Performance control is used when objectives are easily measured, such as increasing the number of participants in an after-school program.

the methods taken to achieve objectives are best left to the individual employee or unit. For example, a local middle school might have an objective to increase participation in an after-school program by 10 percent over the course of the next academic year. How the leaders of the after-school program achieve the outcome is up to them. The ultimate outcome is easily measured and can be used to assess the performance of the program staff at the end of the academic year. The staff members are accountable for their performance in achieving the participation targets outlined beforehand. Performance control works best when the ultimate objective is easily measured, such as an increase in participation.

Both action planning and performance control are intimately connected to the overall planning process. Strategic planning helps an organization to articulate its values, vision, mission, goals, and objectives and to outline key organizational priorities (see chapter 7). Action planning and performance control help to enact the planning process by specifying the processes and outcomes necessary for employees to achieve the goals and objectives of the organization. They fulfill a necessary coordinating function by standardizing processes and outcomes, building accountability for performance, and limiting employee discretion in important areas.

management by objectives (MBO)—Performance control system where managers and supervisors jointly set objectives and evaluate results.

Management by Objectives **Management by objectives (MBO)** is an accountability mechanism that was popularized by Peter Drucker. It is a performance control system where managers and supervisors jointly set objectives and evaluate results (George & Jones, 2002). In Drucker's classic work, *The Practice of Management*, he asserts that the busy work lives of managers help them fall into an activity trap where they focus so much on their daily activities that they forget the bigger picture (Drucker, 2001). MBO keeps managers focused on their responsibilities to the objectives of their unit and the larger organization. A key aspect of MBO is that the manager's objectives should reflect the larger objectives of the organization. MBO also emphasizes participatory decision making; both managers and supervisors have input in determining and evaluating performance objectives. MBO is typically implemented at the management level. However, its principles might be used at other levels of the organization as well.

For MBO to be successful, objectives must be clear, specific, and measurable. Drucker suggests that managers and their supervisors should write SMART objectives (see chapter 3 for more details):

▶ Specific

▶ Measurable

▶ Achievable

▶ Realistic

▶ Time-related

MBO entails a considerable amount of trust between supervisors and managers. Without trust and good communication, managers may try to set objectives that are too easy to achieve, or managers may be vague or unrealistic in their expectations. Finally, organizations and managers must have a clear idea of their objectives in order to implement such a system. That said, MBO can be another tool for coordinating individual efforts and building accountability to organizational goals.

Horizontal Coordination

Horizontal coordination focuses on lateral techniques for integrating the efforts of units or positions across the organizational chart. Horizontal coordination generally uses the following techniques:

▶ Meetings and direct contact

▶ Teams and task forces

▶ Integrated roles or coordinated units

▶ Electronic networks

horizontal coordination—Integrating the efforts of units or positions across the organizational chart.

Meetings and Direct Contact

One method for coordinating the efforts of people or units involves direct contact. In most organizations, this takes the form of regularly scheduled meetings that are used to review goals, discuss progress, assign responsibilities, and address concerns relevant to the group. Regular meetings serve an important integrating function. There may be few opportunities for organizational members to actually meet face to face, especially in highly specialized work environments. In some cases, relatively autonomous units may actually begin to work toward their own goals and purposes because they have little understanding of the roles played by other units. Organizational meetings can be motivating and can help remind people and units of their connection to larger organizational goals. They can help employees get to know the job roles of other people and units in the organization. Regular direct contact between people in different units can facilitate interaction among staff and managers, and it can help develop personal relationships that will facilitate cooperation on difficult goals.

Meetings have a potential downside as well, however. Too many meetings can waste time and organizational resources; time spent in meetings means less time spent taking care of organization or customer concerns. Managers should constantly review their need for meetings, taking into account both the value and cost of such encounters. Craumer (2001) suggests the following checklist for effective meetings:

1. Analyze the purpose of the meeting and set clear objectives.

2. Create and distribute an agenda in advance.

3. Invite the right people and the right number.

4. Set ground rules.

5. Clarify action steps and responsibilities.

6. Follow up and follow through promptly.

Meetings require the right balance of coordination—too many meetings, and time and resources are wasted; too few meetings, and staff can get off track. Often, the default coordinating tool for managers is a meeting. However, there may be more effective ways to achieve organizational integration, depending on the goals of coordination. Continually reviewing the need for and frequency of meetings can help managers achieve the right balance. One example is forgoing long meetings in exchange for short team huddles—opportunities for team members to get together and quickly review key agenda items. Some organizations have called these short huddles *stand-ups,* requiring staff to stand during the duration of the huddle in order to remind them that the meeting will be brief (Krattenmaker, 2003).

Using meetings as a horizontal coordination tool often works best in smaller, less complex organizations. Large organizations with complex operations spread over large geographic areas may be less conducive to face-to-face meetings because of the coordination challenges involved in getting people to attend the meeting in the first place. When used effectively (sparingly and purposefully), however, meetings are a key component for organizational integration.

Teams and Task Forces

Recall that in chapter 5, teams were introduced as a strategy for organizational design. Both teams and task forces are formal work groups put together by the organization in order to meet organizational goals. Teams and task forces differ in their permanence. **Teams** consist of a group of organizational members who work together to accomplish common organizational goals. **Task forces,** also called problem-solving teams, are assembled for the purpose of accomplishing a specific organizational goal. After the goal is accomplished, the task force is usually disbanded, although longer-term goals or organizational problems may be addressed through standing committees or task groups (George & Jones, 2002).

Both teams and task forces aid in horizontal coordination when they comprise members from different functional specializations, departments, or divisions. For example, a team or a task force set up by a city park and recreation department to manage a large community festival might consist of members representing the programming, facilities, marketing, customer relations, risk management, and human resources units within the department. On a larger scale, the city itself might set up a team or task force with members of city departments including parks and recreation, police, emergency medical service, legal counsel, community schools, buildings and grounds, housing, and transportation. Increased coordination and integration occur by including team members from different functional units.

Teams and task forces are highly goal oriented—they exist to achieve specific ends. They require a large degree of commitment and interaction among group members. Teams or task forces are usually created for the following purposes:

▶ To coordinate work processes across various functions (management teams)

▶ To study an overarching organizational concern and recommend action (task forces or problem-solving teams)

teams—Groups of organizational members who work together to accomplish common goals.

task forces—Organizational members who come together for the purpose of accomplishing a specific organizational goal and normally disband after the goal has been achieved.

▶ To produce a specific product that requires input from a variety of organizational functions (work teams)

▶ To examine and refine organizational policies or address organizational problems (quality circles)

The coordination and control challenges that teams and task forces are designed to alleviate may also negatively affect team functioning. Some challenges to team performance include the following.

Lack of Leadership   The lack of strong leadership is one of the many challenges to team performance and can be the cause of many of the other challenges listed below. In some cases, teams may be assembled without an officially designated leader—there is no one person who articulates the team's vision, sets the agenda, guides the work process, or holds team members accountable for performance. This challenge might be resolved merely by designating a team leader. However, if the leader does not have official authority to engage in the functions of leadership, or if the person does not have the respect of the other team members, team performance is bound to fail.

Lack of Shared Values Among Team Members   Teams are often based on the desired qualities and competencies of people from various units within the organization. Because of this, team members may not share the same values or have a unified sense of purpose. High-performing teams have a strong shared vision and purpose (Argyris, 1990).

Lack of Resources and Commitment to the Team's Purpose   Organizations must commit to the goals and work processes of teams and task forces. Much like larger organizational units, teams and task forces must have resources in order to effectively meet their goals. Resources could include office space, administrative assistance, financial support, workload allocation for team tasks, or some combination of each. For teams to effectively solve problems, provide solutions, and achieve their goals, they must have the commitment of the organization.

Lack of Accountability for Team Members' Performance   One of the reasons teams fail is a lack of accountability. Most people have had the experience of working with team members who did not pull their weight. This often results in a lack of trust in individual members, and if the problem is widespread, it can severely affect team morale and undermine the team's ability to function properly. When individual team members do not make meaningful contributions to the team's work, their capacity and talents are wasted, ultimately diminishing the team's effectiveness. Effective teams have built-in accountability mechanisms for individual and group performance. Organizations should include team or task-force duties in the performance appraisal process, and they should consider the feedback of team leaders and members. Team or task-force leaders can be evaluated on their ability to meet the team's charges.

Ultimately, organizations need to devote resources to team and task-force duties; that is, teamwork should not be seen as simply one more thing to do. It should have meaning for both the employee and the organization, and it should be job enhancing rather than just job enlarging. Team tasks and duties should be incorporated into the overall scope of an employee's job responsibilities.

Lack of Synergy   **Synergy** refers to the idea that the talents and capacities of individuals are maximized when working with others—that production outcomes are maximized through shared effort rather than working alone. Sometimes organizational cultures favor individual effort. From a management perspective, it may be easier to evaluate an employee's effectiveness, and from an individual perspective, an employee need not worry about coordinating efforts with others. Although structuring work for individuals may have some advantages, it can also lead to wasted energy, duplicated efforts, and, ultimately, inefficiency. In addition, individual talents are often amplified when working with others. Effective teams coordinate efforts, but they also draw on the unique capabilities of members to achieve group goals, motivate team members, and help to develop individual talents.

Lack of Group Cohesiveness   In order to achieve synergy, teams need to function as cohesive units. This can be difficult to achieve, especially when teams are made up of members from different organizational divisions. Sometimes teams can provide forums for turf fighting or other kinds of disagreements, and conflict among team members may undermine group efforts. Teams often react to conflict by attempting to keep disagreement to a minimum or trying to arrive at compromises that ultimately do not resolve problems (Senge, 1994).

The talents and capacities of individuals are maximized when working together with others, as in the case of this synergistic work team.

Surprisingly, though, conflict does not necessarily undermine productivity or team cohesiveness. Conflict among members can be good for organizational effectiveness, up to a point. Acknowledging conflict can facilitate team and organizational learning, redirect organizational efforts, and lead to shared understanding (Jones, 2004). Of course, team leaders need to be able to effectively manage group conflict before it begins to undermine team goals or render the team completely ineffective. This can be accomplished by discussing team goals and working toward shared understanding from the beginning, as well as depersonalizing discussions so that they focus on team goals rather than on individual ones.

Coordination of Units

One answer to some of the challenges that face formal work groups is the creation of coordinating units or the designation of specific people with integrating roles. These organizational members or units are designed to help other organizational members with the integration effort. For example, the University of California at Berkeley's Department of Intercollegiate Athletics and Recreational Sports is a large, complex collegiate athletics organization. The department sponsors approximately 27 intercollegiate sports, 26 sport clubs, and 20 different intramural sport opportunities for students. It also provides open recreation and fitness opportunities.

Recreational sport and intercollegiate athletic opportunities take place at more than 20 different facilities on campus. In many cases, these facilities are shared by multiple sports and across multiple programs (e.g., intercollegiate, intramural or club, open recreation). In order to coordinate the facility needs of the various sport and program areas, a coordinating unit has been set up to manage facility scheduling and access. Before each semester, meetings are held with representatives of various program areas to discuss facility and other space needs. A facilitator is present to manage the process and work out conflicts. During the course of the semester, the facility coordinating unit handles additional requests, troubleshoots problems, and works with the diverse program areas to ensure that facility needs are being met.

In this way, individual program areas are able to express their facility needs while the entire process is integrated by a centralized coordinating unit. Needless to say, given the diverse programming areas and needs, the facility management process could easily devolve into intergroup fighting over specific needs and priorities. Using a coordinating unit to help bridge the gap between diverse program areas, handle the details of facility scheduling, and take facility management out of the hands of individual programs has helped to alleviate conflict and develop a coherent approach to a complex process. Using a coordinating unit or designating a person to serve in an integrating role works when the process is relatively complex, such as the example described here. Simple group tasks probably do not require such an involved step.

Electronic Networks

Many of the horizontal coordinating roles that are described here can be easily retooled for use with virtual or electronic networking. Consider the facility management example in the previous section. The large athletics and recreational sport department combined the use of a work team (facility management working group) with a coordinating role (facility management unit) and used face-to-face meetings to achieve integration of a complex system. It is possible to replace both the work team and the regular meetings with an internal electronic network that guides the facility management process.

For example, representatives of various sport programs (e.g., athletic teams, intramural sport, sport clubs, informal sport) might have access to a dynamic online scheduling system, such as the one used by the University of New Hampshire (see figure 6.3a). All potential users of the network are able to log in and view available athletic facilities. Clicking on available days and times triggers a pop-up window calling for additional information (see figure 6.3b). Filling out the requested fields and hitting *send* places the request in a queue and allows the facility manager to review the request, follow up with the person making the request, and check to see if the request is allowed based on preset criteria. Electronic networks can be used for other types of scheduling, purchasing requests, inventory control, group communication, or product development as well. This kind of network can also be used in a vertically coordinated organization; however, the ideal organization is both vertically and horizontally coordinated, using a balance of these strategies.

Figure 6.3 University of New Hampshire facility management electronic network.
Used with permission of the University of New Hampshire.

External Organizational Coordination

Leisure services organizations, and municipal park and recreation agencies in particular, have a long tradition of engaging in partnerships with other entities to deliver recreation programs and services. Municipal recreation departments and schools in many communities throughout the United States and Canada, for instance, have historically been linked through shared programs, staff, and facilities. Following World War II, public investment in municipal parks and recreation precipitated a shift away from the joint provision of recreation services and led to the proliferation of standalone park and recreation departments responsible for the direct delivery of community recreation (Crompton, 1999; Glover, 1999). Publicly funded park and recreation facilities, programs, and services arose to meet the demands of a growing population.

However, a climate of dissatisfaction with government spending and tax increases since the 1970s has put pressure on municipal recreation departments to do more with less and to find ways to meet the demands of the community without adding to the already overburdened public funding base. One result of this shift has been a return to the collaboration networks of the past and the potential of partnerships for increasing leisure options.

Intersectoral Partnership

Leisure services delivery in communities involves a complex system of service providers in three primary institutional sectors—public, nonprofit, and commercial (see chapter 5 for more on these three sectors). Municipal park and recreation agencies, YMCAs, voluntary youth sport organizations, state or provincial park systems, commercial sport and fitness businesses, nonprofit/voluntary youth organizations, and community schools are all examples of leisure services providers. Meeting the leisure and recreation needs of a community is not the sole responsibility of any one organization. Rather, a multitude of direct and indirect service providers form an interdependent web of leisure services in communities. In many cases, organizations from all three sectors coordinate their efforts and engage in partnerships to help facilitate leisure services delivery. The term **intersectoral partnership** refers to partnerships that occur among organizations in different institutional sectors.

> **intersectoral partnership**—Partnership among organizations in different institutional sectors.

Although there are considerable differences in the service mandates, organizational philosophies, and funding mechanisms for each sector, there are many examples of collaboration and cooperation between sectors to enhance recreation services. Even well-funded organizations find that they need to work with other providers to better meet the needs of their constituents. Suppose a municipal park and recreation department has primary responsibility for sport and athletics facilities throughout the city. They operate indoor and outdoor swimming pools, several outdoor multisport complexes, baseball and softball fields, a skate park, an ice arena, and an indoor gymnasium. They also offer a variety of in-house youth sport programs, such as a league basketball program for middle and high school students.

Provision of youth sport programs, however, is not the sole responsibility of the municipal recreation department. A number of parent-led, voluntary sport organizations also provide youth sport opportunities in baseball, softball, cheerleading, soccer, football, lacrosse, and ice hockey. These voluntary sport organizations work with the recreation department to secure facility space, partner with the local business community for funding support, and affiliate with national organizations (such as Little League Baseball) for competitive structure, insurance, and standardized rule sets.

What seems at first to be a fairly simple service is actually a complex set of relationships that needs to be managed. It would be nearly impossible for any one organization to provide such services in isolation. Given the interdependence that exists in the delivery system, some form of partnership must exist in order to effectively and efficiently manage the process. The term **partnership** describes the relationship between two or more parties for the purposes of addressing a common need (Barcelona & Carroll, 2007). Partnerships can be classified by both the levels and areas of integration between organizations (Kohm, La Piana, & Gowdy, 2000). The partnership matrix in figure 6.4 depicts the range of partnership classifications.

> **partnership**—Relationships between two or more parties for the purposes of addressing a common challenge.

Figure 6.4 **Partnership matrix.**

Adapted with permission from La Piana Associates, Inc.

Collaborations

> **collaboration**—Two or more stakeholders working together to solve problems that neither can do alone.

Collaboration anchors the left side of the partnership matrix. It is the process of two or more stakeholders working together to solve a set of problems that neither can solve alone (Crompton, 1999). In the context of the partnership matrix, collaborations leave high levels of autonomy to each partner organization. Although the organizations work together to achieve mutual goals, authority and decision making are left to the individual organizations. Collaborations tend to lack permanent structures. This does not suggest that collaborations are informal structures—they can be highly formalized—but each organization retains the right to act on its own behalf.

In the previous municipal park and recreation example, collaboration takes place among the various members of the local recreation delivery system. Each organization works together to achieve its own individual goals and retains ultimate decision-making authority. For example, the park and recreation department may decide to limit the number of voluntary sport organizations it works with, or a sport organization may choose to change affiliations with its national governing body.

Alliances

> **alliance**—Strong partnership effort categorized by high levels of commitment between organizations and some sharing of authority and decision making.

> **administrative consolidation**—Alliance where organizations agree to share, exchange, or contract administrative functions to increase efficiency.

An **alliance** is a stronger partnership effort and is categorized by higher levels of commitment and some sharing of authority and decision making. Whereas collaborations may be driven by formal agreements, alliances are defined by such agreements. Alliances may include **administrative consolidation,** where organizations agree to share, exchange, or contract administrative functions to increase efficiency (Kohm et al., 2000). An example might be to share fund-raising efforts between organizational members or to pool purchasing decisions in order to receive bulk discounts. Alliances may also include joint programming and facility use. **Joint programming** and **joint facility use** focus on the combined management efforts of organizational partners to further the mission of the alliance. An example of joint programming might be an after-school program run by a community youth development alliance, where administrative, fiscal, personnel, and facility resources are pooled to facilitate program design and delivery.

Alliances are often formed by organizations that are already collaborating through formal or informal channels or are linked through mutual webs of connections. These **networks** of organizations can often be the seeds of alliance formation in the future. An example of this type of coordinated effort is the formation of the Dover Kids Cabinet, a grassroots alliance of youth development organizations in the Dover, New Hampshire community (see the sidebar on page 135).

Partnership Integrations

Partnership integration is the strongest level of partnership and is typified by a structural change in one or more partners to create an entirely new organization (Kohm et al., 2000). Integration includes both joint ventures and organizational mergers. A **joint venture** is a shared project between two or more organizational partners that results in a new corporate entity represented by each partner organization. In this arrangement, partners typically share governance of the new corporate entity. An example of a joint venture is the Generations Sports Complex, a regional sport and recreation complex near Williamsport, Pennsylvania. The joint venture is a partnership between private developers and three nonprofit organizations, resulting in a new 501(c)(3) corporation. The focus of the joint venture is to enhance quality of life, promote positive youth development, and stimulate economic investment in the area (www.gensports.org).

A **merger** refers to the dissolution of one or more organizational partners. Mergers can either result in

▶ the incorporation of all or part of one or more organizations into another organization, or

▶ a new organization that includes some or all aspects of the old organizations.

A defining characteristic of mergers is that one or more of the original partners gives up autonomy and decision-making authority to the new organizational entity. Mergers may be the result of a desire to increase efficiency, better manage scarce fiscal resources, or improve the coordination of related management efforts. Some scholars note that these reasons have led to an increased number of mergers in the past decade (Yoder & Ham, 2004). An example of a merger between recreation organizations is Recreation Nova Scotia, which resulted from the merger of three organizations: the Recreation Association of Nova Scotia, the Recreation Council on Disability in Nova Scotia, and Volunteer Nova Scotia. The new organization advocates for access to quality recreation services on behalf of all Nova Scotians (www.recreationns.ns.ca).

Partnership as Exchange

Typically, partnership efforts are best viewed as exchange relationships—they must provide benefits to all parties in order to flourish. Partnerships are advantageous when organizations receive benefits that they might not otherwise receive and when

---

joint programming (joint facility use)—Alliance that focuses on the combined management efforts (shared programming or facility use) of organizational partners to further the mission of the alliance.

networks—Organizations that are connected through formal or informal channels or are linked through mutual webs of connections.

partnership integration—The strongest level of partnership, typified by a change in organizational structure in one or more partners to create an entirely new organizational entity.

joint venture—Shared project between two or more organizational partners that results in a new corporate entity represented by each partner organization.

merger—Strong partnership that occurs when one or more organizational partners dissolve themselves into an existing partner, resulting in a new organization.

individual players would not be able to function as effectively or efficiently (or in some cases, at all) if the partnership did not exist. This is an important consideration in managing partnerships because it forces managers to think in terms of what they can offer to the partnership as well as thinking about what they may gain. When partnerships are one-way efforts, they tend to break down.

Consider cases where organizations must engage in some level of partnership as a precondition for existence. For example, organizations that do not have access to their own facilities to run programs, such as the Boston Ski and Sports Club (BSSC), must seek out partners to provide facility access. The partnership arrangement benefits the BSSC—joint facility-use agreements allow their programs to happen—and the host organization receives a facility rental fee that provides an additional revenue source. In some cases, this type of arrangement allows a host organization, such as a large municipal park and recreation department, to outsource the day-to-day operations of a specific program (in this case, adult sport and recreation) to an outside group while still providing some level of service to the existing customer base. This type of arrangement represents a classic win–win scenario that typifies partnerships as exchange relationships. Organizations in both the commercial sector and the public sector benefit from the arrangement.

Benefits of Partnerships

The list of benefits from partnerships goes beyond resource acquisition. Partnerships have been justified by their ability to yield a number of organizational benefits, including the following (Andereck, 1997; Crompton, 1999; Glover, 1999):

▶ Gaining access to new resources (facilities, staff, equipment, financial capital)

▶ Creating synergy between partnering organizations where joint efforts produce more than what either partner could produce alone

▶ Avoiding duplication of services and unnecessary competition for scarce resources

▶ Enhancing efficiency by creating a more flexible organizational structure

▶ Better meeting the needs of customers by being able to offer a wider range of services

▶ Enhancing expertise in specialized areas

▶ Building and developing community

▶ Enhancing organizational prestige

Several of these benefits speak to the importance of coordination as a key component in the formation and functioning of partnership efforts. For example, public and nonprofit or voluntary organizations may find it advantageous to coordinate efforts so they are not unnecessarily duplicating services, competing for scarce resources, or unintentionally creating gaps in service provision for underserved groups (Barcelona & Carroll, 2007). Organizations may also find it necessary to coordinate their efforts to maximize talents and capitalize on the strengths of other organizational partners (through pooling or sharing physical, financial, technological, or human resources). Coordinating efforts may also allow smaller organizations to achieve more power for influencing the causes they care about.

Dover Kids Cabinet: An Alliance for Youth

The Dover Kids Cabinet was formed in response to cuts in funding to the Dover Middle School Leaders' Project, an after-school program that served more than 200 children per year. In response to these changing conditions, Leaders' Project staff and friends identified other youth development organizations and support organizations and called a meeting to discuss the implications of losing the program. The network members represented at the meeting, including the park and recreation department, community schools, the local teen center, the police department, the YMCA, the public housing authority, university faculty, parent volunteers, and stakeholders from the business community, decided to form an alliance to influence youth development programming in the area. The Dover Kids Cabinet is an alliance of organizations representing all three institutional sectors (public, nonprofit, and commercial) and the voluntary, frontline, local, state, regional, and national levels.

The Dover Kids Cabinet identified five primary goals for the alliance:

1. To coordinate community resources and agency activities to improve health, education, and recreational opportunities for children, youth, and adolescents in the Dover community

2. To promote collaboration between youth-supporting programs and agencies in the Dover community

3. To facilitate the participation of community members in a positive agenda for the development of children, youth, and adolescents in the Dover community

4. To provide leadership and advocacy for comprehensive and efficient services for children, youth, and adolescents in the Dover community

5. To provide leadership on issues involving sustainability for programs serving children, youth, and adolescents in the Dover community

Almost all of the benefits of partnerships noted in this chapter are represented in the goals of this alliance, including collaboration, coordination to avoid duplication, community building, shared resources and expertise, and creation of a synergistic relationship among network members.

Making Partnerships Work

For collaborative relationships to succeed, network partners need to benefit individually and collectively from the arrangement. These relationships often fail because the partners do not feel they have benefited from their involvement. Collaborative relationships also tend to break down—or fail to get off the ground—because they do not respond favorably to what Ferguson and Stoutland (1999, p. 44) refer to as the four trust questions:

1. What are the motives of current or potential allies?

2. Are they competent? Can they do the job, or are they at least willing to learn?

3. Will they be dependable in fulfilling their responsibilities?

4. Will they be collegial? Can partners get along?

According to the authors, these four trusts—motive, competence, dependability, and collegiality—are the foundation for partnerships. Unless these basic questions are answered in the affirmative, most will fail.

Bocarro and Barcelona (2003) provide six suggestions for encouraging effective partnership formation:

▶ Encourage different types of partnerships. Not all partnerships are built around resource acquisition. Indeed, many partnerships are focused on other goals, including coordinating shared efforts, sharing resources and expertise, leveraging power in numbers, and creating synergistic relationships among network partners.

▶ Ask "What can I offer?" as well as "What can I gain?" Partnerships need to be viewed as mutually beneficial relationships. Thinking of partnerships as a meaningful exchange with both parties giving and receiving helps to frame the relationship.

▶ Clearly articulate the needs, roles, and responsibilities of each partner. Who is responsible for what? What talents, skills, and responsibilities does each partner bring to the group? What are the unique needs of partners that need to be accommodated? Considering these questions up front can help prevent trust breakdowns later on.

▶ Make partnerships more formal. Formalized, written agreements that detail the responsibilities of all partners can help coordinate a diverse group of network members. Many of the coordination strategies discussed earlier in the chapter can help formalize the relationship, including designating group goals and holding regular meetings. Partnership agreements should attempt to address at least some of the following areas: the purpose of the partnership, partner roles and responsibilities, governance and the decision-making process, the communication process, deliverables (products of the partnership), time lines, resource transfers, and evaluation of the partnership results. It is always advisable for managers to consult with legal counsel when entering into formal, written agreements.

▶ Engage in power-with rather than power-over relationships. In partnerships, power issues will arise. Partnerships will have little chance to get off the ground if partners engage in power struggles and feelings of superiority.

▶ Create an organizational commitment to partnering. It is often easy to work in isolation; however, collaborating with other organizations can result in more effective and efficient provision of services. Managers should recognize the value of partnerships and devote organizational resources to developing these types of relationships.

Conclusion

▶ The ability to coordinate organizational resources is one of the core competencies of leisure services managers. Coordination includes all four functions of management—planning, organizing, leading, and controlling. Balancing coordinating mechanisms is an important consideration for managers. Vertical coordination focuses on formal systems of control, whereas horizontal coordination focuses on lateral techniques that integrate the efforts of units or positions across the organizational chart.

▶ Partnerships can also coordinate the efforts of organizations operating in interdependent systems. Leisure services in a community are typically delivered through public, nonprofit, and commercial providers. Although these providers are distinct entities, sometimes organizations must collaborate to provide services to their clientele. Intersectoral collaboration can maximize resources, create synergy among network partners, avoid duplication of services and unnecessary competition, enhance efficiency, consolidate power, and strengthen community. Organizations engage in partnerships because there are mutual benefits to such relationships. Partnerships are built on trust and depend on the motives, competence, dependability, and collegiality of network partners.

REVIEW QUESTIONS

1. What is the difference between structural differentiation and integration?

2. What is suboptimization? How can effective coordination be used to limit this organizational challenge?

3. What tools and techniques can managers use to enact both vertical and horizontal coordination?

4. Define and differentiate the concepts of policies, procedures, rules, and standards.

5. What is accountability? How can action planning, performance control, and management by objectives (MBO) be used to increase accountability?

6. What is the difference between a team and a task force? What are their general purposes?

7. What are the main coordination and control challenges that face teams and task forces? What can managers do to avoid these challenges?

8. Provide an example of an intersectoral partnership in leisure services. Is this partnership a collaboration, alliance, integration, joint venture, or merger? Why?

9. What are the main benefits of partnerships?

10. How can managers maximize partnership effectiveness?

 Check out the online student resource at www.HumanKinetics.com/LeisureServicesManagement for additional material, including sample documents, case studies, Web links, and more.

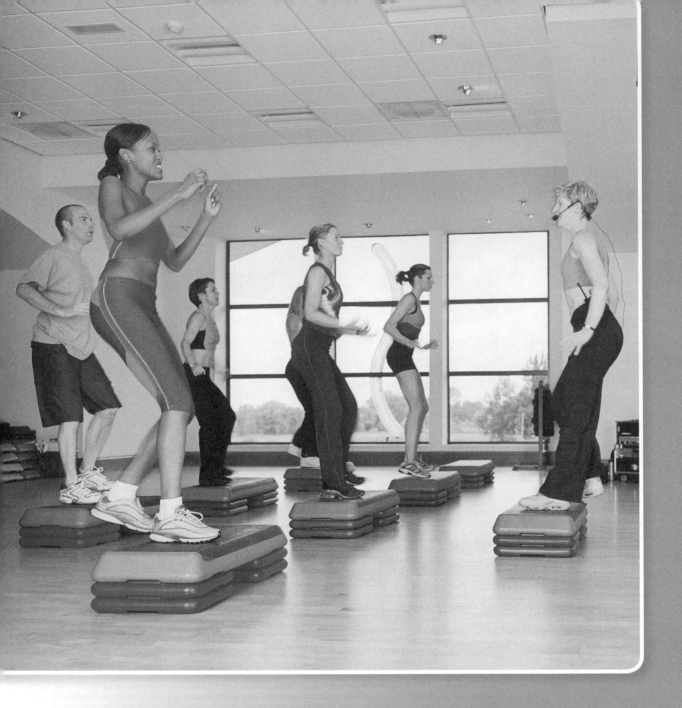

KEY WORDS

strategic planning, performance analysis, SWOT analysis, focus group, master planning, business plan, revenue facilities, decision making, problem solving, programmed decisions

COMPETENCY CHECK

Take another look at table 1.3 (page 9) to see how you assessed these related competencies.

24. Use effective problem-solving and conflict-resolution skills.

25. Make ethical decisions.

38. Provide input on strategic, master, recreation, marketing, and technology plans.

CHAPTER 7

Planning and Decision Making

LEARNING OUTCOMES

1. Compare and contrast the six plans most used in the recreation profession.
2. Describe the decision-making process.
3. Differentiate between programmed and nonprogrammed decisions.
4. Explain the four approaches to ethical decision making.

I oversee all floor and front desk operations of the museum. With this comes a variety of responsibilities. I complete daily information sheets for every floor of the museum so that staff members can find out what floors they are assigned to, what programs are being offered, and any other detailed information needed for guest service concerns. I also meet regularly with various full-time staff members to discuss what is going on for the upcoming weekend, including birthday party details, field trips, education programs and classes, and so on. I also take care of the front desk operations.

Before the museum opens for the day, I access the safe and properly distribute money to cash registers. I also take care of setup needs during this time for various programs and activities for the day. I also have the chance to meet and greet all guests and help customers in our gift shop, aid the usually busy first floor, or help with equipment and supplies for the scheduled birthday parties or planned programs.

Antoine Edwards
Museum Weekend Manager
Children's Discovery Museum
Normal, Illinois

This chapter presents two tightly linked management practices that serve as a foundation for management and the operation of an organization. In management, planning is the process of creating a direction for one or more parts of the organization. Planning guides decision making—when decisions need to be made, managers will look to their plans to ascertain what can be done to solve the problem that best meets the goals, objectives, and future direction of the agency. This chapter goes through the process of planning and decision making, including ethical decision making.

Planning

In addition to guiding decision making, planning serves several purposes. First, agencies make plans to achieve their vision. The vision statement is a declaration of where the organization wants to be in 5 to 10 years, and planning outlines the necessary steps to reach this vision. Chapter 3 discussed the role and importance of having a vision, and planning is the path to accomplishing this vision.

Agencies also plan in order to enhance efficiency and effectiveness. As discussed throughout this book, efficiency and effectiveness involve using resources to minimize waste and reach goals and objectives. Neither would be consistently possible without a plan outlining both resource use and the goals and objectives to be accomplished over a certain time frame.

In addition, planning helps agencies deal with change. Change is inevitable and often difficult. When establishing a vision for an organization, change is always at the forefront. Planning helps the organization and the people within it to change. It can be a step-by-step process to deal with something such as a major change in technology, or it can serve as a guide for more complex issues such as shifting population demographics in a community.

Planning also helps agencies to be proactive. Solid organizations are proactive rather than reactive. Good managers envision trends in the field and develop a plan to meet these trends. Being proactive means solving problems before they occur, and planning helps managers anticipate community needs, changes, and desires. Reacting to a situation instead of being proactive places undue stress on both financial and human resources.

For example, for the past 10 years, a school district has leased an unused elementary school to the local park and recreation department for use as a community center. The school district has given notice that due to projected population increases, the district is being proactive and terminating the lease to the facility in 3 years. In this situation, a plan is necessary to determine where all the recreation programs will go, how the building will be converted back to a school, and whether the park and recreation department should look for a different facility to lease or build a new one. This is a situation where good planning can help ease the stress of decision making and allow the agency to be proactive rather than reactive.

There are a number of plans within the park and recreation profession, including master plans, recreation program plans, marketing plans, and capital development plans, just to name a few. Regardless of the type of plan, the main purpose is to have a written document of what the organization wants to achieve in the future. Some agencies are equipped with the staff expertise to develop their own plans, and others hire a consulting firm to facilitate the planning process. It is impossible to thoroughly cover all of the plans that may be used by an organization. In this chapter we'll look at six types: strategic, master, business, marketing, program, and technology plans. Strategic plans and master plans are more comprehensive and might involve consultants. The other four are less comprehensive and are more likely to be created by staff.

Strategic Plan

Probably the most widely used type of plan in parks and recreation, **strategic planning** involves envisioning a future state of the organization and designing strategies and tactics to reach that vision. Strategic planning relies on managers' conceptual skills to see the big picture of the organization. The term *strategy* is used because this type of plan is a purposeful process to make the organization better.

Strategic plans cover anywhere from 3 to 5 years and establish guidelines on what organizations need to do, why they need to do it, and how they will get it done (Alliance for Nonprofit Management, 2007). These plans are not designed to make decisions for the organization but are used as reference points to guide decision making. Strategic planning guides decision making by establishing priorities for the organization. This is a difficult process, but it assists the organization in determining what is most important, what goals should be accomplished, and how to manage resources in doing so.

Although strategic planning could be done by the staff within an organization, it is probably best to hire a consultant to facilitate the process. This is not to say that the consultant will develop a plan and tell the organization what it needs to accomplish; rather, the consultant will facilitate the planning process with the staff. Consultants see the organization from an unbiased perspective, which is difficult, if not impossible, for staff. Furthermore, consultants who do this type of work are trained facilitators and can move a group through the process more efficiently and effectively than a manager within the organization can.

strategic planning— Envisioning a future state of the organization and designing strategies and tactics to reach that vision.

Although the consultant is facilitating the strategic planning, staff at all levels of the organization must be involved. This increases the amount of information available for making decisions, and it increases buy-in from the very staff members who will be responsible for implementing the plan. In addition to staff, stakeholders should help formulate the plan. Stakeholders are those people who have a vested interest in or impact on the organization, including stockholders, users, neighbors, or volunteers.

Several models can be used in the strategic planning process. Regardless of the model, McLean et al. (1999) argue that a strategic plan should answer three questions.

1. *Are we doing the right things?* Managers must examine what services or products are currently offered, what the quality of those services and products are, and whether enough products and services are being produced.

2. *Are we doing things right?* This question analyzes delivery systems, efficiency, and effectiveness. The planning process explores how programs are delivered, where they are delivered, what goals are being met, and how resources are being used.

3. *What should we do next?* The final question is a direct result of the other two and focuses on the outcomes (discussed in chapter 2) the organization is seeking. This is the vision piece of the plan and includes an outline of strategies to reach the vision.

These three questions can be answered by following the six steps of our strategic planning model (figure 7.1).

Step 1: Develop and Clarify the Values, Vision, and Mission

Previous discussion on values, vision, and mission outlined the interconnectedness of these three concepts and how each one drives the next. The premise of strategic planning is to show organizations how they can achieve the vision set out by the staff. Without this step, the plan will have no direction and will not be grounded in a solid philosophical foundation. This step is paramount to answering the first question: "Are we doing the right things?" The actions of the organization need to match the values, vision, and mission statement. If they do not, then the strategies developed in a later step should address the inconsistencies.

Figure 7.1 Strategic planning model.

Step 2: Complete a Performance Analysis

During a **performance analysis,** an organization studies its core competencies. Much has already been said about competencies in relation to individual employees, but an organization itself has core competencies, too. Organizational core competencies are the things that an organization does well that are difficult for competitors to imitate, and they are a source of competitive advantage (Prahalad & Hamel, 1990).

performance analysis—Examining core competencies to determine strengths and weaknesses of an organization.

In addition to examining core competencies, the performance analysis step addresses the question, "Are we doing things right?" (McLean et al., 1999). Each area of the organization will go through its programs, products, and services to ascertain whether it should continue what it is doing. Divisions may find they are providing services that they should not be based on their mission or they do not have the core competencies to be offering such services. In essence, this step in the planning process looks at whether the agency should be in the business of providing certain products or services. For example, the mission of Toronto Parks, Forestry, and Recreation is as follows:

> **The Parks and Recreation Division's mission is to ensure that people in the diverse communities of Toronto have full and equitable access to high-caliber locally responsive recreational programs, efficiently operated facilities, and safe, clean and beautiful parks, open spaces, ravines and forests.**

www.toronto.ca/parks/

Given this mission, the agency can complete a performance analysis of the programs currently offered or desired, such as the analysis depicted in table 7.1.

Table 7.1 **Sample Performance Analysis**

DOES THIS PROGRAM, PRODUCT, OR SERVICE SUPPORT THE VALUES, VISION, AND MISSION OF THE ORGANIZATION?

	Definitely supports	Moderately supports/not sure	Does not support
Miniature golf course			✔
Zoo	✔		
Youth-at-risk programs		✔	
Youth scholarship program	✔		
Programs specifically for people with disabilities		✔	
Open space	✔		

Step 3: Complete a SWOT Analysis

A **SWOT analysis** of strengths, weaknesses, opportunities, and threats (SWOT) is the next step in the strategic planning process. Strengths and weaknesses are considered to be internal to the organization whereas opportunities and threats are external to the organization. The strengths and weaknesses of the organization include

- ▶ its products and services;
- ▶ the organization, training, and education of the staff;
- ▶ management of the organization, including training and education, number of managers, and abilities;
- ▶ budget and financial resources;
- ▶ information and communication, including reports, records, and access to information; and

SWOT analysis—Planning tool that identifies the strengths, weaknesses, opportunities, and threats of an organization.

▶ customers, especially meeting their needs and having customer knowledge (Gray & McEvoy, 2005).

All of these strengths and weaknesses focus on the organization and its operations, which is why they are considered internal operations. Table 7.2 is a sample SWOT analysis. The agency lists elements of operations and rates the elements as strengths or weaknesses.

Opportunities and threats are external factors that have an impact on the agency (table 7.3). This sort of analysis would focus on

▶ demographics of customers and the community;

▶ economic trends and factors that could affect the organization;

▶ demand trends such as an increase or decrease in demands for products;

▶ technological trends;

▶ government and public policy trends such as limitations on taxing authority or child care regulations;

▶ macroenvironmental trends such as ethical and legal concerns, population growth, and the obesity epidemic (Gray & McEvoy, 2005).

Table 7.2 Sample Strengths and Weaknesses Analysis

	Major strength	Minor strength	Neutral	Minor weakness	Major weakness
MARKETING					
1. Company image					
2. Product demand					
3. Media relations					
4. Public relations					
BUDGET AND FINANCE					
5. Cash flow					
6. Accounting procedures					
7. Investment policies					
SERVICES					
8. Facilities					
9. Variety of services					
10. Reputation of services					
MANAGEMENT					
11. Trained and knowledgeable staff					
12. Trained and knowledgeable managers					
13. Visionary staff					

Table 7.3   Sample Opportunities and Threats Analysis

	IMPACT LEVEL		
	High	**Medium**	**Low**
1. Growth in baby boomers			
2. National obesity rate			
3. Economic decline			
4. Ability to grow			
5. Aging population			
6. Increased competition from nonprofit agencies			
7. Funding received from federal government			
8. Changing family structure			
9. Risk management and increased lawsuits			

Opportunities and threats in particular could be identified by external stakeholders such as user groups or volunteers because they may be more open-minded and less ingrained in the organization itself. It is not unusual and most often beneficial to include the public in the planning process. They may serve on planning subcommittees or as participants in a **focus group** or community meeting.

> **focus group**—Means of gathering information from a group of participants where semistructured questions are asked and responses from the group are received.

Step 4: Identify Strategic Issues and Implement Strategies

Thus far in the strategic planning process, the agency has gathered information from managers and stakeholders, solidified a vision for the future, and analyzed the current state of the organization and its environment. Using this information as a foundation, the organization identifies strategic issues and then creates strategies to address the issues. Strategic issues are the guiding forces behind the strategic plan. They are the overarching step to achieving the vision, which is the purpose of the strategic plan. The issues and strategies are the major outputs of the entire plan. Here is an example to get a better understanding of this step.

> St. Paul Parks and Recreation Department updated their strategic plan, which was originally completed and implemented in 2002. In the plan, the issues and strategies are divided according to year they will be completed, with the plan spanning from 2006 to 2010.

www.stpaul.gov/depts/parks/administration/comp-plan.html

STRATEGIC ISSUE

Need to increase cultural unity and build community relationships.

Strategy: Provide 20 new community outreach programs to underserved communities.

Responsibility: Parks and recreation administration, division managers, parks and recreation commission, numerous community organizations, staff

Budget impact: Staff time

Strategy: Develop signage, media print, marketing print, and voice plan for using multiple languages and disability access in presenting information.

Responsibility: Parks administration, division marketing coordinator, all sections, commission, city marketing coordinator

Budget Impact: Staff time

STRATEGIC ISSUE

Need to strengthen safety and security in parks.

Strategy: Implement program for pedestrian accident reduction.

Responsibility: Parks and recreation administration, bicycle and pedestrian coordinator, city marketing director, mayor's communication director, public works traffic safety officer, safe streets organization

Budget impact: Staff time

Strategy: Work with neighborhood groups (surveys, meetings, focus groups) to identify security concerns within the park system.

Responsibility: Parks and recreation managers, support services section, police department

Budget impact: Current staff time

Como Park Zoo and Conservatory has seen its aging infrastructure dramatically upgraded over the past several years because it was highlighted as a key priority in St. Paul Parks and Recreation's strategic plan.

Notice that the strategies in the example also outline who is responsible for implementing them and how they will affect the budget. These things help make the strategy actionable. Remember when the functions of a manager were discussed in chapter 2? The responsibility and budget elements in the example are the organizing part of those functions that result from the overall planning.

Step 5: Approve and Implement the Plan

Once the strategic issues and strategies are identified, the plan is ready for approval and implementation. Depending on the type and structure of the agency, various approval processes must be followed. The plan may need the approval of the board of directors, the advisory council, or top management. This approval process should not be lengthy since the approving body and staff should be involved in the development of the plan from the beginning.

Implementing the plan means integrating each strategy into the daily responsibilities of the appropriate staff. A well-written plan that includes the responsibilities and dates for accomplishing each action makes implementation easier than if these things were left up to the staff to determine after the plan was approved. The strategic plan of the St. Paul Parks and Recreation Department will be easy to implement because the responsible entities know what and when they should accomplish each strategy.

Countless agencies have ended their strategic planning efforts right before implementation. They spent hundreds of hours formulating the plan just to let it sit on the shelf to gather dust. Some agencies do this because they lack support for the plan from staff. Others only complete strategic plans so they can be eligible for grants and awards or as a public relations tool so that the community thinks they are attempting to be better. When a strategic plan is created but not implemented, a great deal of money and other resources are wasted. If the plan is done well, it can improve the overall efficiency and effectiveness of the organization.

Step 6: Monitor, Review, and Update the Plan

The final step in the strategic planning process occurs once the plan has been implemented. The plan should be continually monitored to ensure that the responsible staff members are following through on the strategies and that the strategies are achievable. This monitoring can be done as an entire agency, by a department, or at the individual level. The main goal of monitoring the plan is to determine what outcomes have occurred as a result of accomplishing the strategies.

The plan should be reviewed and updated annually. Even with all of the foundational information used to formulate strategies, a strategic plan can require changes. The annual review of the plan should highlight accomplishments. Many agencies use their plan as a report card for their customers. It gives them an opportunity to celebrate accomplishments and brag a little about what they were able to achieve over a certain amount of time.

During this review process, major changes in the agency may require modification of the plan. In a sense, a mini-SWOT analysis is done to determine any major shifts to address in the plan. For example, a major change that had a large impact occurred within the City of Las Vegas Department of Leisure Services. It was determined that parks would be better housed in the Department of Public Works, and less than a year later they were moved to a newly created department—Field Operations —which included fleet services, building maintenance, park maintenance, and streets. Losing a major part of an agency or department such as this requires a change in the strategic plan.

Lastly, the annual review serves as a launching point for the strategies to be accomplished during the next year. This monitoring and review step is an ongoing process and must be done in order to carry out the strategic plan and reach the ultimate goal of achieving the vision set by the organization.

Master Plan

The terms *strategic planning, comprehensive planning,* and **master planning** are often used interchangeably. The differences among them vary with the agency, geographic location, and setting (Wolter, 1999). For our purposes, the master plan covers land, facilities, and natural resources, whereas the strategic plan focuses on the entire organization. Master planning includes such factors as how land will be used; what facilities will be purchased, built, or renovated; what park land will be purchased; and preservation and conservation initiatives.

master planning—Planning for land, facilities, and natural resources.

Master plans are generally updated every 10 years and are completed for several reasons. First, master planning is a means of getting public input on facilities and parks. As is the case in strategic planning, involving the public is beneficial. Public input gives a different perspective and provides valuable insight into the process.

Second, master plans are created so that agencies can apply for grants. For example, the Land and Water Conservation Fund (LWCF) provides matching grants for states to acquire and develop outdoor recreation sites and facilities. These funds are usually distributed to departments of natural resources and local park and recreation departments. In order for states to be eligible, they must have a statewide comprehensive outdoor recreation plan (SCORP), and the applying agencies must have a master plan for the proposed site of development. In addition, the project must fit with the SCORP.

Master planning is also done to establish a capital improvement plan over an extended length of time. A master plan will show major projects to be completed as well as land acquisition, facility construction, and large-scale maintenance. This planning purpose is vital to developing annual budgets and establishing priorities for capital development.

Finally, master plans are developed to protect historical, ecological, and environmental areas. Natural resources are shrinking because of urban sprawl, overuse, and exploitation. Master plans outline how to protect these resources.

The master planning process is quite similar to strategic planning. Wolter (1999, p. 164) outlines the planning-policy-management process (PPMP) of master planning, which includes four steps:

1. *Survey and analysis:* This step examines current natural resources, inventories programs and services, identifies trends in the field that affect parks and recreation, ascertains the needs of the community, and defines administrative concerns (e.g., budget) that affect the agency.

2. *Development of strategies and policies:* This step is much like step 4 in the strategic planning process (identify strategic issues and implement strategies). Goals are clarified, issues are identified, strategies and policies for addressing the issues are created, and priorities are established.

3. *Implementation:* This step is achieved through the allocation of resources and assigning staff and other resources to carry out the strategies, mirroring the implementation step in strategic planning.

4. *Monitoring and evaluating:* The last step is monitoring and evaluating progress on the plan, just as is done with a strategic plan.

After reading about both strategic planning and master planning, it may seem as though there is considerable overlap between the two processes. This is true—they follow the same steps. In addition, the master plan may be a part of the strategic planning process or vice versa. Together the plans give an organization a more comprehensive look at what it must do to reach its vision.

As with a strategic plan, a master plan can be done by the staff without the aid of a consultant. However, a more detailed plan requires the hiring of an outside group to facilitate the process. Consultants can quickly become expensive, but a well-developed plan is worth the resource expenditure. Due to the nature of these two plans, they will most likely require different planning consultants. Master planning requires consultants with specific expertise such as architecture, landscape design, engineering, and accessibility knowledge.

Business Plan

A **business plan** details how a business venture will operate. Business plans are created for two reasons. First, the business plan serves as a blueprint for success because the plan requires managers to look at all aspects of the business and think about how the organization will operate. Second, a business plan is needed if loans or investors are being sought. The plan will give the details needed to make financing decisions. Although this type of plan is for commercial businesses, this does not mean that nonprofit and public agencies do not have business plans. Agencies in each sector may have entrepreneurial elements, such as **revenue facilities,** that operate as businesses.

A quick Web search will overwhelm you with the hundreds of companies and commercial software that help develop business plans for a fee. There are also various formats for business plans. In this section we will use the format developed by SCORE as an example. SCORE is a nonprofit organization partnered with the U.S. Small Business Administration that provides free advice to people interested in starting a new business. They have helped start such businesses as Vermont Teddy Bear, Vera Bradley Designs, and Jelly Belly Candies (SCORE, 2007b). They have approximately 39 offices throughout the United States and provide how-to advice and business templates for new entrepreneurs. Canada's version of SCORE exists as a provincial agency in British Columbia. Small Business BC helped establish such businesses as Jorg & Olif—The Dutch City Bike Company and Sheets Ahoy Boat Bedding Company (Small Business BC, 2008). A standard SCORE business plan contains the following sections (SCORE, 2007a).

> ▶ *Executive summary:* The executive summary summarizes everything contained within the plan. It is a stand-alone document that may be the only section read by a decision maker. Executive summaries are found in many types of plans and reports, not just business plans.

> ▶ *General company description:* The description details what the business will be, including the mission statement, goals, objectives, philosophy, description of the industry, company core competencies, and ownership (e.g., sole proprietorship, partnership).

> ▶ *Products and services:* This includes a detailed description of products and services, factors that give the organization a competitive advantage, and pricing details.

> ▶ *Marketing plan:* A marketing plan outlines market research on the products and business, economics of the industry, features and benefits of the product, who the customers are, who the competition is, marketing strategy, distribution, and sales projections. Marketing plans are discussed in more detail in the next section.

> ▶ *Operational plan:* This section of the plan describes how and where the business will function. It includes product development, inventory control, production

business plan—Document detailing how a business venture will be operated, what will make it successful, and what short- and long-term finances are needed.

revenue facilities—Facilities that are expected to make a profit and are not supported by taxes or other means.

Companies such as bicycle and fitness equipment retailers rely on a business plan to serve as a blueprint for success.

techniques and costs, accounting systems and policies, type of location (such as storefront, Internet, or mail order), and so on.

▶ *Management and organization:* This portion of the plan outlines the personnel and their structure, any contractual personnel, and the board if applicable.

▶ *Personal financial statement:* Because people starting businesses often have to draw on their own financial resources, a personal financial statement is included in a business plan. This section would be omitted in some business plans, such as those developed for public agencies.

▶ *Financial plan:* The financial plan is completed with a 12-month profit and loss projection, start-up costs projection, cash-flow projection, a projected balance sheet, and other financial indicators.

A business plan is an extensive undertaking but one that will increase the chance of success for an organization.

Marketing Plan

In this chapter we focus on the planning aspects of marketing; for more on the importance and details of marketing, see chapter 8. Marketing plans are common in the public, nonprofit, and market sectors. Similar to the other plans discussed, marketing plans can be created by staff or by a hired consultant. Marketing plans can range from 2 to 5 years, with most covering just a couple of years at a time.

They have several sections, some of which are the same as other planning documents discussed.

▶ *Executive summary:* This is the same as described for the business plan; it summarizes the entire plan.

▶ *Situational analysis:* This includes the values, vision, and mission of the organization; history of the organization; a SWOT analysis; and a product analysis.

▶ *Customer analysis:* This includes demographics, psychographics, segmentation strategies, and the target market.

▶ *Marketing issues and strategies:* This includes short- and long-term marketing goals and strategies to address them.

▶ *Implementation and control:* This includes the action plan for who will do what and when it will be accomplished. It also details the budget required to complete the strategies and the evaluation procedures for the plan.

Here is an example of marketing strategies from the Newfoundland and Labrador Tourism Marketing Council Marketing Plan.

GOAL

Use the Internet to enhance and extend our market reach and to position Newfoundland and Labrador as a compelling and unique destination.

OBJECTIVES

1. Develop a target market advertising campaign aimed at driving inquiries to the Web site.
2. Obtain research data to support effective Internet marketing campaigns in target markets.
3. Obtain research.

www.tcr.gov.nl.ca/tcr/nltmc/strtmarketingplan20042008.pdf

The following example is from the South Carolina Department of Parks, Recreation, and Tourism. Rather than using the term *strategies,* the agency uses *tactics;* they use *strategy* in place of *goal.*

STRATEGY

Advertising: Reach and influence travelers with the highest propensity to travel to South Carolina by using a multimedia campaign. Select quality media venues that will convey an effective advertising message and influence targeted audiences in order to raise awareness of South Carolina as a travel destination and ensure its place in the traveling consumer's consideration set.

TACTIC 01: MEDIA SCHEDULE FOR SPRING, SUMMER, AND FALL 2006

Develop and implement a domestic consumer media plan for spring, summer, and fall using magazine, newspaper, television, radio, and Internet advertising opportunities. Pursue opportunities that exceed recommended media objectives beyond the negotiated rate to ensure a maximum return on media investments.

Lead: Marketing director
Timeline for Completion: Fourth quarter

TACTIC 02: CREATIVE AND PRODUCTION—SPRING, SUMMER, AND FALL 2006

Develop creative consumer advertising that will continue to showcase the state's diverse tourism products in an effort to influence targeted audiences.

Lead: Marketing director

Timeline for completion: Ongoing

www.scprt.com/files/Marketing%20Partners/Marketing%20Plan%20FY%2005-06%20no%20budget2.doc

Recreation Program Plan

A recreation program plan follows the same format as the others but with an emphasis on recreation programs and services. Rather than reiterate the planning process, the more unique features of program plans will be explored.

A recreation program plan uses public input to a greater extent than the other planning processes. Needs assessments are done via a number of methods, including community surveys, focus groups, Web surveys, public meetings, and surveys of nonusers. Advisory boards (see chapter 5) also play a key role in giving community feedback.

In addition to public input, a recreation plan inventories and analyzes what other recreation providers offer the community in order to minimize duplication of services. This means looking at agencies from all three sectors to determine what they do and how well they do it. Duplicating services that others offer may not be an efficient use of resources, particularly for agencies with limited funds. This part of the recreation plan helps make those decisions.

Finally, a recreation program plan includes a service segmentation analysis, which requires the agency to look at its programs from four perspectives (DiGrino & Whitmore, 2005).

1. Programs should be categorized according to their target market. For example, they can be categorized as preschool programs, teen programs, and programs for people with disabilities, among others.

2. Programs can be divided according to type, including arts, sports, outdoor recreation, and aquatics.

3. Programs can be categorized by the facility in which they are held, such as at an ice rink, community center, or resort.

4. Programs can be classified by the geographic region in which they are held.

Categorizing programs in so many ways reveals weaknesses in service offerings. For example, when categorizing the programs in each of the ways suggested, it may be easier to see that arts programs are missing for teens in the northwest section of the city.

A recreation plan allows an organization to examine its services from a multitude of perspectives, analyze what the community needs, and plan recreation services accordingly. This plan may be part of the overall strategic plan and is also likely to interface well with a master plan in terms of what programs and services can be offered in facilities and parks.

Technology Planning

Technology planning is not much different from other organizational planning efforts. Similar to other plans, the technology plan should be a component of the overall strategic plan and work with the larger strategic initiatives and goals of the organization. Successful technology plans demonstrate how an investment in technology contributes to the mission of the organization. For example, a municipal park and recreation department might have a mission to increase the health and well-being of the community by encouraging active participation in community resources. A plan that specifies how technology might be used to achieve that mission—making more information available through the Internet, perhaps, or reducing participation barriers by streamlining activity registration using online applications—is more effective than simply stating that the organization needs to buy more computers. Ultimately, technology planning maps the path between where an organization is currently and where it wants to be in the future.

Technology should not be seen as an end in itself. It must provide technological solutions that enhance organizational effectiveness; otherwise, investments in technology may be unnecessary and a waste of scarce resources. Just because a tool exists does not mean that it has to be used or that it is the most effective tool for the job. Like any tool, the solution that is chosen will be based on a variety of factors, including availability of the resource, time, budget, competence of the user, and so on. By linking the technology plan with the strategic plan, technology becomes a tool for achieving the mission of the organization.

Technology planning helps provide the technical direction of the strategic plan (Farris, 2006). The strategic planning process is typically conducted every 5 years or so, but the technology plan should be revisited more frequently to keep up with the rapid pace of technological change. Consider Moore's Law, which suggests that computing power is essentially doubled for half the cost every 18 months (Drucker, 2002). Despite this, only 45 percent of municipal governments are using an active technology plan that has been updated since 2002 (Center for Digital Government, 2004).

Technology planning involves the following steps:

- ▶ Assembling a planning team
- ▶ Examining the vision, mission, goals, and objectives of the organization
- ▶ Assessing current technology infrastructure
- ▶ Identifying new technology solutions that work to achieve organizational goals
- ▶ Developing implementation strategies, time lines, and costs
- ▶ Understanding and involving end users
- ▶ Assessing effectiveness
- ▶ Making adjustments by repeating the process

Each step of the process is described in the following sections.

Assembling a Planning Team

As in any planning process, involving key stakeholders is critical for receiving input, understanding needs, assessing alternatives, and creating buy-in. The leader of the technology planning team should be familiar with a broad range of technological applications. This person may be the chief information officer (CIO), director of computing technology, managing systems administrator, or other staff member with leadership, planning skills, and technological competence. In some cases it may be advantageous to work with an outside consultant who specializes in technology planning and solutions. This option may be cost intensive; however, if the organization is committed to technology planning and considers the expense to be a necessary component of strategic planning, the organization may benefit from fresh ideas and outside-the-box thinking. Either way, it is important that technology planning be conducted at the organizational level and include representatives from all relevant units in order to achieve a system that is integrated and creates the kind of boundaryless structures that encourage innovation.

Examining the Vision, Mission, Goals, and Objectives

As stated previously, technology planning should be seen as an extension of the strategic planning process. It needs to be connected to the overall mission, goals, and objectives of the organization. Clearly articulating the goals of an organization and how technology might be employed to achieve them is at the forefront of technology planning.

Assessing Current Technology Infrastructure

Technology planning should take stock of existing technological infrastructure, including digital hardware, software, and networks. Hardware consists of the physical components of computers and other digital or electronic systems. Typically, computer hardware includes the monitor, keyboard, and central processing unit (CPU). Hardware can also include peripheral machinery such as printers, faxes, modems, docking stations, and the concept can be extended to an array of computing, communications, and multimedia devices. Software consists of the programs that allow these devices to function. Computing software may include operating systems as well as specific technological functions such as word processing, spreadsheets, databases, Web site development, presentations, and multimedia applications.

The ability to develop networks connecting customers, organizations, and employees is a powerful tool, and the wider the network, the more powerful the tool (Lovelock, 2001). Organizations should examine their access to and use of the Internet, extranet, and intranet. The Internet is publicly accessible by everyone who can log onto a computer. Open-access Web sites that provide information can be viewed anywhere there is a computer with Internet access. A German citizen who is planning to take a trip to Canada can access the National Parks of Canada Web site from Berlin and find public information related to Glacier National Park, for example.

Extranets have more restrictive access. Organizations define the boundary of the network and provide access to specific users through secured portals. For example, a sport organization may make general information publicly accessible through its Internet site but make specific information available only to season-ticket holders or club sponsors through a password-protected security system. Intranets are the most restrictive and are generally only accessible by employees or members of the organization. System administrators provide network security to prevent access from unauthorized parties. Intranets may link or network different employees or units within an organization and can greatly enhance communication and the exchange of information.

Identifying New Technology Solutions

In examining the strategic plan of the organization, the technology planning team should devise technological solutions that help advance the organization's goals and objectives. These solutions may include using current technology resources more effectively, integrating existing systems, or adopting brand-new technological applications. Regardless of the proposed strategy, the planning team must demonstrate how the technological solution can help bridge the gap between where the organization is currently and where it wants to be.

For example, the recently released technology plan of the U.S. Department of Education (2006) includes a strategy for integrating student data. In recommending a plan of action, the department identified the current state of student records management (isolated silos of incompatible, incomplete, or redundant data on student attendance, academic performance, involvement in extracurricular activities, free and reduced lunch status, and so on), articulated a vision for the future (aggregation and alignment of data accessible by parents, teachers, administrators, students, governments, and so on), and proposed a technological solution for getting there (data warehousing). Such a plan could benefit after-school program directors by improving the effectiveness of targeting and referring children for extracurricular involvement based on a specific set of indicators, abilities, or deficits.

Developing Implementation Strategies, Time Lines, and Costs

Technology solutions need implementation strategies. As a rule, complex solutions requiring major additions to the existing technology infrastructure or changes in organizational systems need to be phased in over time. Managers should expect some resistance to changes in technology and systems, and a realistic time frame should be allowed for wholesale buy-in of new technology solutions. Managers must also consider the costs involved in implementing new technology. They extend beyond just the cost of the technology and include staff (or customer) training and the potential for lost productivity while personnel get up to speed on new systems. The following steps represent a plan for implementing new technology within an organization.

1. Develop a time line and budget for implementation of new technology.
2. Develop an information campaign for staff and customers.
3. Train a few personnel or customers on the new technology as a test run.

4. Install new technology systems.

5. Test new systems solutions in mock or artificial environments.

6. Evaluate performance, obtain feedback from stakeholders, and make adjustments where appropriate.

7. Pilot test new systems in a limited manner.

8. Evaluate performance, obtain feedback from stakeholders, and make adjustments where appropriate.

9. Train all staff and customers on the new technology.

10. Implement the new system.

Understanding and Involving End Users

Technology planning should develop strategies with the end user in mind. Each step of the process should involve users such as employees or customers to ensure a successful transition to new technological systems. Personnel and key customers should be included in the process of designing strategies or systems, provided with training on new systems, and asked to provide input for the purposes of evaluation and as a precursor to future change. By including staff and customers in the planning process, resistance to change can be reduced.

It is also important to consider the current capacity of people to use new technologies. Staff and customers will undoubtedly need information, orientation, or training on the use of new systems. Access is another factor to consider. For example, if an organization is planning to go paperless by moving program registration, facility reservation requests, and payment for services online, then it is imperative that potential users be able to access those systems. Although Internet use is growing, it is still not a universally accessed technology. The U.S. Census Bureau reported that 62 percent of American households have at least one computer in the home, and 55 percent of those households have Internet access (U.S. Census Bureau, 2005b). Moving to an Internet-based registration and payment system may be a good idea for a variety of reasons; however, the organization must create an implementation plan for ensuring that all customers can access and use the new system. For example, in trying to bridge the digital divide, a public park and recreation organization might provide digital kiosks in convenient locations throughout a municipality, allowing constituents without Internet access to register for programs, reserve facilities, and make payments.

Assessing Effectiveness, Making Adjustments, and Repeating the Process

Technology planning is a process. As with any plan, organizations should continually evaluate, revisit, and adjust their strategies and solutions. Obtaining feedback from key users is a valuable method for evaluating the effectiveness of technology strategies. A system for data collection and ongoing assessment of organizational systems and technology use can help drive future planning efforts.

Summary of Plans

The plans discussed in this chapter are used in all sectors of the leisure services profession. Different agencies may have different plans depending on their needs.

An agency might also have one comprehensive plan that encompasses a strategic plan, a master plan for facilities, a recreation program plan, a marketing plan, and a technology plan.

Problem Solving and Decision Making

The ability to solve problems and make decisions is a highly rated competency for both entry-level and top managers (Hurd, 2005). Furthermore, decision making falls within the planning aspect of the managerial functions.

The terms *problem solving* and *decision making* are often used interchangeably due to their close relationship. **Decision making** is choosing between two or more alternatives whereas **problem solving** is determining solutions to correct the discrepancy between a desired state and current reality (Dumler & Skinner, 2005). When problems arise that need to be solved, a decision must be made on how to solve the problem. However, not all decision making deals with problems. We make hundreds of decisions every day without even thinking about them—we choose what clothes to wear, what route to take to work, what to have for dinner, and so on.

Decisions fall on a continuum from programmed to nonprogrammed (Certo, 2003). **Programmed decisions** are the routine decisions managers make. These decisions may be policy or planning driven, so the manager already knows what to do. Programmed decisions are usually less time consuming and difficult to make than nonprogrammed decisions. For example, a programmed decision may be whether to close a pool and spa in an electrical storm or whether to cancel a class based on low enrollment.

Nonprogrammed decisions are more challenging because they are often new or unique. Problems usually require nonprogrammed decisions. These situations take more thought and time to look at every angle of the situation in order to make the decision and solve the problem. Nonprogrammed decisions could include how to define *family* for membership purposes or how to deal with an undesirable group that requests the use of a park for a controversial rally.

Making decisions requires a process. Although programmed decisions will be made without consciously thinking about these steps, nonprogrammed decisions require careful consideration and follow six steps (figure 7.2).

Step 1: Identify and Define the Problem

Identifying and defining a problem is not as easy as it may appear. Sometimes when managers look at problems, what they are really seeing are symptoms of a larger problem. This requires that the manager look deeply into the situation. To identify the real problem, managers must see what barriers are standing in the way of achieving goals and get multiple viewpoints of the

> **decision making—** Choosing from two or more alternatives through a process of analyzing the situation, evaluating options, and selecting a course of action.
>
> **problem solving—** Creating solutions to correct the discrepancy between a desired state and current reality.
>
> **programmed decisions—** Routine decisions that managers face on a daily basis.

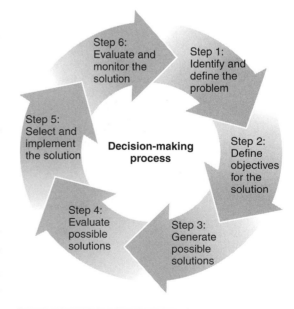

Figure 7.2 Decision-making process.

situation (Arnold, Heyne, & Busser, 2005). Multiple viewpoints provide a different perspective from what the lone manager sees. These multiple viewpoints can come from fellow managers or from people external to the agency. Someone without any history of the situation may shed new light on the root of the problem rather than the symptoms.

To illustrate the decision-making model, assume you are a manager in the Jefferson Parks and Recreation Department. You are faced with the question of whether or not to ban sledding in parks. The major concerns are liability and damage caused to the golf course.

Step 2: Define Objectives for the Solution

The next step is to determine the objectives of the solution, or what the end result should achieve. In determining the objectives, it is important to consider everyone involved with the problem. More people may be affected than those within the agency; there are also customers, community members, shareholders, and other stakeholders to consider. Their reaction to the solution may require consideration. For our sledding problem, here are a few examples of objectives:

▶ Protect the golf course from turf damage.
▶ Provide safe activities for city residents.
▶ Provide a variety of indoor and outdoor free winter activities for city residents.

Each objective is specific enough to guide you through the next step of generating possible solutions.

Step 3: Generate Possible Solutions

Few problems have only one solution, so looking for multiple solutions is advised. Inexperienced managers may be too timid to generate creative solutions for fear of rejection. However, creative problem solving makes you a better manager. We have all heard the phrase "think outside the box." This is especially true when generating possible solutions for a problem.

Sometimes the generation of solutions is inhibited for various reasons. Ideas may be stymied because of emotional attachments to programs, products, or places. For example, a popular preschool arts program instructor was fired for insubordination, not following through on responsibilities, and not staying within the program budget over several years. This instructor was so popular that upon her firing, past program participants spoke out expressing their disbelief. They caused quite a media stir and much headache for the agency. The solution to this problem is inherently connected to

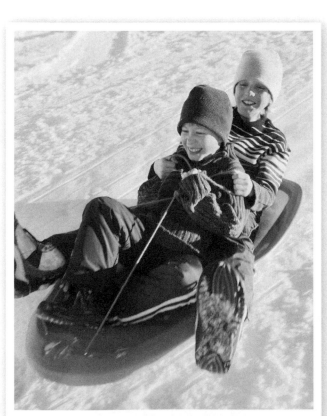

As a manager, how would you balance activities such as sledding against concerns involving liability and damage to city parks?

emotional ties from the community. When generating solutions, the agency needs to consider such emotional ties but should not be held hostage by them.

Solution generation can also be inhibited by change. People have varying degrees of success when dealing with change. Walk into any agency as a new manager and listen to people describe processes in the organization. Undoubtedly, the phrase "we've always done it that way" will emerge. When ways of doing things become ingrained in the culture of the organization, they are sometimes difficult to change. A radical solution to a problem may be a great idea, but if it is not the typical response, it may cause some resistance. However, this is not an excuse to avoid generating good ideas. Change is the only constant within an organization!

Here are some possible solutions to the sledding problem:

▶ Ban sledding at the golf course and allow it at other parks.

▶ Post signs at dangerous sledding spots to warn of dangers and take extra precautions to protect sledders, such as fencing in areas where sleds go off course.

▶ Hire a supervisor at the golf course to monitor for safety and damage.

▶ Stop sledding at all parks and golf courses.

Step 4: Evaluate Possible Solutions

All solutions need to be screened based on the objectives for the solution. This step allows managers to compare the solutions, adapt them if needed, and even combine possible solutions. Once a change is made to a solution, it needs to be evaluated just as the original solutions were. In this step, all solutions should have a devil's advocate to think of the alternatives, the what-ifs of a solution. Here is one example of how to evaluate the solutions to the sledding problem (table 7.4).

Table 7.4   Evaluation of Solutions

Solution	Pros (+)	Cons (−)
Ban sledding at the golf course and allow it at other parks.	– Stops damage to the golf course. – Keeps sledding as a free winter activity.	– Damage occurs in other parks. – Liability is still an issue.
Post signs at dangerous sledding spots to warn of dangers and take extra precautions to protect sledders, such as fencing in areas where sleds go off course.	– Keeps sledding as a free winter activity. – Does not necessarily prevent injuries and accidents.	– Makes people aware of the dangers. – Somewhat protects the agency in case of lawsuits.
Hire a supervisor at the golf course to monitor for safety and damage.	– Reduces injuries. – Reduces damage if sledding is stopped in time.	– Does not eliminate injuries and accidents. – Adds the expense of a supervisor. – May need to charge to sled, thus eliminating a free winter activity.
Stop sledding at all parks and golf courses.	– Stops turf damage at the golf course and parks. – Eliminates a liability issue.	– Eliminates a free winter activity. – Major elimination for a minor and controllable problem.

Step 5: Select and Implement the Solution

After evaluating possible solutions, one is chosen and implemented. Each solution will have some level of risk. Selecting a solution means determining which one will be the most beneficial and least detrimental to achieving the goals, objectives, mission, and strategic plan of the organization. After much thought and discussion with staff, board, and community, sledding is banned from the golf course and extra safety precautions and signage are installed at other parks.

Step 6: Evaluate and Monitor the Solution

Decision making does not end with the implementation of the solution. Managers learn a lot from evaluating and monitoring their decisions. Once implemented, managers should measure whether the desired effect occurred with the solution. Evaluating and monitoring means examining the consequences of the decision, measuring the outcomes, and determining if it was the right decision. If it was not the right decision, then the process begins again.

As for our sledders, after the first winter the agency evaluated the new policy and how it met the needs of the community. The solution seemed to work. However, if it did not, the agency could go back and look at other solutions to the problem.

Even following this decision-making process does not automatically result in the right decision every time. Decision making is not foolproof because there are so many uncontrollable and sometimes unforeseeable aspects to various situations. Using the sledding example, a number of variables could have come into play to affect the quality of the decision. It could have been a snowy winter and the number of sledders was well beyond projections and turf suffered; it could have been a mild winter with little snow, yet many sledders used the park and destroyed turf; or unforeseen risk areas in the park might have resulted in a higher number of injuries than in the past. As managers gain experience, they become better at identifying problems, defining objectives, developing creative solutions,

To determine if a ban on sledding on a hilly golf course was a good decision, look at the objectives for the solution, the desired outcomes, and the consequences of the decision.

predicting consequences, and choosing the right solutions. This takes experience, and it takes making both good and bad decisions.

Ethical Decision Making

The decision-making process covers all decisions regarding everything from human resources to participants. It is impossible to discuss decision making without discussing the ethical implications of decisions. Ethics are principles of behavior encompassing goodness, fairness, and doing what is right. Ethical decision making takes into account the results of a decision and how it affects others.

Rather than reinventing the decision-making process, it is only necessary to consider the ethical implications. To do this, the manager assesses the situation to see if there are legal, personal, or social issues that could cause conflict. For example, it is unethical for a supervisor to ask a staff member to do personal errands or jobs for the supervisor. A supervisor asking a landscape specialist to plant a flower bed at the supervisor's house while being paid by the agency is considered unethical.

When an issue is defined as ethical, extra care must be taken during the decision-making process. When generating possible solutions (step 3) for an ethical decision, the solutions can be categorized in several ways. Let's use the following scenario to look at the various ethical decision-making approaches. The local YMCA has a competitive soccer program for young people. This program has a widespread reputation for being one of the best for player development. Many players in the league went on to earn college scholarships and even play professional soccer. The teams are ranked in terms of talent. A local businessperson is upset to hear that his son made the second team and not the first, which has the top players and gets the most exposure to large universities. This person offers the YMCA $25,000 to make much-needed renovations to the soccer fields. The only thing the agency needs to do is move his son to the first team.

The first approach to ethical decision making is the utilitarian approach, where the decision results in the greatest good for the greatest number. It can be viewed as the decision that does the least amount of harm. In this situation, the manager would place the son on the top team. It is only adding one more person, and the young man has talent since he was originally placed on the second team. The most good will come to future players because they will have state-of-the-art facilities on which to play.

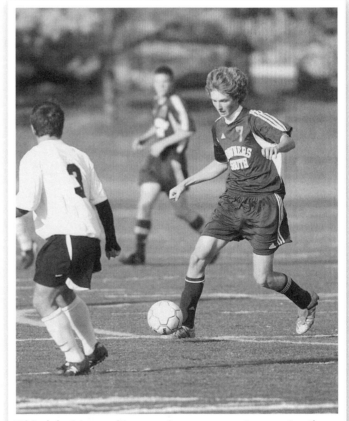

Ethical decision making requires managers to examine the impact on all involved. How would you determine whether to place a soccer player on the top team in exchange for a donation to renovate the soccer field?

A moral approach to ethical decision making requires the manager to do what is right regardless of the consequences. If using a moral approach, the manager would not move the player to the top team or accept the donation, because the young man did not earn the spot on the first team and the money was not given in good faith.

A universalist approach requires the manager to look at the situation and how it affects everyone else. In this case, the manager must assess how everyone else would feel if they knew how the new soccer fields were funded and that the player was moved up to the first team. This requires thinking like those who are affected to determine whether they would rather have new fields or give the space on the first team to a more talented player.

Finally, a cost–benefit analysis requires the manager to examine the costs and benefits of the decision. The manager would need to look at the cost of this move to the reputation of the program and how the ability to buy a child's way into a program goes against all that the organization stands for in its mission. The benefits of accepting the money include the ability to put other resources originally earmarked for field renovations into other aspects of the program and the ability to draw state and national tournaments on much-improved fields (Poznak Law Firm, Ltd., 2007).

Ethical decision making requires an extra step to identify the issue as ethical and then determining what ethical approach to take in the situation. All other aspects of ethical decision making follow the presented process and should result in a decision meeting the needs of the organization.

Conclusion

▶ This chapter focused on two concepts that are strongly interrelated. First, planning was introduced as a guide to reach the vision an agency sets for itself. Planning goals, objectives, strategic issues, and strategies help an agency prioritize what it should do, why it should do these things, and how they should be done. Second, decision making and problem solving are affected by planning and policies. Although planning does not determine decisions, managers refer to plans when evaluating the solutions to problems.

▶ Planning and decision-making skills are interwoven with many aspects of being a manager, from setting goals and objectives to creating budgets. Neither will be instantaneous skills for new managers; they will build over time and with experience. They require the involvement of others both inside and outside the organization to be effective.

REVIEW QUESTIONS

1. Compare and contrast strategic planning, master planning, and recreation program planning.

2. Explain the four approaches to ethical decision making.

3. Explain a SWOT analysis and give an example of each element.

4. Why should organizations plan?

5. Discuss the role of public input in planning and policy making.

6. Explain programmed and nonprogrammed decisions and give an example of each.

7. Discuss the decision-making process.

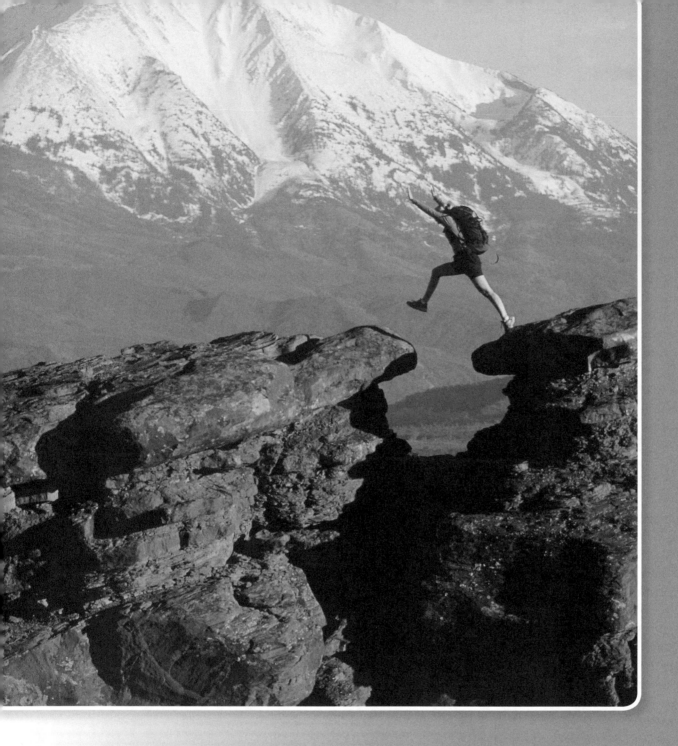

KEY WORDS

marketing, market segmentation, target marketing, demographics, psychographics, marketing mix, product life cycle, direct distribution, indirect distribution, intensity of distribution, penetration pricing, neutral pricing, skim pricing, promotion, promotions mix, advertising, sales promotions and incentives, personal selling, publicity, public relations, media relations, community relations

COMPETENCY CHECK

Take another look at table 1.3 (page 9) to see how you assessed this related competency.

9. Implement marketing techniques.

CHAPTER 8

Marketing and Public Relations

LEARNING OUTCOMES

1. Explain marketing and its importance in leisure services.
2. Differentiate between market segmentation and target marketing.
3. Examine the marketing mix and describe how to incorporate it into leisure services organizations.
4. Outline the role of public relations and its related activities.

On any given day, my job has me heading in multiple directions and juggling multiple roles for any number of events. My job is to design an event that will not only attract the target market but also create a setting where the targeted consumers can enjoy our product once they are at the brewery; all the while the event must communicate Redhook's mission, "Defy ordinary." The job requires long hours. In terms of marketing, each event demands band booking, ticket sales, advertising, overseeing creative marketing, meeting with promoters and cosponsors, creating and maintaining budgets, maintaining Web site listings, coor-

dinating advertising schedules with print and radio outlets, and the list goes on. At the end of the day, it's rewarding to see an event that I created from start to finish serve the greater purpose: The brewery gained new consumers who started their visit as concert attendees, and these consumers have not just sampled the brand but also had a taste of the brewery's mission, its home, and the entire Redhook lifestyle and experience.

Jessica Watts
Special Event Coordinator
Redhook Ale Brewery
Portsmouth, New Hampshire

For many years, marketing was not a part of the park and recreation profession in the public and nonprofit sectors. Agencies hired people to plan and implement programs but no one to tell the public about them. Marketing was left up to the programmer and may have consisted of developing a flyer, distributing a brochure, or sending out a news release.

Until the last decade or so, few park and recreation curricula required students to take a marketing course. However, this has changed, as has the concept of marketing. Marketing in leisure services has moved beyond flyers and brochures to integration of the marketing mix, marketing plans, target marketing, and market research.

Marketing can take on many faces within an organization. Some agencies have employees whose only job is to market products and services. Other agencies have an employee who is responsible for some marketing but also has other responsibilities, and then there are agencies where staff members do their own marketing. Marketing is an innovative area, and rarely can an agency attract too many people to use its programs and services. Thus, it is important to know the fundamentals of marketing in order to increase use of programs and services to the desired level.

For those who have the luxury of a marketing department to carry out marketing functions, it is still necessary to understand marketing basics. This knowledge allows for a team approach to marketing with input from the manager as well as the marketing staff. The manager has much more intimate knowledge of the product, service, or program than the marketing staff does, and vice versa in terms of marketing. If the two sides can come together and speak a common language through an understanding of marketing, the organization will be able to better utilize resources and capitalize on marketing efforts than if the manager does not understand marketing beyond a flyer and news release. This chapter outlines the foundations of marketing and introduces concepts needed in order to market programs and services effectively.

Definition and History of Marketing

Marketing can be defined as the purposeful planning and execution of the pricing, place, and promotion of ideas, goods, and services to create an exchange of time or resources that results in the satisfaction of individual needs and organizational objectives (figure 8.1).

Marketing has not always been defined and executed in this fashion. Marketing history can be divided into four eras (O'Sullivan, 1991). These include the production era, the sales era, the marketing era, and the service marketing era (figure 8.2).

marketing—Purposeful planning and execution of the pricing, place, and promotion of ideas, goods, and services to create an exchange of time or resources that results in the satisfaction of individual needs and organizational objectives.

Production Era

The Industrial Revolution changed how people worked and spent their money. More and more people worked in factories and were able to mass-produce products for consumers. In this era, businesses focused on what they did best and produced those products while trying to reduce costs. People were able to buy things for the first time, and demand often exceeded supply. There was little regard for what customers wanted, and goods were the focus rather than services. Manufacturers simply had to put the product on the market and people bought it.

Figure 8.1 **Definition of marketing.**

Sales Era

Beginning in the 1930s and during the Great Depression, supply exceeded demand for most products. Companies were still producing the products they wanted based on their own strengths. Sales techniques were used to stimulate demand and align customer wants with production capabilities. During this era, sales and marketing became synonymous. Also during this time, a lot of advertising was done by people who had virtually no control over the product. This approach is still seen today in many leisure services agencies where the responsibility of the marketing staff is to sell programs to users without having any input on the programs.

Marketing Era

This era, which began in the early 1980s, derived from increased competition and saw organizations becoming more responsive to the needs of consumers. Marketing staff studied consumer needs and then developed products to meet those needs. Marketing thus became an integrated function of product development because it was customer driven rather than product driven. It was also during this era that park and recreation agencies saw the value in marketing and started marketing their programs.

Service Marketing Era

The service marketing era is similar to the marketing era, except it has increased the focus on marketing services and ideas in addition to products. This era started in the early 1990s and continues today. It remains customer focused, and the value of services as a product is strongly emphasized.

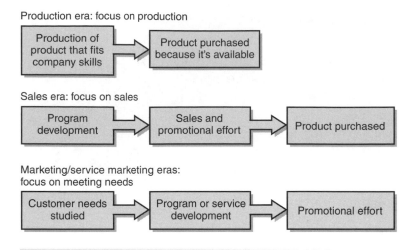

Figure 8.2 **Eras of marketing.**

Adapted from D.R. Howard and J.L. Crompton, 1980, *Financing, managing, and marketing recreation and park resources* (Dubuque, IA: Wm. C. Brown Publishers), 307, by permission of The McGraw-Hill Companies.

Summary of Eras

The leisure services profession has moved through all four eras of marketing. The commercial sector was ahead of the public and nonprofit sectors in doing so, but the latter two sectors are quickly catching up and valuing the benefits of marketing as much as the commercial sector does. This is especially true now that the marketing of services has become a focus.

Goods Versus Services

Marketing for all three sectors only became prominent during the marketing and service marketing eras. As indicated, both eras have many similarities with the main difference being a product or a service orientation. When looking at a good versus a service, there are four main differences: intangibility, inseparability, heterogeneity, and perishability.

Services are considered intangible whereas goods are considered tangible. A tangible good can be sensed through touch, such as a bicycle, a football, or hiking boots. On the other hand, services are considered intangible. The consumer experiences a service, such as a swim lesson, but the service cannot necessarily be physically touched.

Second, services and products differ based on the inseparability of services and their creators or producers. Services must be consumed at the place they originate, and they must be used at the time they are produced. Using the swim lesson example, the lesson must be used when the instructor creates it at the pool. Consumers cannot take this service home and use it when they want, unlike a product such as a bicycle that can be ridden at any time the buyer chooses.

Third, there is more heterogeneity, or inconsistency, in services than in goods. For example, let's say you have decided to purchase a Trek Navigator 100 bicycle. There are four bicycles on the floor, each in a different color. Because the products are homogenous, there is no reason to ride a bicycle in each color to determine which one feels best. The bikes are standardized, and production and assembly are rigidly controlled and inspected before distribution. Conversely, most services do not have the luxury of these control factors, making them more heterogeneous. The swim lesson will change based on the preparation, mood, or experience of the instructor; the aesthetics or location of the facility; and even the weather. Since people cannot be totally standardized, services will always have some variability.

Finally, services differ from goods in terms of perishability. Services are highly perishable because they cannot be inventoried or stored. The unsold bicycles remain available for consumer purchase long after their production, whereas a swim lesson held on Tuesday for an hour is gone once the lesson time passes. Furthermore, bicycle manufacturers can mass-produce their bicycles in advance for the summer

Although many see parks and recreation as a service industry, another important aspect of the field is the sale of tangible goods.

season. Due to perishability, swim lessons cannot be mass-produced in the winter, stored, and then used in the summer.

The recreation profession deals with both goods and services, whether it is selling outdoor adventure equipment or running the Thunderbird Lodge in Manitoba. Because of this, *goods* and *services* will be used interchangeably throughout this chapter.

Market Segmentation and Target Marketing

Because not everyone has the same wants and needs, watches the same television programs, or uses the same products and services, market segmentation and target marketing are needed. **Market segmentation** is the process of dividing a heterogeneous market into smaller homogenous subgroups that are similar in terms of wants, needs, demographic profiles, and how they respond to the marketing mix (Mullins, Hardy, & Sutton, 2000). **Target marketing** selects one or more market segments to focus on.

Before target marketing is possible, the market must first be segmented. A market is all the actual or potential buyers of a product (Kotler, Bowen, & Makens, 2006). Market segmentation allows an agency to look at its different markets, their individual needs, and the products that meet those needs rather than taking a mass-marketing approach. Mass marketing assumes that all people want the same things, and one product is expected to appeal to all people.

For example, let's say the local senior center offers a trip to New York City that includes airfare, a hotel room for five nights, tickets to two Broadway shows, and all meals at a cost of $2,500 per person. In a mass-marketing approach, the

market segmentation—Process of dividing a heterogeneous market into smaller homogenous subgroups who are similar in terms of wants, needs, demographic profiles, and how they respond to the marketing mix.

target marketing—Selecting one or more market segments and focusing the market mix on this segment.

organization would direct promotions for this trip to the entire community of 250,000 people rather than focusing on likely buyers. Market segmentation would allow the agency to identify market segments in the community based on such characteristics as income, age, and travel interests. Then the specific segments that are most likely to take this trip would be targeted and marketing efforts developed. Market segmentation is a better use of time and money because efforts are aimed at groups that are most likely to respond.

Shifts in Demographics in the United States and Canada

The demographic profile of the United States is rapidly changing. Minority groups are growing so quickly that there is no majority race in the states of California, Hawaii, New Mexico, and Texas (U.S. Census Bureau, 2006). The same is true in Canada, where it is projected that by 2017 (Canada's 150th birthday), 19 to 23 percent of the population will be a visible minority. Already in Toronto, one of the world's most diverse cities, 43 percent of the population identified as a visible minority (Toronto, 2007). A visible minority is a person who is non-Caucasian in race or nonwhite in color (Statistics Canada, 2007b).

Given this growth in minority populations, it is easy to see that targeting minority markets is a necessity. Not only is there a desire to meet the needs of these markets, but there is a wealth of buying power as well. Buying power is the total posttax, personal income of residents that is available to spend on goods and services, also called *discretionary income* (Humphreys, 2004). For example, it is estimated that by 2009, buying power for Caucasians will be $8.9 trillion, followed by Hispanics ($992.3 billion), African Americans ($964.6 billion), and Asians ($528.2 billion) (Humphreys, 2004). Clearly, minority groups have a large amount of disposable income to spend on leisure services, which makes targeting minority markets a necessity.

Selecting a Segmentation Strategy

When determining whether to segment a market, it is important to establish whether the market is identifiable, sustainable, accessible, and responsive. In addition, the market must have a perceived need. In a market segment that is identifiable, the people within the segment can be distinguished from the general population, which will reveal the size of the market and its purchasing power, or its sustainability. The market should not be so small as to be a poor use of resources but not so large as to resemble a mass market.

A viable market segment should also be accessible. The people within the segment must be able to be reached by distribution and promotion of the product. For example, isolated seniors or homeless people may prove to be difficult groups to access regardless of the value of offering recreation services to them.

A market segment should also be responsive to the marketing mix. There are two aspects of responsiveness: the ability of the program to meet the needs of the segment and the responsiveness of the segment to the marketing initiatives. Both aspects need to occur for the segment to be viable.

The last segmentation criteria for the park and recreation profession is perceived need. Youth at risk, inactive children, and low-income families are just a few examples of segments that may be excluded based on the other three guidelines but are in need of services provided by the profession and represent a fair portion of the community (McCarville, 2002).

Bases of Segmentation

Bases of segmentation are ways in which a mass market can be segmented into smaller, more homogenous groups. Although this can be done in a number of ways, typically leisure services use five different bases: demographics, geography, psychographics, behavioral characteristics, and benefits.

The most common base is **demographics** and includes income, age, gender, race and ethnicity, sexual orientation, education, and family life cycle (how people progress through various stages of life; table 8.1). Many leisure services providers use demographics to segment their market. For example, the Carmel Clay Parks and Recreation Department in Indiana divides programs into parent–child, preschool, youth, and adult programs. Demographics data are available through most cities, libraries, and census bureaus.

demographics Population characteristics used to gather data on groups of people (e.g., sex, age, race).

Table 8.1 Demographic and Geographic Segmentation Variables for Consumer Markets in the United States

Variable	Typical breakdown
GEOGRAPHIC	
Region	Pacific, Mountain, West North Central, South Central, East North Central, South Atlantic, Middle Atlantic, New England
City or metro size	Under 5,000; 5,000-20,000; 20,000-50,000; 50,000-100,000; 100,000-250,000; 250,000-500,000; 500,000-1,000,000; 1,000,000-4,000,000; 4,000,000 and over
Density	Urban, suburban, rural
DEMOGRAPHIC	
Age	Under 6; 6-11; 12-19; 20-34; 35-49; 50-64; 65+
Family size	1-2; 3-4; 5+
Family life cycle	Young and single; young, married, no children; young, married, youngest child under 6; young, married, youngest child 6 or over; older married, with children; older married, no children under 18; older single; other
Income	Under $10,000; $10,000-$15,000; $15,000-$20,000; $20,000-$30,000; $30,000-$50,000; $50,000-$100,000; $100,000+
Occupation	Professional and technical; managers, officials, and proprietors; clerical, sales; craftspeople, foremen; operatives; farmers; retired; students; stay-at-home wives or husbands; unemployed
Education	Grade school or less; some high school; high school graduate; some college; college graduate; postgraduate work; postgraduate degree
Race	African American; American Indian; Asian; Caucasian; Hispanic; other
Nationality	American; British; French Canadian; German; Italian; Japanese; Australian; Latino
Social class	Lower lower; upper lower; working class; middle class; upper middle; lower upper; upper upper

A second segmentation base is geography. This variable considers such factors as geoclusters and proximity. Geoclusters, or how closely people live to each other, assumes that people living close together, as in neighborhoods or zip codes, share many of the same characteristics. It is possible to develop a market segment based on a neighborhood and determine a demographic profile of this geocluster to learn even more about it. Similar to geoclusters, proximity identifies how close people are to the service. There is a strong relationship between proximity to a service and use of that service. A person who lives 5 minutes from a beach is much more likely to use the beach than someone living an hour away. Because of proximity concerns, the YMCA of Greater Des Moines has seven branches located throughout the city. Members can use any branch, but most will use the one closest to where they live or work.

psychographics— Values, attitudes, beliefs, personality, motivation, and lifestyle variables that define a person.

Psychographics include personality, motivation, and lifestyle or social class variables. Psychographic data can be difficult to gather, yet they can be beneficial if used in conjunction with demographic data. Lifestyle variables are of particular interest to park and recreation professionals. These variables are a combination of activities such as vacations, hobbies, and entertainment; interests such as family, community, and work; and opinions such as politics, social issues, and culture. The Ventana Inn and Spa in Big Sur, California, provides an elegant resort experience that caters to a high-end lifestyle, including formal dining with caviar, oysters on the half shell, and foie gras as appetizers; rooms starting at $1,500 per night; and a spa featuring massages, body treatments, and Reiki therapy (Ventana Inn, 2007). This type of vacation destination would appeal to a specific lifestyle and market segment. Businesses such as the Ventana Inn and Spa would greatly benefit from psychographic data.

A market segmented according to behavioral characteristics considers how much and how often consumers purchase a product, their skill level related to the product, and their product loyalty. In response to the different segments of buyers, the Indiana Fever Women's professional basketball team understands the value of behavioral segmentation by offering different ticketing options for different levels of users. The options include a season ticket (18 games), half-season ticket (9 games), minipackage (5 games), choose-and-go plan (8 tickets redeemable for any game desired), and single-game tickets (Indiana Fever, 2007). These options are offered in response to attendance behaviors of several segments.

In addition, skill level plays a significant role in targeting people for certain activities based on their experience. For example, Clear Creek Rafting Company in Idaho Springs, Colorado, offers trips for a variety of abilities, including beginner trips, intermediate trips, advanced trips, evening trips, and multiday trips (Clear Creek Rafting Company, 2007). Each user level has different trip expectations and different desires for increased challenges. To a business such as Clear Creek Rafting Company, behavioral characteristics are a better determinant of market segments than demographics.

Finally, benefits-based segmentation separates homogenous groups based on what they want to gain from the product. For example, Dagger Kayaks offers a fit guide that asks potential buyers what benefits are important to them and then finds the kayak that is the best choice based on those benefits, such as a touring kayak that is durable, affordable, and stable with a lot of storage (Dagger Kayaks, 2007). The company has a full line of kayaks and targets benefits rather than demographics, psychographics, or other segmenting methods.

Selecting a Target Market

Once a market has been segmented into different groups, target markets must be selected. Determining which segments to target will depend on several factors, including resources available and likelihood of the segment to respond to marketing efforts. However, there are three basic strategies to selecting a target market: undifferentiated, differentiated, and concentrated strategies (figure 8.3). An undifferentiated approach ignores the different market segments and focuses on all of them. This approach assumes the mass-marketing mentality that everyone will be reached by one marketing mix. Of the three sectors, the public sector is most likely to use this method because market research skills, time, and money limit a better segmentation strategy.

Differentiated market segmentation recognizes that market segments require different marketing strategies. A number of segments are identified and specific marketing plans are developed for each segment.

The commercial and nonprofit sectors are more likely to use a concentrated target marketing strategy than the public sector. This selection approach identifies a clearly defined target market and focuses its resources and marketing mix on that particular market. The Ventana Inn and Spa, for example, knows that its target market is educated, high-income, middle to older adults who value prestige, relaxation, and escape. This is the market they will target, and though others are always welcome to come to the inn, they are not the focus of the marketing mix.

Many leisure services agencies show their marketing weaknesses by disregarding market segmentation and target marketing. Managers are expected to use limited resources as best as possible, and any manager attempting to mass-market a product is wasting resources. All people are different and want different things. By clustering people into groups and then focusing on those segments that would

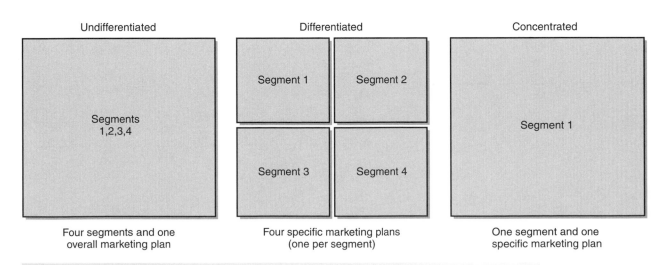

Figure 8.3 **Target marketing strategies.**

best be served by the product, the manager is making wise use of time, money, and effort. Furthermore, with target marketing there is a far better return on the marketing investment if the manager understands who the prime candidates are for the marketing exchange.

Marketing Mix

marketing mix—Integration of product, place (or distribution), pricing, and promotion.

product life cycle—Phases that products go through from inception to death, including introduction, growth, maturation, saturation, and decline.

Once a target market is selected, the **marketing mix** for that market must be outlined. The marketing mix encompasses the four Ps—product, place, price, and promotion. It is the careful and purposeful combination of these elements that makes marketing effective. Although many people view marketing as simply advertising, several additional aspects are required in order for it to work. A logical starting point is the product. As previously discussed, for the purpose of this chapter the term *product* also includes programs, events, services, and facilities.

Product

From the time a product is first offered until its discontinuation, it goes through a **product life cycle.** As it passes through each of the five phases—introduction, growth, maturation, saturation, and decline (figure 8.4)—the marketing strategy is adjusted to respond to customer behaviors. Inexperienced managers might focus solely on advertising a product, but there are several strategies that can be used to extend the life cycle of the product. In order to make these adjustments, an understanding of what happens in the life cycle is needed.

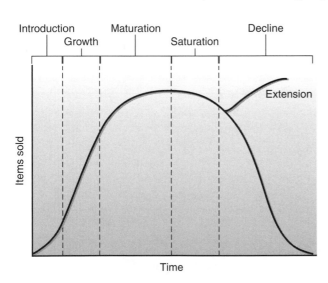

Figure 8.4   Product life cycle.

Introduction

During the introduction phase, the product is first released to the market. Typically there are only a small number of participants and little profitability. Marketing efforts are employed to expose people to the product and convince them to try it. This is done through heavy promotions, such as two-for-one deals, buy one get one free, a month's free membership, or Sunday nights free with a Friday and Saturday stay.

Growth

The product begins to experience a rapid growth in the number of participants as the early consumers continue participating and new consumers emerge. During this phase of the life cycle, there is a heavy reliance on word of mouth and various promotional efforts to lengthen the growth phase as long as possible.

Maturation

Growth slows in this phase, and products stay in this stage the longest, sometimes for several years. Most marketing efforts are directed at mature programs because they are solid programs that are still seeing growing numbers. At this stage, different markets can be explored and program modifications made (Rossman & Schlatter, 2003), and advertising campaigns are changed to accommodate these two changes or to simply attract more people.

Saturation

At the saturation stage, sales level off and the number of consumers peaks. Those who are loyal to the product keep purchasing at a steady rate; this is called *brand loyalty.* Any people who drop out are replaced by new purchasers, thus keeping steady numbers of consumers. Promotional efforts may change to attract new users and maintain loyalty.

Decline

When there is a steady decrease in consumers, the product has moved into the decline phase. During this phase, decisions on what to do with the program need to be made. Program options include petrification, death, and extension. If petrification is chosen, the program is left as is and will phase itself out until there are no more consumers. The program can also experience a death in that it is simply stopped. The most elaborate response to the decline phase is to use extension strategies that manipulate the product or the target market (figure 8.5): market penetration, market development, product development, product replacement, and diversification (Howard & Crompton, 1980).

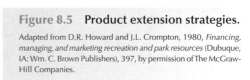

Market Penetration When an existing product that has been targeted to a specific market slides into the decline phase, market penetration can be used to extend the life of the product. Market penetration leaves the existing product as is and goes deeper into the existing target market. This may mean adjusting the marketing strategies to attract competitors' consumers or using heavy promotion to convince nonusers within the target market to become consumers. For example, the Greater River Area Family YMCA in Chillicothe, Missouri, offers an aquatics fitness program called Rusty Hinges that targets seniors who need a low-impact aerobic workout. With market penetration, increased promotional efforts are used to target people in this market who have the intention to participate but have not yet done so.

Figure 8.5 **Product extension strategies.**

Adapted from D.R. Howard and J.L. Crompton, 1980, *Financing, managing, and marketing recreation and park resources* (Dubuque, IA: Wm. C. Brown Publishers), 397, by permission of The McGraw-Hill Companies.

Market Development Market development looks for a new market segment for the existing product. Using the Rusty Hinges example, if attendance began to drop, the YMCA could target a younger population with physical disabilities who would benefit from the program.

Product Development and Product Replacement Both product development and replacement are extension strategies for a new product and an existing market. With product development, the old program is replaced by an entirely new program, whereas with replacement, the old program is replaced by an improved version of the same program. Using the Rusty Hinges example, a product development strategy would replace Rusty Hinges with another program aimed at the same target market, whereas a replacement strategy would make improvements to Rusty Hinges and reintroduce the improved version to the same target market.

Diversification   Diversification, the last extension strategy, begins the product life cycle over again since it introduces a new product to a new market segment. For example, the Rusty Hinges program would no longer be offered and its time slot and pool space would be used for a different program targeted toward a different segment, such as young people. With diversification the decision is made to move in an entirely different direction.

Place

The second *P* in the marketing mix is place. Sometimes referred to as *distribution,* place is how organizations get the product to the consumer. Place may include parks, recreation centers, golf courses, resorts, stores, and so on.

It is not by chance that a business finds itself in a certain section of the community or that certain programs are only offered in select recreation centers. In-depth research is carried out on distribution channels and intensity, community composition, location accessibility, and atmosphere (figure 8.6).

Distribution Channels and Intensity

Since parks and recreation is a diverse profession and encompasses the public, nonprofit, and commercial sectors, distribution channels vary widely. Distribution channels are either direct or indirect. In **direct distribution,** a product goes directly from the producer to the consumer, whereas an **indirect distribution** channel has a facilitating agent between the producer and the consumer. All those involved in the distribution of products are considered channel members. The public and nonprofit sectors usually have fewer channel members and a more direct distribution route. For example, the Bloomington Parks and Recreation Department in Indiana runs a premier farmers' market on Saturday mornings. They deliver the farmers' market directly to area residents without involving any other channel members—they plan and implement the program for the community without going through any other leisure services providers or distributors (figure 8.7).

Commercial recreation agencies such as a resort will also use a direct channel of distribution for many services such as room nights or meeting and convention services. However, the commercial sector in particular may also use an indirect channel of distribution. This means of distribution involves wholesalers and retailers. The wholesaler serves as a broker who works for the producer to get products to retailers. For example, a sporting goods store will work with a wholesaler of Nike products to get the equipment in the store in order to sell it to the customer. Since the equipment comes from a wholesaler rather than directly from Nike, the distribution method is indirect.

Another example of indirect channels of distribution in the commercial sector occurs within resorts. Many resorts do not provide their own recreation programs and services but hire companies to do this for them. For example, the American

Figure 8.6   Elements of place.

direct distribution—
Sending products straight from the producer to the consumer.

indirect distribution—
The means by which a product reaches the consumer; there is an intermediary entity between the producer and the consumer.

Hospitality Academy hires recreation workers who are assigned to various resorts where they plan and implement activities and events (American Hospitality Academy, 2007).

Although an indirect channel of distribution is widely used in the commercial sector, the public and nonprofit sectors use this distribution method as well. For example, Portland Parks and Recreation in Oregon offers adult basketball leagues. Because the agency owns limited gym space, the leagues use local elementary and middle school gymnasiums. In another example, the Champaign County YMCA in Illinois wanted to offer swim lessons for people with disabilities in order to meet the needs of an underserved market segment. Since the YMCA did not have staff expertise in this area, they contracted with Champaign-Urbana Special Recreation to offer programs at the YMCA. These are both examples of public and nonprofit agencies using an indirect channel of distribution as well as collaborative efforts.

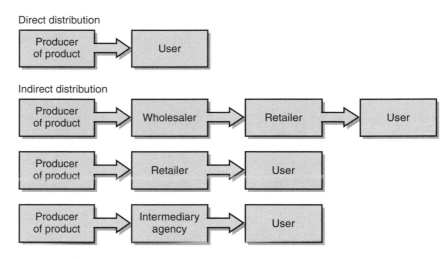

Figure 8.7 **Direct distribution versus indirect distribution.**

In addition to the channels of distribution, there is intensity to consider within the marketing mix (figure 8.8). **Intensity of distribution** is the "relative availability of a service to the consumer" (Crompton & Lamb, 1986, p. 193). Given the nature of the recreation profession, intensity is a factor regarding both facilities and services. Facility intensity is concerned with such things as the number and location of golf courses, pools, resort rooms, and bike trails. Also of interest for many agencies is the location of facilities. Many large communities, for example, are cognizant of the need to have recreation centers in different neighborhoods, including low-income neighborhoods. Service distribution has many of the same concerns regarding the number and variety of programs offered in each location.

> **intensity of distribution**—Number of events, programs, services, and facilities available in a community.

Not all service providers in the recreation profession have the same intensity of distribution. Three levels of distribution intensity are used in the leisure profession—intensive, selective, and exclusive (McCarville, 2002). *Intensive distribution* "creates maximum numbers of opportunities to enjoy a program" (p. 182). Parks and playgrounds are prime examples of intensive distribution because many communities strive to provide both within a short distance of all residents in a community. For example, Dallas Parks and Recreation in Texas has 374 parks and 183 playgrounds throughout the city (Dallas Parks and Recreation, 2007).

At the other end of the spectrum is exclusive distribution, where facilities or programs are limited to a select few. An elite golf league, an ice rink, and an urban white-water rafting facility are examples of exclusive distribution. In Dallas, a city of almost 1.2 million people, the park and recreation department has only six golf courses.

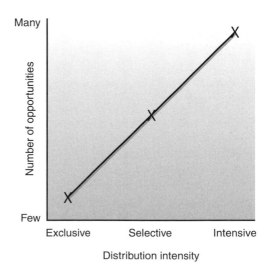

Figure 8.8 **Intensity of distribution.**

In the middle of these two intensity levels is selective distribution. Selective distribution assumes that a program can be held at a few locations or a few sessions of a program are offered throughout the year at one or more facilities. For example, the Wisconsin Department of Natural Resources has 53 state parks distributed within its borders. Although there is not a state park in every city, there are quite a few within 45 to 60 minutes of residents (figure 8.8).

Equitable Distribution of Resources

Equity of programs is a major issue in public recreation and refers to how programs, services, facilities, and other resources are distributed throughout the community. Three models of equity are used to distribute these resources (McCarville, 2002).

▶ The compensatory model provides resources based on who needs them the most. For example, an agency may determine that more free youth programs are needed in a low-income segment of the community.

▶ The equal opportunity model dictates that resources are distributed equally to all residents. This would mean that neighborhood parks are distributed within a certain distance of every home in the community so everyone has access close to home.

▶ The market equity model provides services for those who are willing and able to pay for them. This means of distribution is most often used by the commercial sector, but it is also seen in the public and nonprofit sectors for such things as fitness memberships or aquatics facilities.

Community Composition

Understanding the composition of the community is an important element that cannot be emphasized enough. Most communities have several neighborhoods, each with its own characteristics, people, and work and leisure activity. What goes on in a neighborhood and what is located there will have a tremendous impact on whether it is a good distribution channel. Gaining a clear picture of community composition includes breaking down the city by neighborhood and investigating

▶ what businesses are in the community,

▶ the nature of the businesses (i.e., industrial, technological, or large versus small businesses),

▶ overall education of the community and potential workers for the business,

▶ cost of living,

▶ economic viability and a plan to either maintain or grow economically, and

▶ direct and indirect competition in the area for the proposed business.

All of these factors set the stage for whether the proposed business will succeed or fail. For instance, a nonprofit organization whose mission is to provide services for teens from low-income, single-parent families would not choose a highly industrialized neighborhood with many high-tech businesses where the few households that are in the area belong to senior adults. The organization would miss its target market segment simply by choosing the wrong location. However, this same location may be well suited for a hotel that caters to business travelers.

Location Accessibility

Location decisions for service distribution may mean finding a new facility to buy and renovate, finding land on which to build a new facility, or choosing which of the current facilities to offer programs through. Regardless of the situation, several things need to be considered when addressing the accessibility of current and future locations.

Transportation is the main factor concerning location accessibility. It includes bus systems, train systems, airports, interstates, ease of traffic flow, and availability of parking. Even with the best marketing efforts, if people cannot easily get to a location, the product is bound to fail. The adage "Build it and they will come" is risky at best and probably not the most sound means of addressing location.

Even within the same industry, different transportation concerns affect where a business is located. For example, Motel 6 builds properties near major highways because its customers are most likely to be driving, whereas Sheraton Hotel knows a large portion of its guests are businesspeople, thus driving the decision to locate hotels in business districts (Kotler et al., 2006).

Transportation barriers that hurt businesses can be physical, such as unbridged rivers, mountains, or freeways without access ramps, or they can be social, such as congested traffic, unsafe neighborhoods, or industrial areas (Hsu & Powers, 2002). Agencies use several tactics to overcome these barriers. For instance, consider Disneyland. This amusement park sits directly off the Santa Ana Freeway, which allows easy access. Imagine if Disneyland were located at the end of a two-lane road! In another example, the Chicago Cubs' Wrigley Field is located on the north side of the city and has no parking deck or designated lots. The Cubs organization uses DeVry University lots on weekends and evenings and runs shuttles, but fans are strongly encouraged to use public transportation such as buses, trains, and shuttles from the suburbs. Although locals are used to the parking situation, it can be difficult for people from out of town.

Atmosphere

The last element of place involves the facility itself. The atmosphere, or the appearance of the facility and its neighborhood, can attract or eliminate potential customers. Our perception of a business is derived through the senses. Colors, brightness, smells, noise level, and shape are a few ways we use our senses to develop perceptions. A low-lit, quiet, elegant restaurant and a multicolored, bright, noisy bar are different experiences and create different expectations. Taking this example a step further, a loud bar and an elegant restaurant will most likely have different smells. We can expect the elegant restaurant to smell of freshly cooked food, flowers, and cleanliness, whereas a bar will more likely smell of beer, smoke, and fried foods. Using these sensory elements together can create the desired image of a facility.

a

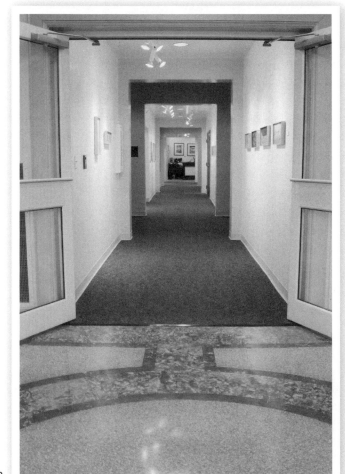

b

The Springer Cultural Center in Champaign, Illinois: *(a)* The bottom floor was designed to be child oriented with bright colors and a fun atmosphere; *(b)* the top floor was designed to project a gallery image with cool colors, a quiet atmosphere, and works of art on display.

For example, the Champaign Park District in Illinois renovated a historic post office in the downtown area. The purpose of the Springer Cultural Center was twofold: To provide a place for art programs to reach a specific target market and to offer a variety of general preschool and youth programs. These two program types were sometimes in conflict in terms of image. To remedy this problem, the top floor of the building was set aside for art programs and was decorated formally with off-white walls, cool colors (i.e., blues and grays) on the floors and furniture, dark wood trim and flooring, and professional artwork on the walls. This floor was somewhat quiet even with a large number of people in the building. The bottom floor became the youth floor and was painted with primary colors. It had tile floors for easy cleanup and smelled of tempera paint, clay, and many other things associated with high-energy children's programs. This noisy, fun floor was quite a contrast to the one above it simply because of its atmosphere. The atmosphere of each floor created the image desired by the park district.

Pricing

The third *P*, pricing, is the total value assigned to a product. It is the only element of the marketing mix that brings in revenue, yet it is the least understood aspect of the four Ps (Kotler et al., 2006). Price is far more complex than simply assigning a dollar amount to a product or service. Recreation products have monetary, opportunity, effort, and psychological costs that make up the total value of products and influence the marketing mix (Brayley & McLean, 2001).

Monetary costs are the typical costs associated with a product. Let's use an Indianapolis Colts football game as an example. The direct monetary costs for attending the game include the game ticket, parking fees, a Colts sweatshirt to show fan loyalty, and visits to the concession stand. There are also indirect costs such as gas to get to the game and a babysitter for the children at home. All of these things require an exchange of actual money. Opportunity costs also exist. In other words, what is the fan giving up in order to attend the game? For students, it may mean time studying or working on a project. For parents, it may mean missing their child's soccer game.

Effort is also a cost to consider, including physical energy expended, logistics of participation, and commitment. Effort costs for Colts games may be high if the game is sold out and tickets are difficult to get, if personal schedules need to be arranged, or if it is hard to find someone to attend the game with. In terms of effort costs and commitment, attending a game requires a large time and resource commitment. If the Colts fan is a season-ticket holder, considerable time and money are given to the team in comparison to attending just one game.

The last aspect of cost is psychological. Psychological aspects can be both positive and negative and may include how much fun the game will be, uncertainty of whether the Colts will win or lose, and embarrassment if they lose by a wide margin. For a volleyball league or fitness program, another psychological cost may be that people experience low self-esteem or feel they lack the skill needed to participate in activities such as these.

These four cost elements make pricing quite complex. Remember that the definition of marketing is creating an exchange to satisfy wants and needs. Before Colts fans will commit to buying the ticket and going to the game, they need to think about whether the game experience will outweigh all of the costs. That is where marketing comes in. Effective marketing helps a potential customer see the value of the product, eases participation through such things as distribution, and communicates how the product meets the needs of the consumer, thus helping the consumer decide to make the purchase. Knowing the costs associated with a product and realizing how few of them are strictly money driven aids in understanding how instrumental pricing is to the marketing mix. Other aspects of pricing include pricing strategies, psychology of pricing, and changing prices.

Pricing Strategies

Chapter 12 discusses how to set prices to meet financial objectives. However, as pricing pertains to marketing, there are three basic strategies for setting prices. These strategies include penetration pricing, neutral pricing, and skim pricing, as shown in figure 8.9 (McCarville, 2002).

With **penetration pricing,** agencies set prices low to attract consumers. This strategy is often used in the public sector where agencies have the luxury of using tax dollars to subsidize programs. It is aimed at attracting new users and competitors' customers and then trying to retain them. Penetration pricing can start price wars. For example, Wal-Mart and Toys "R" Us entered into price wars over such toys as Tickle Me Elmo where each continued to lower prices to lure customers away from the other retailer. Although good for the consumer, price wars often are not good for businesses because they boost sales on a particular item but do not necessarily increase market share or revenue (Byrnes, 2007).

Another downside of penetration pricing occurs in the nonprofit and commercial sectors. The public sector can subsidize programs with tax revenue, but the nonprofit sector needs to break even and the commercial sector needs to

penetration pricing— Setting prices intentionally low to attract new customers; sometimes leads to price wars when other companies must match the low price to stay competitive.

Pricing strategy	Focus
Penetration pricing	Price
Neutral pricing	Value, service, quality, and reliability
Skim pricing	Revenue generation

Figure 8.9 **Pricing strategies.**

generate a profit. If all three of these sectors offer fitness facilities that compete against each other, the public sector is most capable of using penetration pricing to lure customers away from the commercial and nonprofit sectors, which cannot operate facilities at a deficit. This issue has been a heated one in all three sectors, but the biggest battle has been between YMCAs and commercial health clubs (Cohen, 2000).

Rather than setting prices extremely low as in penetration pricing, if an organization sets prices that are not exceptionally low or exceptionally high, it is using a **neutral pricing** strategy. This middle-of-the-road strategy reduces the importance of price in product selection and relies on other things such as quality and customer service to attract customers. Although the price is not excessively high, in neutral pricing it is rarely set below the break-even point so revenues still pay for the product, thus eliminating the unfair advantage that some public agencies have with penetration pricing.

Spending an hour in a major department store is enough to realize that there is another pricing strategy—skim pricing. The focus of **skim pricing** is revenue generation. With this strategy, products are priced based on what the market will bear. This usually means that revenues will far outdistance actual product costs. The commercial sector uses this approach more often than the other sectors because of the need to make a profit. However, the public and nonprofit sectors can also use this strategy. They might use skim pricing to generate revenue from a popular program that they can use to subsidize another program that will not break even but is beneficial to the public. Both of these sectors may also use skim pricing to reduce the demand for a product. For example, raising the price of a round of golf at an overused course may decrease the number of rounds played to a more manageable level.

Psychology of Pricing

Psychological aspects of price move beyond the economics of setting a price and cost recovery and appeals to emotions more than logic. The psychology of pricing focuses on how people respond to set prices.

Consumers establish a price–quality relationship where they perceive price as equal to value. In other words, a more expensive service may appear to be better. For example, in searching for a hotel room in San Francisco, a $50 room and a $250 room are found to be available. Right away, most travelers would doubt the

neutral pricing—Setting prices in the middle and not too high or low; reduces the importance of price to focus more on product benefits.

skim pricing—Setting prices based on what the market will bear, meaning that typically revenue will far outdistance actual product costs.

quality of a $50 room in a major city and they would assume that the $250 room offers many amenities. In another example, when buying a global positioning system (GPS) without much knowledge of the equipment, a person will most likely rely on the detailed descriptions on the boxes in combination with price comparisons to determine which one is of higher quality. The price of the GPS, the promotional efforts, and the perceived value sell this product to the consumer.

Odd–even pricing also falls within the psychology of pricing. Products priced at $19.95 or $19.99 are perceived as more attractive than if they were priced at the rounded-up $20. Even though the price difference is minute, people perceive it as a greater difference than what it actually is. This is why stores rarely price their products at even dollar amounts and price just below the rounded-up price. This slightly lower price results in increased revenue because of the odd–even pricing phenomenon.

Changing Prices

People experience reference, objective, and subjective pricing regarding products and services. Consumers assign a price to an item based on what they think it should cost. This is the reference price. The actual price is the objective price and the subjective price is whether the actual price of the item is perceived as cheap or expensive. If the objective price is much lower than the reference price, the item is perceived as inexpensive. If the reverse is true and the objective price is much higher, then the item is perceived as expensive. Organizations want to set prices so that the reference price and objective price are close to the same. This makes the price of the product appear to be fair.

Rarely will a price remain the same throughout the entire life cycle of a product. Adjustments will be made, most likely to increase the price. For many products, people establish a tolerance zone where a slight increase in price has no impact on purchasing patterns. For example, raising the cost of pool admission from $3.50 to $3.75 may not influence customers unless $3.75 is outside of their tolerance zone and judged as expensive. When a price is outside of this tolerance zone, some people will leave and never return, whereas others will take some time to get used to the price increase, adjust their tolerance zone, and return as customers.

Increasing prices is a difficult decision to make. It is tricky to know if the increased revenue will offset the customers lost due to price increases. However, careful marketing can reduce the number of lost customers and enable people to more easily adjust their tolerance zone.

One way to aid the acceptance of a price change is to explain the details and benefits of the program and the reasons for the change. Let's say the after-school program of the city park and recreation department decides to raise its price from $60 per month to $80 per month. In order to help parents understand the price increase, the program supervisor can show that the new price is $2 per program hour, with which children get quality staff trained in recreation leadership, a daily snack, a monthly field trip, and daily education and recreation activities. Without the price increase, the snack, field trip, and two leaders would be eliminated from the program.

A different approach with the same program is to compare the after-school program with others like it. For example, the park and recreation department can compare its after-school program to those offered at the YMCA and the private sport complex in town. This comparison should highlight the advantages of the after-school program of the park and recreation department.

The last approach to helping customers accept price increases is expanding program benefits and explaining what changes were made to the program. This approach goes back to the price–quality relationship where people equate price with quality. If the price goes up, people will want to know what added value they are getting for the increased fees.

Given the different aspects of actual costs, psychology of pricing, and different pricing strategies, it is easy to see why pricing is so complex and a major factor in marketing. It is never easy to align all of these factors and set a price that entices consumption of a product. However, when pricing is used in conjunction with the other parts of the marketing mix, the chance of successfully marketing a product increases.

Promotion

promotion—Communication designed to facilitate an exchange between potential consumers and an organization.

The last piece of the marketing mix is promotion. Although many people equate marketing and promotions, this assessment is inaccurate. **Promotion** communicates the value of the product—it is the mouthpiece of the program, so to speak.

With parks and recreation in particular, many products are actually services. As discussed, a major difference between the two is tangibility. When a tangible product is promoted, the product can be displayed in advertisements. However, a service does not have that luxury. Instead, a benefits approach is taken to make a service seem more tangible. A benefit is anything of value to a consumer, so rather than promoting a service as just a service, it should be promoted as a bundle of benefits that a consumer will receive from the service.

The NRPA and the Canadian Parks and Recreation Association (CPRA) have been at the forefront in helping leisure services professionals understand that their true product is not a swim lesson or an aerobics class but rather a bundle of attributes, characteristics, and outcomes that people get from these programs. These benefits can be likened to the outcomes component in outcomes-based management (chapter 2).

The NRPA and CPRA outline four categories of benefits—individual/personal benefits, economic benefits, social benefits, and environmental benefits (figure 8.10).

Not every program has all four types of benefits, but many have several. For example, a midnight basketball league for teens has several individual and social benefits, including increased self-esteem for players, lower vandalism rates in the city, increased skill and fitness levels for players, and an opportunity for players to interact with each other in a positive environment. A new park built within a city has a number of benefits as well, particularly economic and environmental benefits. The new park increases the property values of neighboring houses, the mature trees provide shade and reduce power bills, green space is preserved in

BENEFITS CATEGORIES AND EXAMPLES

Personal and Individual Benefits

- Fitness and wellness
- Relaxation and stress relief
- Skill building

Social Benefits

- Reduced loneliness
- Strong families
- New friends

Economic Benefits

- Preventative health
- Reduced costs of vandalism
- Increased sales revenue into a community

Environmental Benefits

- Conservation
- Environmental rehabilitation
- Lower energy costs

Figure 8.10 Benefits categories and examples.

a rapidly expanding city, and environmentally conscious products and equipment were used to build the park. Good promotions would focus on all of these benefits.

The **promotions mix** is the means by which the organization communicates the benefits of its products. This is done through advertising, sales promotions and incentives, personal selling, and publicity. To be successful, the promotions mix should follow the AIDA approach (Mullins et al., 2000):

▶ Increase awareness (A)

▶ Attract interest (I)

▶ Arouse desire (D)

▶ Initiate action (A)

promotions mix—Use of advertising, sales promotions and incentives, personal selling, and publicity to communicate an exchange between potential consumers and an organization.

This acronym is a sequential process where the manager strives to increase awareness of products. Exchange of resources cannot happen if people do not know about the product. Once awareness exists, promotion is designed to attract interest. This phase of promotion requires more in-depth information about the product in order to develop promotions that will arouse the desire to purchase or participate. This phase will most likely focus on conveying the benefits of participation. It is hoped that people will begin to move from intent to participate to action where the actual exchange of resources takes place.

This approach leads a potential consumer from learning about a product to consumption. Different elements of the promotions mix help marketers achieve different aspects of AIDA.

Advertising

Advertising is any paid form of communication through the media that is paid for and controlled by the sponsoring agency. This means that an organization buys ad space and has control over what goes into that ad. There are many options for buying media, including television, radio, newspaper, magazines, display boards, Internet advertising, and logo placement opportunities such as dasherboards on ice rinks.

Choosing which media to buy is a difficult task at best. First, consider the preferences of the target market. Find out what media they watch, read, or listen to as a group. Media preferences differ significantly by market segments. For instance, consider the differences between students and professors. Compared with professors, students are more likely to read the university paper than the local paper. Professors are more likely to watch the evening news than students, and students are more likely to pay attention to chalked sidewalks and flyers hanging around campus.

Second, the type of product dictates what type of media to buy. Some products are better suited for certain types of media. For a new luxury resort, a luxury travel magazine might be a good option if the advertisements are targeted to the right groups. A local bar advertising a band playing on a Friday night would choose media that best reflect the activity, such as flyers on campus or radio ads.

Cost is also a media determinant and the one that may be the most influential for park and recreation agencies. Television ads can be expensive, whereas radio and newspaper ads may be more affordable. This is not to say that television would be prohibitive for public and nonprofit agencies; there are deals and less expensive ads that may be perfect for a certain target market. However, the price of some media and the return on that investment may be prohibitive. For example, Troy Parks and Recreation in Michigan offers Buzzy Bugs, a class for 10 children at a cost of $5 per child. Given the product, the registration fee, and the low maximum number of participants, running advertisements on television would not be the best use of money.

The last media buying consideration is the message. If the message to be communicated is simple, then newspapers and billboards may be good options because of the limited space available and the short amount of time people can look at a billboard while driving. If the message is more complex, then radio or television might be a better option. Let's say there is a major special event coming up. This event has been going on for years and is well known throughout the area. It would require a simple message letting people know the date and time of the event and maybe an activity or two that will be going on during the event. This simple message opens a lot of opportunities for advertising. A billboard on a major

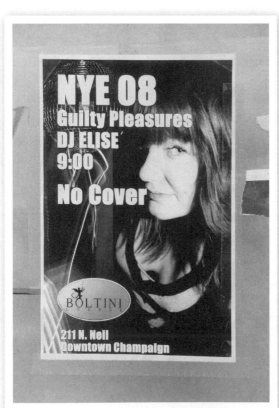

Posting flyers on campus announcing a DJ at a local bar is a good way to reach the desired target market.

Flyer courtesy of Boltini's Lounge.

thoroughfare, posters placed around town, and carefully placed ads in the newspaper may be all that is needed to advertise the event.

However, the first year this event was held would have required far more complex advertising since it was in the introductory stages of its life cycle. Advertisements had to be more complex since more information was needed about the new event. This detailed information would not be effective on a billboard where the information people can absorb while driving by is limited. This event may have required larger, more detailed newspaper ads, as well as ads on television and radio.

Sales Promotions and Incentives

Sales promotions and incentives have a financial value to the consumer and are used in the short term to stimulate awareness or lead people to participation. This type of promotion can be categorized as promotional pricing, free offers, prizes, and celebrities.

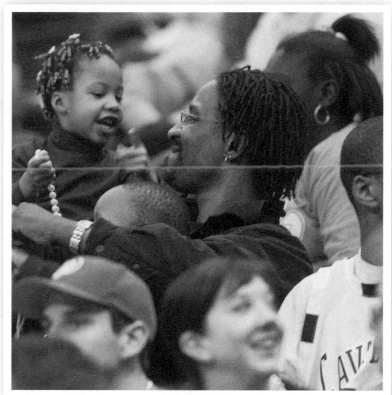

Sporting events often use sales promotions and incentives such as memorabilia giveaways, autograph sessions, or a free child's ticket with the purchase of an adult ticket.

▶ Promotional pricing—Buy two get one free, half-off admission, family discount night, discounted entrance fees with a soda can

▶ Free offers—First lesson free, children under 6 free, passes for free admission

▶ Prizes—Free T-shirts, door prizes, contests, giveaways

▶ Celebrities—Local or national celebrities used as spokespersons or available at events or for autograph signings

sales promotions and incentives—Promotion of a program or service that has a financial value to the consumer.

Sales promotions and incentives are most often used to introduce new programs by offering free trials, attract new clients to programs, stimulate more frequent use through such offers as participate in five programs and get the sixth free, and stabilize fluctuations in demand by offering discounts for off-peak times such as inexpensive indoor tennis-court time in the summer.

Personal Selling

Direct, face-to-face communication with the intention of creating an exchange is considered **personal selling.** Although many customers dislike the idea of salespeople, personal selling is an everyday part of many jobs in the leisure services industry. Some people will be involved in hard-core selling such as being a part of the sales staff at a major hotel with the job of bringing in large conferences and meetings.

personal selling—Use of direct, face-to-face discussions to promote a product or service.

Other jobs in the field focus less on sales and more on providing information that leads to sales. For example, the youth sport coordinator at the YMCA may talk daily to parents whose children are interested in learning a new sport. The coordinator discusses the benefits of the program as well as details on how to register. Although it may not seem like direct selling, that is what the program coordinator is doing: using face-to-face communication with the intention of convincing the parent to register the child for the program.

Publicity

publicity—Unpaid communication through a media outlet where the agency is not identified as the direct sponsor of the message.

Publicity is any form of exposure that is not paid for by the agency and over which the agency has no control. This exposure is most often received through the media and is instigated by the agency in the form of a news release or public service announcement. A news release is sent to print media (i.e., newspapers or magazines) whereas a public service announcement is sent to broadcast media (i.e., television or radio). The news release and public service announcement offer basic information about the event or program and are sent to the media in hopes of obtaining free coverage on an upcoming event. The downside to this free coverage is the lack of control. The media may run the information at their discretion, including when, where, and what information is announced. Although positive publicity received in this manner is helpful, it cannot be the sole promotions effort.

In addition to positive publicity, negative publicity can also occur. Obviously an agency would not seek negative publicity, but certain events occur that are reported in the newspaper or through other media outlets. This may include such things as a death on the river with a white-water rafting company, a staff member arrested on child pornography charges, or unsafe practices at an ice rink. Agencies must learn to deal with these situations and be as proactive as possible in dealing with the media.

The promotions mix is complex and must be planned out thoroughly in order to best utilize the resources available. Not all programs, events, and attractions will be promoted in the same way since they have different target markets, have different message needs, and are at different places in the life cycle. A well-thought-out promotions campaign can go a long way in ensuring a successful product, especially if that plan follows the AIDA approach using a balanced mix of promotions to move the consumer from awareness to action.

For example, let's say you are running a special event: the world's largest musical chairs fund-raiser. A minimum of 5,000 people will play musical chairs over 24 hours to raise money for a local playground for people with disabilities.

The objectives of the event are as follows:

▶ Attract 5,000 players and 200 volunteers to the event.
▶ Attract community members to watch the game as well as enjoy other entertainment and activities at the event.

Table 8.2 demonstrates how an event can use the promotions mix to create awareness.

Table 8.2   Sample Promotions Plan

Promotions Mix	Weeks from event	Task	Budget
Personal selling	1-16	Planning committee presentations to local service clubs, major employers, fraternities and sororities, and university service clubs	—
Publicity	8	News releases to area newspapers announcing the event	—
	8	Public service announcements to area television and radio stations announcing the event	—
	1	News releases to area newspapers announcing event setup and arrival of 5,000 chairs for a photo opportunity	—
	1	Public service announcements to area television and radio stations announcing event setup and arrival of 5,000 chairs for coverage	—
	1	Chalked sidewalks at the university	$10
Sales promotions and incentives	—	T-shirt giveaways to first 500 game participants	$5,000
	—	T-shirts to all volunteers	$2,000
	—	Two airline tickets to the game winner	$600
	<1	Local celebrity chairs game to start event	—
Advertising	4	Billboards	$1,000
	4	Bus boards	$1,000
	8	Flyers	$100
	6	Posters	$300
	6	Radio ads	$2,000
	6	Newspaper ads	$2,000
	6	Television ads	$4,000

Programming note: This promotions mix is budgeted at more than $17,000. Since this event is a fund-raiser, sponsors would most likely be used to offset a portion of these costs.

Public Relations

Often the terms *public relations* and *marketing* are used interchangeably when in fact they are different yet integrated functions within an organization. Andreasen and Kotler (2003, p. 471) distinguish the two as follows:

▶ Public relations is mainly a communication tool, whereas marketing includes communication and the marketing mix.

▶ Public relations seeks to influence awareness and attitudes, whereas marketing tries to elicit specific behaviors, such as purchasing, joining, and donating.

▶ Public relations does not define the goals of the organization, whereas marketing is intimately involved in defining the mission, customers, and services of the organization.

public relations—Multifaceted communication used to create a positive image of an organization for its internal and external publics.

Given these differences, **public relations** can be defined as a multifaceted form of communication used to create a positive image of an organization for its internal and external publics. Internal publics include staff, board members, and volunteers, whereas external publics include such groups as users, residents, and community members. Public relations primarily deals with internal and external communication, media relations, and community relations.

External and Internal Communication

External and internal communication promotes understanding and acceptance of the organization. It cannot be assumed that just because people work for the company, they understand what the company does or support company causes, programs, and business practices. Internal communication such as newsletters, weekly reports, or e-mail lists serve to heighten employees' knowledge about the organization.

External public relations provides information to increase knowledge about what the company does. It is not to be confused with advertising; it consists of information that is more general and addresses the image of the organization as a whole and not just one program or event. Communication pieces for this group may include newsletters, annual reports, brochures, and informational DVDs.

Media Relations

media relations—An established relationship between an agency and the media with which the agency works.

The media play a prominent role in shaping public opinion. As such, positive **media relations** are an important part of public relations. Organizations can take three approaches to the media: the reactive approach, the proactive approach, and the interactive approach (Gonring, 1997).

A reactive approach is used to respond to requests from the media for interviews, queries, and so on. In sport, this may include requests for interviews with coaches or players, photo sessions, or profiles (Mullins et al., 2000). A proactive approach occurs when the organization gives the media information in advance of an event or activity. In the hotel industry, if a new hotel is about to open, a press kit containing information about the property, the grand opening, and other interesting amenities is sent to the media in hopes of gaining publicity. An interactive approach involves developing partnerships and relationships that are mutually beneficial to the agency and the media. For example, a local park and recreation department holds a major event each summer. An interactive approach with the radio station creates a partnership where the station promotes the event on air and then is given a role in the event with a tent on site, logos on shirts, and on-air personalities serving as MCs for the event or as judges for some type of contest. In this situation, both the media and the event benefit from the relationship.

Marketing managers seek to develop positive media relations with local television, radio, and newspapers.

Community Relations

The last piece of the public relations puzzle is the relationship of the organization with the community as a whole. **Community relations** involve outreach programs to the public to gain support for the organization. These programs create goodwill within the community, generate publicity and media attention, and help create a positive image of the organization. Organizations participate in community events, sponsor activities and facilities, and raise money for charities in order to be associated with a good cause. Professional sport uses community relations extremely well to generate support that can ultimately lead to ticket sales. For example, the Indiana Fever WNBA team donates courtside tickets and a meet-and-greet session with any player or coach for charities to auction off. Peyton Manning, the Indianapolis Colts quarterback, established the PeyBack Foundation to provide leadership and growth programs for disadvantaged children (PeyBack Foundation, 2007). For other examples, see the sidebar on the Arizona Cardinals on page 192.

community relations— A positive relationship developed between an agency and the community in which it exists that is enhanced by communication, education, and provision of services to the community.

Summary of Public Relations

Public relations is an integral part of marketing because of its ability to expose people to an agency and its products. Good public relations reflects positively on the organization so that people may be more likely to exchange time and money for services. For public relations to be effective, a plan should be developed and implemented for communicating with the public. Developing a positive public image will go a long way in attracting the support of the community, potential users, and current customers.

Arizona Cardinals Community Relations Programs

Here are just a few of the programs the Arizona Cardinals football team uses to develop community relations.

- ▶ In 2005, 53 different players took part in 123 community events and distributed more than 8,000 pieces of Cardinals memorabilia.
- ▶ Several Cardinals players have their own foundations, including Edgerrin James and Kurt Warner.
- ▶ The Cardinals Wives Club works to improve the community by volunteering for the Salvation Army food drive, visiting the local children's hospitals, and serving food at homeless shelters.
- ▶ Several youth programs are run by the Arizona Cardinals, including Milk and Cookies, where players go into local schools and read to classes while they have milk and cookies; Punt, Pass, and Kick programs to develop football skills in young children; and a free kicking, punting, and snapping camp for high school players.

www.azcardinals.com/community/program.php

Conclusion

▶ Marketing is the purposeful planning and execution of the pricing, place, and promotion of ideas, goods, and services to create an exchange of time and resources that results in the satisfaction of individual needs and organizational objectives. Marketing is far more complicated than running an advertisement in the local paper or creating a flyer to hand out. It involves developing programs for the target market; making complex distribution decisions; setting prices; and establishing the right promotions mix to attract people.

▶ Marketing is not just for the commercial sector. It is an important part of any organization and requires managers who are knowledgeable in marketing principles. A well-developed marketing plan will enable the agency to see the big picture of how resources for marketing efforts are being used. Knowledge of marketing also allows managers to market their own programs or work cooperatively with a marketing staff.

REVIEW QUESTIONS

1. Describe how marketing has changed from the Industrial Revolution to today.

2. Discuss the differences between market segmentation and target marketing. Why should managers care about these concepts?

3. Explain the various ways to segment a market.

4. What is the difference between a product and a service?

5. Define the marketing mix and how each component can be used to market a product or service in recreation.

6. Describe the steps of the program life cycle. What strategies can extend the product in the decline stage?

7. Differentiate among the three levels of distribution intensity. Use an example not included in the book to explain each level.

8. Explain the promotions mix and give examples of each element.

9. Describe public relations and how it fits into marketing.

KEY WORDS

communication, encoding, communication channels, decoding, feedback, communication noise, external noise, internal noise, external–internal noise, sociocultural noise, downward communication, rumors, upward communication, horizontal communication, informal communication, grapevines, social networks, crisis, external communication, persuasion, information richness, dynamic Web sites, positioning, repositioning

COMPETENCY CHECK

Take another look at table 1.3 (page 9) to see how you assessed these related competencies.

6. Clearly communicate with staff, customers, and the public.

7. Possess effective written and oral communication skills.

36. Network within and outside the profession.

Communications and Customers

1. Explain what communication is and why it is a critical competency for leisure services managers.

2. Understand the process of communication and be able to identify potential communication breakdowns.

3. Apply the various uses for communication, including management communication (internal), marketing communication (internal and external), and positioning and repositioning strategies (external).

Organization and communication are instrumental in my position. I can always count on my clients to start my day off with a variety of messages containing changes, event details, and more. It's routine to have a department meeting three or four mornings a week. After the meeting, I check in with my staff to see how their events are progressing, and then it's off to check on event sets once again. When I return, I begin a slew of e-mails and phone calls with planners, vendors, attendees, and promoters. A good portion of the day will be spent organizing and filtering the information obtained through the correspondence and using the information to advance future events. As the day progresses,

I make my way to the event space periodically to work with my current client on site. Planning ahead is key, but even more important is your ability to roll with the punches and think on your feet. Confidence in your decisions and knowledge is essential. From scheduling event staff to organizing vendors and event details, it is important to have open communication with others, strong organizational skills, multi-tasking abilities, and attention to detail. The best part about my job is that there is no typical day!

Sasha Shutter, CMP
Event Sales Director
The Wildlife Experience
Parker, Colorado

Communication is a critical competency for leisure services managers. Successful communication can provide information, coordinate efforts, motivate employees, educate customers, and express organizational values. Communication is about more than just talking. It is an ongoing, dynamic process that involves multiple levels of action, including strategy, message design, message delivery, interpretation, and response. Communication is also about exchange. It is a give-and-take-and-give relationship shaped by the dynamics of the shared process. It is difficult to underestimate the importance of effective communication for leisure services managers; most studies of organizational behavior rate communication as the key competency of effective management. This chapter focuses on the processes of communication and how managers communicate effectively.

Functions of Communication

communication—The process of exchanging information between people or groups to achieve mutual understanding (George & Jones, 2002).

Communication is the process of exchanging information between people or groups to achieve mutual understanding (George & Jones, 2002). Two distinct functions underlie the communication process: conveying information and achieving mutual understanding. Merely conveying information is not enough. To communicate effectively, the parties involved in the communication process must understand the information that is conveyed. When information is misunderstood or misinterpreted, the communication process breaks down.

Conveying Information

Suppose a leisure services organization has a distinct dress code for all frontline service employees—khaki pants and a staff polo shirt with the logo of the organization on the front. Let's also suppose that the organization makes all new employees aware of the dress code as a component of orientation and provides written information on the dress code in an employee handbook. In this case, the organization has informed employees of certain standards through both verbal and written forms. On the surface, communication appears to be a one-way process—the organization is conveying information to new employees. Although conveying information is important, the communication process must go further in order to be effective.

Achieving Mutual Understanding

Deeper examination of the previous example shows a more dynamic process at work. The employees receive the message about the dress code by attending the orientation session, reading the handbook, and interpreting the messages that they contain. Let us assume that they respond to the request by asking questions about the policy, and they receive clarification from their manager on the importance of a unified agency image for good external communication. The new employees demonstrate their understanding of the message through their compliance with the standards. In this case, the communication process has achieved mutual understanding—a true exchange, or a two-way relationship. This is the second function and the critical component of effective communication. This simple example demonstrates how the basic communication process works. It is both a process of conveying information and arriving at a mutual understanding.

Communication Process

Communication is an active process. It requires individuals and groups to make sense of information and to respond to this information. Communication is also a dynamic process. Effective communicators often adapt their message or delivery to achieve the understanding that they seek. Consider the example of the dress code. Suppose that the new employees did not comply with the various standards that the organization had outlined in orientation and in the employee handbook. Communication occurred, but the results did not yield mutual understanding. The organization would need to examine its communication process, including the message, the delivery of the message, and other factors that may have prevented mutual understanding.

The active and dynamic nature of the communication process often befuddles managers. The organization might be convinced that it clearly communicated the dress code and why it was important. How could such plainly spoken and written words not be understood? Understanding the communication process requires breaking down and analyzing the various layers of the process. The communication process involves senders and audiences, and it includes message design, message delivery, message interpretation, and feedback mechanisms.

The communication process (figure 9.1) starts with senders, the individuals or groups who begin the communication process. They take the information they intend to convey and encode it by finding ways to make it easy to understand. **Encoding** can involve turning ideas into written or spoken words, or it can involve representing

encoding—Turning ideas into written or spoken words and communicating information through the use of signs, symbols, or images.

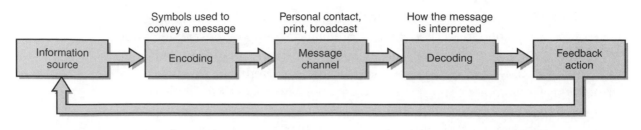

Figure 9.1 Communication process.

communication channels—Methods for delivering messages, including personal contact or print, broadcast, or electronic mediums.

decoding—The process of interpreting a message; how the audience makes sense of the signs, symbols, or images associated with a message.

feedback—A dynamic process of providing information and message evaluation back to a sender.

information through the use of other signs, symbols, or images. Senders also need to deliver the information through an appropriate communication channel. **Communication channels** can involve personal contact, such as presentations, orientations, training, and one-on-one conversations; they can involve print media, such as an employee handbook; or they can involve broadcast media, such as radio, television, e-mail, and other electronic forms of communication.

After the message is received, audiences must decode the information. The **decoding** process focuses on how the message is interpreted, or how the audience makes sense of the signs, symbols, and images associated with the message. After the message is decoded, the audience responds to the message via **feedback,** or providing information and message evaluation to the sender. The feedback process demonstrates the dynamic nature of communication. If the audience does not respond in the manner intended, the sender must evaluate the message strategy. Perhaps the initial message design was encoded inappropriately or the communication channels were inadequate in reaching the intended audience. The audience reaction to the message conveys valuable information to the sender. Managers who ignore the two-way nature of communication miss important information that can be used to refine existing messages or craft new ones.

Communication Breakdowns

Sometimes communication breaks down despite our best efforts. Messages go unheard or get misinterpreted. Think of the game Telephone, where a message is whispered to one person, who then whispers the message to the next person. This sequence repeats itself over and over, and the last person who receives the message must repeat it to the group. Invariably, the final message gets distorted to such an extent that it is unrecognizable from the original message. This game gives us insight into how messages get distorted. Recognizing the sources of **communication noise**—the internal and external factors that affect the communication process—can help managers craft communication strategies to minimize message distortion.

communication noise—The internal and external factors that affect the communication process.

External Noise

A number of external distractions can interfere with the communication process. For example, when playing the game of Telephone, perhaps an actual telephone was ringing while the initial message was being delivered, or perhaps the person who was delivering the message had a thick accent and was difficult to understand. Factors that interfere with the interpretation of the message and are external to the intended audience are **external noise.** Managers should be especially careful when communicating in the presence of external noise. For example, managers should be aware of their surroundings when giving instructions or feedback to employees. Providing information in a busy work environment with several other distractions might lead to misinterpretation or misunderstanding not because of the message itself, but because of the manner and context in which the message was communicated.

external noise—Factors that interfere with the interpretation of a communicated message and are external to the intended audience.

Internal Noise

Internal distractions are also responsible for misinterpretation. **Internal noise** refers to those factors that are internal to the message recipient that cause misunderstanding. For example, an employee who is under considerable stress, such as an illness in the family or a sudden change in a child care schedule, might not be in the best position to receive a message regarding job performance. Managers should con-

internal noise—Factors that are internal to the message recipient and cause misunderstanding.

sider the timing of a message to allow it to resonate and have the most positive impact on the receiver.

Multiple methods of communication can be helpful in minimizing internal noise. Written communication may be misinterpreted because an employee might focus on certain parts of the message to the exclusion of others. For example, an employee might focus only on the positives of a written performance review and minimize or disregard the manager's concerns. Combining a written review with face-to-face contact can help a manager reinforce the key components of the message, and it can allow for personal feedback to ensure that the message was properly received.

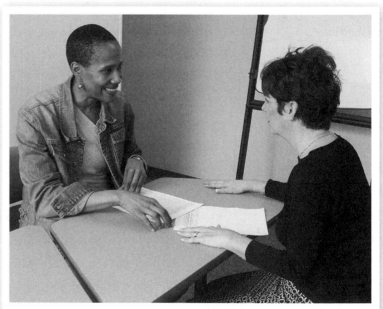

A quiet meeting place is essential to help reduce external noise.

External–Internal Interaction

External–internal noise refers to miscommunication that occurs due to the social context in which a message is delivered, or how external factors affect internal interpretations of a message (Hersey, Blanchard, & Johnson, 2001). The social context in which a message is delivered can amplify, blunt, or fundamentally alter a message. Consider the employee dress code discussed earlier in the chapter. The organization may have felt that it clearly communicated the dress code in both the orientation process and the employee handbook. However, perhaps veteran employees suggested to their rookie counterparts that although the dress code is official policy, it is rarely enforced. This might alter the new employees' perception of the message and its importance. Managers must be aware of the social context and culture of the

external–internal noise—Miscommunication that occurs because of the social context in which a message is delivered; how external factors can affect internal interpretations of a message.

organization when attempting to communicate with employees because messages are often interpreted by the larger group as well as the individual employee.

Sociocultural Noise

Many times noise comes from the message itself. **Sociocultural noise** sometimes occurs because of cultural misunderstandings. For instance, an organization that tries to engage in team building by adopting certain Native American symbols and terminology might have a specific communication strategy in mind, but that strategy might be lost on team members who view the use of such imagery as offensive (George & Jones, 2002). The meaning of events is often misinterpreted because of the loose coupling between activity and meaning (Bolman & Deal, 2003). People have different perceptions and are likely to assign different meanings to different events. A manager who holds a staff picnic on a weekend might intend to build esprit de corps, yet an overworked staff might interpret this message as an infringement on valuable weekend family time.

Language Choices

Finally, language choices such as the specific words or phrases that are used to represent ideas are sometimes vague and open to multiple meanings. When a city manager talks about accountability, what does that mean? When the governor tells the state parks director that the system needs to be more efficient, how should that efficiency be interpreted? When a campus recreation director talks about organizational effectiveness, how should that effectiveness be measured? Each of these terms—accountability, efficiency, and effectiveness—has multiple meanings and can be interpreted in many ways. After all, efficiency can mean cutting staff, or it can mean using less paper in the office. Using specific, descriptive language that is commonly understood is critical for effective communication. Developing shared understanding with employees and constituencies about what words mean, such as clearly defining what efficiency, effectiveness, or accountability mean within the context of your organization, can reduce confusion and misinterpretation.

Strategic Approach to Communication

A strategic approach to communication can reduce the impact of noise and facilitate an exchange of information that develops mutual understanding. Managers can employ this strategic approach to communication by doing the following:

▶ Identifying the intended audience
▶ Understanding the needs and information capacity of the audience
▶ Encoding information in a way that is as clear and unambiguous as possible
▶ Choosing communication channels likely to be effective in distributing and reinforcing the message
▶ Surveying the communication landscape to determine whether the message has been adequately received

▶ Developing a system for multiple levels of feedback

▶ Adjusting, reinforcing, or changing the message accordingly

Ultimately, avoiding noise is about creating a good feedback system. At its simplest, good communication comes from recognizing that communication is an active, dynamic, multiparty process. Communication should also be multidirectional—it should be an upward, downward, and horizontal process. Renowned management scholar Peter Drucker once said, "The harder the superior tries to say something to his subordinate, the more likely is it that the subordinate will mishear. He will hear what he expects to hear rather than what is being said" (2001, p. 214). The functions of communication include opportunities for multiparty dialogue and feedback. Effective communication aimed at both internal and external customers must be an ongoing, dynamic process.

Downward Communication

Providing information to employees is typically accomplished through **downward communication,** characterized by the movement of information from superior to subordinate on an organizational chart. One strength of downward communication is that it allows organizations to convey information that is important for employees and constituents to know. Organizations control the flow of information in this system, so messages are often carefully disseminated to serve particular strategic goals. Ultimately, all forms of communication should enhance organizational effectiveness. Downward communication that is clear, concise, synthesized, and easily understood can help organizations achieve message consistency and keep employees and constituents on the same page.

> **downward communication**—The movement of information from superior to subordinate on an organizational chart; used to convey information.

Certain difficulties are associated with this method of communication, however. In this system, employees are placed in passive roles as recipients of information. They may not have access to complete information, and they may feel as if they are lacking some of the information they need to do their jobs effectively.

In the bigger picture, employees want to know that what they are doing in their jobs is contributing to a larger goal of organizational effectiveness—in other words, that they are making a difference. Employees may need access to a wide range of information to be able to see how they fit within the larger organizational system. In his book *Stewardship,* Peter Block contends that employees "cannot contribute to what they cannot see" (1996, p. 92). He suggests that all employees should have access to information related to how they, their unit, and their organization are doing. Imperfect or incomplete information can lead to **rumors,** or unofficial information that is often distorted, inaccurate, or damaging to people or the organization.

> **rumors**—Unofficial information that is often distorted, inaccurate, or damaging to individuals or the organization.

In many cases, managers have access to a tremendous amount of information relating to organizational practices. As you may recall from chapter 2, Peter Senge developed the concept of the learning organization. Adequate information flow is critical for organizational learning. That said, managers are often bombarded with so much information that paying attention to all of it would waste time, create inefficiencies, and lead to confusion. Rather than overloading employees, managers need to be able to organize and synthesize this vast amount of information and communicate it in a way that sheds light on important issues. Determining what information is important for employees to have in order to do their jobs effectively and to help groups or teams develop shared understanding is a key competency of effective communicators (Senge, 1994).

Senge is not suggesting that managers withhold information or engage in situational communication; rather, they should decide which variables enable employees to contribute to effectiveness and which ones just contribute to noise and distract employees from their intended goals. Part of the manager's role is to be a monitor, and monitoring information flows is not in itself bad for the organization (Hersey et al., 2001). Managers must exercise judgment in this area since any information that is withheld can lead to confusion, disconnect, or rumors. Thinking about how information can help employees do their jobs more effectively, communicate with customers, and connect to the larger goals of the organization can be useful when attempting to organize and synthesize information for consumption.

Upward Communication

upward communication—The movement of information from subordinate to superior on an organizational chart; helps to create shared values.

Whereas downward communication is effective for conveying information to subordinates, **upward communication** allows for information to go up from subordinate to superior. Strong upward communication systems help to build shared values. The basic idea behind upward communication is that there is a considerable distance both in physical and experiential terms between upper-level management and frontline or support staff. It is difficult to develop a system of shared values when there is such distance between members of an organization.

Managers can enable upward communication by providing systems that allow employees to share information, provide insights and perspectives, and give feedback on organizational goals. Upward communication needs to go beyond the employee suggestion box where employees drop their ideas into what often resembles a black hole—the information goes in but almost never comes back out in the form of recognition or organizational improvement. Upward communication can take place in many forms, including team meetings, task forces, network structures, and other mechanisms that allow for significant input from the people in the organization who are most affected by organizational policy or management practices.

Upward communication systems can act as a bridge and provide useful information for managers. Honesty and trust are hallmarks of this communication system; employees must trust that the manager will recognize and address information that is provided. Creating a system where employees are encouraged to speak the truth to people in positions of power is a key characteristic of upward communication. That does not necessarily mean that all upward communication will be acted upon; that still lies in the hands of the decision makers. However, a system that requests information yet does not acknowledge the information that is generated will eventually lose credibility.

horizontal communication—The movement of information across an organizational chart between peers or managers in different organizational units.

Horizontal Communication

Horizontal communication is communication between peers or between managers in different units. It is communication across the organizational chart. Much like upward communication, horizontal systems can be formalized through meetings, task forces, or networks (see chapter 6). The key distinction is the goal of the communication process. Horizontal communication is often used to coordinate efforts between units or individual employees and build on knowledge or resource gaps that cannot be filled without some form of cooperation.

It should be noted that downward communication systems can also be used to coordinate work processes. Providing information on employee roles, demonstrating relationships among jobs, and articulating performance standards are all types of communication that can be distributed in a downward system. However, downward systems are not as effective when units are fairly autonomous yet work processes are highly interdependent. In these cases, horizontal systems are also needed to achieve effective communication.

For example, a large municipal park and recreation department might have a facilities unit and a programming unit, both of which have their own hierarchies, supervisors, employees, and jobs. Both units perform their own job functions, yet what they do has an effect on each other. Communication needs to flow both downward (providing information on roles, scope of responsibility, reporting lines, and quality standards) and horizontally in order to effectively coordinate the efforts of various units. Poor communication could lead to the wrong facilities being prepared for a weekend soccer tournament or the destruction of outdoor facilities because games were played in inclement conditions.

Horizontal communication can also be informal. Strong working relationships can enhance the exchange of information. Conversely, managers must guard against the tendency of semiautonomous units to become insular and closed. Even within the same unit, employees may form cliques or subgroups that can become impediments to the fast and accurate transfer of information.

Informal Communication

Informal communication passes unofficial information through unofficial communication channels. These systems are characterized by grapevines and social networks. **Grapevines** grow naturally, consist of diverse organizational members, and flourish in environments where there is little access to information. They pass along unofficial information such as rumors or falsehoods.

Social networks consist of the relationships among specific organizational members. Networks may pass along unofficial information, but they can also be used as part of an official communication strategy. For example, if the boundaries of a social network can be defined and the network consists of opinion leaders, a manager might test a message to see how it plays among employees. In this way, the manager is able to both communicate information and get feedback about how the message was received.

> **informal communication**—The movement of information through unofficial communication channels.
>
> **grapevines**—Informal communication systems composed of organizational members; used to pass along unofficial information, such as rumors or falsehoods.
>
> **social networks**—Social relationships that exist between specific organizational members; can be used to transmit both unofficial and official information.

Internal Communication

As noted earlier, managers must ensure that employees operate in an environment where there is ample access to information. Good internal communication is a key leadership competency. Successful communication strategies that allow information to move freely up, down, and across the organizational chart help to create and strengthen organizational culture (Gardner, 1993).

Internal communication functions include

▶ providing, synthesizing, and organizing information;

▶ expressing values;

▶ coordinating and controlling organizational systems; and

▶ crisis communication.

Providing, Synthesizing, and Organizing Information

At a basic level, employees need enough information to be able to perform their jobs effectively. For example, employees need information to understand

▶ how to perform job tasks,

▶ how job roles relate to one another,

▶ policies and procedures of the organization, and

▶ whether their performance meets organizational standards.

Such information might be communicated in a variety of ways, including orientation and training sessions, employee manuals, regularly scheduled meetings, organizational charts and other documents, and frequent performance reviews. Employees also need continual access to information to understand changes in organizational structure or practice, trends, and potential issues that might affect their ability to perform their jobs. Continual access to information can be accommodated through team meetings, written memos, e-mail, continuing education and training, and organizational networks.

In the decoding process, an organization uses language, signs, and symbols to help convey a message and articulate its values.

Expressing Values

In addition to providing information, communication can help organizations define themselves. As discussed in chapter 3, values help the organization and its members know what it stands for. In large, complex organizations, clear expressions of values can assist employees in understanding how their daily tasks add to the organization. For example, a maintenance worker in a public park system needs to understand what safe, clean, accessible parks mean to the overall quality of life in the community. In this way, communication can be motivating—it can strengthen the feeling that employees are part of something bigger than themselves.

An organization communicates its values through writing, speaking, signs, symbols, and rituals. It is also important for organizations to develop a system of shared values, or values that are common to the leaders, employees, and external constituents of the organization. Creating a system of shared values requires more than downward communication. It practically begs for a system that is dynamic, provides feedback, and allows an organization to respond to changes.

Coordinating and Controlling Organizational Systems

Communication is also used for coordinating and controlling complex organizational systems. As organizations increase in size and scope, they become more complex, and as complexity increases, the need for coordination increases. Effective communication and efficient information flow can help coordinate and control various organizational efforts. Good communication between disparate and somewhat autonomous units, for example, can increase efficiency by eliminating duplicated efforts and streamlining work processes. Communication among group members can increase access to critical information without having to rely on third parties to distribute the message. When work tasks are highly interdependent—when the work of one member or group affects the work of another member or group—communication that helps to coordinate and control efforts becomes more important (George & Jones, 2002).

Crisis Communication

An important component of communication for coordination and control is crisis management. Recreation facilities and programs can be fertile ground for crises. A **crisis** is any incident that has the potential to negatively influence public perceptions of the organization. Imagine the impact that the following crises might have on an organization:

> crisis—Any incident that has the potential to negatively affect the public's perceptions of the leisure services organization.

- A lost child at a summer day camp
- A drowning incident in a public swimming pool
- The theft of money and valuables from the locker room of a commercial fitness facility
- An injury resulting from violence in a youth sport contest
- A bus accident that happens during a Special Olympics basketball team's road trip
- A major natural disaster that strikes during a group tour

The key to successful crisis communication is for the organization to immediately gather as many facts related to the incident as possible. Good management procedures in other areas of the organization can help this process immeasurably. For example, consider a bus accident that occurs during an athletic team's road trip. If the athletic organization has effective policies for team travel, including knowing itineraries, bus assignments, and schedules, it will be easier to handle difficult questions regarding the impact of the incident and who was affected.

In the immediate aftermath of a crisis, the organization should focus on fact gathering, and this focus should be clearly communicated to the media. Having a designated organizational representative clearly state that facts are being gathered and that the organization will issue a response by a certain date can help manage the critical time right after a crisis occurs. Being truthful, honest, and upfront, as well as not jumping to conclusions or offering unsupported opinions, is critical. "Don't go where you don't know" is the gold standard for crisis communication in the initial stages.

Once a crisis occurs, the organization needs to involve upper-level management, legal counsel, and the marketing or media relations team in reviewing the facts. The crisis team's responsibility is to coordinate a communication strategy and decide on a clear and consistent position related to the cause of the crisis incident. After reviewing the facts, the organization may come to the conclusion that the crisis incident was caused by any number of factors, including human or clerical errors, the use of unauthorized procedures, inadequate supervision, lack of quality control, judgment errors, or inadequate implementation of standard operating procedures (Clawson Freeo, 2007).

Managers should remember to be truthful, honest, upfront, and timely when dealing with crises. In addition to communicating effectively to external constituents such as the media or general public, it is also important for managers to provide adequate information and instructions for their own employees to ensure that everyone in the organization is on the same page.

Dealing With the Media in a Crisis

1. Coordinate media coverage and know exactly what is being released to the media.

2. Always be honest. State the facts that can be released and no more. Never speculate on the situation.

3. Prepare a written statement and read it. Look for sound bites of 5 to 10 seconds that could be pulled out by the media in the editing process and take extra care to make sure these are well constructed.

4. Never say "No comment." It implies guilt and dishonesty.

5. Return phone calls from the media and understand that they have the right to ask questions.

6. Prepare for interviews and try to anticipate what questions reporters may ask. It may be beneficial to do a mock interview with another staff member.

external communication—Communication that is targeted primarily to external constituencies: customers, the general public, policy makers, or other stakeholders.

External Communication

Communication that is targeted primarily to external constituencies, including customers, the general public, policy makers, and other stakeholders, is **external communication.** It is important to recognize the connection between internal communication and the ability of an organization to communicate with its public. Consider the previous crisis communication examples. Frontline service staff and staff with high customer contact must possess accurate and up-to-date information, be consistent in delivering message content to both users and nonusers of leisure services, and understand the scope of their positions and how far they are able to go in their communication with customers.

External communication generally comprises two areas: marketing communications and positioning and repositioning strategies. Both of these areas are related; positioning and repositioning efforts are components of overall marketing and communication efforts. However, each area is discussed separately in the sections that follow.

Marketing Communication

A manager's ability to communicate effectively to external constituents can be seen as a component of marketing (see chapter 8). At the most basic level, consumption of leisure services cannot happen if a consumer does not know what services are offered, when they occur, where they take place, or why they should be important to the consumer in the first place. Marketing communication can help a leisure services organization answer those questions and encourage and direct customer behavior (McCarville, 2002). Effective marketing communication gets constituents to consume the leisure services offered by the organization. Communication efforts—informing, educating, persuading, reminding, and continuing contact—are designed to move constituents from stages of increased awareness through repeated initiated action.

Organizations must ensure that their external communication strategy is linked to their overall marketing efforts. A leisure services organization that invests time and energy in developing a new program targeting a new market demographic will find it difficult to get the program off the ground if inadequate information is available to customers or if customers do not readily understand its benefits. New services, distribution strategies, pricing strategies, and promotions will fail unless there is a strong communication effort to inform, educate, persuade, remind, and maintain contact with new, existing, and potential customers (Lovelock, 2001).

Information

At a basic level, managers need to provide information to their customers about the programs, services, and resources that they provide. Without access to adequate information, customers cannot begin the consumption process. A good information campaign will provide customers and potential customers with information about the following:

▶ What services are available
▶ Where services occur
▶ How to access services (including registration options, transportation information, and so on)
▶ When services take place
▶ What cost, if any, is involved

▶ What choices and options are available

▶ How to follow up or obtain additional information

Research on constraints to leisure participation (or why people do not participate in leisure) often reveals that unawareness of the programs and services that are available is one of the strongest reasons given for nonparticipation. Without access to information on the services offered, consumption of those services cannot occur.

Education

Closely related to information, a good communications strategy will educate consumers about the potential benefits of participating in leisure services. For example, cardiorespiratory activities and other types of fitness activities are often strenuous, and this can dissuade consumers of fitness services from regularly taking advantage of the opportunities available to them. A communication strategy that educates consumers about the benefits of regular physical activity can help provide a more tangible set of outcomes than the ones that they immediately experience following a difficult workout (e.g., weight control versus fatigue; cardiovascular health versus boredom). This also helps consumers more effectively evaluate the service, especially when the positive attributes of the service are not easily discernable.

Education can also be used to direct consumer behavior. For instance, it is easy to see how members of a health club who engage in the same workouts day after day might become bored with their daily fitness routines. An education campaign that directs the club members to different services that yield the same fitness results (for example, varying workouts by running on a treadmill on day 1, swimming on day 2, and taking a group fitness class on day 3) can help prevent

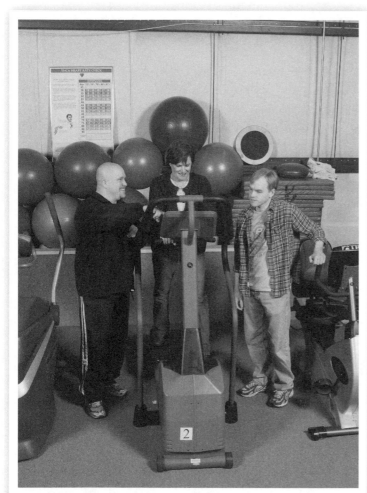

Educating new customers about the benefits of regular physical activity is a key communication objective for the personal fitness industry.

boredom and at the same time enhance the demand for other services that the agency offers.

Persuasion

persuasion—Convincing customers to purchase or use an organization's services rather than not using them at all or using the services of a competitor.

Persuasion is convincing customers to purchase the services of an organization rather than not using them at all or using the services of a competitor (Lovelock, 2001). The point of marketing communication is to convince consumers and potential consumers to use the services of a specific organization. McCarville (2002) suggests that persuasion takes place via two types of routes:

▶ Deliberative routes appeal to consumers' logic by providing them with sufficient information to make a sound decision about the attributes of potential services relative to their needs.

▶ Nondeliberative routes are less rational, more emotional, and based more on the trustworthiness of the message source than the quality of information that is provided.

It is easy to see the importance of having a frontline staff that is properly trained to provide the up-to-date information necessary to help persuade a potential consumer to take action. Frontline staff also must be able to connect with potential consumers on an emotional level because quality information by itself might not be enough. Ultimately, persuasion is about communicating the value of a service and highlighting its benefits to the customer.

Reminders

In order to close the consumption loop and keep customers coming back, communication must remind consumers about their past experiences and encourage them to use the same services in the future. Customer assessment of the service experience is a critical component in encouraging repeat participation. Because services are intangible and often difficult for consumers to evaluate, communication efforts must provide tangible evidence that reminds consumers of their experience. For example, a women's triathlon event might contract with a photography service to take pictures of triathletes at various stages of participation, such as getting out of the water, getting off the bike, and finishing the run. They might send proofs of these pictures to participants to remind them of their experience, along with an opportunity to purchase the pictures. They might also include information related to the past event (e.g., standings, times), as well as information for future participation opportunities (e.g., save-the-date reminders, online registration information).

Leisure services organizations might also have participants formally evaluate their experience and gauge future intentions to participate. Participants in a 5K road race designed to raise money for charity may be asked to evaluate their experience and provide the following information:

▶ Participants' demographic profiles (age, running level, household income)

▶ Participants' evaluation of event organization (registration, cost, check-in, volunteers, course, prizes, sponsors, the overall event)

▶ How participants learned of the event

▶ Past participation in the event and intent to participate in the future

By analyzing the information provided by participants, the race organizers are able to modify the event to enhance the race experience. The evaluations also provided valuable market segmentation information and feedback on how the marketing message was received.

Maintaining Contact

Marketing communication should not only remind participants of their experience, it should also include ongoing contact to help guide consumers to other services based on their past participation behavior. Databases can be effective tools for keeping track of past consumption patterns and providing tailored information that can directly appeal to a consumer's needs. Figure 9.2 shows a sample online form where customers of Amelia Island Plantation Resort can provide information that allows resort managers to better understand the unique needs of specific clients.

Figure 9.2 **Web-based data form.**
Used with the expressed permission of Amelia Island Plantation.

Disaggregating data by targeting individual consumers can be advantageous because customers are generally more responsive to services that meet their specific needs (Wedel, 2001). Online book retailers such as Amazon.com have mastered this technique by developing database software that tracks individual purchases and makes individual recommendations to customers based on past consumption. This level of sophistication need not be prohibitive for leisure services organizations. Suppose an adventure organization has a flat-water kayaking program and offers trips for beginner, intermediate, and advanced paddlers. A database containing contact information for the customers who went on the beginning kayaking trip can be harvested and personal reminders sent out with information on upcoming intermediate kayaking trips. By maintaining contact and tailoring the message based on past consumption patterns, the organization can be more effective at meeting individual consumers' needs.

Communication Mix for Leisure Services

In many cases, leisure services organizations only rely on a few communication strategies to get their messages out to their consumers. Municipal recreation agencies in particular often rely on print messages, such as seasonal program brochures, as their primary promotional communication tactic (Tew, Havitz, & McCarville, 1999). This might be an effective method for delivering certain types of messages, but employing a range of communication strategies and tactics can help extend both the reach and depth of the message.

Chapter 8 discussed the traditional promotion mix for communicating benefits to customers, including advertising, personal selling, sales promotions and incentives, and publicity. These four areas are part of a larger communication mix that can help drive communication strategy by highlighting a variety of strategic elements and specific communication tactics. Strategic elements of the communication mix include the following (Lovelock, 2001):

- ▶ Personal communications
- ▶ Advertising
- ▶ Sales promotion
- ▶ Publicity and public relations
- ▶ Instructional materials
- ▶ Corporate design

Figure 9.3 provides communication tools and tactics that can be used for the six strategic elements of the communication mix. For example, Planet Fitness, a large commercial fitness organization, uses multiple methods of communication to reach its customers. To attract new customers, the organization uses staff to help sell new memberships (personal communications), buys ad space in the local newspaper (advertising), offers discounted membership options during certain times (sales promotions and incentives), runs open houses at facilities to increase customer traffic (publicity and public relations), prints brochures (instructional materials), and communicates its mission through its corporate logos and facility

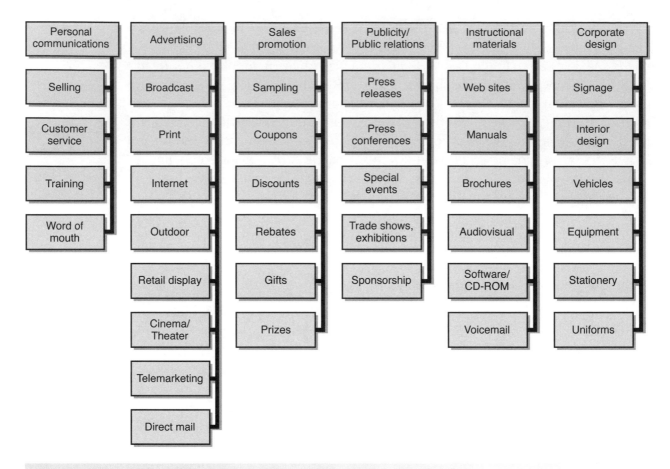

Figure 9.3 **Lovelock's (2001) communications mix.**

Reprinted, by permission, from C. Lovelock, 2001, *Services marketing*, 4th ed. (Upper Saddle River, NJ: Prentice-Hall), 296.

design (corporate design). Each technique broadens customer recruitment efforts, and the overall communication strategy is integrated so that each technique delivers a cohesive message.

> **information richness**—The breadth and depth of information that a communication method can carry and the extent to which it enables a common understanding (George & Jones, 2002).

Different communication choices vary in their **information richness,** or the breadth and depth of information that a communication method can carry and the extent to which it enables a common understanding (George & Jones, 2002). Information richness can be plotted on a continuum from high to low. A ranking of communication media from high to low based on information richness follows:

▶ Face-to-face communication (frontline staff, personal selling, personal conversations)

▶ Personalized verbal communication (telephone, voice mail)

▶ Personalized written communication (letters, e-mails, interactive Web sites)

▶ Broadcast communication (brochures, flyers, Web sites)

Face-to-Face Communication Face-to-face communication, such as information passed from frontline service staff to the customer, has the potential to yield a much higher level of information richness than impersonal information designed for a mass audience, such as a brochure that details available programs and services. Face-to-face communication allows for feedback and a two-way exchange of information. Both parties can ask questions and provide responses. Face-to-face communication is not particularly effective when an organization needs to communicate on a mass scale. Also, this communication method relies on staff members having access to a wide range of information so that they can respond to consumer needs and requests.

Personalized Verbal Communication   Personalized verbal communication, such as information that is given over the phone, can also be high in information richness. Live phone conversations provide immediate feedback, and messages can be changed or altered depending on the dynamics of the conversation. The major drawback of phone conversations is that they are one-dimensional—they focus solely on verbal communication. It is difficult to gauge body language or other forms of nonverbal communication, which detracts from the information richness of the medium and minimizes the personal aspect of the communication experience. Remember, persuasion can be as much about trusting the source of the information as the information itself!

Another drawback of phone conversations is again a matter of scale—most leisure services organizations do not have the resources to phone bank or telemarket. The use of automated voice-mail services solves this dilemma. For example, a college intramural sport program might post daily schedules of intramural games, including matchups, game times, and game locations, on a voice-mail system. The message can be updated based on program factors such as weather, forfeits, and other contingencies. The voice-mail system can provide up-to-the-minute information for participants, and anyone can access the system by simply dialing a phone number. In this system, the problem of scale is solved, but the feedback loop is closed—there is no way for customers to respond to an automated message, and questions about information in the message would need to be directed elsewhere.

Personalized Written Communication   Written information that is personally addressed allows an organization to tailor a message to the needs of a particular customer. Using databases with information on past consumption patterns can help generate personalized messages inviting customers to participate in upcoming programs or to take advantage of certain services. With a good database of information and the right technological system in place, this communication medium can be effective at reaching a large number of customers while still being perceived as a more personal form of communication than a standard brochure or flyer.

A drawback of personalized written communication is that it can be difficult for leisure services organizations to develop the sophisticated data management and tracking system that is required to generate such information. Another drawback is the lack of feedback potential, although the use of electronic media, such as e-mail or dynamic Web sites, can provide mechanisms for immediate response to these written communication forms. **Dynamic Web sites** change content frequently, usually as a result of user choices and preferences. Such sites allow user feedback and

dynamic Web sites—
Web sites that change content frequently, usually as a result of user choices and preferences; they allow user feedback and interaction between the customer and the organization.

permit interaction between the customer and the organization. For example, an organization might send a personal e-mail to a parent whose child took beginning swimming lessons inviting the child to participate in upcoming intermediate swimming lessons. The e-mail might include a link to the Web site of the organization and its online registration system for easy payment and sign-up. Of course, such a system is contingent on widespread Internet access and usage patterns. For example, only 55 percent of American homes have Internet access, creating a digital divide between those who can benefit from such a system and those who cannot (U.S. Census Bureau, 2005b).

One further note on personal written communication—it is important that customers perceive these messages as personalized. Form letters with standardized information that only pretends to be personalized by using word-processing software to change the address field, for example, do not count as personalized written information.

Broadcast Communication Broadcast communication is the lowest in information richness. This communication method relies on moving information to as many customers as possible. The advantage of broadcast communication is that an organization can communicate with a large number of constituents with relatively little effort. Most mass-media strategies fall into this category, including the use of broadcast, print, outdoor, and electronic media. In some cases, these communication media are limited by the amount of information they can contain. For example, communication through paid television, radio, or print advertisements can be cost prohibitive for many leisure services organizations, especially those operating in the public or nonprofit/voluntary sectors. Even if organizations can afford the cost, they are limited in how much information they can communicate by either time (television, radio) or space (print, outdoor media). Web sites, however, can communicate a large amount of information at a relatively low cost. By including additional functionality, such as discussion boards and blogs, an organization can add a level of interactivity that also creates an opportunity for feedback.

Positioning and Repositioning Strategies

Positioning is a component of marketing strategy, but it is critical to understand here because it helps to drive communication efforts. **Positioning** refers to the place of leisure services in the minds of stakeholders relative to their perceptions of competitors. A leisure services agency can position itself based on specific issues that are of fundamental importance to its community. These issues are often related to the larger concerns that a community faces, such as contributing to economic development or alleviating social problems (Crompton, 1999). Similarly, an agency might try to position its services and facilities based on strategies that appeal to individual consumers. The set of positioning strategies (McCarville, 2002) is listed here, along with corresponding communication implications:

> ▶ *Attributes:* These are the characteristics of the service that are valued by the customer, such as safety, quality, perceived risk, staff competence, and so on.

positioning—The place that leisure services and programs hold in the minds of stakeholders relative to their perceptions of other services provided by competitors (Crompton, 1999).

Communication strategies highlight the desired attributes in order to appeal to customer needs.

▶ *Price:* This strategy focuses on how much the service costs in relationship to competitors. Communication strategies use price as a differentiator and can be based on low-cost provision (community swimming pools) or high-cost luxury (expensive resorts).

▶ *Comparison with competitors:* This position focuses on services the agency provides that competitors do not. Communication strategies highlight the strengths of the service provided relative to competitors.

▶ *Product class:* This strategy differentiates the service from a range of other options. For example, a state beach might focus on the desirability of swimming in the ocean versus hiking in the mountains. Communication strategies highlight the differences between the services of the organization and a broad range of competing leisure opportunities.

▶ *User:* This positioning strategy is based on the interests and needs of particular user groups. Communication strategies demonstrate how the services meet those unique needs and interests.

▶ *Use-related:* This strategy focuses on how the product is consumed. Communication strategies remind customers about the reasons for their consumption. An example might include focusing on patriotism and national pride as a reason for visiting a national park over the U.S. Independence Day weekend.

Leisure services organizations must effectively communicate with both users and nonusers of their services. This is particularly true for organizations that compete for public tax dollars. Taxpayers in a city are stakeholders in the municipal park and recreation department regardless of whether they use any of its leisure services. Because some stakeholders do not use the services available to them, they are unaware of the benefits that such services provide. For example, citizens might agree that reducing traffic, providing green space, and reducing the amount of energy consumed by residents are important public priorities. However, citizens might not realize how public investment in park and recreation services can achieve these important policy objectives. By using effective communication strategies, organizations can better position their programs and services at a larger level beyond the needs of those who already use their services. In this way, positioning can demonstrate the value of a leisure services organization in relation to other community services that compete for scarce public resources.

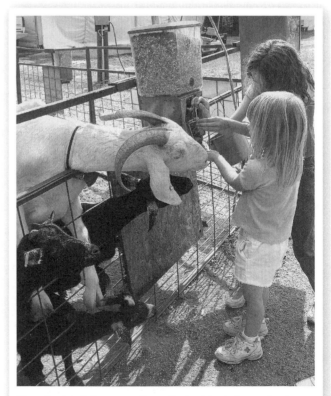

Developing leisure services that address important community issues, like this environmental education program, helps to position the organization positively in the minds of its stakeholders.

Three Axioms of Positioning

To further understand positioning, managers need to take into account three fundamental axioms (Kaczynski & Crompton, 2004):

▶ Positioning is concerned with stakeholder perceptions about what an agency does rather than what an agency actually does.

▶ Position is not considered in isolation but in relationship to competitors.

▶ Message consistency is key because effective positioning and repositioning take time to solidify.

Positioning Affects Perceptions   Good communication will influence stakeholders' perceptions about what a leisure services agency does. In the previous example, citizens in a community have identified three major public policy issues that concern them: reducing traffic, providing green space, and reducing the amount of energy consumed by city residents. At first glance, these issues might be addressed through any number of public agencies, including the department of transportation, local energy cooperative, and city conservation commission. However, many public park and recreation departments offer multiuse trail networks that link various parts of the city. Although the majority of users access these trail networks for recreational purposes (e.g., walking, jogging, bicycling, inline skating), there is evidence that some users rely on the trails for commuting. An effective communication strategy should help connect the dots for the public. It should highlight issues that the public is concerned about (traffic and reduction of energy use) and provide accessible evidence that demonstrates the ability of the service to address those issues.

Positioning Is in Relation to Competitors   In the example of multiuse trails, stakeholders might have thought of other municipal services before parks and recreation when considering how to tackle tough questions such as traffic control or energy reduction. This is a challenge for leisure services agencies, especially those operating in the public sector, because they have to be seen as an effective solution to community problems in order to continue receiving scarce public tax dollars. When leisure services are seen as nonessential, they become more vulnerable to flat funding or budget cuts. By developing a communication strategy that emphasizes the potential of parks and recreation in solving community challenges, a leisure services organization can improve its position against other competitors for public tax dollars. Figure 9.4 shows an effective communication strategy for educating the public and highlighting the value of park and recreation programs for young people in high-risk environments (Crompton, 1999).

Not only does the communication campaign clearly articulate the services that the city offers to young people, it clearly positions parks and recreation as a more effective and efficient option for dealing with youth crime than the juvenile justice system. In this way, the Oxley Nature Center and the City of Tulsa Park and Recreation Department are able to position themselves as players worthy of financial support in the city's crime-prevention efforts (figure 9.4).

Message Consistency Is Key   Consistency in messaging is a key to effective positioning. A leisure services organization must first choose the community issues it

It costs approximately $30,000 to incarcerate a juvenile offender for one year. If that money were available to the Park and Recreation Department, we could:

Take him/her swimming twice a week for 24 weeks

Give him/her four tours of the Zoo plus lunch

Enroll him/her in 50 Community Center programs

Visit Oxley Nature Center twice

Let him/her play league softball for a season

Tour the gardens at Woodward Park twice

Give him/her two weeks of tennis lessons

Enroll him/her in two weeks of day camp

Let him/her play three rounds of golf

Act in one play

Participate in one fishing clinic

Take a four-week pottery class

Play basketball eight hours a week for 40 weeks

After which we could return to you:

$29,124 and one much happier kid.

Figure 9.4   Positioning Oxley Nature Center: City of Tulsa marketing plan.

Adapted, by permission, from J. Crompton, 1999, *Financing and acquiring park and recreation resources* (Champaign, IL: Human Kinetics), 134.

wants to position itself on and then make sure that its communication strategies clearly reflect those positions. Figure 9.4 is a good example of a clear and consistent message—community recreation is an efficient and effective investment in youth development. This message resonates in an environment where youth crime is an important community consideration. It may not work in a different community with different needs. Identifying important community issues is the first step in the process of developing a consistent communication strategy. The usual array of data collection techniques can be used to identify these issues, such as surveys, focus groups, town meetings, secondary data sources, and environmental scans.

Positioning drives communication strategy. Communication efforts should focus on the agency's most salient contributions to important community issues. This can be accomplished through the use of text or verbal descriptions, visuals (pictures, video), statistics, slogans, symbols, sponsorship alignments, and so on. The key is consistency—clearly communicating what the agency does to address the important issues facing the community. Ambiguous positions lead to an unclear organizational identity and cause an agency to get lost in the clutter of competitor organizations, programs, and services. Poorly chosen positions are also dangerous because they miss the mark in connecting with the priorities of stakeholders and do not provide stakeholders with a clear reason for supporting an agency's contribution to pressing community concerns.

Repositioning

repositioning—Changing the frame of reference that stakeholders have about what an agency does and how it aligns with issues that are important to the broader constituency (Crompton, 1999).

Sometimes the priorities of a community change and a leisure services organization finds itself in a poor position relative to its competitors on the key issues affecting its stakeholders. In this case, an agency might find that it needs to reposition itself. **Repositioning** means changing its stakeholders' frame of reference about what the agency does and how it aligns with issues that are important to the broader constituency (Crompton, 1999). Consider the commercial bowling industry. White Hutchison, a leisure consulting firm, notes that the number of people bowling in leagues has declined by two-thirds since 1980. Traditionally, league bowlers helped to drive the industry. As times have changed and preferences have shifted, bowling alleys have had to reposition themselves as indoor recreation centers catering to families and singles. Successful businesses have repositioned themselves to cater to this shift in the marketplace by eliminating smoking, focusing on customer relations, changing the physical layout and functionality of their facilities, and promoting themselves as indoor recreation and bowling centers rather than bowling alleys. Finding ways to connect to the needs of constituents is the critical piece in this process.

The axioms described in the positioning discussion are all relevant to repositioning efforts. Because repositioning attempts to change existing perceptions of what an agency does, it can be a much more difficult and time-consuming process. Changing existing frames of reference requires clear, consistent, frequent, and reliable messaging.

Conclusion

▶ Communication is a critical competency for leisure services managers. The ultimate aims of communication are to convey information and achieve mutual understanding. Managers must engage in internal communication within their agency, crafting strategies to communicate with superiors, other managers and organizational units, and staff. Good communication strategies are active and dynamic; they provide feedback and minimize noise. Communication should occur downward, upward, and horizontally within an organization depending on whether the communication is providing information, expressing values, or coordinating and controlling organizational practices.

▶ External communication includes informing, educating, persuading, and reminding consumers and potential consumers about the services that the organization provides. External communication strategies are also designed to position and reposition leisure services in the minds of users and nonusers.

REVIEW QUESTIONS

1. What is communication? Why is effective communication one of the key competencies for leisure services managers?

2. Describe how effective communication works using the communication process model.

3. What are some examples of external, internal, external–internal, and sociocultural noise? How might these examples change or alter the communication process?

4. What are the strengths and weaknesses of downward, upward, and horizontal communication for leisure services managers?

5. Provide an example of how a manager might use informal communication channels (such as social networks) to help amplify an official organizational message.

6. What are some examples of crises in leisure services organizations? How can leisure services managers ensure a clear, consistent organizational message in the face of a crisis incident?

7. Provide some examples of communication strategies that a leisure services organization might use to inform, educate, persuade, and remind their customers about their program and facility offerings. What strategies can be used to maintain contact with customers after they finish the consumption process?

8. Provide an example of a communication tool or tactic related to each of the six communication mix strategies proposed by Lovelock (2001).

9. How can a leisure services organization most effectively use a technology (such as a Web site) to enhance the communication process?

10. Why is positioning and repositioning important for leisure services managers to understand?

 Check out the online student resource at www.HumanKinetics.com/LeisureServicesManagement for additional material, including sample documents, case studies, Web links, and more.

KEY WORDS

personnel, Taylorism, law of diminishing returns, human resources capacity,
cross-training, cost-of-living adjustments,
technical skills, conceptual skills, human
relations skills, knowledge, skills, abilities,
stage-based screening process, employee
training, employee development, high-
threshold training, low-threshold training,
volunteers

COMPETENCY CHECK

Take another look at table 1.3 (page 9) to see
how you assessed these related competencies.

26. Understand the hiring process.
27. Supervise, discipline, and evaluate a
    diverse staff.

CHAPTER 10

Personnel Procedures and Practices

As the coordinator of a program offering several therapeutic recreation programs to children in multiple municipalities, I often have a lot of balls in the air at once, sometimes literally. On a daily basis I check in with program staff to offer any support necessary. I also try to connect with the other program coordinators in our organization who may be assisting with a youth program or whose programs I am assisting with. Most days, I find myself in at least one meeting or speaking with a group at a conference, support group, potential funding source, or partnering agency. I also try to stay on top of documentation, billing, and the other paperwork that comes with working in school systems. Keeping a full therapeutic recreation caseload, as well as planning and implementing after-school programs and special events, means that I have to pursue my management responsibilities when the opportunities arise. Rather than setting aside a specific time to do all of this, I try to work it into the natural course of my day. With today's technology, I am able to check my e-mail and voicemail from just about anywhere, and I feel that I can stay informed and effective without being at my desk all the time.

Matt Frye
Program Coordinator Therapeutic Recreation
Empowering Kids (TREK)
Northeast Passage
Durham, New Hampshire

In many ways, the lifeblood of an organization is the human resources that it employs. Service organizations, especially those with high customer contact such as parks, recreation, and leisure services enterprises, are judged by the knowledge, skills, and abilities of their personnel as much as they are by the size and scope of their physical or fiscal resources. In his book, *Good to Great,* Collins (2001) talks about the value of "getting the right people on the bus." According to Collins, finding the right employees and providing them with the tools and resources necessary for their continual development is one of the fundamental traits of great organizations.

Much of what managers do revolves around personnel. One of the four functions of management—leading—focuses on encouraging personnel to contribute to the success of an organization. However, as we have seen in other aspects of management, the other three functions play a critical role in personnel procedures and practices as well. Managers must be able to plan for personnel needs based on the capacity of the agency and its needs for particular sets of knowledge, skills, and abilities. They must be able to organize and coordinate the work output of staff members to avoid inefficiencies and maximize the talents of the staff. Finally, managers must be able to control the process by evaluating the contributions of staff and providing feedback to keep the organization on track to achieve its goals.

What we now think of as accepted practice in personnel or human resources management began with behavioral school theorists, such as Elton Mayo, Mary Parker Follett, and Chester Barnard, and continued with thinkers of the human relations era, such as Abraham Maslow, Frederick Herzberg, and Douglas McGregor (see chapter 2). Chapter 10 deals with the processes and procedures of personnel management.

Human Resources Perspectives

In general, the term **personnel** refers to the people employed within an organization, agency, or institution. Personnel may also be referred to as *human resources,* a term that stems from the ideas of the behavioral school and human relations era by emphasizing the fact that personnel are, first and foremost, human. Contrast this thinking with that of classical era thinkers such as Frederick Taylor. **Taylorism** was a principle based on the notion that people could be managed as if they were machines. According to Taylorism, through the application of scientific principles (known as *scientific management*), personnel could function similar to the physical machinery of an assembly line or factory. Specific job tasks could be managed, deskilled, and routinized to such an extent as to render the individual employee as little more than a cog in a large machine controlled and supervised by a group of top-level managers.

> **personnel**—People employed within an organization.
>
> **Taylorism**—Based on the notion that through the application of scientific principles, personnel can function in a manner similar to the physical machinery of a factory.

The problem with this approach is that people are not machines. Unlike machines, employees have needs that may not be directly linked to the specific job they are attempting to perform. Consider the following examples. What are the consequences to the organization if these needs are not met?

- ▶ A single, working mother who has to balance her job with the after-school activities of her children might have a real need for a flexible work schedule.
- ▶ An entry-level employee working in an area with a high cost of living needs to be paid enough to cover basic living expenses.
- ▶ A facilities manager who has a job that contains physical risk needs a safe work environment to minimize the chance of injury.
- ▶ A new father needs to spend time with his family upon the birth of his first child.
- ▶ A middle manager has a need for organizational advancement and building new knowledge and skills through continuing education and professional development.

Repercussions on Effectiveness

Human needs are powerful motivators. When not addressed, they also can be significant demotivators and can have repercussions on effectiveness in the following ways.

Underperformance

When certain employee needs go unmet, underperformance in terms of work quantity and quality may increase. Underperformance also can have a ripple effect on other employees or units within the organization. Disgruntled employees require more attention—time that would be better spent on key management tasks.

Increased Employee Attrition

Poor work environments and employee dissatisfaction can lead to higher rates of employee attrition (leaving the organization). As the conventional wisdom goes, it is most efficient for an organization to do what it can to minimize employee attrition, and especially to retain its best employees. Job searches, staff development, orientation, and training are inefficient when they have to be repeated over and over for the same position. It is in the best interest of an organization to hire the right people and do its best to keep them.

Underutilization of Employee Capacities

In some cases, an organization may underuse its employees' knowledge, skills, and abilities. If employees' talents have value, then it stands to reason that a manager would want to maximize that value by using those talents. Just as managers would be wasting organizational resources by buying an expensive computer program and only using part of its capabilities, so too are managers inefficient when they only use a portion of an employee's abilities. Tapping into the knowledge and talents of all employees in an organization can improve product quality and organizational efficiency and effectiveness, and thus it is a major goal of management.

Process and Philosophy

Human resources management has been created to help organizations meet employees' needs and prevent minor situations from becoming significant problems or draining effectiveness later on. Human resources management is both a process and a philosophy. Bolman and Deal (2003) lay out the core assumptions of a human resources philosophy:

▶ Organizations exist to serve human needs rather than the reverse.
▶ People and organizations need each other—organizations need the talents and energies of people, and people need careers, salaries, and professional opportunities.
▶ When the fit between individuals and organizations is poor, one or both suffers.
▶ Good fits benefit both the employee and the organization. A relationship of mutual exchange is created that benefits both.

Ultimately, human resources management is about understanding the human side of organizations. Human resources management is a process that helps to determine how both individual and organizational needs can be managed in a system that is clear, unambiguous, fair, and legal.

Personnel Planning

As with virtually every other aspect of management, managing human resources requires significant planning. Adding human resources without a clear plan for what to do with them is counterproductive. The **law of diminishing returns** from basic economics theory says that when we add additional variable inputs (for example, new employees) while keeping fixed inputs constant (for example, numbers of supervisory or administrative staff), each new input will contribute less and less after

law of diminishing returns—When new variable inputs (for example, new employees) are added while fixed inputs remain constant, each new input will contribute less and less.

a certain point. Consider some of the fixed inputs of the youth unit in a commercial resort (e.g., fiscal resources, activity space, office areas, support services, supervisory contact). Given these conditions, adding additional staff may continue to increase unit effectiveness up to a point. Lacking adequate supervision, pay, office space, scope of responsibility, or administrative support, new staff members are likely to become dissatisfied. At the same time, the organization may find itself overstaffed given the size and scope of its programming efforts and wasting scarce resources.

Figure 10.1 illustrates this law. The ideal number of program staff for this organization given its existing resources is probably four. Adding a fifth staff member may not contribute to overall productivity, and overall productivity may actually decrease due to the strains that come with managing and supervising this additional human resource.

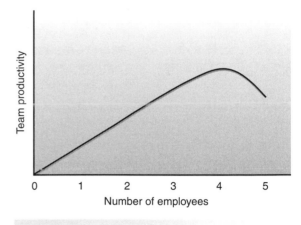

Figure 10.1 Law of diminishing returns.

Organizational Capacity

Understanding the capacity of an organization to meet the needs of additional staff members is an important first step in human resources planning. **Human resources capacity** refers to the resources, supervision, and systems that an organization has in place to meet its human resources needs. Adding human resources without addressing the capacity to manage them can result in inefficiency, as described previously. In addressing organizational capacity, the following areas should be considered:

human resources capacity—Resources and systems that an organization has in place to meet its human resources needs.

▶ Existing staff levels

▶ Fiscal resources

▶ Supervisory resources

▶ Physical resources and administrative support systems

Existing Staffing Levels

One of the first steps in assessing capacity is analyzing current staffing levels of the organization. Managers must ask themselves whether current organizational tasks and functions can be met by existing staff resources. Arriving at the answer to this question can be more complex than it appears, and a definitive yes-or-no answer does not necessarily lead to a particular course of action. For example, suppose the recreation director of a midsized department is conducting a human resources analysis of the aquatics unit. In consultation with the aquatics coordinator and assistant coordinator, the director comes to the conclusion that the tasks of the aquatics unit—pool operations, life guarding, and swimming instruction—are not adequately met by existing personnel resources. The next step is to examine why this is the case.

Numbers It is possible that the existing number of staff is inadequate to meet the needs of the program. For example, the number of lifeguards needed during the summer when both outdoor and indoor pools are in operation means that more lifeguards need to be hired when demand increases. The decision to add staff in this case would be an appropriate response. Of course, the decision to add staff must take into consideration the capacity of the organization to accommodate the needs of new employees.

Expertise   It could be that existing staff are not able to meet unit goals because they lack the expertise to carry out their job duties. For example, the aquatics unit might lack enough certified pool operators or staff with specialized expertise in aquatics facilities management. In this case, a course of action might be to recruit and hire additional staff with the needed expertise. Another solution would be to cross-train present personnel in the specialized skills needed to accomplish the tasks. **Cross-training** refers to preparing staff to perform the tasks associated with various jobs in an organization. In this example, the assistant aquatics coordinator could be trained as a certified pool operator and given responsibilities for pool operations and maintenance. Or entire job categories could be cross-trained to handle varying responsibilities—for instance, lifeguards might be certified as water safety instructors so that they could provide swim lessons.

By cross-training existing staff, the size of the workforce may not need to change and problems with capacity are diminished. This solution is most effective when there is room to add responsibilities to existing workloads, when the required expertise is fairly easy to obtain, and when combining job functions (job enlargement) makes sense. Adding new staff to address gaps in expertise makes more sense when the needed skill sets are highly specialized or when the nature of the work makes job enlargement impractical.

Work Allocation   Sometimes staff members are not able to meet their goals because work is not allocated in a way that maximizes efficiency and effective-

cross-training—Preparing staff to perform the skills and tasks associated with different jobs within an organization.

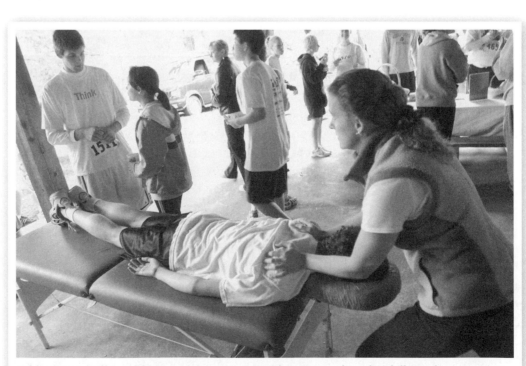

Adding new staff to address gaps in expertise makes sense when the skill sets for a position are highly specialized, as in the case of a massage therapist.

ness. This indicates that there might be a structural problem that requires personnel reorganization. Let's continue with the aquatics example. Suppose that the assistant aquatics manager's job duties were largely redundant with the supervisor's and that there was room for subordinate staff to take on additional responsibilities. If the organization eliminated the assistant aquatics coordinator's position, it might be able to reallocate its personnel resources by hiring additional lifeguards (or swim instructors, or pool maintenance staff) to address current demands.

Or, suppose that the aquatics unit was overstaffed in one area and understaffed in another. Reorganizing pool maintenance staff by eliminating or downsizing full-time positions could help supplement personnel resources in another program area. It might be that only a small crew of full-time pool maintenance staff is needed year-round with additional part-time help needed in the summer, whereas swim instructors are in high demand year round. Assessing the organization and allocation of personnel resources is a critical component of human resources planning.

Fiscal Resources

When resources are limited, as is commonly the case with leisure services organizations, fiscal and budgetary realities often dictate personnel decisions. Decisions to add personnel may be constrained by tight budgets and, particularly in public or nonprofit organizations, by strict approval processes for adding personnel. Even when additional personnel resources are clearly needed in response to increasing demand or gaps in existing expertise, decision makers may be reluctant to commit financial resources to permanent benefits-eligible positions. This may be due to political realities related to taxation in the public sector, constraints on spending decisions in the nonprofit sector, or a concern that future demand may not be strong enough to justify increasing personnel costs in the commercial sector. In all of these cases, fiscal and budgetary realities are the driving force behind personnel decisions, especially when staff additions are being considered. The result is that existing staff are often asked to shoulder the burden of doing more with less.

Conducting a careful analysis of fiscal resources is an important step in determining the capacity of an organization for adding personnel. Before determining the capacity to invest in new personnel, managers and decision makers must consider the types of positions that are needed. Different job types will require different investments of fiscal resources. For example, many staff positions in leisure services organizations are part time, hourly wage, seasonal, and benefits exempt. Lifeguards, sports officials, front-desk attendants, camp counselors, coaches, and group fitness instructors can be hired with less financial investment and generally less financial risk than program, management, executive, and certain support and technical staff positions. Not only do part-time and seasonal positions cost less, they are also more easily eliminated during times of lower demand.

Full-time, permanent, salaried, and benefits-eligible positions require a greater fiscal commitment. This commitment extends beyond the increased salary that such positions are likely to command. The commitment begins during the search process, where the organization may be required to lay out thousands of dollars recruiting qualified candidates. Salaries must be competitive in order to attract the best candidates, especially for positions that are in high demand or that require specialized skill sets. Benefits, including health care, retirement savings, life insurance, and paid vacation time, can cost employers up to 40 percent on top of the employee's salary, meaning a $30,000 entry-level position could cost an organization more than $40,000 in total compensation.

Organizations must also consider fluctuations in the larger economy, including increases in cost of living, or the cost of goods and services that a household is expected to be able to purchase at an average level of consumption. In order to ensure that employees are able to keep up with the cost of inflation, many organizations provide annual **cost-of-living adjustments.** Such salary adjustments help to ensure that employees continue to be adequately compensated even as the price of goods and services in the larger economy increase. Finally, ongoing training costs and professional development that are required for employees to do their jobs effectively must also be considered as part of the employee's cost to the organization. Much like other assets, human resources are investments that organizations must carefully consider in order to maximize efficiency and effectiveness.

cost-of-living adjustments—Salary increases for employees in order to offset losses in purchasing power due to inflation.

Supervisory Resources

When assessing the capacity of an agency to accommodate additional personnel resources, managers must take into account the level of supervision that is needed to manage new employees. An assessment of supervisory resources is important because coordination is needed to ensure efficient work processes. Employees also need adequate access to their supervisors to enhance communication and avoid misunderstandings.

Coordination and Control   As organizations grow, they become more complex, creating structural dilemmas and questions regarding how best to coordinate and control staff activities. Recall that in chapter 6, we discussed how increasing the number of supervisors (decreasing spans of control) generally leads to greater coordination. When adding new personnel, managers must assess whether current supervisory resources are adequate to achieve the proper balance between coordinating staff and providing enough autonomy for staff to demonstrate expertise and tap into their potential.

This assessment will depend on the nature of the position that is being considered. Some staff positions may require increased supervision and narrower spans of control, whereas other positions may be better served by creating autonomous structures that allow for more individual freedom and greater accountability. Sales positions, for example, might benefit from such freedom, with quotas serving as the principal accountability mechanism for ensuring adequate job performance. Additional sales staff might not require additional supervisory resources; salespeople often work independently and overcoordination can hinder such flexibility.

However, hiring additional maintenance staff might also require a new maintenance supervisor, because maintenance tasks are often highly interdependent with other organizational functions (such as programming, facilities management, or even marketing). Because of this interdependence, there is a greater need to coordinate and control maintenance efforts. Failing to plan for the integration of new maintenance staff could lead to structural dilemmas.

Supervisor–Employee Relationships   Employees look to their supervisors for guidance, feedback, and resources so they can do their jobs effectively. In highly interdependent positions where the actions of one person greatly affect the actions of others, staff must be able to rely on their supervisors to frame their job roles, coordinate the activities of their unit, and advocate for them in times of conflict. When considering organizational capacity to handle new personnel, managers must ask whether existing supervisor–staff relationships will be adversely affected by the addition of new positions. Noneconomic costs are involved in adding new staff, especially with respect to the time that is spent orienting, training, coordinating, and managing their efforts. Failing to account for these noneconomic costs may create new inefficiencies, especially if management feels strained in the ability to handle new staff or if new staff members feel that their needs are not being met by their supervisors.

Physical Resources and Administrative Support Systems

Organizations also need to provide employees with the tools to do their jobs effectively. For some positions, this means providing adequate office space, computing resources, and communication systems. Other positions may have specialized equipment or specific physical space needs. Without access to the proper resources, employees may find it difficult to accomplish their tasks. Before adding new staff, managers must be sure that the organization has the physical resources to accommodate job-related needs.

In addition to physical resources, employees need administrative support systems that help them to navigate their often-complex job roles. Administrative support means assisting staff in areas that may or may not be directly related to their everyday tasks. For example, some staff positions may require administrative support consisting of typing letters, making copies, organizing office systems, scheduling meetings, taking registrations or payments, answering phones, handling employee payroll, or responding to e-mails. Administrative support can also mean assisting employees with more general personnel needs, including assistance with benefits or questions regarding organizational policy. Questions related to capacity must consider whether staff levels can be provided with the administrative support needed to effectively perform necessary job functions.

Organizational Needs

In addition to considering their capacity, organizations must also think about their personnel needs. One of the classic personnel dilemmas is whether to think about personnel needs in terms of specific positions and technical skill sets or whether to think about such needs more broadly by considering the qualities that an organization wants its employees to possess. Although this dilemma does not necessarily present itself as an either–or proposition—a candidate can be both technically skilled and possess the qualities that the organization is seeking—sometimes finding the right combination of conceptual, human, and technical skills can be a daunting task.

In the process of assessing human resources needs, organizations should clearly define the qualities that they most value in their employees. These qualities should fit the vision, values, mission, and culture of the organization. Remember one of the propositions of human resources philosophy—when the fit between employee and organization is a good one, both tend to benefit.

Personnel Needs Based on Position

Often, personnel needs come in the form of specific expertise. In this model, personnel decisions stem from the vision and strategic planning efforts of an agency. When a position becomes vacant in a specific unit, the organization often seeks a replacement with the same technical skill sets as the previous employee. For example, if a fitness organization needs to replace a personal trainer, management may seek qualified candidates who possess the competencies, certifications, and experiences that best meet the fitness and personal training needs of the clients.

The specialized nature of many jobs in leisure services organizations, especially at the program level, may lead managers to think in terms of position needs first. Organizations may have a need for aquatics coordinators, sport programmers, fitness directors, turf maintenance specialists, youth development professionals, or marketing managers. Each of these positions requires a specialized set of skills. If the organization needs an aquatics coordinator, it needs someone with proper certifications, training, competencies, and experience in lifeguarding, swim instruction, and pool operations and maintenance.

Though it is important for managers to consider the job-related competencies that they expect their employees to possess, it is equally important to remember that skill sets extend beyond the technical. **Technical skills,** which include the job-specific knowledge and techniques that enable an employee to do a job effectively, are important, but so are conceptual skills and human skills. **Conceptual skills** include the ability to analyze situations, determine causes and effects, come up with solutions to programming or organizational challenges, and see the big picture. **Human relations skills** include the ability to work with, lead, and understand other people, including both individuals and groups. Each of these skill sets should be considered when analyzing the personnel needs of the organization, and, as we consider in the next section, sometimes the best candidate for the organization may not be the candidate who possesses the highest level of technical expertise at the time of the hire.

Considering personnel needs primarily based on position and technical qualifications is appropriate under the following conditions:

▶ When a particular job function requires highly specialized skill sets

▶ When the acquisition of the required technical skills are difficult or costly to obtain

▶ When recruiting efforts yield a deep enough pool of candidates who possess the technical, conceptual, and human relations skills to meet the needs of the organization

technical skills—Job-specific knowledge and techniques that enable employees to do their job effectively.

conceptual skills—Ability to analyze situations from multiple perspectives, determine cause and effect, and come up with solutions to challenges.

human relations skills—Ability to work with, lead, and understand other people, including both individuals and groups.

> ▶ When the organization is required by law or policy to justify hiring decisions based on an objective set of criteria such as certification, licensure, specific academic degrees, or specific technical expertise

Because many of the jobs in leisure services organizations are highly specialized, considering personnel needs primarily based on the qualifications needed for a specific job is often the most pragmatic means for personnel planning. However, it is important to go beyond the technical requirements for the position and consider a broad range of competencies that often are not skill specific. In chapter 2, we discussed the importance of competencies that cut across many of the job types found in leisure services organizations. Many of these competencies are not job or skill specific yet are still considered to be vital for employees to possess. Although some competencies, such as technical skills, can be obtained through training and education, many interpersonal competencies, such as conceptual or human relations skills, can only be obtained through experience and professional perspective.

Personnel Needs Based on Qualities

What if the best fit for the organization is not the candidate with the highest level of technical skill but the candidate who possesses the right mix of conceptual and human relations skills? What if the best fit is the candidate who possesses the qualities that the organization values the most? In his book *Good to Great* (2001), Jim Collins found that the best organizations focus on getting the best people first—they think about specific jobs later. Collins found that this works because of three reasons:

> ▶ Hiring based on desired qualities rather than specific technical skills allows the organization to be more flexible in times of shifting demand.
>
> ▶ Hiring based on desired qualities renders questions of motivation relatively moot—the right people tend to be self-motivated and do not need to be tightly managed.
>
> ▶ Great vision without great people is irrelevant—great organizations ultimately need great people.

The general concept that underlies Collins' research is the idea that people who possess the right mix of qualities that are valued by the organization (e.g., robust work ethic, commitment to team, strong communication ability) can be trained in the technical skills that a specific job requires. For instance, employees with a strong work ethic can be trained in a variety of job-related tasks, but it is difficult to train someone to have a strong work ethic.

This method is admittedly difficult to implement for leisure services organizations. Training and employee development, especially in specific programming areas that require specialized skills or certifications, may be too difficult, expensive, or time consuming for the organization. For example, it takes years of study and experience to be a turf maintenance specialist. It may also be difficult for organizations to justify hiring decisions based on criteria that are difficult to measure, such as values, work ethic, or team focus. Hiring based primarily on an employee's perceived qualities can also open the door to various forms of discrimination or abuse. However, considering the personnel qualities that are most important to the organization and significantly weighing those qualities during a job search is a critical step in the personnel planning process.

Employee Diversity

Part of the personnel planning process includes thinking about the diversity of a workforce. Beyond being the right thing to do, developing and maintaining a diverse workforce makes good business sense. Demographic trends show a changing workforce in the United States. By 2010, women are expected to increase their proportion of the labor force faster than men. With respect to race, Asian, Black, and Hispanic populations are expected to increase their percentages of the labor force at a rate higher than non-Hispanic whites by 2010. Although the median age of the labor force will increase as the baby boomers near retirement, the percentage of young workers (aged 16-24) is expected to grow faster than the labor force as a whole (Fullerton & Toosi, 2001). According to the U.S. Census Bureau (2006), all residents of California, Hawaii, New Mexico, and Texas are technically members of a minority group since the percentage of non-Hispanic whites as a proportion of the population is less than 50 percent in those states (U.S. Census Bureau, 2006).

Similar demographic trends can be seen in Canada as well. Visible minorities, or non-Caucasians, have increased from 1.1 million to 4 million since 1981. The most recent figures show that visible minorities now make up 13 percent of the Canadian population—an 8 percent increase in the past 20 years. Further, indigenous people continue to make up a sizable portion of the population in the north and west, even holding a majority in the Northwest Territories and Nunavut (Statistics Canada, 2007a).

The labor force in the United States and Canada is clearly growing more diverse. Leisure services organizations must continue to focus on the diversity of their workforces, both to reflect the diversity of their constituents and to benefit from the skills of the broadest array of potential job seekers.

It is important for organizations to recognize the moral imperative and good business practices behind workforce diversity, but it is also important to recognize that federal, state, and provincial laws in the United States and Canada prohibit organizations from discriminating against employees and job seekers. For example, in the United States, it is unlawful for employers to discriminate against employees or job seekers based on race, color, religion, sex, national origin, disability, or age. Many states broaden these areas through their own laws and statutes, barring

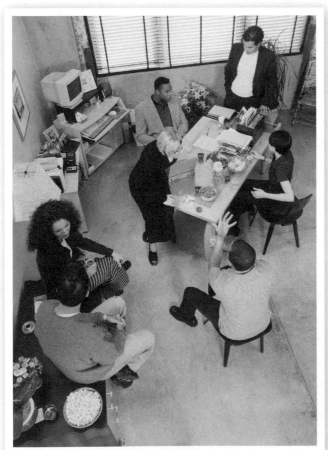

The labor force in the United States and Canada is growing more diverse as the number of women and minority employees as a percentage of the labor market is increasing.

discrimination based on sexual orientation, marital status, or status as a veteran. Many individual organizations have also adopted antidiscrimination policy that goes beyond the legal requirements.

Federal legislation in the United States forbids discrimination in the following areas:

▶ Hiring and firing

▶ Compensation, assignment, or classification of employees

▶ Transfer, promotion, layoff, or recall

▶ Job advertisements

▶ Recruitment

▶ Testing

▶ Use of company facilities

▶ Training and apprenticeship programs

▶ Fringe benefits

▶ Pay, retirement plans, and disability leave

▶ Other terms and conditions of employment

Similar rights are extended to workers in Canada. The Canadian Human Rights Act prohibits federally regulated employers or service providers from discriminating against employees or potential employees based on race, national or ethnic origin, color, religion, age, sex, sexual orientation, marital status, family status, disability, and conviction for which a pardon has been granted. Provincial and territorial legislation offers similar protection for most employees who are not federally regulated.

Discriminatory practices covered by the Canadian Human Rights Act are numerous, and leisure services managers are encouraged to familiarize themselves with the provisions of the act, including exceptions. Provisions of the act related to discrimination in the workplace include the following:

▶ Employment

▶ Employment applications or advertisements

▶ Employee organizations

▶ Discriminatory policy or practice

▶ Equal wages

▶ Assessment of the value of work

▶ Harassment and sexual harassment

▶ Workplace accommodations

Legislation involving human resources is complex and extensive. As such, the discussion here is a general overview focused specifically on employment discrimination and equal opportunity laws. Recall that we discussed many of the key employment laws in chapter 4. You can also refer to figure 10.2 and the sidebar on page 235 for a brief discussion of important equal opportunity legislation in the United States and Canada.

Equal Employment Opportunity is

THE LAW

Employers Holding Federal Contracts or Subcontracts

Applicants to and employees of companies with a Federal government contract or subcontract are protected under the following Federal authorities:

RACE, COLOR, RELIGION, SEX, NATIONAL ORIGIN

Executive Order 11246, as amended, prohibits job discrimination on the basis of race, color, religion, sex or national origin, and requires affirmative action to ensure equality of opportunity in all aspects of employment.

INDIVIDUALS WITH DISABILITIES

Section 503 of the Rehabilitation Act of 1973, as amended, prohibits job discrimination because of disability and requires affirmative action to employ and advance in employment qualified individuals with disabilities who, with reasonable accommodation, can perform the essential functions of a job.

VIETNAM ERA, SPECIAL DISABLED, RECENTLY SEPARATED, AND OTHER PROTECTED VETERANS

38 U.S.C. 4212 of the Vietnam Era Veterans' Readjustment Assistance Act of 1974, as amended, prohibits job discrimination and requires affirmative action to employ and advance in employment qualified Vietnam era veterans, qualified special disabled veterans, recently separated veterans, and other protected veterans.

Any person who believes a contractor has violated its nondiscrimination or affirmative action obligations under the authorities above should contact immediately:

The Office of Federal Contract Compliance Programs (OFCCP), Employment Standards Administration, U.S. Department of Labor, 200 Constitution Avenue, N.W., Washington, D.C. 20210 or call (202) 693-0101, or an OFCCP regional or district office, listed in most telephone directories under U.S. Government, Department of Labor.

Private Employment, State and Local Governments, Educational Institutions

Applicants to and employees of most private employers, state and local governments, educational institutions, employment agencies and labor organizations are protected under the following Federal laws:

RACE, COLOR, RELIGION, SEX, NATIONAL ORIGIN

Title VII of the Civil Rights Act of 1964, as amended, prohibits discrimination in hiring, promotion, discharge, pay, fringe benefits, job training, classification, referral, and other aspects of employment, on the basis of race, color, religion, sex or national origin.

DISABILITY

The Americans with Disabilities Act of 1990, as amended, protects qualified applicants and employees with disabilities from discrimination in hiring, promotion, discharge, pay, job training, fringe benefits, classification, referral, and other aspects of employment on the basis of disability. The law also requires that covered entities provide qualified applicants and employees with disabilities with reasonable accommodations that do not impose undue hardship.

AGE

The Age Discrimination in Employment Act of 1967, as amended, protects applicants and employees 40 years of age or older from discrimination on the basis of age in hiring, promotion, discharge, compensation, terms, conditions or privileges of employment.

SEX (WAGES)

In addition to sex discrimination prohibited by Title VII of the Civil Rights Act of 1964, as amended (see above), the Equal Pay Act of 1963, as amended, prohibits sex discrimination in payment of wages to women and men performing substantially equal work in the same establishment.

Retaliation against a person who files a charge of discrimination, participates in an investigation, or opposes an unlawful employment practice is prohibited by all of these Federal laws.

If you believe that you have been discriminated against under any of the above laws, you should contact immediately:

The U.S. Equal Employment Opportunity Commission (EEOC), 1801 L Street, N.W., Washington, D.C. 20507 or an EEOC field office by calling toll free (800) 669-4000. For individuals with hearing impairments, EEOC's toll free TDD number is (800) 669-6820.

Programs or Activities Receiving Federal Financial Assistance

RACE, COLOR, RELIGION, NATIONAL ORIGIN, SEX

In addition to the protection of Title VII of the Civil Rights Act of 1964, as amended, Title VI of the Civil Rights Act prohibits discrimination on the basis of race, color or national origin in programs or activities receiving Federal financial assistance. Employment discrimination is covered by Title VI if the primary objective of the financial assistance is provision of employment, or where employment discrimination causes or may cause discrimination in providing services under such programs. Title IX of the Education Amendments of 1972 prohibits employment discrimination on the basis of sex in educational programs or activities which receive Federal assistance.

INDIVIDUALS WITH DISABILITIES

Sections 501, 504 and 505 of the Rehabilitation Act of 1973, as amended, prohibits employment discrimination on the basis of disability in any program or activity which receives Federal financial assistance in the federal government. Discrimination is prohibited in all aspects of employment against persons with disabilities who, with reasonable accommodation, can perform the essential functions of a job.

If you believe you have been discriminated against in a program of any institution which receives Federal assistance, you should contact immediately the Federal agency providing such assistance.

Publication OFCCP 1420
Revised 2004

Figure 10.2 Equal employment opportunity poster.

Reprinted from The Office of Federal Contract Compliance Programs (OFCCP), Employment Standards Administration, U.S. Department of Labor.

Major Discrimination Laws in the United States and Canada

The following federal laws provide general guidelines for employee rights and discrimination in the United States and Canada. Leisure services managers should make the effort to understand each of these laws and should consult appropriate legal authorities if questions arise.

United States

- ▶ Equal Pay Act of 1963: Prohibits sex discrimination in payment of wages to women and men performing substantially equal work in the same establishment.

- ▶ Title VII of the Civil Rights Act of 1964: Prohibits discrimination in hiring, promotion, discharge, pay, fringe benefits, job training, classification, referral, and other aspects of employment on the basis of race, color, religion, sex, or national origin.

- ▶ Age Discrimination in Employment Act (ADEA) of 1967: Protects applicants and employees 40 years of age or older from discrimination on the basis of age in hiring, promotion, discharge, compensation, terms, conditions, or privileges of employment.

- ▶ Rehabilitation Act of 1973: Prohibits job discrimination because of disability and requires affirmative action to employ and advance in employment qualified people with disabilities who, with reasonable accommodation, can perform the essential functions of a job.

- ▶ Title I and Title V of the Americans with Disabilities Act (ADA) of 1990: Protects qualified applicants and employees with disabilities from discrimination in hiring, promotion, discharge, pay, job training, fringe benefits, classification, referral, and other aspects of employment on the basis of disability. The law also requires that covered entities provide qualified applicants and employees with disabilities with reasonable accommodations that do not impose undue hardship.

Each of these laws prohibits retaliation by an employer against an employee who files a charge of discrimination, participates in an investigation, or opposes unlawful employment practice.

For more information, visit the United States EEOC Web site at www.eeoc.gov.

Canada

- ▶ Canadian Charter of Rights and Freedoms: Requires employers to ensure that equal employment opportunities exist for both job applicants and current employees; guarantees the rights of aboriginal peoples, the right to equality for men and women, and the right to use either of Canada's official languages (French and English).

- ▶ Canadian Human Rights Act: Requires employers to ensure that equal employment opportunities exist for both job applicants and current employees. Prohibits discrimination based on the following protected classes: race, national or ethnic origin, color, religion, age, sex, sexual orientation, marital status, family status, disability, and conviction for which a pardon has been granted.

- ▶ Employment Equity Act: Requires that employers identify and eliminate employment barriers for designated group members that result from the employer's employment systems, policies, and practices; designated groups include women, aboriginal peoples, people with disabilities, and visible minorities.

For more information, visit the Labour Program in Human Resources and Social Development Canada at www.hrsdc.gc.ca/en/labour/index.shtml.

Personnel Processes

A considerable amount of planning is required before actually addressing the personnel needs of an organization. Consideration of organizational capacity, needs, and legal requirements is the necessary first step. After the organization and its management team carefully consider these factors, they need to develop a process for staffing the organization. In general, personnel processes follow these steps:

1. Development of the job description
2. Creation of the job announcement
3. Candidate recruitment
4. Candidate selection
5. Orientation, training, and employee development
6. Performance appraisal

Developing a specific plan to navigate through each step can help an organization be purposeful about its personnel decisions, and it provides a blueprint to guide personnel decisions.

Developing the Job Description

Developing a written job description is the culminating act of the various planning steps discussed previously. The job description is the formal, written definition of the essential functions of a job, as well as its required qualifications and competencies. The job description is the basis for personnel recruitment, candidate selection, training, and performance appraisal. A well-written, thorough description clearly communicates the scope of responsibilities associated with a particular job. It sets the expectations for employment and provides a framework for personnel supervision.

At a minimum, a job description should list the essential functions and competencies required to perform the duties associated with the job. Even the best job descriptions cannot capture every responsibility assigned to a particular job; thus, a job description should be an overall summary of the duties assigned to a particular position and should leave room for additional assignments as needed. Different agencies may have unique formats for job descriptions. However, the following sections are usually included:

▶ *Salary range:* Job descriptions may include a salary range that represents the minimum and maximum salaries that can be earned by an employee in a specific job class. This is particularly important in public and nonprofit organizations, where organizational or political mandates require specific salary ranges.

▶ *General definition:* This is a general definition of the job and its overall scope of responsibility within the organization.

▶ *Supervision:* This statement details the supervision the position receives and exercises.

▶ *Job segments and functions:* Most job descriptions provide a detailed list of the essential job functions that the position is responsible for within the organization. Job segments might include program planning, personnel supervision, budgeting, accounting, marketing, policy making, and so on. Job descriptions should go beyond just listing broad job segments, however. They should be fairly descriptive in specifying the functions that are associated with each particular segment. For example, instead of merely listing *marketing* as a job segment, a job description might also state that the position is responsible for all aspects of marketing and publicity for recreation programs, including developing and distributing brochures and press releases, updating the program Web sites, customer service, and communicating with the media.

▶ *Working conditions:* Some job descriptions include a statement regarding the conditions that the employee is expected to work under. This is particularly important for jobs that require specific physical or manual labor or that require the employee to work in somewhat dangerous settings.

▶ *Qualifications:* Job descriptions must outline the minimal qualifications necessary for the particular job, including both level of formal education and length and type of experience. If there are any additional qualifications for the position, such as specific licensure requirements, certifications, background checks, or physical abilities, they should be listed here as well.

▶ *Competencies:* This section focuses on the specific attributes that are needed to fulfill the essential functions of the job. They generally derive from a combination of education and experience. Some job descriptions will focus on general competencies, whereas others will focus on specific knowledge, skills, and abilities (KSAs) associated with the job. In general, **knowledge** refers to the body of information that directly applies to specific job functions, such as knowledge of the recreation needs of a particular community or understanding of program evaluation techniques. **Skills** are physical or psychomotor competencies required for a particular job, such as operating certain types of machinery or typing on a keyboard. Finally, **abilities** are the aptitudes for a position, or what and how well a person is able to perform a certain task. Examples of abilities might be communicating effectively with the public or establishing effective interpersonal working relationships.

knowledge—Information required to perform a job.

skills—Physical or psychomotor competencies, such as operating certain types of machinery or typing on a keyboard.

abilities—The aptitudes for a position; what and how well a person is able to perform a certain task.

Job descriptions are not static documents. Jobs evolve over time, and as organizational needs change, new knowledge, skills, and abilities are required. Organizations should conduct regular job reviews, especially if position descriptions are out of date and incongruent with the actual job duties being performed.

Creating the Job Announcement

Following the personnel planning process and the development of the job description, the leisure services organization should have a clear idea of its personnel needs. The first step in the candidate selection process is the development of an open job announcement. Job announcements serve several purposes:

▶ They provide notification of available positions to potential job seekers.

► They provide a template for organizational decision making in candidate selection.

► They act as a marketing tool for the organization.

The job announcement sets the tone for the hiring process. As such, it plays an important role in communicating what the organization wants in an employee and what the organization is about. The job announcement should be viewed as a two-way communication tool. It should clearly delineate the employment need of the organization but should also be developed to attract the best candidates. In this way, the job announcement can be seen as part of marketing and communication efforts. Poorly written job announcements reflect negatively on the organization.

Many organizations have standard formats for job announcements or require that certain information be included. An example of this might include statements affirming the commitment of the organization to equal employment opportunity and workforce diversity. Leisure services managers should first consult with their human resources division, if one exists, to ensure that job announcements conform to whatever standard formats might exist. When developing a job announcement from the beginning, consider including the following components.

Title of the Position

Job announcements should include the title of the open position. In some cases, organizations may have an official position title that corresponds with specific employment classifications within the larger organization but is not representative of common job titles in the field. For example, for human resources purposes, a city or municipality might generically categorize all agency heads as unit managers, but their working titles might be more specific (e.g., chief of police, director of housing, director of parks and recreation). In these cases, it is wise to include both the official title and the more common working title for the position. Remember, the job announcement is a communication tool, and job titles often help communicate the scope of responsibility.

It is also important to remember that job titles may differ from organization to organization. This is especially true of organizations in different leisure services settings. For example, campus recreation organizations often use titles such as director, associate director, assistant director, and program coordinator to designate scope of responsibility. Municipal recreation departments may use titles such as recreation director, recreation superintendent, assistant superintendent, and program manager. Using titles that are common in the institutional setting of the organization helps prospective job seekers understand the scope of the position.

Overview of the Organization

Job announcements should include basic details about the organization that have relevance for the scope of responsibility. Consider briefly describing the mission, structure, facilities, personnel, or other areas of potential interest to prospective candidates. In many cases, this is the first contact that a prospective job seeker will have with the organization, so a brief overview can help create interest in potential candidates.

Brief Overview of the Position

In addition to the position title, the announcement should include a general description of the position and its scope of responsibilities. This information could be similar to the general definition of the position discussed earlier. For example, a brief overview of the position might state the following: "Under the direction of the recreation director, the youth sport program supervisor is responsible for all phases of the design and delivery of a comprehensive community recreational sport program for young people, including but not limited to program design, facility management, tournament administration, supervision of coaches and officials, communication with parents, program evaluation, budgeting and accounting, risk management, and program evaluation."

Academic and Professional Qualifications

Job announcements should clearly state both the required and preferred academic and professional qualifications for the job. In general, academic qualifications include education levels, degrees, and areas of study. Professional qualifications include requirements for licensure, certification, or other credentials. A rule of thumb to consider is that as requirements become more specific, the potential applicant pool shrinks. For example, requiring an undergraduate degree in a specific academic area or requiring an advanced graduate degree may limit the pool of applicants. A benefit to this is that it can discourage underqualified applicants from applying, and it eliminates them from consideration early in the process if they do decide to apply. A drawback is that stringent qualifications may prevent good candidates from applying because of their inability to meet the specific requirements for the position. Another potential drawback is that stringent qualifications may reinforce existing inequities in employment based on sex, race, or other areas. For example, if certain racial or ethnic minorities are underrepresented in graduate degree programs in leisure services management, then requiring an advanced degree may further limit the pool of otherwise qualified minority candidates.

In figure 10.3, the position of recreation superintendent responsible for community sport and special events requires candidates to possess a bachelor's degree in recreation management, sport management, or a related field. This obviously limits the applicant pool to candidates who possess academic qualifications in the general field while still allowing a search committee some flexibility in deciding if a degree in a different but related academic area (such as physical education or public administration) could be substituted. The position announcement also states that the organization prefers candidates to possess a master's degree in recreation administration, sport administration, or a related field. Such a statement might give weight to an advanced degree during the selection process but does not completely eliminate otherwise qualified candidates who might not hold a graduate degree. Discussing the required and preferred academic qualifications for the position during the personnel planning process can provide insight into the benefits and costs to the organization when making these decisions.

POSITION ANNOUNCEMENT: RECREATION SUPERINTENDENT FOR COMMUNITY SPORTS AND SPECIAL EVENTS, ANY TOWN, USA

Any Town, USA, seeks a qualified and enthusiastic individual for the position of recreation superintendent for community sports and special events. The Parks and Recreation Department offers a wide range of programs and facilities servicing the tri-town area, including New Town, Young Town, and Old Town. The Any Town Parks and Recreation Department sponsors youth and adult sports, special events, community festivals, art, music, drama, after-school programming, summer camps, senior recreation, and inclusive recreation for persons with disabilities. The Parks and Recreation Department operates the new $10 million Any Town Community Center, as well as the Any Town Outdoor Sports Complex and Tennis Facility. In addition, the Parks and Recreation Department oversees numerous outdoor recreation areas, parks, and hiking/walking/biking trails that serve residents of the tri-town area.

- *Position overview:* Under the direction of the recreation director, the recreation superintendent for community sports and special events is responsible for all phases of the design and delivery of a comprehensive community recreational sport program for youth, adolescents, adults, and seniors in the tri-town area. Programs under the direct supervision of this position include recreational and travel youth sport, Camp Fun in the Sun, and adult sport and special events. Facilities under the direct supervision of the recreation superintendent include the Community Center, the Outdoor Sports Complex, and the Tennis Facility. The position oversees a full-time program supervisor, as well as numerous part-time and volunteer staff.

- *Academic and professional qualifications:* A bachelor's degree in recreation management, sport management, or a related field is required, and a master's degree in recreation administration, sport administration, or a related field is preferred. The position requires 1 to 3 years of demonstrated experience in recreation program design and supervision. More than 3 years of experience is strongly preferred.

- *Certifications and other credentials:* Certification in CPR and standard first aid from a reputable national certification agency (i.e., American Red Cross) is required. Preferred credentials include certified park and recreation professional (CPRP) and certified youth sports administrator (CYSA).

- *Competencies:* The successful candidate will have demonstrated experience in the following areas: policy development, tournament design and administration, program design and delivery, staff supervision (including both paid staff and volunteers), risk management, facility maintenance and management, budget development and financial accounting, marketing and publicity, program evaluation, personal computing, and Web publishing. In addition, the successful candidate must have the ability to provide high levels of customer service, to speak in front of large audiences, to connect personally with the public and fellow staff, and to communicate effectively in written reports and other forms of written communication. Experience supervising full-time staff is strongly preferred. CONTINUED ▷

Figure 10.3   Position announcement for recreation superintendent.

- *Compensation:* $43,472 to $57,345, depending on experience and qualifications. A full benefits package, including paid vacations; health, dental, and life insurance; and 401(k) contributions are included.

- *Application deadline:* Completed applications received before November 1, 2009, will be given priority. Applications that are received after November 1 may be considered.

- *Application process:* Submit a cover letter expressing qualifications and interest in the position, along with a résumé and the names, addresses, and phone numbers of three professional references, to: Human Resources Director, PO Box 1234, Any Town, USA 55555. For questions about the application process or about the position, contact Recreation Director Jane Smith at (603) 555-5555, or by e-mail at jane.smith@anytown.us. You can also visit the Any Town Parks and Recreation Department Web site at www.anytownrec.org.

The Any Town Parks and Recreation Department welcomes females and minority applicants to apply.

The Any Town Parks and Recreation Department is an equal opportunity employer.

Figure 10.3 *(continued)*

Required and Preferred Competencies

Similar to academic qualifications, job announcements should list the competencies that are both required and preferred for the position. When listing required competencies, consider the base level that the position requires. Preferred competencies are those that the organization desires but are not absolutely critical.

Compensation

Some organizations list salary ranges and other forms of compensation on the job announcement, especially for entry-level and middle-management positions. Others merely state that compensation is "commensurate with experience and qualifications." The decision on whether to list compensation on the job announcement is tricky. By providing specific information on salary and benefits, organizations may be either attracting or discouraging job seekers from applying for the position. Providing specific compensation information also means that the organization goes public with its salary structure, which it may be reluctant to do for any number of reasons. In general, if an organization believes its salary structure is competitive with other organizations or believes that providing specific compensation information may help attract good candidates, then it makes sense to provide that information. If an organization does not want salary to be the deciding factor in whether a job seeker applies for the position, or if it has the flexibility to negotiate salary with a successful candidate, then it may make sense to limit the information provided in this section.

Application Process

The job announcement should be extremely clear about the process that candidates must follow to apply for the position. This section should include the contact person to send application materials to, the materials required to apply (e.g., cover letter, résumé, references), specific formatting requirements for application materials, and the deadline for receipt of materials.

Deadlines may be hard (all application materials must be received by a specific date), soft (application materials are encouraged by a specific date, but applications received after the date may still be considered), or open (application materials will be considered until the job is filled). Advantages of hard deadlines are that they encourage job seekers to get their applications in early, they make organization of the application process easier, they help to achieve fairness in the process, and they help to limit large applicant pools. Soft and open deadlines allow greater flexibility on the part of the organization and potential job seekers, but they can also be more difficult to manage, especially with large numbers of applicants for a given position.

Additional Information

Job announcements should include contact names, phone numbers, physical and e-mail addresses, and Internet links for candidates to obtain more information about the position. If the organization has specific requirements for candidates to follow (e.g., no phone calls), this information should be clearly stated. For professional or career positions, many organizations include information pertaining to lifestyle interests, including information about the area, local amenities, access to cultural events, and other areas of interest to potential job seekers. This can also be helpful in attracting the best candidates for a particular position.

Recruitment

The job announcement might be seen as the first step in recruiting qualified candidates. The recruitment process is about finding the best possible candidate for the position. Recruitment strategies should be proactive—that is, organizations should invest both time and resources in the candidate search process. Organizations are generally best served when their applicant pools for open searches are wide and deep, because this puts them in the best position to choose the best fit among qualified candidates.

When open positions arise, organizations are faced with two recruitment options: Fill the position with an internal candidate (an existing employee), or fill the position with an external candidate (someone from outside the organization). The decision whether to recruit internally or externally depends on the specifics of the situation, and there are trade-offs when choosing either approach.

The following are benefits of internal recruitment:

▶ Provides in-depth knowledge of existing employee skills, abilities, and work habits.

▶ Less time and fewer resources need to be designated for candidate recruitment.

▶ Creates a performance incentive for existing employees and may increase motivation.

▶ Less time and fewer resources are devoted to getting new employees oriented and trained.

▶ Creates long-term attachments to the organization and deepens organizational loyalty.

There are also benefits to attracting candidates from outside the organization:

▶ Allows organizations to choose from a wider range of qualified candidates to achieve the best fit for the position.

▶ Adds skills and abilities that may not be present in existing employees.

▶ Fresh ideas and perspectives are brought in from outside the organization.

▶ Can help change the existing organizational culture.

▶ Can promote diversity in the existing workforce.

If the organization chooses to recruit externally, it should employ a range of strategies to attract potential candidates. Keep in mind that an external job search does not exclude internal candidates from applying for the position. Recruitment strategies may be extremely targeted, such as the use of personal and professional networks, or they may be more wide ranging, such as the use of newspaper advertisements or generic Web-based job sites. Both targeted and wide-ranging approaches to recruitment can be advantageous. For example, using trusted personal or professional networks to seek candidates for an open position can increase confidence that the candidate will be a successful hire. Wider recruitment strategies can help extend communications beyond traditional search boundaries and may yield candidates with skills and expertise that might have gone unnoticed.

Overreliance on any one strategy can have negative consequences for the organization. Focusing on personal or professional networks to identify potential candidates can create an insular search and can perpetuate existing hiring biases and patterns. Relying on newspaper advertisements or generic job search Web sites can be cost prohibitive and creates a passive approach to candidate recruitment. A mix of recruitment strategies provides multiple advantages to the organization.

Possible methods for candidate recruitment from the most targeted to the least include the following:

▶ Using personal and professional networks

▶ Posting the job announcement on the Web site or through the internal human resources system of the organization

▶ Utilizing a services search or other third-party firms

▶ Posting positions at career fairs or using career services through professional organizations

▶ Disseminating job announcements over e-mail distribution lists affiliated with professional organizations

▶ Placing advertisements in professional publications or Web sites

▶ Placing advertisements in relevant newspapers or other print sources

▶ Advertising the position on generic job Web sites

Organizations should also reach out to traditionally underrepresented groups through networks and professional organizations to capitalize on diverse talents and expertise that might go undetected through traditional recruitment strategies.

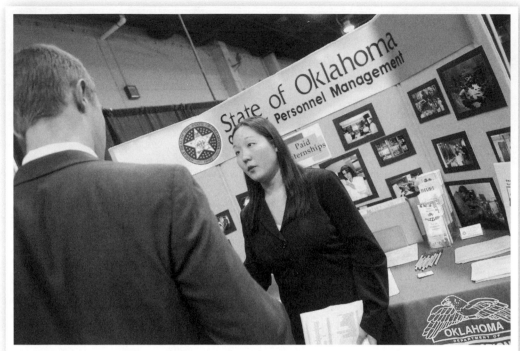

Utilizing a mix of employee recruitment strategies, such as having a presence at a job fair, can help an organization build wide and deep pools of talented and diverse candidates.

Selection

The job search is about selecting the right candidate for the job. If the organization does a thorough job identifying its needs, articulating them in a formal job announcement, and recruiting a large pool of prospective candidates, it stands a better chance of bringing the right candidate on board. To select the right candidate from among the pool of prospective applicants, the organization must develop a selection process, screen applicants, interview top candidates, and make an official offer to the top candidate. Although the specifics might differ, the general steps in candidate selection are usually the same regardless of whether an organization is filling positions at the entry, middle, or upper levels.

Developing a Process

One of the first steps in developing a candidate selection process is deciding who will be responsible for making the hiring decision. In most cases that involve professional staff positions, a search and screen committee is put together to narrow the candidate field. Organizations may take different approaches to putting together the search and screen committee. A typical model for committee development includes a committee chair, who is usually the person responsible for supervising the position, along with approximately three to five committee members who represent various interests that intersect with the open position. It can be advantageous to allow broad organizational input on candidates, especially where other employees might be affected by the hire; however, large search and screen committees with too many decision makers are difficult to manage and can become unwieldy.

The search and screen committee should agree upon a reasonable time frame for candidate selection. It is important for committees to have enough time to identify the ideal candidate and make the proper hire. However, taking too much time can lead to losing good candidates because other organizations may move more quickly in making them an offer.

Screening Candidates

One of the roles of the search and screen committee is to narrow a large group of applicants to a more manageable number of candidates that the organization would like to examine more closely. The committee should develop a process for screening applicants that is unambiguous and fair. Being purposeful about the screening process and avoiding arbitrary decision making can help to avoid potential conflict over specific candidates. One method for narrowing an applicant pool is through the use of a **stage-based screening process.** Stage-based processes set specific benchmarks for applicants to meet based on their qualifications for the position. Each stage sets more stringent benchmarks, narrowing the applicant pool as the process moves along. Figure 10.4 shows the benchmarks set for the first two stages of a search and screen process.

Committee members evaluate applicants based on their application materials (e.g., cover letter, résumé, letters of reference, written application). All committee members score a candidate based on their impression of the candidate's qualifications. When the committee convenes, the group identifies areas where they have consensus to pass an applicant to the next stage and can discuss disagreements about particular candidates. How disagreements are settled is based on the committee process. Some methods could include averaging committee members' scores, attempting to come to a general agreement about an applicant, or putting the final decision to a vote.

> **stage-based screening process**—Candidate screening process that sets specific benchmarks for applicants to meet based on their qualifications for the position. Each stage sets more stringent benchmarks, narrowing the applicant pool as the process continues.

Interviewing Candidates

After the applicant pool has been narrowed to the top group of promising candidates, the process should include some formal contact between the organization and the top candidates. Usually this contact comes in the form of an official job interview, where both the organization and candidate are able to formally evaluate the potential employment opportunity in a deeper way. As with other forms of management communication, interviews are two-way processes. While the organization evaluates the candidates, the candidates should also evaluate the fit between themselves and the organization. Just as some job applicants look better on paper than they do upon closer scrutiny, so do some organizations.

The number of candidates that an organization decides to interview will depend on various factors, including the nature of the position, the number of qualified candidates left in the applicant pool, and the time and financial costs of the interview process. There are three specific types of interviews: screening interviews, phone interviews, and face-to-face interviews. Each type usually takes place at different times during the search process and involves different numbers of potential candidates.

Screening Interviews   Screening interviews typically occur at the beginning of the search process and are used when organizations have easy access to applicants.

SEARCH AND SCREEN COMMITTEE: RECREATION SUPERINTENDENT

CANDIDATE SCORE SHEET

Name: _____

Stage I: Initial Screen

For yes-or-no questions: Indicate whether the candidate meets the criteria and place the point total assigned to the *yes* or *no* value in the last column.

Criteria	Evaluation	Total
Bachelor's degree in recreation management, sport management, or related field	Yes (50) No (0)	
1-3 years demonstrated experience in recreation program design and supervision	Yes (50) No (0)	

Total points needed to pass to stage II = 100 points: (circle)   Pass   Does not pass

Stage II: Secondary Screen

For yes-or-no questions: Indicate whether the candidate meets the criteria and place the point total assigned to the *yes* or *no* value in the last column.

For rating questions, use the following as a guide:

5 = Candidate has superior experience or ability in competency area.

3 = Candidate has some experience or ability in competency area.

1 = Candidate has no experience or ability in competency area.

Criteria	Evaluation	Total
Experience supervising full-time staff	Yes (15) No (0)	
More than 3 years of experience	Yes (15) No (0)	
Master's degree in recreation administration, sport administration, or related field	Yes (10) No (0)	
Certified park and recreation professional	Yes (5) No (0)	
Demonstrated experience in policy development	1 2 3 4 5	
Demonstrated experience in tournament design and administration	1 2 3 4 5	
Demonstrated experience in program design and delivery	1 2 3 4 5	
Demonstrated experience in staff supervision for part-time and volunteer staff	1 2 3 4 5	
Demonstrated experience with risk management protocols	1 2 3 4 5	
Demonstrated experience with facility maintenance and management	1 2 3 4 5	
Demonstrated experience in budget development and accounting	1 2 3 4 5	
Demonstrated experience in marketing and publicity	1 2 3 4 5	
Demonstrated experience in program evaluation	1 2 3 4 5	
Demonstrated experience working with personal computers and Web design	1 2 3 4 5	
Demonstrated ability to communicate effectively in written form	1 2 3 4 5	
	Total	

Total points needed to pass to stage III = 55 points: (circle)   Pass   Does not pass

Figure 10.4   Screening committee score sheet.

For example, a city park and recreation department might use the NRPA National Congress to meet briefly with delegates who might be interested in an available position. Screening interviews allow organizations to talk more about themselves and their job openings, and they allow applicants to ask questions. Screening interviews may be informal discussions with prospective candidates, or they may use formal questions designed to elicit specific responses.

Screening interviews can be informal (face to face) or they can be a written response to specific questions, a phone interview (see the next section), or a video interview where candidates submit recorded responses to predetermined questions. During screening interviews, the organization can get a sense of the human skills that potential applicants possess, and the applicants can get a sense of the people they might work with someday. Screening interviews may not be possible unless the organization can obtain access to potential job applicants in one location. For positions that require a national search, this is obviously a difficult task.

Phone Interviews   Phone interviews typically occur before bringing the final list of candidates in for face-to-face interviews. Phone interviews usually involve 5 to 10 candidates, with the intent of narrowing the final field to 3 to 5 candidates. These interviews may be conducted as conference calls with all members of the search committee taking part, or they may be conducted with smaller subsets or individual members of the committee.

In some cases, phone interviews may not be necessary. For example, part-time or seasonal staff positions, such as lifeguards, youth coaches, group fitness instructors, and similar positions where candidates are easily accessed might not require this step. For professional positions, national searches, and searches where organizations do not have easy access to candidates or where time and money are obstacles to hosting more than two or three top candidates, phone interviews can be useful in narrowing lists of potential candidates. Phone interviews can also allow an organization to more deeply evaluate candidates beyond their written application materials.

Advantages of phone interviews include the following:

▶ They allow organizations to follow up on questions related to application materials.

▶ They provide a two-way exchange of information between the candidate and the committee.

▶ They are less expensive than face-to-face interviews.

▶ They can eliminate poor fits without wasting time and money by bringing candidates in for a face-to-face interview.

▶ They are more flexible and require less commitment on the part of the organization and candidate than face-to-face interviews.

Disadvantages of phone interviews include the following:

▶ They are limited to verbal communication between candidates and the search committee.

▶ The committee is unable to evaluate other aspects of a candidate's communication ability (e.g., nonverbal communication) or other sets of desired skills (e.g., person-to-person interaction).

▶ Technology limitations can create confusion with multiple-party dialogue over phone lines.

Face-to-Face Interviews   The last step before arriving at a final ranking of top candidates is the face-to-face interview. As with other job interviews, face-to-face interviews provide an opportunity for an exchange of information and should be seen as a chance for both organization and candidate to get to know one another. At this point, candidate qualifications should be well known from their application materials, screening interview, and phone interview. Face-to-face interviews are as much trial runs as they are fact-gathering forums. In other words, during the interview experience, both the organization and the candidate will be finding out whether a good fit exists.

Face-to-face interviews can be categorized into three types: individual interviews, group interviews, and assessment centers. These formats do not necessarily need to be mutually exclusive. Organizations may find it useful to combine interview formats to assess the suitability of a candidate for the position.

The standard format is the individual interview. The individual, in this case, is the candidate. One or more people from the organization interview the candidate regarding the job. Individual interviews generally use standard question-and-answer formats. The types of questions that are asked during an interview will vary depending on the position. However, questions should go beyond asking candidates to restate the technical qualifications that are already listed in their application materials. Many interview questions seek deeper insight into an employee's potential work behavior or various skills they have that might not easily translate onto a résumé or job application. For example, interview questions should attempt to illuminate the candidate's conceptual or human relations skills through scenario or application formats. Consider the differences between these two questions:

▶ What are your experiences with budget preparation and financial management?

▶ Following your first budget approval process, you have been told that appropriated funds toward your operating budget for programs and services will be cut by 5 percent. What ideas do you have for recovering the lost revenue or balancing your budget?

Both questions attempt to understand the candidate's experience with budgeting and financial management. The first question focuses solely on the technical experiences of the candidate. Although this is important, these experiences should be apparent from reading the candidate's application materials. The second question attempts to more deeply understand the candidate's approach to budgeting and financial decision making, and it delves into the candidate's competencies. To answer the question, candidates will still need to speak to their technical skills in this area, yet they have an opportunity to reveal more insight into their actual work behavior and decision-making ability. This approach can be used to reformulate almost all standard interview questions and provide greater insight into the competencies that candidates possess relative to the job. Keep in mind that interview questions should be based on the job description.

Ordering Interview Questions

When deciding on an order for interview questions, start with general questions about education and experience to put the candidate at ease. As the interview goes along, make the questions increasingly more specific and challenging. At the end, always ask if they have any questions for you.

The second major type of face-to-face interview is group interviews, which are conducted with a number of candidates answering questions in the same interview session at the same time. In a group interview, an interviewer or panel of interviewers asks the same set of questions to each candidate in some random order, and candidates provide answers to the questions in the presence of each other. Each candidate gets to hear the answers of every other candidate, and the interviewers can evaluate answers in relation to the other answers provided. Group interviews can be advantageous because they can reveal candidates' ability to adjust their approach based on what others have already said. Group interviews work well in situations where there are a number of highly qualified candidates for the position, when the position requires candidates to think outside the box and come up with different solutions to challenges, or when candidates are relatively similar and there is a desire to see how they differentiate themselves from one another. However, group interviews are high-stakes endeavors. As such, they can be overly stressful on candidates and may lead to highly competitive exchanges or place candidates and interviewers in uncomfortable positions.

The third major type of face-to-face interview is the assessment center. Often the traditional candidate evaluation and selection process is conducted away from the context of the position. The assessment center is a response to the critique of the traditional question-and-answer interview format that focuses more on a candidate's knowledge than on the candidate's actual work behavior and processes. As noted, standard interview questions can be reformulated to gain insight into the latter, but the assessment center takes this a step further. The assessment center attempts to understand a candidate's work behavior in context. It utilizes a mix of evaluation approaches that can provide more understanding of a candidate's work behavior within the context of the job that is being hired. Some of these approaches include the following:

▶ *In-box exercises:* A simulated in-box is put together by interview teams with a variety of tasks that are associated with the day-to-day duties required of the position. The candidate is given a set amount of time to respond to the various tasks contained in the in-box. The candidate is then evaluated on criteria such as the quality of the work performed, the decision making behind the tasks selected, and the ability to prioritize tasks in a limited time frame.

▶ *Team project:* A simulated team project asks the candidate to function as part of a group with the intent of producing a piece of work within a given time frame. The simulated team could comprise other candidates for the position,

What Can I Ask?

Not all interview questions that an employer may ask are appropriate or legal. The critical question for employers to ask themselves is, "What do I really need to know about these candidates to judge their competence to do the job in question?" Interview questions must be directly applicable to the job vacancy. Some examples of legal and illegal interview questions follow. These are just guidelines; individual states or provinces may expand this list. Be sure to refer all questions about legality to the legal counsel of your organization.

Age

Illegal: How old are you?

Legal: Are you over the age of 18?

Disabilities

Illegal: Do you have any disabilities?

Legal: Are you able to perform the functions of the job with or without reasonable accommodations?

Nationality

Illegal: Where are you from? Where were your parents born? What is your native language?

Legal: Are you authorized to work in the United States?

Armed Forces

Illegal: Which branch of the military did you serve in? Were you honorably discharged?

Legal: What type of experiences did you gain in the military? What type of training did you receive?

Height and Weight

Illegal: How tall are you? How much do you weigh?

Legal: Can you lift 60 pounds (27 kilograms)? Do you need any special accommodations for the job? (Questions about ability need to be related to the job.)

Marital Status and Dependents

Illegal: Are you married? Do you have children? Do you plan to have children? Whom do you live with?

Legal: Are you willing to relocate for this job? Are you willing to travel? Are you able to work weekends? (Again, questions need to be related to the job.)

No legal questions may be asked about the following categories:

▶ Race

▶ Religion (except whether one can work on a specific day, if it is related to the job)

▶ Sex

similar to a group interview, or it could comprise members of the organization who might be required to work with the person who is hired. Through simulated team projects, the organization can gain insight into the candidate's leadership skills, ability to listen to others' ideas, personal relationship skills, ability to handle conflict, and ability to produce under a deadline.

▶ *Demonstrations:* Candidates may be asked to perform various tasks associated with the position, including mock budget hearings, staff trainings, presentations, or demonstrations of specific skills or abilities (e.g., fitness instruction, sport officiating skills, outdoor adventure leadership). Through these demonstrations, the organization can more accurately evaluate the candidate's competence related to the requirements of the position.

All three of these assessment center techniques can be used together to enhance candidate evaluation. Each technique should be used to understand the candidate's competencies within the context of the job. The goal of this process is to select the candidate with the best skill set (technical, human, and conceptual) for the position, as well as the best fit for the organization.

Making an Offer

At the conclusion of the interview process, it is time for the organization to make an offer to its top candidate. This process can be more complicated than it seems because the top candidate may not accept the job offer. At the end of the process, the search committee should have a clear sense of who would fit with the organization and who would not. For example, among the three finalists for a position, which of the three would be the best hire? If the top candidate does not accept the offer, is the second candidate an acceptable choice? If the second and third candidates would not be acceptable, the organization needs a contingency plan in case the top candidate refuses the job offer. This contingency plan often includes regrouping and starting the search over again.

The organization needs to make some decisions before making an offer to its top candidate. For example, what parts of the offer are open for negotiation? Is there room to negotiate compensation, such as starting salary or fringe benefits? Is there room to negotiate moving expenses? Start date? Vacation time? To a large extent, the answers to these questions will depend on the position that is being hired. Top-level executives may have more leeway to negotiate than entry-level employees, and full-time employees may have more room to negotiate than part-time employees. Negotiation of compensation might be more acceptable in the commercial sector than in the public or nonprofit sector, where salary levels may be regulated by policy or statute. Positions where there is a scarcity of qualified employees may require more flexibility in reaching a final offer. Organizational planning is critical before making a job offer. The organization needs to fully understand the ramifications behind its decisions both in terms of landing the ideal employee and the implications for existing staff.

Orientation and Training

Orientation and training are critical steps in employee development. Organizations that do not invest in training and development waste human potential. New employees who are not properly oriented to the policies, rules, and culture of the organization can feel anxious, out of place, or undervalued. Poorly trained or unprepared employees can lead to poor work performance, waste of organizational resources, and could even create dangerous situations for customers or other staff members depending on the position. In organizations where employee orientation and training are shortchanged, supervisors may need to spend more time teaching and correcting performance errors. In short, investing in employee development through orientation and training can help to maximize potential more quickly, create greater job satisfaction, create a sense of organizational stewardship, and reduce the need for constant supervision by management.

Hiring the best person is only the beginning of the staff development process. Regardless of how well new employees fit with the organization, they will most certainly have questions related to policies, rules, culture, values, and the nature of their job in relation to others. For new employees, orientation provides an introduction to the organization and is often focused on two areas: general orientation and job-specific orientation. For some positions, new employees may need training in specific technical skills to perform their jobs effectively. Regardless of their tenure with the organization, all employees need ongoing support, knowledge, and skills development in order to maximize their talents as professionals. Thus, training can be broken down into two categories: skills training and ongoing learning and development.

Orientation

The purpose of most orientation programs can be seen as helping new employees fit into their new organizations. Orientation programs should provide employees with information about the organization and the job that the employee has been hired to do. They should also integrate new employees into the social fabric of the organization by building esprit de corps.

The following components should be included in a general organizational orientation program for new employees:

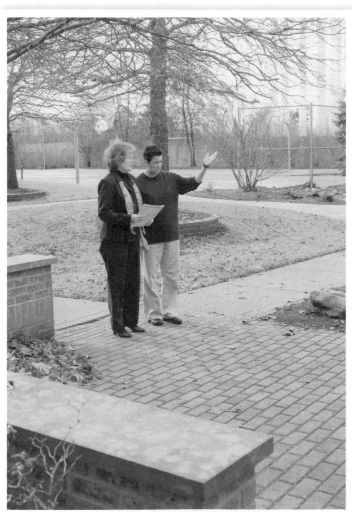

A new employee gets a tour of the organization's facilities during orientation, providing her with a sense of place and understanding of the organization's scope of operations.

▶ *Organizational values:* Although new employees should already be aware of organizational values from the application process, orientation programs are opportunities to further articulate the areas that the organization cares deeply about (e.g., history, tradition, excellence, community development, customer service, safety). These areas also contribute to organizational culture.

▶ *Organizational structure:* Orientation programs are good places to educate new employees on organizational structure and layout, including reporting lines. New employees should also become aware of how their position relates to other positions up, down, and across the organizational chart.

▶ *Work-related policies, procedures, and rules:* Orientation programs should clearly articulate the major policy areas that employees should understand. If the organization has an employee manual or handbook, and it should, orientation programs are good opportunities to share and discuss the critical content areas.

▶ *Facility tours:* To understand the scope of the organization, new employees should be given tours of the facilities. These tours can also be an opportunity to provide keys or other forms of access to secure facilities. This is particularly important for organizations with large or multiple facilities.

▶ *Compensation and benefits:* New employees will need to spend some time with a benefits counselor or other human resources expert to discuss options for health and life insurance, retirement plans, tax withholding, and other aspects of employee compensation. See the sidebar for examples of employee benefits.

▶ *Bonding:* Orientation programs should provide opportunities for staff to become acquainted with one another and should attempt to quickly integrate new employees into the organization. Adding a social component to the orientation either on- or off-site can help build relationships and can ease the transition of new employees into the organization.

Examples of Employee Benefits

▶ Vacation and holiday pay

▶ Domestic partner benefits

▶ Pension plans

▶ Use of agency facilities

▶ Paid education fees

▶ Child-care services

In addition to a general orientation, new employees need information related to the basic functions of a particular job. The following components should be included in a job-specific orientation for new employees:

▶ *Supervisor:* New employees should have significant time to meet with their direct supervisor to discuss the boss–employee relationship. This is a time for supervisors to discuss their management philosophy and their approach to running their unit, including any unit-specific policies, procedures, guidelines, or protocols.

▶ *Scope and duties:* New employees need to be sure that they adequately understand the duties of their position. This can include areas of responsibility, supervisory capacity, and day-to-day job functions.

▶ *Office space and resources:* Employees need the proper resources to do their jobs effectively. One of the areas that new employees tend to get most excited about is their office space and the resources available to them. Orientation programs should introduce new employees to their office space, computing resources, storage files, and other office resources.

▶ *Staff introductions:* As mentioned, orientation programs are opportunities to form relationships and build esprit de corps among staff. Job-specific orientation programs should also include meetings between the new employee and fellow unit coworkers. If the position has supervisory responsibility, the new supervisor should be able to spend time getting to know staff members.

Orientation programs are critical in easing the transition for new employees into an organization. As such, orientation should not be shortchanged. Sometimes organizations try to provide too much information in a compressed amount of time. Too much information can lead to overload and may create more anxiety for the new employee. Mixing methods for delivering orientation programs, including formal presentations, workshops, one-on-one meetings, social gatherings, and alone time for new employees to reflect and digest information, can help keep the process interesting and effective. Some information presented during orientation will not be retained, so to reinforce critical information, ongoing training and development programs are also needed.

Training and Development

employee training—Process of preparing employees for their responsibilities.

employee development—Ongoing process of learning, improvement, and change for workers in an organization.

Employee training refers to the process of preparing employees for the work that they do. **Employee development** is a broader concept and implies an ongoing process of learning and improvement. Block (1996) differentiates between the two concepts by stating that training tends to be management imposed and focused on organizational concerns, whereas learning and development should be employee initiated and focused on the concerns of the employees or their unit.

Training and development programs may focus on the following:

▶ Preparing employees to operate within specific organizational protocols or systems

▶ Providing employees with specific technical skills to do their jobs effectively

▶ Developing competencies that address key organizational concerns (e.g., team building, handling conflict, diversity)

▶ Preparing employees, managers, and units to navigate significant organizational change

▶ Providing employees with the resources and opportunities to continually learn, grow, and develop as both individuals and organizational actors

The goals of employee training and development will differ depending on the situation. New employees may need to focus on learning how the organization does business or building specific technical skills to do their jobs effectively. All employees may need to gain more knowledge on diversity or how to manage conflict in the workplace. Managers may need to spend time understanding larger organizational challenges and preparing their units to handle significant change. Individual employees may desire to take on greater challenges in their jobs or broaden their knowledge for their own self-improvement.

Investing time and resources in employee training and development is a necessary step in preparing employees to do their jobs effectively and to help their organizations meet their performance mandates. Employee training and development programs can be either high- or low-threshold investments. **High-threshold training,** which involves a considerable investment of time, expertise, or resources, includes

high-threshold training—Training methods that involve a considerable investment of time, expertise, or resources.

> ▶ workshops,
> ▶ retreats,
> ▶ clinics,
> ▶ formal education programs (colleges or universities), and
> ▶ professional certification or licensure programs.

Low-threshold training, which can achieve results through modest investments of time or resources, includes

low-threshold training—Training methods that can achieve results through modest investments of time or resources.

> ▶ meetings,
> ▶ job shadowing (observation),
> ▶ job coaching (observation, practice, and feedback),
> ▶ employee mentoring programs,
> ▶ providing access to professional resources (trade magazines, Internet and intranet access),
> ▶ professional association involvement and conference attendance,
> ▶ networking,
> ▶ job enrichment (adding responsibilities that provide opportunities for professional growth),
> ▶ job rotation (providing opportunities to work in different positions or units), and
> ▶ committee or task-force assignments.

Performance Appraisal

Performance appraisal, also referred to as *employee evaluation,* is used by managers to achieve several goals:

> ▶ Provide feedback on performance.
> ▶ Provide opportunities for ongoing learning and education.
> ▶ Stimulate employee motivation.
> ▶ Help make decisions related to commendation, promotion, discipline, or termination.
> ▶ Draw connections between an employee's individual job performance and unit or organizational goals.

Employees need information related to their job performance in order to effectively fulfill the responsibilities of their position. Without access to this information, employees may continue to repeat mistakes, waste resources, or underserve customers. Managers may find it difficult to make decisions about pay increases or promotions without documented information related to an employee's job performance. Absent such information, these decisions may be perceived as arbitrary or unfair. Employees also cannot seek out opportunities for further development if they are unaware of their strengths and weaknesses. In some situations, employees who are terminated or disciplined without regular, documented performance reviews may legitimately perceive that they have been denied due process or, worse, discriminated against. Regular performance assessment benefits both the employee and the employer, and it can be used as an employee development tool as well as a framework for managerial decision making (George & Jones, 2002).

Performance appraisal can be formal, informal, or a mix of both. Examples of informal performance reviews include frequent meetings to discuss progress, pats on the back, constructive criticism, short handwritten notes, and e-mails for jobs well done or a performance that missed the mark. In some cases, informal performance reviews can be documented—copies of handwritten notes can be placed in employees' files, e-mails can be saved and copied, and meetings can be noted. However, the purpose of these informal reviews is to keep lines of communication open and to be sure that expectations are clearly articulated, problems are addressed, and good performance is recognized. Informal methods are useful because they provide immediate feedback for employees and allow flexibility in adjusting to the information that is exchanged.

Formal performance appraisal takes place less frequently and typically relies on specific methods of measurement and feedback. For example, an organization may conduct formal performance reviews twice per year, or perhaps more frequently during an employee's introductory probation (if one exists). Formal performance reviews rely on either objective or subjective measures of performance. Objective measures are used when performance is determined by specific numeric results, such as participation counts, dollars raised, or new members signed up. Subjective measures are used when performance cannot be objectively measured. They rely on an evaluator's interpretation of performance based on preestablished criteria.

One of the main challenges of formal performance appraisal, especially when subjective measures are used, is the accuracy of the assessment.

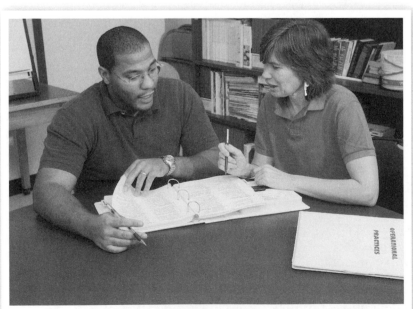

A manager conducts a formal performance appraisal with an employee, providing him with feedback on his job performance and resources that will enhance his development.

Different people have different perceptions of performance, and bias is possible unless there are multiple measures of assessment. One way to help prevent bias is to develop a process that adds a variety of voices to the assessment process, a method George and Jones (2002) call *360-degree appraisal*. In this process, performance appraisal is conducted by those who come in contact with the employee or are in a position to assess performance. This includes "peers, superiors, subordinates, and customers or clients" (p. 156). It may also make sense to include the employee's perspective through self-appraisal. By providing multiple measures of assessment, supervisors can look for patterns in the results, as well as note where there might be areas of disagreement among assessors.

As part of performance appraisal, employees should have the opportunity to discuss the results with their supervisors, ask questions, request resources to help them improve performance, and set goals with the supervisor to be achieved by the next appraisal. Supervisors should be sure to document questions, requests, and future performance goals in writing and have the employee sign off on the process.

The personnel process is time consuming but one of the most important management functions in any agency. The value of human resources has been demonstrated throughout the entire text and should be understood by all professionals for the sake of agency efficiency and effectiveness.

Managing Volunteers

Volunteers are people who provide labor or services for the benefit of the community through their own free will and without monetary reward. A recent study in Canada revealed that approximately 12 million Canadians over the age of 15, or 45 percent of the population, engage in volunteerism (Statistics Canada, 2006). In the United States, more than 61 million people over the age of 16, or about 27 percent of the total population, volunteered for an organization in 2006 (U.S. Bureau of Labor Statistics, 2006).

volunteers—People who provide labor or services for the benefit of the community through their own free will and without monetary reward.

For many leisure services organizations, volunteers are important staff members. Volunteers provide critical functions, including program delivery, administration, logistics, and advisory roles (Mull, Bayless, & Jamieson, 2005). It is difficult to discuss specific volunteer positions in leisure services because responsibilities are so different from organization to organization and from community to community. However, volunteer management is not much different from other forms of personnel management. Leisure services managers should think in terms of four broad areas regarding volunteers: recruitment, training, supervision, and retention.

Volunteer Recruitment

Leisure services organizations need to ask two key questions when thinking about recruiting possible volunteers. The answers to these questions will help guide the organization in developing a sound volunteer recruitment strategy:

▶ What types of volunteer positions are needed? Different organizations have different volunteer needs. For example, some organizations with limited full-time staff may rely on volunteers to take on significant administrative or program responsibilities. Other organizations may rely on volunteers for logistical or support purposes, such as coordinating travel, fund-raising, publicity, or maintenance. Still others may use volunteers as board members or on policy-making teams. As with full-time staff, volunteers may serve different clientele or program areas. For example, volunteers may work specifically with youth, the elderly, or people with disabilities. They may serve as sport coaches, program leaders, or personal care attendants. Carefully considering the types of volunteer positions that are needed will help the organization search for the volunteers who are best suited to the jobs.

▶ What competencies and skills are needed for the position? Developing competency sets for volunteer positions is just as important as identifying needed competencies for full-time staff. As we have noted, volunteers can fulfill a range of roles within the organization, and many of these roles require specific competencies. Depending on the position, it may not be enough to settle for anyone who is willing to do the job. Certain volunteer positions require specific competencies, such as the ability to teach sport skills, write grant proposals, speak effectively in public, or drive a 15-passenger van. Considering the necessary competencies associated with each volunteer position is critical in attempting to recruit the right person for the position. Furthermore, having a job description for volunteer positions can better match the volunteer and the job.

Each of these questions is important because the answers help to create strong matches between position and volunteer. Research shows that the motivation to volunteer can best be understood as a leisure choice (Strigas, 2006) and that satisfaction from volunteerism is derived in part from the job setting and the psychological benefits that are gained from the volunteer experience (Silverberg, Marshall, & Ellis, 2001). In other words, identifying volunteers that are committed to the role that they are about to fulfill is an important consideration in the recruitment process.

In answering these two questions, leisure services organizations need to decide whether it is appropriate to narrowly target or broadly advertise for volunteers. Some positions are best suited to a careful, individualized, tailored recruitment process. Recruiting an advisory board member, for example, might best be accomplished by talking individually to program leaders who have established track records as friends of recreation. On the other end of the spectrum, recruiting volunteers for a 5K road race might include advertising in newspapers, connecting with the local school district, and engaging the local business community.

Depending on the position and the role that the volunteer is expected to fulfill, it might be prudent to conduct some form of background screening, such as checking work references, conducting criminal background checks, verifying physical addresses and social security numbers, drug testing, and checking the public sexual offender registry. The NRPA (2006) recommends that all volunteers who are working with vulnerable populations (e.g., youth, elderly, people with disabilities) should be subject to background screening. Despite this recommendation, a recent study in Michigan found that only 25 percent of park and recreation agencies required background screening for all volunteers, and only 34.6 percent required screening for volunteers who work with children (Ellard, Geisthardt, & Schilling, 2004).

Training and Supervision

Too often, volunteers are left without proper training to fulfill their roles effectively. For example, it has been estimated that up to 90 percent of volunteer youth sport coaches have not gone through a formalized coach training program (Ewing, Gano-Overway, Branta, & Seefeldt, 2002). This is a concern in the broader field of youth development; volunteers often report feeling unprepared to work effectively with children and adolescents (Huebner, Walker, & McFarland, 2003). Other groups of volunteers, including those working with the elderly, with participants with disabilities, and in administrative positions, often experience the same lack of training support.

Once volunteers are recruited and selected, the leisure services organization is responsible for orienting and training them for the role they are going to perform. The type of training provided for volunteers is going to depend on the nature and scope of the position. For example, event volunteers working a 5K road race will need a basic orientation and training for the duties that they will perform on the day of the race. Volunteers who have more frequent contact with participants, work with vulnerable populations, or perform roles that require significant responsibility will need more in-depth training. The following can be helpful guides to structuring a volunteer training program:

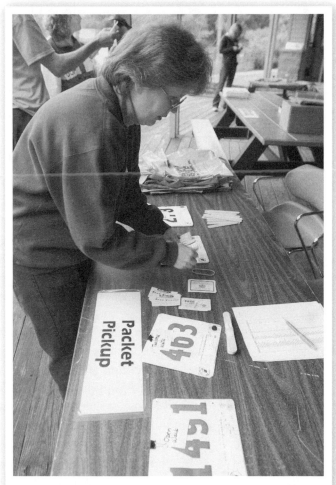

Volunteers play a critical role in many leisure services organizations, often providing direct service to customers, as is the case with this volunteer for a 5K race.

- ▶ Provide volunteers with information on the agency, including the mission, vision, goals, and objectives.
- ▶ Develop volunteer job descriptions that list specific job roles and scope of responsibilities.
- ▶ Develop a set of expectations for the position, including estimated time commitment, meeting requirements, and behavior and ethical standards.
- ▶ Provide a list of policies and procedures applicable to the position, including purchasing guidelines, communication protocols, and risk management plans.
- ▶ Develop a system for communication, including one-on-one meetings to clarify expectations and provide feedback.
- ▶ Where applicable, require or encourage attendance at a training program that is applicable to the volunteer position (e.g., youth coach training, inclusion training, first aid and CPR training).

▶ Provide support for attendance at relevant professional conferences or workshops that are applicable to the position.

It is important to provide the support and resources to help volunteers do their jobs. Many volunteers want access to training and development resources, and developing these systems can maximize the volunteer experience and lead to higher levels of volunteer retention.

Retention

Keeping a solid core of volunteers is important for leisure services organizations because then the organization doesn't need to start over with new volunteers each year. This is especially important for programs that require continuity or that focus on building and maintaining relationships with participants. To a large extent, retention is dependent on sound recruiting, access to training and development, and effective supervision. If significant resources are devoted to these areas of volunteer management, then the organization is well on its way to a successful retention strategy. In addition, volunteer-recognition programs that recognize the effort and importance of volunteers can aid in the retention process.

Volunteer recognition can take many forms and can include both large-scale events and small tokens of appreciation. Some examples to consider for a volunteer-recognition program include the following:

▶ Thank-you letters
▶ Certificates
▶ Appreciation plaques
▶ Volunteer awards
▶ Staff apparel
▶ Dinners and banquets
▶ Appreciation weeks

Public recognition also plays a valuable role in increasing awareness of the volunteer opportunities that are available through an agency. This process can thus be a valuable recruiting tool for future volunteers.

Conclusion

▶ Much of what leisure services managers do on a daily basis involves planning, organizing, controlling, and leading personnel. Successful personnel management addresses the needs of the organization and the employee and involves both planning and processes. Personnel planning includes considering the capacity of an organization for accommodating staff. This requires analyzing existing staffing levels, fiscal resources, supervisory resources, physical resources, and administrative support systems. Personnel planning also includes considering the personnel needs of an organization. Organizations must consider the composition of their staff and commit to ensuring a diverse workforce.

▶ Personnel processes involve developing a system for staffing and employee training and development. This system includes conceptualizing organizational needs; developing job announcements; recruiting qualified applicants; selecting and hiring the best candidate; creating orientation, training, and development processes; and providing feedback on employee performance through formal and informal appraisal.

REVIEW QUESTIONS

1. What is the difference between the terms *personnel* and *human resources*? What are the core assumptions of Bolman and Deal's human resources philosophy?

2. What are the organizational capacity factors that leisure services managers need to consider before adding additional staff?

3. What are the differences between technical skills, human relations skills, and conceptual skills?

4. What are some of the key diversity trends in the United States and Canada? Why is increasing diversity in society an issue for leisure services managers to consider?

5. What are the key federal and state/provincial discrimination laws in the United States and Canada? What is the impact of each of these laws on the hiring process?

6. What are the key components of a job description?

7. What is a job announcement used for? What content areas should it include?

8. What are the advantages and disadvantages of hiring from inside and outside the organization?

9. What is a competency-based interview question?

10. What are the three main forms of candidate interviews?

11. What should be included in a general orientation program for employees? What about a job-specific orientation program? Why are orientation programs necessary in the first place?

12. What are the main differences between the concepts of training and development?

13. What are some examples of high- and low-threshold training or development programs?

14. What are the key decisions involved in the performance appraisal process?

15. How is volunteer management similar to yet different from managing paid staff members?

Check out the online student resource at www.HumanKinetics.com/LeisureServicesManagement for additional material, including sample documents, case studies, Web links, and more.

KEY WORDS

motivation, three needs theory, equity theory, expectancy theory, rewards, extrinsic rewards, intrinsic rewards, monetary rewards, nonmonetary rewards, performance-based rewards, membership-based rewards, progressive discipline

COMPETENCY CHECK

Take another look at table 1.3 (page 9) to see how you assessed these related competencies.

27. Supervise, discipline, and evaluate a diverse staff.
28. Motivate employees.

CHAPTER 11

Motivation, Rewards, and Discipline

1. Understand foundational and current thinking on motivation in leisure services organizations.
2. Understand how to develop and grow employees in leisure services organizations.
3. Explain ways to reward employees in leisure services organizations.
4. Define the concept of self-care in a management capacity.
5. Discuss the effective use of discipline in leisure services organizations.
6. Understand the steps to take when hiring and terminating employees.

A Day in the Life

A typical day for me at the hotel is supervising the interns in the department. This includes watching over the indoor/outdoor pools, fitness center, bike rentals, kids' camp, and the towel hut. Teamwork is very important in the hotel business. In fact, "Teamwork Works" is one of our 10 basic beliefs at the Crowne Plaza Hilton Head. A manager is expected to run a successful department

in the hotel, and to do this they must rely on several people in their department to help them. To ensure the greatest level of teamwork, a manager should appreciate his or her employees. A little "thank you" or "good job" goes a long way.

Joey Hasselbring
Recreation Supervisor
Crowne Plaza Beach Resort
Hilton Head Island, South Carolina

Throughout this text you have been learning the important skills and knowledge you need to effectively and efficiently manage a leisure services organization. However, organizations do not accomplish goals, satisfy client needs, or create active and involved communities—people do. Employees are the most critical resource in meeting goals and fulfilling the mission of an organization. This chapter gives you a deeper understanding of how to help employees make the most of their talents and achieve organizational objectives.

In this chapter we discuss employees; however, many organizations involved with leisure, sport, and recreation have not only paid staff but volunteer staff as well. The principles for managing, motivating, and rewarding volunteers are similar to those for paid employees. Volunteers are working members of an organization who require motivating, managing, leading, and evaluation, just like paid employees. The term *employee* will be used throughout most of the chapter; however, in most instances the general principles of rewards and motivation apply to both. In addition, a short section addresses rewards for nonpaid staff. Finally, an important part of managing human resources is the effective use of discipline and, less frequently, dismissing employees. This chapter provides an overview of this challenging area of management.

Employee Development

In simple terms, employee development is the strategic investment of an organization in its people. Many organizations spend time and money selecting the appropriate technology or equipment for a facility but neglect a similar investment in their people. Developing employees is a critical management task that begins with the initial stages of hiring. When recruiting, interviewing, and hiring new employees, an organization communicates what it values, what it expects, and how it rewards its employees. This can be done intentionally through carefully orchestrated recruitment and new-employee socialization, or it can be more haphazard if an organization fails to pay attention to the details at this critical juncture in the employee's tenure. Investing time and effort in socializing new employees often pays future dividends by avoiding misunderstandings and developing employees who will be more self-reliant in the future. Employees require not only leadership but also motivation. The following section briefly summarizes the research on motivation in the workplace.

Motivation

Organizations need employees who are willing and skilled. Training and developing competencies is essential; however, without motivation, the willingness to perform may not be present. **Motivation** is one of the most studied areas in organizational behavior, and we have come to view employee motivation in several ways.

A number of foundational theories have laid the groundwork for an understanding of motivation. As you will recall from chapter 2, Maslow's hierarchy of needs, McGregor's theory X and theory Y, and Herzberg's motivation-hygiene theory are all early theories that attempted to explain motivation within the workplace. Maslow suggested that unless people have basic needs fulfilled, they will be unable to progress to the higher-level needs that drive the behavior most organizations expect from employees. McGregor focused on whether the manager views employees as inherently lazy and in need of coercion (theory X) or whether they enter the workplace wanting to contribute and gain personal fulfillment from their work (theory Y). Finally, Herzberg's work focused more on reward systems. He suggested that some benefits, such as pay, are hygiene factors—necessary but not sufficient to motivate employees. Motivators, on the other hand, could have a positive influence on behavior. These early motivation theories have been a springboard to several current approaches that have received significant support. Three of the most prevalent modern theories are the three needs theory, equity theory, and expectancy theory.

motivation—Internal or external factors that affect the direction, intensity, and persistence of behavior.

Three Needs Theory

You may notice that some people are strongly driven to achieve whereas others are more concerned with different things such as friendship or being in control. David McClelland and his colleagues at Harvard University have spent more than a quarter of a century investigating this phenomenon. McClelland's **three needs theory** (McClelland, 1961) proposes that in most work situations, there are three relevant needs or motives for employee behavior: the need for achievement, the need for power, and the need for affiliation.

The need for achievement is the desire to strive for excellence, to meet goals, and to do things better. People with this need seek tasks in which they can be successful and in which they feel they contributed to that success. As such they often avoid extreme tasks—those that are very easy and those that are extremely difficult. The need for power is the need to influence the behavior of others. People with this need focus on being influential; they enjoy being in charge and tend to prosper in situations that are status oriented or competitive. Finally, the need for affiliation is a desire for close relationships and a friendly place to work. People with this need seek to be liked and accepted by others. Not surprisingly, they are more likely to seek out cooperative settings and situations where they can have a high level of mutual understanding. This particular need is the least studied of the three.

three needs theory—Motivation theory proposing that people are motivated by three needs: the need for achievement, the need for power, and the need for affiliation.

Let's look at three hypothetical employees working in a marketing role for a minor league baseball team. Bill is in charge of game-day preparations. He is meticulous in making sure everything is right and often exceeds the standard that management has set for the facility. Bill loves it when his manager recognizes the quality of his work and his commitment to excellence. In the three needs theory, Bill would be driven by a need to achieve.

Jillian, on the other hand, is the corporate sales leader for the team's marketing department. Her job is to sell the corporate boxes at the stadium and develop effective marketing strategies to attract the support of the local corporate community. Jillian loves the public attention and status of this position. She is driven by increased sales numbers and keeping her corporate clients coming back year after year. She has a knack for getting others to help her make the wishes of her corporate clients come true, such as meeting with players, throwing out the first pitch, and even on one occasion having a company bring its employees and families to sleep on the field and watch movies after a ball game. Jillian reflects a need for power.

Finally, James is the team's community and public relations coordinator. He is all about relationships and loves the social nature of his job. He helps bring together the needs of the club and the community. James' rewards are the strong friendships he has developed and the focus on cooperation that his job demands. James would be a prime example of needs affiliation.

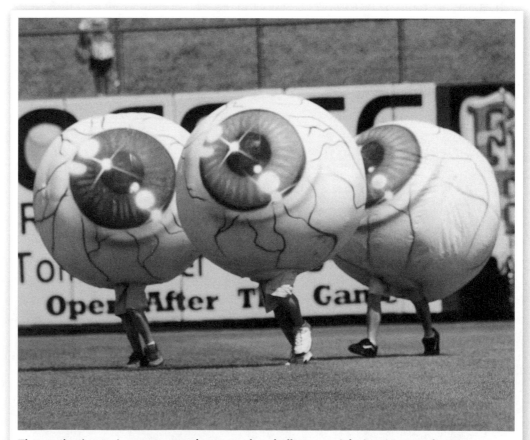

The motivation to increase attendance at a baseball game might inspire a marketing manager to try unusual or intriguing promotions.

Equity Theory

Most people want to be treated fairly, and when they feel that they are not receiving fair treatment, they may act in some way to change the situation. For example, if you worked long and hard developing a new program for your local recreation department and received little positive feedback whereas a colleague quickly threw together a new program idea in a couple of hours and then received a promotion for that work, you might not feel that the promotion was fair. This notion of fairness is what led John Stacey Adams to develop the **equity theory** of motivation (1965).

Equity theory looks at employees' comparison of their inputs (what they put into a job) and their perceived outcomes (what they get out of it). This input–output ratio is then compared with what Adams (1965) called *relevant others*. In simple terms, employees look at their effort and what they get back, whether it is something tangible such as a promotion or intangible such as praise or recognition. They then compare this ratio with someone who matters to them, such as a coworker or a friend in another organization. Adams calls this person a *referent*. A referent can be an other, a system, or oneself (self-referent). Other referents are people with similar roles, such as other lifeguards at the pool and other lifeguards at another facility across town. System referents are a comparison of the situation with the policies and procedures of the organization, such as pay or promotion. Lastly, a self-referent is a unique comparison based on a person's own contacts and experience. For example, an employee may have put in less effort in a previous job and been paid more than at her current job.

If employees assess their situation as inequitable, they can see it as underrewarded or overrewarded. Feeling underrewarded, where the employee gives more than she receives, may be the most common perception. However, overrewarded perceptions are also common. For example, a person who loves tennis, works summers at a tennis club, and gets to play most of the day may perceive this situation as overrewarded. Someone who feels underqualified for a position, such as a new graduate who gets a great job, may perceive an inequity based on greater output than input.

When inputs match outputs, a balance, or equity, is achieved. The theory suggests that this is the desired state and that employees will act in ways to return to a perception of equity if an inequity exists. Employees who are overrewarded may increase their output in order to correct the inequity, whereas employees who are underrewarded may do the opposite and reduce their output. Employees may also change their perceptions of the situation to rectify the inequity.

equity theory—Proposes that employee motivation is based on the comparison of employee inputs to perceived outcomes of a particular action.

Expectancy Theory

Expectancy theory builds on the idea of fairness and holds that people expect certain results from their actions. For example, a runner who trains hard may expect a certain time improvement. The actual behavior (training hard) will be more likely to occur if achieving the fastest route time is something that the runner values. Victor Vroom's expectancy theory addresses these issues and may be the most supported motivation theory. Vroom suggests that the expectation of how a behavior will influence a given outcome and how attractive that outcome is to a person is the best way to understand employee motivation (Vroom, 1964).

expectancy theory—Assumes that motivation is based on employees' comparison of how hard they have to work, what the reward will be, and how attractive that reward is to the person.

Expectancy theory has three parts:

1. The effort–performance link refers to the expectation or probability that a given effort will result in a given outcome.
2. The performance–reward link is the degree to which a person believes that performance at a certain level will lead to the attainment of a desired outcome.
3. Attractiveness refers to the importance a person places on a potential reward or outcome.

For example, say you are a salesperson for a professional sport franchise. You believe that if you work hard, you will perform well. The more calls you make, the more tickets you will sell. You also believe that if you sell a lot of tickets (i.e., perform well), you will be rewarded financially through salary and bonuses and also through a promotion to your dream job of sales manager for the team. This process shows that individual effort leads to performance, which leads to organizational rewards and finally achievement of an attractive individual award.

Conversely, if your actions do not seem linked to performance, you may have reduced motivation. Say you are a student in a leisure management course. You start the course highly motivated and put in a great deal of effort, but when you take the midterm, you score much lower than expected. You may find your motivation lacking in the second part of the term, and you miss more classes and just skim the textbook. What happened? Expectancy theory would suggest that the link between effort and performance was broken with the midterm. You may have perceived the midterm as unfair because trivial questions were weighted too heavily or because it was an essay exam and you felt the instructor's grading was off base. If the link between effort, performance, and outcome is broken, motivation may be reduced. If, however, you felt the exam was fair, then you may have increased your motivation knowing that more effort was required to reach your goal.

Expectancy theory offers several practical applications for managers looking to motivate employees. First, the theory emphasizes rewards and outcomes that an employee values; therefore, managers must provide rewards that employees want, and they must ensure that employees understand what they need to do in order to get the performance and in turn the rewards they desire. Second, expectancy theory is about perceptions, not actual behavior. This requires continual feedback on performance to help employees align their perceptions with the reality of what is required. Looking again at the classroom example, the professor could sit down with you and explain the expectations for getting a desired grade in the class. The professor would want to understand the reward that you desired and what effort you felt was necessary to achieve it. The professor could then help to clarify what was needed and get you on track for a successful second half of the course.

Reward Systems

rewards—The return one receives for engaging in a particular behavior.

One of a manager's most important tools is the ability to select **rewards** and time the rewards properly. Even if managers are not solely responsible for financial rewards, they can use a number of tools to increase the effectiveness of their organization.

Reward systems can address several important managerial objectives as they relate to employee motivation. A solid reward system requires concerted attention in its development. The following sections provide a basis for a well-constructed reward system.

Purposes of Reward Systems

Reward systems serve several purposes in organizations. Effective reward systems help an organization be more competitive, retain key employees, and reduce turnover. Reward systems also can enhance employee motivation and reinforce the image of an organization among key stakeholders or future employees.

People are the most important resource for organizational competitiveness, and keeping them on the job is a key task for any manager. Competition to attract and keep the best employees is intense. For people looking for a career opportunity, that's great news, but as a manager of an organization needing to keep the best and brightest, it is a challenge. It may be even harder in the nonprofit and public sectors where flexibility in providing financial rewards may be more limited than in a commercial context. Retaining employees saves money on retraining costs, improves the consistency of services, and allows for relationships to develop between clients and the organization. In addition, proper rewards systems can reduce absences. Absences cause innumerable headaches for managers. Instructors who don't show up, too few staff members at busy times, and the lack of a cleanup crew can all increase workplace stress. Absences not only affect the manager but also fellow employees who need to pick up the slack and clients who feel the brunt of too few employees on site.

As suggested earlier, understanding who, what, and when to reward can improve employees' performance. However, the improper use of rewards can have a debilitating effect on employee performance. Managers need to understand their employees' perceptions of the importance and fairness of the reward and then clearly communicate what needs to be done to receive the reward.

Effective use of rewards can encourage employees to gain the skills that are necessary to help them and the organization grow. This can also increase their desire to continue being part of the organization. For example, an organization can pay and provide time off for employees who want to take advanced courses in an area that is valuable for the organization. Some organizations may even provide time off or support to help employees advance their own personal goals or skill sets.

Ideally, an organization wants employees who not only show up to work but are excited about being there as well. This passion for work has been referred to as *affective commitment*. Although research is somewhat preliminary, there is some indication that affective commitment can be strengthened by rewards that enhance employee perceptions of being supported and having control of the work situation.

Finally, reward systems can also help with recruiting efforts. Just as happy customers may be the best advertisement for a particular product, happy employees are often a great tool for recruiting new employees and making the organization a workplace of choice. Think about the kind of job you want. Often you will easily be able to identify an organization that stands above the others as a great place to work. As a consequence of this, the organization can attract the best and brightest, creating a virtuous circle whereby it becomes an even more attractive workplace. Hopefully you can see that establishing the right reward structure for an organization is critical to its success. The following sections delve into the details of various reward structures.

Types of Rewards

Understanding how each employee perceives and values different rewards is an essential part of management. Managers need to grasp an understanding of extrinsic and intrinsic rewards.

extrinsic rewards—Tangible rewards such as pay, bonuses, benefits, or extra time off.

Extrinsic rewards are external rewards tied to certain employee behaviors, skills, time, or roles in an organization. How employees perceive these rewards relevant to their performance and the rewards given to others will ultimately determine the effectiveness of the rewards. Managers also need to understand how much value each employee places on specific extrinsic rewards. For example, a well-paid but overworked employee may value additional vacation time or a reduced workload more than a few extra dollars. Money, praise, awards, and incentive prizes such as tickets to a concert or a game are all examples of extrinsic motivators. Whatever motivator the manager chooses, the employee must see the reward as a motivator for it to be effective. For example, if the extrinsic reward is tickets to the opera, an employee who hates the opera likely would not be motivated by the tickets. On the other hand, if the employee is a football fan and the extrinsic reward is tickets to a major game, the motivator might be more effective.

intrinsic rewards—Intangible rewards based on feelings of accomplishment or personal satisfaction.

It is simpler to explain what intrinsic rewards are by discussing what they are not. **Intrinsic rewards** do not have an obvious external incentive; that is, people are not acting to get a tangible reward, be it time off or money. Instead, they act because it feels good or provides some form of internal satisfaction. Intrinsic rewards are often more highly valued and more effective over time, yet using them is a difficult managerial task. Intrinsic rewards derive from employees feeling good about the job they have done, the effort they have put forward, or the role they played in a team project. Intrinsic rewards in the workplace come from the job itself, so to provide intrinsic reinforcement, a manager should enrich the job. Job enrichment involves improving work processes and environments so they are more satisfying for employees, such as eliminating dysfunctional elements or enlarging jobs (increasing the duties and responsibilities of a job).

Developing an effective reward system can be a difficult task. The following sections provide some guidance on the basics of an effective reward system. These sections focus almost exclusively on extrinsic rewards, but intrinsic rewards should also be considered when developing each employee's job.

Monetary Versus Nonmonetary Rewards

monetary rewards—Rewards that have a direct financial price, such as a salary or performance bonus.

Monetary rewards are most commonly given in the form of pay increases, bonuses, or increases in benefits, such as pension or health care premiums. Such rewards can be divided into two categories: direct and indirect compensation (table 11.1). Both contribute to the financial betterment of an employee. Direct compensation is relatively straightforward and consists of increases in hourly pay, increases in hours (for nonsalaried employees), increases in salary, merit pay based on perfor-

Table 11.1 **Direct Monetary Rewards, Indirect Monetary Rewards, and Nonmonetary Rewards**

Direct monetary compensation	Indirect monetary compensation	Nonmonetary compensation
Base salary	Pension contributions	On-site gym
Hourly wages	401(k) (U.S.) RRSP (Canada)	On-site cafeteria
Merit pay	Paid leave	Learning opportunities
Bonuses	Various forms of insurance	Use of recreation facilities

mance, seniority pay based on time with an organization, and bonuses based on the achievement of individual, group, or organizational objectives.

Indirect monetary compensation includes increases to benefits or the addition of benefits such as a dental plan. It can also include paid leave in the form of vacation days, days off for training, or longer time off such as a sabbatical, as well as paid leave for illness, caring for a child, or caring for an elderly parent. Additionally, some organizations may offer services as part of an indirect compensation package, such as on-site child care, an elder care program, an on-site cafeteria, a games room or gym, and confidential counseling services for employees and their families. Again, indirect compensation should be valuable to employees and ideally should offer choices from a range of services.

Nonmonetary rewards cost the organization but do not directly improve the employee's financial position (table 11.1). Supplying employees with the best tools possible to do their job is an example, such as providing a new high-end laptop or having an excellent training facility for coaches at a university. A good office location, choice of furnishings, or special parking place can all be nonmonetary rewards. Employees may not know the full details of pay and other monetary benefits of coworkers, but nonmonetary rewards are often visible and can create perceptions of inequity in an organization. In some cases, this may be the intent of managers who want employees to strive to achieve the stereotypical corner office, but often it may also unintentionally encourage feelings of inequity. That inequity may have positive implications for an organization if employees strive to increase performance, or it can result in turnover and reduced

nonmonetary rewards—Rewards without a financial price attached to them, such as praise.

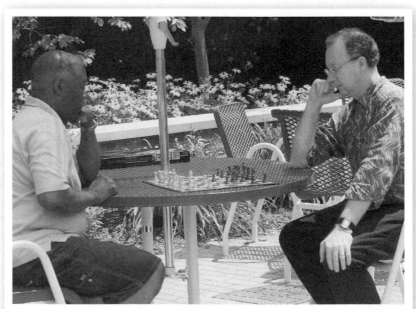

Nonmonetary rewards include such things as an outdoor space for employees to take a break from the stresses of work or an area where coworkers informally gather to socialize.

Creative Low- or No-Cost Ideas

Rewarding employees doesn't need to be expensive, nor should it be boring! Following are some ideas for employee rewards ranging from the simple to the more unique.

- ▶ Write employees a thank-you note.
- ▶ Surprise them with coffee from the best local coffee shop.
- ▶ Hold a staff meeting at an afternoon ball game.
- ▶ Give an afternoon-off pass to be used whenever they want to do something fun.
- ▶ Have the staff develop their own list of great gifts for under $20 and use that list to reward them.
- ▶ Bring in a comedian, magician, or local band at lunch.
- ▶ Give gift cards, which are great and easy.
- ▶ Give away team pedometers and count steps as the team walks across the country, state, or province. Have special lunches celebrating the places reached.
- ▶ Bring a dunk tank in for dunk-the-boss day.
- ▶ Have a treasure hunt.
- ▶ Turn an office into a miniature golf course.
- ▶ Have an employee's car secretly washed and detailed while they work.

performance. As with any reward, nonmonetary rewards need to be carefully thought out before being implemented.

Performance-Based Versus Membership-Based Rewards

One of the most difficult challenges for managers is to decide what to base rewards on. A common distinction is performance-based versus membership-based rewards. As the name implies, **performance-based rewards** are tied to the ability of an individual, team, group, or organization to meet some previously agreed-upon standard of performance. Performance rewards are based on an evaluation of contribution and awards are allocated based on that evaluation.

Membership-based rewards are allocated solely for being part of a group within an organization. These rewards commonly include annual cost-of-living increases to a base salary or support for an equity policy. For example, if a park and recreation department was looking to encourage staff to have master's degrees or obtain certification, they might offer pay incentives for having either or both. Membership-based rewards are also often tied to length of time with an organization. For instance, after a certain length of service with an organization, employees may receive a certain percentage increase to their pay or be eligible for additional benefits. In a unionized environment, many of these rewards are spelled out in a labor agreement.

To illustrate the difference between the two structures, let's look at annual raises. A performance-based structure means that each employee's performance is evaluated and raises are based on performance, with the highest performers getting the

performance-based rewards—Individual or group rewards based on the accomplishment of a certain goal or level of performance, such as a performance bonus for high levels of client service.

membership-based rewards—Rewards received for being the member of a specific group rather than for individual performance, such as an annual cost-of-living pay raise.

most money. A membership-based structure means that all employees receive the same raise regardless of performance. Membership structures can be demotivating to high performers because they get the same rewards despite working harder.

Nontraditional Rewards

As more and more managers understand the importance of individualizing reward systems, the use of nontraditional rewards will continue to grow. Time is often a key constraint, and for many people work is a major time commitment. Ways in which employees can individualize their work schedule are becoming increasingly important rewards. Four methods of individualization are reduced workweeks, staggered daily schedules, flextime, and working from home.

Reduced Workweek

A reduced workweek often sees employees working a 4-day week instead of 5 days. In return for that extra day, employees work longer on their 4 days in the office. For example, in a 40-hour workweek from Monday through Friday, employees would work 8-hour days, but the reduced workweek would see hours increase to 10 hours a day for 4 days. The benefits to the employees are longer blocks of time to take care of their personal lives, less frequent and often less busy commutes, and ultimately more useful time for themselves. The organization has no additional expenses and evidence suggests that absenteeism and time lost for personal reasons decreases.

However, there are also downsides for both employees and the organization. Parents, for example, may find it difficult to find child care that is open late or early enough to accommodate the longer work schedule. The longer work day may also be a constraint to people who are involved in weekly evening activities, be it coaching a team or attending an art class. Some jobs may also not lend themselves to longer days. A lifeguard or sport instructor may be considerably less effective in those last 2 hours, which can lead to decreased performance and in some cases safety risks. Also, the hours and timing of work may affect service to clients. Even if an organization maintains its regular schedule, clients expecting to reach a particular person during traditional business hours may find the new schedule frustrating. Finally, reduced workweeks seem to be most effective when employees themselves are involved in creating the schedule. Understand that employees participating in reduced workweeks need to be scheduled so that the entire organization is not gone on Friday!

Staggered Daily Schedule

An alternative to a reduced workweek may be a staggered daily schedule. Employees still work their designated weekly hours but can allocate those hours in different ways. For example, one employee may want to come in late and leave later to accommodate dropping off children. Someone else may prefer being in the office an hour earlier and leaving an hour earlier. These schedules may even be adapted weekly or monthly to accommodate changing employee needs. This idea meets employees' individual needs but can often be difficult to manage. Again, a staggered daily schedule may not be appropriate in all settings and must consider not only employee needs but also organizational requirements and client desires.

Flextime

Flextime allows some employee freedom while still meeting client and organizational needs. Employees are expected to be in the office during a certain time frame, usually ranging from 4 to 6 hours, such as 9:30 a.m. to 3:30 p.m. Flextime emphasizes productivity and allows the employee some leeway in that flexibility zone (before 9:30 a.m. and after 3:30 p.m.).

For example, take Pat, an aquatics programmer. Pat has two school-aged children and requires some flexibility to drop them off and pick them up at school. Pat has worked with the employer and agreed that he will be at the pool between the hours of 9:30 and 3:30 but will complete the rest of his work elsewhere. This ensures that Pat's coworkers and clients can reach him at predictable times while still allowing him the personal flexibility he requires at this point in his life. This type of arrangement has been effective for many organizations and employees, although obviously it won't work in all situations.

Flextime also allows a staff person more control over their hours. For example, a special events coordinator works 5 hours over the weekend. The following week, the coordinator comes in an hour later than usual each day.

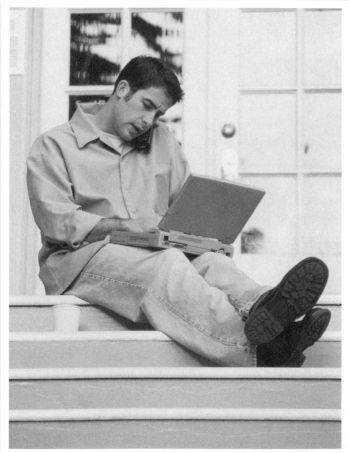

Telecommuting allows an employee the freedom to enjoy the sunshine and a latte while still keeping in touch with the office.

Working From Home

As technology has advanced, the option of working at home for some or all of the workday is becoming increasingly possible. A high-speed Internet connection and a laptop computer connected to the workplace network provide many people with everything they need to do their job. Obviously this arrangement is more suited to some positions than others. A job developing programs for a municipal recreation department would be more suited to a work-at-home plan as opposed to the job of instructing the programs. Working for some or all of the workweek at home can offer fewer workplace distractions, allow employees time to concentrate on projects that are important to the organization, and make more effective use of the day by eliminating the need to commute as well as the usual time killers present in most offices.

However, working from home is not for everyone. The distractions of the home require discipline, and for those who consistently work at home the blurred distinction between home and office can be unsettling. Additionally, monitoring employees at home is nearly impossible. Evaluation needs to be performance based and work-at-home schemes do not work for organizations that want to monitor how employees spend their time. Allowing employees to work at home part of the time, however, may be an excellent compromise for both employees and the organization.

Four Options for Rewards

So far we have discussed the purposes and types of rewards. This section addresses four options that managers can base rewards on: job, skill, seniority, and performance.

Job-Based Rewards

Traditionally, rewards were based on position, or the role employees hold in an organization. A manager evaluates one job in relation to another and gives rewards based on those evaluations. A programming position may be evaluated as more valuable than an instructor and the instructor position as more valuable than the front-desk clerk. Jobs that are more valuable tend to have greater responsibility, but they also may be more intrinsically appealing and offer greater opportunities for achievement and autonomy.

Skill-Based Rewards

Using skills as a basis essentially rewards employees for what they know and do that helps meet the needs of the organization. As employees gain more skills, they can do many more things in the workplace, which can also improve their satisfaction and overall organizational efficiency and effectiveness, much as described in systems theory (see chapter 2). However, paying for skills can be expensive. An employee may continue to add skills that are above and beyond the requirements of a job, which can make the cost to the organization more expensive than is reasonable. It could be argued that the job-based approach already accounts for skills needed; when allocating the work to positions, a manager is paying for skills the jobs require rather than the employees for every skill they have whether those skills are needed or not.

One context where a skills-based reward system may be optimal is where employee flexibility is key, as often occurs in smaller organizations that don't require full-time employees for all the roles that need filling. Nonprofit organizations or small sport organizations are examples where staff with experience in marketing, fund-raising, accounting, and event management may be highly desired rather than specialists in any one of those areas.

Seniority-Based Rewards

Seniority-based reward systems pay people for their tenure in a job or with an organization. This approach is often justified with the argument that time on the job leads to mastery and enhanced skills. Seniority-based systems do not account for changes in technology or best practices that may not always be learned on the job, nor do they account for individual effort in improving skills or performance on the job. Furthermore, seniority-based systems may create inequities between newer and more senior employees. A new employee may be the best fitness instructor yet receive 60 percent of the pay of a longer-serving employee who has much lower ratings. This can reduce motivation, reinforce behaviors that do not enhance organizational effectiveness, and increase workplace conflict.

Performance-Based Rewards

The example in the previous section may work better with a performance-based system where fitness instructors are rewarded based on how well they deliver programs to clients. Higher ratings, more returning clients, and fewer complaints may all be bases upon which to evaluate performance, and the better the rating, the greater the reward. However, this may not always work as planned. Better instructors may face more challenging classes where ratings are lower, or they may be personable and get good ratings but not be as effective at teaching the skills clients desire in the long run. This is not to say that performance rewards do not lead to organizational effectiveness but rather that careful attention must be paid to choosing how to measure performance (these ideas are discussed in more depth in chapters 10 and 14).

Putting It All Together

It may have become evident by this point that no one reward system is effective under all conditions. The most effective systems provide a mix of rewards that are meaningful to employees. For example, a fitness club may give annual salary increases to all employees on a job basis, giving similar increases to each grouping of job. In addition, it may give a small annual increase for seniority to demonstrate a value in staying with an organization over time. Individual or groups of employees may also receive increases based on courses they have taken over the course of a year as well as performance ratings on elements deemed important to their jobs.

This mix includes all four categories of reward bases. It could be further individualized to take into account individual values and desires. Rewards could be distributed through cafeteria-style benefits where employees get to choose how their individual increases will be applied. For instance, take an employee who is expecting a $1,500 increase from the four reward bases. Rather than dictating where that money will go, an organization can let the employee choose. Some may go to annual salary, some to an enhanced dental plan, and some to increased medical coverage. An employee's life circumstances, personal preferences, and life stage all are taken into account in a cafeteria-style approach to benefits.

Rewarding Volunteers

As stated in the beginning of this chapter, the principles of managing, leading, and motivating volunteers are similar to those for nonvolunteers. Managers must understand volunteers' commitment to the organization and convey their expectations to volunteers. Volunteers often come to an organization with a passion or some intrinsic interest in the organization that is their main reward for participation. However, managers should not forget that understanding what a volunteer values is just as important as it is for a paid employee. Volunteer roles require careful attention to job enrichment to help sustain the volunteer's intrinsic motivation. Volunteers' passion for the mission of the organization can also rub off on paid employees, and ensuring that passion remains can be a useful management tool.

Even though volunteers rarely receive monetary rewards, other extrinsic rewards should not be discounted (see chapter 10). Providing the appropriate tools for volunteers to do the job required, such as office space, a place to park, or anything else relevant to a particular context, should be considered. An organization can often unintentionally convey low status to volunteers by making them pay for their own parking, giving them no space to work, or having them borrow an employee's computer or phone. If volunteers are important to your organization, you must treat them that way and ensure that their value is felt throughout the organization.

Rewarding Yourself

The previous sections have been devoted to creating a caring and motivating environment for employees. Even though the leisure services profession focuses on health and well-being, a commonly neglected area of human resources management is caring for yourself, the manager. We can go back to early motivation theorists such as Maslow and Herzberg to understand that if base needs are not met, we are less likely to be high performers. The best thing you can do for your employees is to model the behavior of a high performer.

According to Dr. Jim Loehr and Tony Schwartz in their article "The Making of a Corporate Athlete" (2001), high performers not only focus on the work at hand but also take care of themselves by taking breaks throughout the day, committing to exercise and good nutrition, and remaining connected with family and community. You must be engaged with the workplace if you want your employees to do so. Encourage healthy behavior at work by inviting employees to hold meetings during a walk, making sure lunches at the office

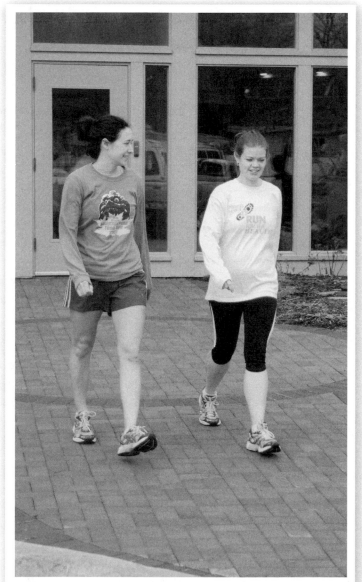

Effective managers promote healthy behavior at work by encouraging employees to care for themselves, such as by taking breaks for exercise.

have healthy options, and offering a fruit basket or healthy whole-grain baked items instead of Friday doughnuts.

Loehr and Schwartz suggest that we need to oscillate throughout the day. We can't run day after day at 110 percent. Instead, you should work like a professional athlete, totally focusing on the task at hand when you are working on it but taking breaks every hour or so to walk around the office, stretch, or grab a healthy snack. Caring for yourself is the best reward you can give your employees. You will find that your energy is more balanced throughout the day, your emotions are more in control, and your productivity is increased.

If these are the ways you want your employees to behave, you need to walk the walk. Particularly in leisure services it is essential for us to demonstrate that we believe in and act on the benefits that a healthy, active life has to offer both professionally and personally.

Discipline

Of course, not all employees are going to be stellar. Those who are not can have a major impact on the agency. They consume a lot of the supervisor's time because the supervisor must deal with the issue. Also, a poor employee probably has lower productivity and morale than a good employee and can cause these same symptoms in average employees through their attitude alone.

Disciplining employees requires that a systematic process be put in place. This system will detail the guidelines all managers are to follow and will also create the documentation needed in case the employee is eventually terminated. A progressive discipline process is outlined along with an improvement plan in this section. Keep in mind that agencies will have the discipline process detailed in their policy manual. However, most will follow a similar process.

Progressive Discipline

progressive discipline—A process of addressing undesirable employee work behaviors in a systematic way with increased efforts to correct the problem.

Progressive discipline is used when disciplinary action is needed because of attendance problems, safety issues, poor performance, or undesirable behaviors. Managers typically follow this progression model:

1. Verbal warning
2. Written warning
3. Intervention
4. Termination

This model becomes more serious with each step, culminating in dismissal from a position. Keep in mind that some infractions may require the manager to skip one or more steps based on the actions of the employee. For example, an employee caught drinking alcohol on the job may automatically be dismissed if this course of action is detailed in the policy manual. There are several behaviors such as this for which the policy manual will dictate how the situation is to be handled, and therefore the policy will supersede the progressive discipline model.

Verbal Warning

When a situation arises that requires the manager to begin disciplinary action, the first step is usually a verbal warning. The manager should set up a meeting with the employee to have a nonconfrontational conversation about the incident. The manager must communicate what is acceptable behavior and then set consequences for further incidents. Although this is a verbal warning, many managers will keep notes on what the situation is, what transpired, and how it was handled. The notes are usually not put in the employee's personnel file but kept by the manager for future reference if the situation escalates.

Written Warning

If the situation occurs again or a similar situation arises, the next step for the employee is a written warning. The manager will formally document the incident, mention the verbal warning, and again discuss acceptable behavior and consequences. A written warning should be discussed in person with the employee, much like the verbal warning. At the end of the meeting, the employee will be asked to sign the written warning to acknowledge that the matter was discussed. If an employee refuses to sign the written warning, a note will be made on the warning that the employee refused to sign. Additionally, an employee is given an opportunity to respond to the warning. The response is then attached to the warning and all documents are placed in the employee's personnel file.

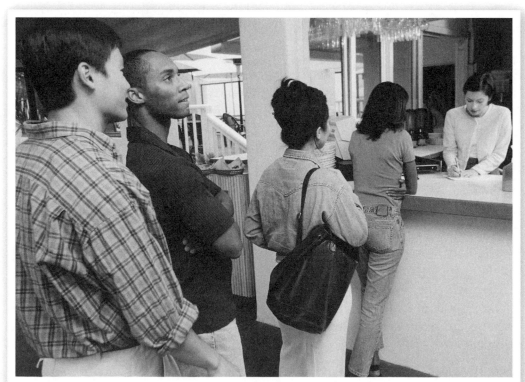

Good customer service is a must in leisure services. If a staff member does not provide a quality service, supervisors must take disciplinary action.

Intervention

The next step in the progressive discipline model is an intervention, which results in an employee improvement plan. Intervention requires the completion of a five-step process. To illustrate the model in action, consider the following situation:

Erin works at the front desk of a fitness service as a customer service representative. She has been there for 3 years. Recently Erin's behavior has grown increasingly difficult. She fluctuates between apathy, complaining, and exhibiting disdain toward the organization. On several occasions, she has been seen moping around the front desk. Little work gets done on those days. At other times, she complains how nothing is ever right or how others are to blame for mistakes. Erin's work productivity has diminished and is half of what it was 6 months ago. Her errors are increasing, and she sometimes handles conversations with callers discourteously. Furthermore, a recent project had numerous mistakes that required correction by coworkers, causing a deadline to be missed.

Step 1: Identify and Define the Performance Problem   Determine what the issues and problems are. Are they attendance problems, safety issues, poor performance, or undesirable behaviors?

The case: Erin is apathetic and complaining; her productivity has diminished; she blames others for mistakes; and she is rude to customers.

Step 2: Explain the Impact of the Problem   Tell the employee how this problem is impacting others both internally and externally to the organization.

The case: Erin is upsetting customers with her attitude; coworkers have to redo her work; this situation requires additional attention from the supervisor; her productivity reduces the organization's productivity.

Step 3: Define the Expected Performance Standard   At this point the manager needs to bring the employee in to talk about the situation and define expectation standards. During this meeting it is imperative to define the level of performance expected in clear and measurable terms. Managers sometimes make the mistake of assuming that the employee knows what is expected. This step is to initially establish performance goals.

The case: Erin is expected to raise productivity to an acceptable level, decrease errors in work completed, and treat customers with respect.

Step 4: Explore Ideas for a Solution   The manager and employee need to explore how to solve this problem together. They should generate ideas and discuss each option as it pertains to each performance standard.

The case: Erin and her manager have determined the best course of action is a change in job tasks for Erin; the manager will set deadlines for projects; Erin will develop customer service skills through training; and Erin will strive to reduce errors.

Step 5: Write an Improvement Plan   An improvement plan is a roadmap aimed at eliminating employee problems and weaknesses. It takes the information gathered in the previous steps and puts it in writing for the employee. An improvement plan will have four elements: the goal or area that needs improvement (step 3), the step-by-step action plans (step 4), positive and negative consequences, and follow-up time.

The case: Here is one example to include in Erin's improvement plan.

Treat customers with respect (goal):

▶ Attend customer service training through XYZ corporation within the next 2 months. (action plan)

▶ Implement five new practices learned in the customer service program within 1 week of attending the training.

▶ Always be courteous with all customers calling the company or walking into the facility.

▶ These tasks will be reviewed at the end of 30 days. (follow-up)

▶ If these tasks are not met, a 2-week suspension is in order. (consequences)

Termination

If all attempts at an intervention are not successful, then termination may be necessary. When firing an employee, a manager can never have too much documentation. Details of the progressive disciplinary action should be in the employee's personnel file. Prior to terminating an employee, the manager needs to prepare for the meeting by discussing the situation with those who are necessary, including human resources staff and the agency attorney. Personnel policies will dictate who should be notified.

Selecting the location for the termination should be given careful consideration. The manager may want to go to the employee's office so that the person fired does not have to walk by other employees if they are visibly upset. It can be in a neutral setting such as a boardroom. If the firing could be confrontational, the manager may want to choose a room that has multiple doors for escape or sit near the door so they can get out easily. Although these situations are rare, they can occur.

During the termination meeting, keep the following tips in mind:

▶ Have a witness in the meeting. It could be a higher supervisor or someone from human resources.

▶ Be direct in telling the employee why he is being terminated. Give facts, but do not elaborate too much and belabor points. Answer all questions honestly and to the point.

▶ Let the employee know the termination is a final decision and that it is not up for debate or negotiation.

▶ Present the employee with a termination letter. This letter should also state the facts and reasons for termination. It should also detail the progressive disciplinary steps that were taken. List the effective termination date and any financial details, including any severance package, the final paycheck, and the date when health benefits will end. A copy of the letter should be signed by the terminated employee acknowledging that he received the letter.

▶ Once the employee has been terminated, give him the opportunity to clean his own office or offer to have two staff members (for witness purposes) clean the office and send belongings to the terminated employee. All company property must be returned, including keys.

▶ During the termination meeting, all access to such things as the computer system or security systems should be stopped. For instance, password changes should be made for the computer to deny access to important company information.

Terminating an employee is arguably one of the most difficult things a manager will have to do. However, sometimes it is the only remaining option. Since employee termination can be a legal issue, agencies will have detailed policies that must be followed. The information presented here is merely a guideline on what you will find in an agency.

Discipline and Dismissal of Volunteers

As noted earlier, volunteers are critical to many leisure services organizations. Just as managers must reward volunteers and treat them as valuable staff members, managers may also need to use principles of discipline and dismissal with volunteers as well. An ineffective volunteer can cause an organization as much trouble as an ineffective paid employee. For instance, take a nonprofit agency where a volunteer answers the phone and is the first point of contact with clients and key stakeholders. This person is in a critical role that requires certain behavior. Just as with any employee, managers should work with volunteers to develop behaviors and skills that meet the demands of their role.

Volunteers differ from paid employees in that they are freely giving their time, and dismissing a volunteer may have negative repercussions as to how other volunteers perceive the organization. A manager's task may be to find volunteers an opportunity that best fits their desires and their skill set even if that opportunity is not within the organization. A proactive, professional, and empathetic approach will go a long way to ensure success in working with volunteers.

Conclusion

▶ Understanding how to motivate, reward, and discipline employees and volunteers is a critical task for managers. As discussed at the outset of this chapter, employees are the key resource in accomplishing organizational goals. Motivation and organizational rewards are topics most people have an opinion on; however, impressions on the topic are often based on incomplete information. A solid understanding of the current thinking in these areas can be valuable for anyone working in a leisure services organization. Equally important is understanding how to effectively use discipline and when to use dismissal. Although often one of a manager's toughest tasks, effective discipline and dismissal is essential to a productive workplace.

REVIEW QUESTIONS

1. Differentiate between performance-based and membership-based rewards.

2. Describe nontraditional forms of rewards and give an example.

3. What are the four primary bases of organizational rewards?

4. What is the cafeteria-style approach to benefits and why might a manager use it?

5. Describe the purposes of reward systems.

6. Compare and contrast rewards for volunteers and paid staff.

7. Describe how you might go about addressing tardiness with an employee who is often late for work.

8. Explain how to use discipline effectively in a leisure services setting you are familiar with.

9. What steps would you take if you needed to dismiss an employee?

KEY WORDS

revenues, compulsory income, real property taxes, personal property taxes, excise tax, gratuitous income, matching grants, earned income, operating expenditures, capital expenditures, subsidy rate, differential pricing

COMPETENCY CHECK

Take another look at table 1.3 (page 9) to see how you assessed these related competencies.

1. Understand financial processes (i.e., purchasing, budget).
2. Develop, monitor, and stay within a budget.

CHAPTER 12

Sources and Methods of Financing

1. Identify the five sources of revenue and their applicability to each sector.
2. Differentiate between operating and capital expenditures.
3. Understand how to price programs using fixed and variable costs, contingency, and demand.
4. Demonstrate knowledge of indirect cost allocation.
5. Apply the concept of program subsidy to pricing.

The focus of my job is to coordinate Kool 2B Fit, a fitness camp for kids 6 to 12. Personnel management is a big part of my job. I have to make sure that the camp is staffed at appropriate levels to ensure program quality as well as safety; we try to maintain a 10-to-1 camper-to-counselor ratio for both of these purposes. Personnel management is connected to almost every other aspect of management, including budgeting, coordination, and scheduling. Planning and organization are also keys to my program's success, but when working with kids, it is essential to be

flexible, have a backup plan, and prepare for the worst! I often have to adapt quickly to situations, whether they are related to campers, counselors, or the program itself. Having the ability to work with kids and having knowledge of fitness and physical activity are important competencies for this position. Most of my job is about management—managing people, facilities, programs, and finances.

Chris Ward
Kool 2B Fit Camp Coordinator
Durham, New Hampshire

Financial management is "the process of planning, acquiring, and using funds to achieve pre-determined organization goals and objectives" (Sellers, Gladwell, & Pope, 2005, p. 493). Regardless of whether the leisure service is in the public, nonprofit, or commercial sector, sound financial management is paramount to the success of the agency. Although each sector has unique financial concerns and regulations, certain basic tenets of financial management are consistent across the sectors. To be a good financial manager, it is not necessary to be an accountant. A basic knowledge of accounting principles as well as revenue streams and expenditures will form the foundation of budgeting. It is these elements that are the focus of the next two chapters. Financial topics to be covered include revenues, expenditures, program pricing, budgeting, and financial analysis.

Sources of Revenue

Fundamental to any recreation product is the budgeting process. However, budgeting is complex and it takes experience to become adept at it. Before discussing budgeting (covered in chapter 13), it is necessary to understand the concepts of revenues, expenditures, and basic program pricing.

Revenues, or income, are the monies coming into an organization. All organizations have some sort of income and these sources vary by sector as well as agency type. Brayley and McLean (2001) identified five common sources of revenue—compulsory, gratuitous, earned, investment, and contractual—and outlined what sources are most important to each sector.

Compulsory Income

Taxes at different levels of government, from the local to the federal, provide **compulsory income.** In both the United States and Canada, public agencies generate most of

revenues—Money coming into the organization from such sources as fees, charges, and taxes.

compulsory income—Revenue generated from taxes at the local, state or provincial, and federal levels.

their revenue from taxes. This tax revenue comes in many different forms, including real property taxes, personal property taxes, sales taxes, and excise taxes.

Real Property Taxes

The most common taxes used by public providers of leisure services are **real property taxes**. In the United States, 96 percent of all property taxes stay at the local level. Local residents are taxed on their property and this tax stays within the community to fund local programs. Property taxes are to local government as personal and corporate income taxes are to federal government—major revenue streams (Howard & Crompton, 2005).

> **real property taxes**— Taxes levied on real estate, including the land, crops growing on the land, and structures built on the land.

In Canada, property taxes are typically divided among the municipality, the county or region, and local school boards. Although organizations such as police departments, fire departments, and libraries can receive property taxes directly, it is more common that they would fall within one of the three taxing entities (Havitz & Glover, 2001). Many provinces in Canada levy property tax on real estate based upon the current use and value of the land. Although property tax levels vary among municipalities, usually common property assessment or valuation criteria are laid out in provincial legislation. A current trend in most provinces is using a market value standard with varying reevaluation cycles. A number of provinces have established an annual reassessment cycle as market activity warrants whereas others have more time between valuations.

Real property that is taxable includes any land owned and whatever is built or growing on that land, including homes, barns, and crops. However, land owned by churches, charitable organizations, governmental entities, and educational institutions are exempt from real property taxes in both the United States and Canada (Crompton, 1999). So, cities with major universities miss out on a large amount of property taxes because the university is exempt from property taxes. In addition to these exemptions, there are also tax abatements, which are tax exemptions given to businesses for a short amount of time. Tax abatements are often used to attract new businesses to a community. For example, a large discount store may choose to build its newest store in one town over another because the chosen town has given the company a 5-year tax abatement during which it does not have to pay taxes on land and structures. Most often this type of tax abatement is worth millions of dollars to the company and incentive enough to influence location decisions.

Property tax owed to the government is based on the type of property, such as residential property, farmland, or open space, as well as the assessed valuation of that property. The valuation of land is determined by a tax assessor and is generally reassessed every 3 to 5 years, depending on the community. Assessed value is the taxable worth of the property and is different than fair market value (Brayley & McLean, 2001). Fair market value is the price the property would be sold for if it was put on the real estate market. In most areas the assessed value is less than the fair market value. Ideally, a homeowner would want a high fair market value and a low assessed valuation. This would ensure a high selling price for the home and lower property taxes. However, in reality there is a direct relationship—the higher the fair market value, the higher the assessed value.

The taxing of all applicable property in a given county, city, or region makes up the tax base for the area. The monies composing the tax base are distributed to local governmental agencies. The higher the assessed value of property in a designated area, the larger the tax base and the more money that local governments have to work with.

Similar to any organization, local government units have budgets they must work within. Once the annual budget is determined, the local government knows how much revenue is needed to operate during the upcoming budget year. Property is then taxed at a rate that will generate the needed revenue. This rate is called the *tax rate*. This is not to say that a municipality can determine that its needs have tripled within a year and charge the property owners a sharply increased rate. Laws set maximum tax rates that local governments cannot exceed without voter approval. Figure 12.1 depicts how all of these tax pieces fit together.

Figure 12.1 Property tax system.

To determine the tax rate, use the following formula:

Tax rate = required taxes / net assessed valuation.

Required taxes are the total expenditures outlined in the city or agency budget after subtracting the revenue received from nontax sources (i.e., fees and charges). The remaining expenditures must be covered by tax money. The *net assessed valuation* is the total assessed value of the property after all tax exemptions and tax abatements have been subtracted out.

The basic unit of taxation is the mill rate. The mill rate is the fraction of the net assessed valuation paid as tax. The tax rate is the mill rate expressed as a percentage.

Example: Consider a community with $7,000,000 in required taxes; that is, it needs $7,000,000 in tax money to cover its expenditures after all other sources of revenue have been accounted for. Suppose the assessed valuation of the property in the community is $520,500,000 with $12,500,000 in tax exemptions. The net assessed valuation is therefore $520,500,000 − $12,500,000, or $508,000,000. The mill rate and tax rates are calculated as follows:

Mill rate = $7,000,000 / ($520,500,000 − $12,500,000)
= $700,000,000 / $508,000,000
= 0.0138
Tax rate = 1.38%

The mill rate expresses the amount of tax paid per dollar of assessed valuation. Since this amount of tax is usually a small number, it is commonly reported in terms of mills, a *mill* simply being a tenth of a penny. The tax rate expresses the amount of tax paid per hundred dollars of assessed valuation.

Example: Continuing from above, the mill rate of 0.0138 indicates that a homeowner would pay $0.0138 in taxes for every dollar of valuation. Since a dollar contains 1,000 mills—there are 100 pennies in a dollar and 10 mills in a penny—the homeowner would pay 13.8 mills (0.0138 × 1,000) for each dollar of valuation. The tax rate of 1.38 percent indicates that a property owner would pay $1.38 for every $100 of assessed value.

> **Taxes paid** = **$0.0138 per dollar of valuation**
> = **13.8 mills per dollar of valuation**
> = **$1.38 per $100 dollars of valuation**

To compute the property tax, multiply the mill rate by the assessed valuation. For example, a homeowner with a home assessed at $100,000 would pay $1,380 in property tax ($1,380 = $100,000 × 0.0138).

The general formulas are as follows:

> **Required taxes** = **Total expenditures – nontax revenue**
> **Net assessed valuation** = **Total assessed valuation – tax exemptions**
> **Mill rate** = **Required taxes / net assessed valuation**
> **Mills** = **Mill rate × 1,000**
> **Tax rate** = **(Mill rate × 100)%**

and

> **Taxes paid** = **In dollars: Mill rate per dollar of valuation**
> = **In mills: (1,000 × mill rate) per dollar of valuation**
> = **In dollars: Tax rate per $100 of valuation**

Tax rates vary each year depending on the amount of taxes needed and the assessed valuation of property within a community. If the amount of taxes needed stays fairly consistent over a few years and assessed value increases significantly, property taxes may actually decrease. New homeowners buy a house knowing what the property taxes are for the year, but they do not know exactly what the taxes will be in the upcoming year.

Local recreation agencies are typically established in two ways. First, the park and recreation agency can be part of city or county government. This means that it is a department within the city or county much like police, fire, and sanitation. This is the only way parks and recreation is established at the local level in Canada. These agencies rely on money distributed via the city or county council. Kaczynski and Crompton (2006) found that parks and recreation typically receives 2.2 to 2.6 percent of the tax revenue of a municipality, which ranked seventh of the nine city services compared; only corrections and libraries ranked lower. Because of the lower-than-desired rankings and the importance of the services provided, park and recreation organizations need to rely on other revenue sources. However, as discussed later in the chapter, such organizations are fortunate that they have more opportunities to generate revenue from sources than do departments such as fire, police, and education.

A second public park and recreation structure in the United States is the special district. Special districts have limited, designated functions. They have enough administrative and fiscal authority to qualify as independent governments (U.S. Census Bureau, 2005a). Park and recreation districts have their own taxing authority and receive tax money directly from property taxes without having to receive their allocation through the city or county council. They set their own tax rate, but they also have legal limits set by the city. Special districts for parks and recreation do not exist in Canada.

Personal Property Taxes

In addition to real property taxes, there are several other taxes that affect leisure services. Some states, but no provinces, have **personal property taxes** in addition to real property taxes. Real property is not easily moved, such as land or barns, whereas personal property is portable, such as furniture. Personal property taxes are divided into three categories:

> **personal property taxes**—Taxes assessed on personal items owned, including intangible property, tangible household property, and tangible business property.

▶ Intangible property—money markets, bonds, loans, stocks; in Canada, these taxes would come in the form of provincial and federal capital gains tax through personal income tax.

▶ Tangible household property—boats, cars, recreational vehicles such as snowmobiles and campers; in Canada, these taxes come in the form of goods and services taxes (GST) and provincial sales tax (PST), which are discussed under sales taxes.

▶ Tangible business property—equipment, fixtures, furniture, computers, software; in Canada, these taxes come in the form of GST and PST.

Not all states tax personal property. These states rely on other types of taxes such as increased real property taxes to make up revenue that would normally be incurred from personal property.

Tax-Increment Financing

Tax-increment financing (TIF) is used by municipalities in the United States to fund redevelopment such as parks, sidewalks, landscaping, or shopping. It is hoped that the redevelopment will attract new business and retain those currently in an area. The premise behind TIF funding is that when an area is redeveloped, its current tax rate increases. When the TIF is approved for a project, the current tax rate is set as the base rate. Once the redevelopment is complete, the base tax rate continues to be assessed with the funds going to the same taxing bodies as before. The increased taxes due to the redevelopment are then used to fund the redevelopment.

Municipalities do not have the freedom to use TIF money whenever they would like; instead there are specified TIF districts where this funding option is available. Many municipalities have TIF districts in their downtown areas. For example, the University North Park TIF district in Norman, Oklahoma, is slated to spend $16,500,000 from TIF funds on a new conference center and cultural facilities and $8,250,000 on Legacy Park, which is a park with a lake, public art, and open space surrounded by shopping and restaurants (City of Norman, 2007).

TIF financing does not occur in Canada. Improvements to areas can be made by the municipality if the municipality itself buys the land, improves it, and then resells it. Essentially the city invests in itself and receives a return on the investment (Havitz & Glover, 2001).

Sales Taxes in the United States

The largest source of state tax revenue and the second largest for municipalities comes from sales taxes (Howard & Crompton, 2005). The exceptions are Delaware, Montana, New Hampshire, and Oregon, which do not have state sales tax.

Sales tax is a combination of both local and state taxes. Although sales tax ranges from approximately 4 to 10 percent, only 1 to 2 percent stays with the local government and the rest goes to the state government. Sales tax is assessed on products and not services, and some states have tax exemptions on such things as groceries and prescription drugs.

Some states and municipalities dedicate a portion of sales tax directly to parks and recreation. For example, the residents of Kirkwood, Missouri, a suburb of St. Louis, voted in 1998 to dedicate 0.5 percent of their sales tax to Kirkwood Parks and Recreation and another 0.10 percent to St. Louis County Parks and Recreation (City of Kirkwood, 2007). Sales tax increases have also been used for funding sporting venues such as renovating the Green Bay Packers Stadium and building Bank One Ballpark for the Arizona Diamondbacks and Coors Field for the Colorado Rockies (Howard & Crompton, 2005).

Sales tax is exceptionally beneficial in tourism-oriented cities since tourists will visit local restaurants, bars, and businesses buying meals, drinks, and souvenirs. The revenue generated from these sales comes from people living outside the community but benefits residents.

Sales Taxes in Canada

Canada has three sources of sales taxes. First, the goods and services tax (GST) is a federal tax on goods and services such as sporting goods, event tickets, and greens fees. GST is not charged on many necessary goods and services such as groceries, rent, and medical services. The United States does not have a GST; however, many other countries have something similar in value-added taxes (VAT). These tax rates tend to change and are used politically.

Second, provincial sales taxes (PST) are assessed on the sale of goods and services in all provinces except Alberta. As in the United States, the rate varies from province to province. The third means of sales tax in Canada is a merging of GST and PST into the harmonized sales tax (HST). Currently there is a flat percentage HST in the three Atlantic provinces of New Brunswick, Newfoundland, and Nova Scotia (Canada Revenue Agency, 2007). All of these taxes are administered at the federal and provincial levels since municipal sales taxes are prohibited in Canada (Havitz & Glover, 2001).

Excise Taxes

Excise tax is assigned to select goods and services in addition to the standard sales tax. There is often a hotel–motel tax, or bed tax, on hotel rooms, as well as car rental taxes in many municipalities. So-called sin taxes are also imposed on cigarettes and alcohol. The revenue from excise tax has been used to develop sport

> **excise tax**—Tax placed on select goods and services in addition to the standard sales tax.

stadiums and promote tourism. For example, Lucas Oil Stadium, the new home of the Indianapolis Colts, was funded by excise taxes generated from legalizing slot machines in Indiana (Stadiums of the NFL, 2007). Furthermore, Wayne County, Pennsylvania, imposed a 3 percent hotel room excise tax in 2005. The revenue is used to fund the Pocono Mountain Vacation Bureau, the official county tourist promotion agency, as well as Wayne County tourism promotion and tourist destination improvement (Wayne County, PA, 2007). Federal tax on gasoline is funneled to the Federal Highway Administration, which funds trail programs (Jensen & Guthrie, 2006).

Although it is easy to equate taxes with organizations in the public sector since much of their funding comes from this source, the nonprofit and commercial sectors indirectly benefit from the funding of such things as convention and visitors bureaus and sport stadiums.

The Alberta Lottery Fund in Canada oversees money generated from provincial lotteries including video lottery terminals, slot machines, and ticket lotteries. In 2007 through 2008 it was estimated that more than $1.3 billion dollars would be distributed to worthwhile community initiatives. Sport, arts, and recreation were major recipients of these funds:

Community facility enhancement program	$38.5 million
Hosting of major athletic events	$.5 million
Alberta Foundation for the Arts	$26.6 million
Alberta Historical Resources Foundation	$8.5 million
Alberta Sport, Recreation, Parks, and Wildlife Foundation	$23.4 million

http://albertalotteryfund.ca/aboutthealf/wherethemoneygoes.asp

Gratuitous Income

gratuitous income— Money obtained through such means as fund-raising and grants that the agency does not have to pay back to the giver.

Gratuitous income is money that an agency does not have to pay back, and this income often results from fund-raising. It can also come in the form of federal grants, such as the Land and Water Conservation Fund or Open Space Land Acquisition and Development, or from private foundations, such as the Ford Foundation or Lily Foundation.

Gratuitous income also comes from corporate sponsorships of programs, events, and facilities; individual donations of land, money, equipment, stocks, and bonds; and bequests from wills or money left from life insurance policies. The nonprofit sector relies heavily on gratuitous income, and the public sector is increasingly using it, especially from grants and sponsorships. The commercial sector is more likely to give away gratuitous income. For example, REI, an outdoor equipment store, gave away $5 million in grants to outdoor recreation and conservation causes (REI community grants, 2007).

Gratuitous income from fund-raising may be directed toward daily operations to offset the cost of programs or events, buy new equipment, or fund special projects. Funds can also be raised in an annual campaign or a capital campaign. In an annual

Grants for Parks and Recreation

The North Carolina Parks and Recreation Trust Fund (PARTF), established in 1994, provides **matching grants** to fund capital projects for state and local parks and recreation and to increase public access to state beaches. PARTF is funded by taxes on real estate deed transfers, a form of excise tax (Gladwell, Anderson, & Sellers, 2003).

The Steve Nash Foundation, founded by professional basketball player Steve Nash, gives grants to projects that help underserved youth in Canada and the United States. Money from the foundation comes from fund-raisers such as the Steve Nash Foundation Charity Classic (Steve Nash Foundation, 2007).

matching grants—Allocations of money from a foundation or other granting agency that is to be equaled by the receiving agency so that the total money for a project is double what the granting agency gives.

campaign the agency sets a fund-raising goal for the year and pursues donors to give to this fund. The United Way runs an annual campaign where communities set goals for the amount of money they want to raise and then encourage people to give to the campaign, which will ultimately fund such programs and agencies as the YWCA and Boys and Girls Clubs.

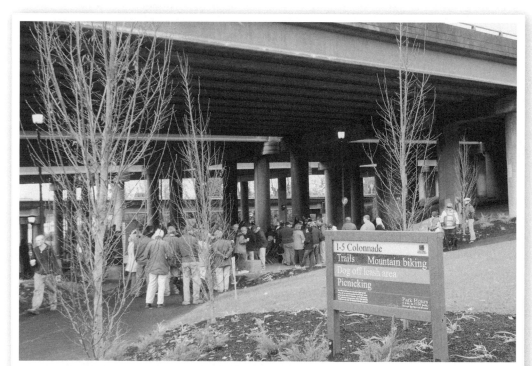

REI provided a $10,000 grant to the Seattle Parks and Recreation Department to help build I-5 Colonnade Park, which is 7.5 acres (3 hectares) of open space located beneath the city's interstate highway. The $1.8 million park includes pedestrian walkways between neighborhoods previously divided by the roadway, an off-leash dog area, public art, and open green space and will expand in the future to include a mountain bike and outdoor sports facility, providing rural recreation in an urban setting.

Planned Giving

Planned giving is an emerging means of fund-raising in parks and recreation. This method of donation focuses on long-term giving over the course of a lifetime or upon the death of the donor. Following are a few examples of planned giving.

Securities

Donors may give stocks and bonds to agencies to use as they see fit. Agencies may hold onto the securities in hopes that their value will increase or sell them and use the revenue from the sale.

Real Estate

Donation of land is common and is especially prevalent in public agencies where families donate land for use as a park or natural area. However, mortgaged land often is not accepted until the mortgage is fully paid.

Life Insurance

An organization can be named as the beneficiary of life insurance policies. Once the purchaser dies, the life insurance turns over to the organization. This is one way a person can give a substantial amount of money while only paying a small annual premium.

Personal Property

Tangible personal property such as jewelry, cars, or artwork may be donated to an organization that can then use the property as is or sell it. Nonprofit organizations occasionally are given automobiles for use or resale. Public agencies have been given such things as houses and valuable collections.

Life Income Gifts

The main purpose of life income gifts is to provide a fixed income for an organization for the life of the donor. Although there are numerous ways to set up life income gifts, one of the most common is the charitable gift annuity where the donor gives cash, securities, or real estate to an organization and the organization then gives the donor and up to two beneficiaries an annual payment for the life of the donor. This payment is generally accrued from interest made on the invested gift.

From selected text in B.L. Ciconte and J.C. Jacobs, 2001, *Fundraising basics: A complete guide,* 2nd ed. (Gaithersburg, MD: Aspen Publishers, Inc.).

Capital campaigns are longer term. The goal for this type of campaign is usually much larger and may include establishing a foundation that operates off the interest from the account, building a new facility, or making major renovations to existing facilities. Although all amounts of donations are accepted in capital campaigns, a special emphasis is usually on larger or long-term donations.

Earned Income

Revenue generated from fees and charges is the main element of **earned income.** The commercial sector relies heavily on earned income by selling its services. Both the nonprofit and public sectors rely on earned income to supplement their fund-raising efforts and/or compulsory income. The main classifications of earned income include entrance and admission fees, rental fees, user or program fees, sales revenue, license and permit fees, and special fees (Brayley & McLean, 2001).

> **earned income**—Revenue generated from fees and charges for services, programs, and products.

Entrance and Admission Fees

Entrance and admission fees are paid either at the door or gate of a facility, through ticket sales or gate receipts, or in the parking lot. Many state, provincial, and national parks in Canada and the United States have entrance fees that are paid at the gate. Individual states and the NPS also offer annual passes for frequent users of parks. Eight states do not have state park entrance fees, but California generates more than $40,000,000 per year in gate receipts (McLean, 2006). Parking fees in place of gate fees are also popular. For example, the Lincoln Park Zoo in Illinois has free admission to the zoo but charges visitors to park.

Rental Fees

Rental fees are charged in all types of leisure services. In the public sector, pavilions, pools, and other facilities can be rented for reunions, parties, and meetings. At the University of Arkansas, the Outdoor Adventure Program rents outdoor equipment from tents to kayaks at low prices to students, faculty, staff, and the community. In the nonprofit sector, places such as the YMCA can rent their pool, meeting rooms, or gymnasiums. For example, the Howard County Historical Society in Kokomo, Indiana, rents the Seiberling Mansion house, kitchen, and grounds for meetings, weddings, and other events (Howard County Museum, 2007). The commercial sector also may be in the rental business. Special-event companies rent equipment such as tables, chairs, and sound equipment. Sporting goods stores can rent equipment, such as Bike Chicago Rentals and Tours, which rents bikes, rollerskates, and inline skates to tour Navy Pier and other Miracle Mile attractions (Bike Chicago Rental and Tours, 2007).

User or Program Fees

User or program fees are assessed to people who use services or programs. Personal trainers and specialized fitness classes at health clubs; leadership and self-esteem programs through the Girl Scouts; and youth and adult softball at the local park and recreation department are all examples of user and program fees. These fees make up varying percentages of revenue depending on the type and philosophy of the agency. A commercial agency will generate a much higher percentage of revenue than the other two sectors, and the variances within these two sectors will fluctuate considerably based on the organizational philosophy regarding how much of the program cost should be recovered. For example, 23.3 percent of the budget for the Seattle Parks and Recreation Department came from program fees, charges, and concession revenue in 2005 (Seattle Parks and Recreation, 2007). In outdoor recreation, the Michigan Department of Natural Resources generated $19,836,061 in camping revenues on top of $12,403,636 in gate receipts. These two sources of revenue account for almost 92 percent of the total revenue of $35,056,281 (McLean, 2006).

Sales Revenue

Sales revenue is acquired from the sale of goods and services through concessions, pro shops, stores, and so on. The commercial sector comes to mind first in terms of revenue generation through sales, especially businesses such as sporting goods stores, restaurants, and hotels. However, the public and nonprofit sectors have their own share of sales revenue through snack bars, pro shops in places such as golf courses and ice arenas; gift shops in museums or zoos; and souvenir shops at national and state park visitor centers. For instance, Kentucky State Parks generates more than $13 million per year from restaurant sales (McLean, 2006). Keep in mind that sales revenue is different than sales taxes. All sectors directly benefit from the sales of their products whereas the tax assessed on the item is diverted to the local and state government and may not necessarily be a source of revenue for parks and recreation.

License and Permit Fees

Outdoor recreation agencies often receive funding from license and permit fees on licenses for snowmobiles, hunting, all-terrain vehicles, special environmental license plates, and so on. In addition to outdoor recreation, the sport industry capitalizes on revenue generated through licenses. This lucrative revenue source derives from the organization selling the rights to its name or logo for use on apparel, collectibles, and other novelties that are then sold to the public (Sawyer, Hypes, & Hypes, 2004). For instance, North Carolina has special vehicle license plates with proceeds supporting the Blue Ridge Parkway Foundation, Friends of Great Smoky Mountains, and Friends of the Appalachian Trail (North Carolina Department of Transportation, 2007).

Special license plates have proceeds supporting the Blue Ridge Parkway Foundation, Friends of Great Smoky Mountains, and Friends of the Appalachian Trail.

Special Fees

Special fees are assessed for out-of-the-ordinary services. For example, ticket brokers such as Ticketmaster charge a special fee for using their service, universities may charge special technology fees to students for computer services, and the sport industry charges personal seat license (PSL) fees to generate large amounts of money. With PSLs, people pay a one-time fee for the right to buy season tickets for a specific seat during a defined time frame. The primary purpose of PSLs is to reduce the debt incurred from major facility renovations or building a new facility. The Green Bay Packers, for example, charge between $600 and $1,400 per seat, a fee that is considered well below market value.

Investment Income

All three sectors have the opportunity to generate revenue by investing some of their assets into money-market certificates, stocks, and mutual funds. Revenue from these investments supplements income from other sources. Although it is easy to associate investment income with the commercial sector, it is used frequently in the other two sectors as well. For example, the NRPA, a nonprofit organization, earned $1,287,643 in 2007 from investments, which contributed 10 percent of its overall budget that year.

Contractual Receipts

A major source of revenue for all three sectors, contractual receipts are agreements with outside organizations that provide services and monetary resources. These contracts can come in many forms, but some of the more common ones include contracting with an outside agency to operate concessions stands, golf and tennis pro shops, and ice arenas. The Austin Parks and Recreation Department in Texas brings in more than $200,000 each year from its contracts (table 12.1).

Table 12.1 Contracts of the Austin Parks and Recreation Department

Contract	Commission paid to city	2004-2005 city revenue from contract
Contract 1: Barton Springs Food and Beverage in Zilker Park	$90,000 annually ($7,500 per month), 8% of gross annual sales up to $265,000, and 28.5% of gross annual sales exceeding $265,000	$75,762
Contract 2: Butler Pitch and Putt short irons golf course	$13,200 annually ($1,100/month), 1% of gross annual sales up to $80,000, and 1.5% of gross annual sales exceeding $80,000	$12,300

Adapted, by permission, from City of Austin Parks and Recreation Department, 2005, *Parks and recreation department annual concession report: 2004-2005* (Austin, TX: Author), 3.

Summary of Revenue Sources

Agencies use a variety of the discussed revenue sources. Some sectors are more prone to use one source than another. Take a look at figure 12.2 to see the breakdown of revenue sources for the NRPA, a nonprofit professional association. The YMCA, on the other hand, counts on revenue from membership fees, program fees, and contributions, among others (figure 12.3).

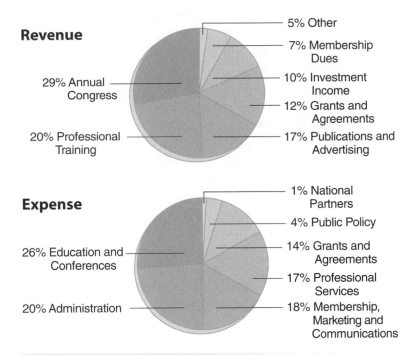

Revenue

- 5% Other
- 7% Membership Dues
- 10% Investment Income
- 12% Grants and Agreements
- 17% Publications and Advertising
- 29% Annual Congress
- 20% Professional Training

Expense

- 1% National Partners
- 4% Public Policy
- 14% Grants and Agreements
- 17% Professional Services
- 18% Membership, Marketing and Communications
- 26% Education and Conferences
- 20% Administration

Figure 12.2 NRPA generates 10% of its income from investments and 49% from trainings and conferences.

From National Recreation and Park Association's FY2007 Annual Report.

Income

	Financials are unaudited
Contributions	$8,713,226
Membership dues	$21,081,521
Program fees	$19,069,283
Sales of merchandise and service	$1,078,464
Government grants	$1,661,345
United Way	$819,111
Investment income	$318,038
Other	$29,908
Total income	**$52,770,896**

Expenses

	Financials are unaudited
Health and wellness	$14,620,141
Child care	$14,026,979
Youth development and aquatics	$9,393,475
Camping and outdoor education	$4,748,818
Teens and at-risk youth	$3,364,028
College scholarships	$323,800
Management and general	$4,294,305
Fundraising	$870,395
Transfer to reserves	$1,128,955
Total expenses	**$52,770,896**
Capital assets, net of depreciation	$67,091,798

Figure 12.3 The YMCA of Metropolitan Dallas uses a multitude of revenue sources including gratuitous income, earned income, and investment income.

Reprinted, by permission, from YMCA of Metropolitan Dallas, 2006, *YMCA of Metropolitan Dallas 2005 annual report* (Dallas, TX: Author), 7.

Expenditures

All organizations have expenditures, or money going out of the organization to pay for staff, facilities, program needs, and so on. Expenditures fall into two broad categories: operating expenditures and capital expenditures.

Operating Expenditures

Operating expenditures, also called *operating costs,* are recurring costs associated with doing business. Operating costs include personnel, utilities, office supplies, equipment, and program supplies, which can be divided into fixed and variable costs (see figure 12.4). Fixed costs are incurred regardless of the volume, or number of participants. For example, if a youth basketball league is cancelled due to low enrollment, there are still costs associated with the program, such as utility costs for the unused facility or staff salary for those directly or indirectly involved in planning the program. Variable costs, on the other hand, change based on volume. If the youth basketball program actually runs, there are several variable costs, including referees, team jerseys, and basketballs. All of these costs will change based on the number of players and teams in the league. Fixed

> **operating expenditures**—Recurring costs associated with doing business.

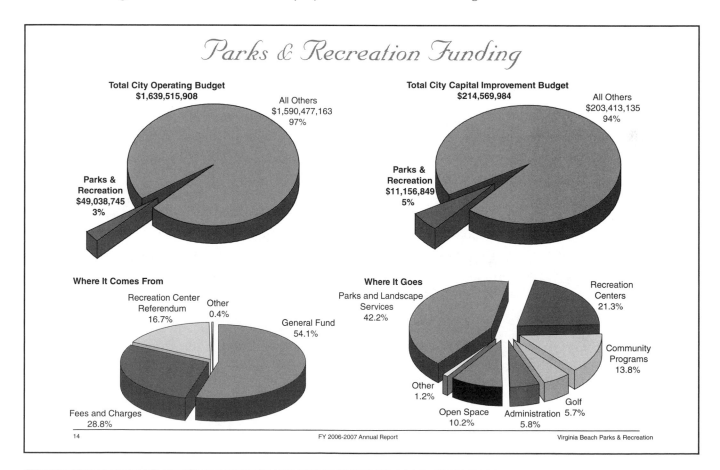

Figure 12.4 Virginia Beach Parks and Recreation Department expenditure sources for 2006 through 2007. Note: Figures do not add up to 100% due to rounding.

Reprinted, by permission, from Virginia Beach Parks & Recreation Department, 2007, *Virginia Beach parks & recreation department 2006-2007 annual report* (Virginia Beach, VA: Author).

and variable costs are important when determining the cost of a program, as is discussed later in the chapter.

Capital Expenditures

capital expenditures—
Costs incurred by large-scale purchases such as land, facilities, or expensive equipment.

Capital expenditures are costs incurred by large-scale purchases, such as playground equipment, updates to a facility to meet ADA standards, new facilities, or park land. The previously discussed streams of revenues will more likely be used to cover the cost of operating expenses and maybe some capital expenditures. Large-scale capital expenditures in the nonprofit sector must rely on fund-raising efforts, and this is often when capital campaigns are instituted.

In the public sector, exceptionally large capital expenditures reach beyond what the tax base and other revenue streams can cover. These expenditures are financed most commonly through bonds. Although several types of bonds are available, two in particular are used to fund capital projects such as a new golf course or minor league baseball stadium: general obligation bonds and revenue bonds.

General obligation bonds (United States) and debenture bonds (Canada) allow a public agency to borrow large amounts of money over a longer length of time, even as long as 30 years, with the intention of paying back the principal and interest. Payments are budgeted for and paid annually; however, because these bonds impose a burden on taxpayers via a temporary increase in property taxes to pay for the bond, general obligation bonds require voter approval through a bond referendum. In addition, there are state limitations on the amount of debt a local governmental agency can assume.

In the United States, revenue bonds are issued for projects where the revenue generated from the completion of the facility will be sufficient to pay back the debt. Since the project itself generates the revenue rather than taxpayers, no bond referendum is needed. Table 12.2 outlines the advantages and disadvantages of obligation and revenue bonds. See figure 12.5 for an example.

In Canada, general revenue bonds are called *debentures* and operate in much the same way as revenue bonds in the United States. However, there are three types of debentures. The serial debenture has a fixed schedule to repay the debt and accrued interest. Serial debenture is the most common type, but there are also sinking fund debentures. Sinking fund debentures require no payment until

General Obligation Bonds

The City of Albuquerque, New Mexico, routinely places park and recreation general obligation bond questions on the ballot for voter consideration. They prepare a general obligation bond program every 2 years, including a variety of public works from streets to community centers to information technology to parks and recreation. Since 1999, city residents have voted to fund more than $103,000,000 in park and recreation projects (City of Albuquerque, 2007).

Table 12.2 General Obligation Bonds Versus Revenue Bonds

	Advantages	**Disadvantages**
General obligation bonds	Taxes are used to pay back the debt, resulting in a more secure guarantee, and they have a lower interest rate than many other nonguaranteed debt options. Funding sources through tax levies results in virtually no risk of default.	Voter approval is required through a bond referendum. All taxpayers pay regardless of any direct benefit from the project. Debt ceiling limit.
Revenue bonds	Reflects a user pay philosophy—those who use, pay. Voter referendum not required.	Higher interest rates due to nonguaranteed status. Restricted to facilities that can generate a profit.

Used with permission of Fitness Information Technology, Inc., from *Financing sport,* D.R. Howard and J.L. Crompton, 2nd ed., 2004; permission conveyed through Copyright Clearance Center, Inc.

the final year of the loan and then the entire amount is due in one payment. In order to meet this obligation, the agency will set aside the annual amount owed so the money is available when the payment is due. Lastly, balloon issue debentures require a set payment for a certain length of time (usually to the halfway point), then a balloon payment, and then the set payment is resumed. This sort of debenture is the least common for financing municipal entities (Havitz & Glover, 2001).

Capital improvements in the commercial sector rely on investors or the business owners themselves for funding. They can also use corporate bonds where a loan is secured with the expectation that the lender will receive a fixed rate of return on investment. The bonds are sold with different maturity dates indicating when the lender can expect payment. Corporate bonds can either be mortgage bonds, where real estate is used as collateral; equipment trust certificates, where the corporation pays off the loan and is issued a clear title; or income bonds, where interest is only paid if it is earned. Income bonds are usually issued to corporations in bankruptcy (Brayley & McLean, 2001).

Pricing

Pricing has several marketing implications, as previously discussed, and it also drives the fiscal processes of an organization. Pricing of programs and services is done for several reasons.

1. Pricing may recover the costs of offering programs and services.
2. Programs can generate additional resources that could be used to fund other programs or simply serve as the profit margin for commercial agencies.
3. Prices establish value based on the price–quality relationship (see chapter 8).

Referenda Results - November 7, 2006

Fourteen of the hundreds of referenda proposals submitted to voters for the general election held November 7, 2006 concerned park, recreation and conservation issues. Seven of the 14 passed. Two of the successful propositions dealt with issues of expanding an agency's boundaries or using public land for park space. Five of the 12 proposals that sought to increase agency income met with voter approval. Three bond issues and two tax measures passed.

The following table details the types of initiatives, the amounts requested and vote totals. Data for this report were obtained from county election authorities after all precincts were counted. If you are aware of an initiative that is not included, please contact me at pmurphy@ILparks.org.

Park and Forest Preserve Referenda Results

DISTRICT	JURISDICTION	TYPE	DESCRIPTION	PASS/FAIL	VOTES YES/NO
Berwyn Park District	Cook	Bond	Shall bonds of the Berwyn Park District, Cook County, to the amount of not to exceed $790,000 be issued for building, maintaining, improving and protecting the existing land and facilities of the District?	PASSED	3,638/2,427
Chicago Ward 35 - Precincts 1,2, 5,7-12,15-19,21...	City of Chicago	Misc.	Shall the Alderman of the 35th Ward use the eminent domain process he has started at the site of the Mega Mall for the public purpose of developing a park as opposed to benefiting a private development?	PASSED	4,162/1,363
Forest Preserve District of DuPage County	DuPage	Bond	Shall the Forest Preserve District of DuPage County borrow money and issue general obligation bonds in the amount of $68,000,000 to acquire natural areas and other land?	PASSED	166,048/ 88,443
Glen Ellyn Park District	DuPage	Bond	Shall bonds or notes of the Glen Ellyn Park District, DuPage County, to the amount of $11,900,000 be issued for the purpose of the payment of land purchased for parks or boulevards?	PASSED	6,982/5,961
Godley Park District	Grundy, Will	Tax	Shall the extension limitation under the Property Tax Extension Limitation Law for Godley Park District, Will and Grundy Counties, be increased from the lesser of 5%?	failed	52/57
Maywood Park District	Cook	Misc.	Shall the Maywood Park District annex all property located in the corporate limits of the Village of Maywood that is not a part of any park district?	PASSED	1,498/461

Figure 12.5 Here is an example of the partial 2006 referenda results for park and forest preserve districts in Illinois. Five of the six referenda listed passed and focused on such issues as tax increases, land acquisitions, and annexations of property.

Reprinted with permission of the Illinois Association of Park Districts.

4. Pricing can influence behavior through damage deposits on rental facilities, late fees for rental equipment returns, early-bird registration opportunities that give discounts for registering by a predetermined date, and so on.

5. Prices promote efficiency and can shift demand from peak times to off-peak hours. For example, Northstar-at-Tahoe Resort Golf Course offers a $10 discount for golfers teeing off after 2:00 p.m., a $29 discount after 3:30 p.m., and a $44 discount after 5:00 p.m. (Northstar-at-Tahoe Resort, 2007). Resorts and tourist destinations offer less expensive room rates during the off-peak season to draw people to the area during less busy times. Pricing for efficiency is also used by membership-driven agencies, such as tennis or yacht clubs. Members are given monthly discounts for signing annual contracts and paying through direct withdrawal from a bank account. This method ensures long-term program revenue and saves staff time collecting and processing monthly on-site payments. Sport organizations sell season tickets for the same reasons—to ensure a revenue stream while simultaneously reducing staff costs for selling individual tickets.

Approaches to Pricing

Price setting can be approached in different ways. Prices can be set arbitrarily because the programmer thinks the price sounds right. They can also be set based on what the competition is charging or what the market will bear. However, the most sound and logical approach is cost recovery, which is "based on the principle of seeking a return from the consumers that represents a predetermined portion of resources that are required to provide the sport or leisure service to them" (Brayley & McLean, 2001, p. 70).

Pricing a Program

Cost recovery requires understanding how to price a program. A program or service can be priced using a three-step process:

1. Determine pricing variables.
2. Determine the cost of one unit of production.
3. Determine the subsidy rate.

Step 1: Determine Pricing Variables

Pricing a program is similar to solving a word problem in math class. Several variables and their values are needed before solving the final equation. In terms of pricing programs, information is needed on demand, contingency costs, fixed and variable costs, and direct and indirect costs.

Program demand is an estimate of how many people will attend a program. Some programs have minimum and maximum enrollment figures that determine when to cancel a class as well as when to stop taking more participants. For example, a program with a minimum of eight participants would be cancelled if only five people registered. Conversely, if a theater only had 500 seats, that would be the set maximum. The maximum number of participants for programs such as plays, sporting events, or trips using buses is fairly simple to set because it is based on seating. Other programs may set maximums based on room capacity, the amount of equipment or gym space available, or the maximum number of people an instructor can handle. Setting minimum numbers is not any easier than setting maximum numbers. Part of this decision will come from determining a break-even cost where revenues and expenditures are equal, which is discussed later. Many programs determine the break-even point and set the minimum at that point so that any people above that level will be added revenue.

In addition to demand, decisions on contingency costs need to be made. Contingency costs are included in programs in order to cover unexpected costs. This may mean replacing a broken backboard for the basketball program, making unexpected major repairs to the Zamboni machine used at the ice rink, or replacing nets that were vandalized on the tennis courts. Contingency costs can be assessed on a per-person basis, such as $1 per registrant, or added into the cost of the program on a percentage basis, such as 5 to 10 percent of expenditures.

Variable costs are those costs that change in proportion to a change in volume. Thus, each person registering for a program will increase the cost of expenditures like supplies that are allocated per person. For example, a soccer clinic would have such variable costs as team t-shirts, soccer balls, and a booklet with drills and exercises because these items are given to participants. As each person registers for the clinic, these costs increase proportionately per person.

Fixed costs, on the other hand, do not change with volume. They remain steady regardless of the number of participants. For the soccer clinic, fixed costs include such things as facility rental and field maintenance. With some programs there are also changing fixed costs. These costs can increase but not proportionately to the volume. For example, this soccer clinic exceeded projected registration. In order to accommodate those on the waiting list, additional instructors must be hired so that the ratio of instructors to players remains at 1:10. So, while the wage for the instructor is fixed, the change in this fixed cost occurs after every eleventh soccer player is added.

Determining price variables requires understanding the fixed and variable costs of a program. These fixed and variable costs include both direct and indirect costs of a program. A direct cost results from actual operation of a particular program. For example, a direct cost for a tennis program would be tennis balls. The tennis program needs this equipment to operate, so the tennis ball cost is directly attributed to its operation. A direct cost can be both fixed and vari-

Pricing programs such as tennis requires consideration of several variables, including demand and direct and indirect costs.

able, depending on what the item is. A direct fixed cost for tennis would be the tennis professional's salary, whereas a direct variable cost may be the t-shirts for each participant.

Indirect costs are attributable to the program, but indirectly. A tennis pro will directly oversee the tennis programs; however, most likely a supervisor will oversee the tennis pro. Although this supervisor does not directly work with tennis programs, some of her salary and fringe benefits will be attributed to all tennis programs. Another common indirect cost is marketing. The marketing staff is responsible for marketing all programs, including developing a seasonal program brochure listing all available programs and services. Each tennis program must include a portion of the cost of the marketing department, including staff, supplies, and printing of brochures, when calculating the total cost of operating the program. These additional costs are considered indirect costs, sometimes referred to as *overhead costs*. As with direct costs, indirect costs can be either fixed or variable. The indirect cost of the supervisor may be fixed if 5 percent of her salary is assigned to the tennis center. However, it may be variable if $1 is added to all program registrants to cover her salary.

Deciding how to allocate indirect costs is a complicated process. Rossman and Schlatter (2003) outlined several methods for this decision making, but three are used more than others in the field: equal share, percentage of budget, and time-budget study.

The first method is equal-share allocation of indirect expenses. With this approach, the indirect costs are equally split among all the departments. To demonstrate allocation costs, assume a sport club has a general manager who oversees the supervisors in each of the four program areas—tennis, golf, fitness, and bowling. If the sport club is using equal-share allocation, then each of the four areas would assume 25 percent of the general manager's salary into their budgets and must account for this indirect cost in the programs offered. This method would be used if all four units were similar in size and ability to generate revenue (table 12.3).

A second allocation method is percentage of budget. If the units are exceptionally unequal in size, cost, or the ability to generate revenue, then this approach may be better than the equal-share system. With percentage of budget, each program is assigned a percentage based on their share of the budget. This same percentage is used to divide the indirect costs. In our example, because tennis has 40 percent of the budget, it must account for 40 percent of indirect costs, or $40,000.

Table 12.3 Cost Allocations of a $100,000 Salary

Allocation method	Tennis	Golf	Fitness	Bowling
Equal share	$25,000	$25,000	$25,000	$25,000
Percentage of budget	40% $40,000	25% $25,000	30% $30,000	5% $5,000
Time-budget study	10% $10,000	25% $25,000	45% $45,000	20% $20,000

A more accurate method of cost allocation may be a time-budget study where time spent on tasks is measured and then assigned to that unit. This process assumes that some units require more attention than others. Though this system may be a better reflection of what the general manager actually does, it takes considerable money and time to complete the study, and it will no longer be accurate as job responsibilities and requirements change over time. Furthermore, this method of allocation works well with salaries but can get more complicated with some other indirect costs such as equipment.

Looking at the comparisons of the three methods in table 12.5, you can see how determining cost allocation could be tumultuous. The tennis unit would prefer the time-budget study because it is the least expensive to them, fitness would prefer equal share, bowling would prefer percentage of budget, and golf would not see a difference with any of the methods. This is where it is a management decision to determine which method is best for the organization.

Step 2: Determine the Cost of One Unit

Once the variables are identified, the cost of one unit of production can be determined. This unit might be cost per hour, cost per person, cost per park, and so on. Cost per unit is determined using the following formulas, where

P = price,
F = fixed costs,
V = variable costs,
C = contingency costs, and
N = demand.

If there is no contingency cost, the following formula should be used:

$P = (F + V) / N.$

The data in the tennis center cost summary (table 12.4) can be used to determine the cost of operating the facility without any programs, reflecting the number of hours the facility will be open rather than the number of people participating in programs. At this point in the pricing process, we are trying to determine how much it costs to keep the facility open rather than looking at individual programs. The individual programs will be accounted for in the budgeting process.

For this example, the facility will be open 350 days a year, 16 hours a day—or 5,600 hours per year. In this example, 5,600 hours is the program demand. Calculating the unit price using these figures results in a cost of $52.64 per hour to open the doors to the tennis center.

$P = (126,800 + 168,000) / 5,600,$
$P = \$52.64.$

Next, assume a 5 percent contingency cost is associated with the facility. Calculating contingency costs modifies the formula.

With contingency cost,
$P = (F + V + C[F + V]) / N.$

Table 12.4 Tennis Center Cost Summary

	Cost	Months or hours	Subtotal	Total
FIXED COSTS				
General obligation bond payment	$3,500	12	$42,000	
Facility maintenance	$1,700	12	$20,400	
Head professional	$50,000	1	$50,000	
Administrative overhead	$1,200	12	$14,400	
Total fixed costs				$126,800
VARIABLE COSTS				
Utilities	$15	5,600	$84,000	
Front-desk staff	$7	5,600	$39,200	
Custodial staff	$8	5,600	$44,800	
Total variable costs				$168,000
Total fixed and variable costs				$294,800

The per-hour facility cost now changes to the following:

$$P = (126{,}800 + 168{,}000) + .05(126{,}800 + 168{,}000) / 5{,}600,$$
$$P = 294{,}800 + 14{,}740 / 5{,}600,$$
$$P = \$55.28.$$

For every hour the tennis center is open, it will cost the organization a base rate of $55.28. So each program that is offered on the courts will need to generate $55.28 on top of the program costs in order to break even. Table 12.5 outlines a youth tennis clinic for 30 people that will be held for 2 hours. The clinic would be priced at $9.85 to break even, including the per-hour court rate.

Take this example one step further and assume there is an additional $1 charge per person that will be used as a program contingency fee for unexpected program-related occurrences. With this $1 program surcharge, each participant would pay $10.85.

Step 3: Determine the Subsidy Rate

The **subsidy rate** is the percentage of unit cost that will be covered by sources other than the consumer (Brayley & McLean, 2001). For the public sector, costs may be subsidized using tax dollars; nonprofit organizations may use money from fund-raising or sponsors; and the commercial sector can use cross-subsidization. In cross-subsidization, revenue generated from other programs offsets the expenses of a program that will not break even. Assume that the tennis center is going to offer the youth tennis clinic free of charge in order to get more people interested in playing the sport. As such, the program needs to be subsidized by $295.56 without the $1 contingency fee in order to break even. If cross-subsidization is used, money

subsidy rate—Percentage of the program, service, or product cost that will be covered by sources other than the consumer.

Table 12.5 Youth Clinic Unit Cost

	Cost	Months or hours	Subtotal	Total
FIXED COSTS				
Tennis balls (1 case)	$60.00	1	$60.00	
Court time	$55.28	2	$110.56	
Total fixed costs				$170.56
VARIABLE COSTS				
Supplies	$25.00	1	$25.00	
4 instructors	$25.00	4	$100.00	
Total variable costs				$125.00
Total costs				$295.56
Cost per person				$9.85

Demand: 30 kids on 6 courts.

$P = (\$170.56 + \$125.00) / 30$

$P = \$9.85.$

generated from a program such as an adult tennis tournament that had a $1,000 profit could subsidize the clinic.

Subsidy rates are usually based on the type of program being offered—public, merit, or private. A public service is offered to the public at large and benefits everyone, such as parks, sidewalks, or walking trails. These services benefit both users and nonusers; both users and nonusers see increased property value, community aesthetics, and overall health of residents. Public services are usually free and totally subsidized with tax dollars.

Merit services, on the other hand, usually see a partial cost recovery as well as a partial subsidization. These types of services directly benefit the people who use them, but they also indirectly benefit the community as a whole. For example, an after-school program benefits participants by providing structured programs, help with homework, and a safe place to stay until parents finish their workday. Indirect benefits come from decreases in vandalism or criminal activity that results when children do not have after-school supervision or decreases in public funding needed if parents can take full-time jobs knowing their children are adequately cared for.

Private services see at least a full cost recovery and many times they turn a profit. These programs mostly benefit the person who is participating in the program. An all-inclusive weekend getaway to Mexico benefits the person taking the trip but not the rest of the community. This trip is a luxury rather than filling a need for the good of the entire community and should be paid for by the person benefiting.

Classifying all programs and services that an organization offers helps establish their subsidy rate. A commercial agency may see that all of its programs are private and must make a profit; its conundrum is deciding how much of a profit to make.

Conversely, the public and nonprofit sectors must first determine which programs to subsidize and then decide how much to subsidize them.

Table 12.6 demonstrates subsidy levels for tennis programs as well as hourly rates for the courts. A 0 percent subsidy is the break-even price since no portion of the fee is subsidized whereas a 100 percent subsidy means the entire cost is subsidized and the program is free.

Table 12.6 Subsidy Levels and Hourly Rates

Program	Program type	Subsidy rate	Court price
Open court time	Public	100%	Free
Adult team tennis	Private	–25%	$69.10
Youth beginner lessons	Merit	60%	$22.11
Teen traveling team	Private	–20%	$66.34
Youth intermediate league	Private	0%	$55.28

In table 12.6 some of the programs list a negative subsidization rate. This means that a profit will be made. For example, the teen traveling team has a –20 percent subsidy rate. Rather than paying a break-even cost of $55.28 per hour, the program would actually cost $66.34. There are two ways to calculate this cost (S = subsidy rate).

Method 1:

$P = (1 – S)(F + V + C[F + V]) / N)$,
$P = (1 – S)(294,800 + .05[294,800]) / 5,600$,
$P = (1 – S) \times 55.28$,
$P = 1.20 \times 55.28$,
$P = \$66.34$.

Method 2:

$P = \text{Unit cost} \times (1 – S)$,
$P = \$55.28 \times 1 – (–20)$,
$P = \$55.28 \times 1.20$,
$P = \$66.34$.

Both methods will give the same end result within a few cents because of rounding the prices.

Pricing Trends and Issues

Pricing can be a sensitive subject for many park and recreation agencies. Each agency has its own philosophy on cost recovery, who should be charged what, and how to increase revenues and decrease costs. Here are a couple of issues regarding pricing in leisure services organizations.

Subsidies and Double Taxation

For public and nonprofit agencies in particular, subsidy rates can be complex. Subsidies have been a point of discussion in the field for many years because public and nonprofit recreation agencies are expected to continue to increase services to their constituents. It is unrealistic to think that park and recreation services should be free. If all programs and services are free, then their quality and quantity are limited.

In order to provide the services needed, fees and charges must be assessed for some programs. The downside of fees and charges is twofold. First, they can eliminate some groups from participating, such as low-income community members. Second, fees and charges are sometimes viewed as double taxation because property taxes are used to fund many of the services.

To avoid eliminating people from participating, fees charged for some programs can either generate revenue for funding free or low-cost programs or tax dollars can be used for the same purpose. Termed *cross-subsidization,* this method of shifting resources allows for increased service provision for all people.

The double taxation perception is actually inaccurate. For most public agencies, tax dollars are used to provide basic public services such as parks and special events. As discussed previously with public, merit, and private services, a portion of merit programs are paid with taxes to represent the benefit to the community as a whole, and the remaining portion of the fee is paid by the person who most directly benefits.

More and more agencies are examining how fees and charges are assessed and how subsidies are used. For example, Denver Parks and Recreation has begun to develop a cost-recovery pyramid to demonstrate how cost-recovery levels are set as well as to demonstrate how tax dollars are used in the community (figure 12.6).

In Denver's initial draft of the cost-recovery pyramid, the basic services that have up to 20 percent recovery of direct costs are at the base of the pyramid. They are seen as the foundation of the agency and serve the largest portion of the community. They include such things as special events and facility drop-in hours. Moving up the pyramid means that an increased portion of direct costs are assessed to the user. For example, the remaining four levels have established cost recovery of 20 to 50 percent, 50 to 75 percent, 75 to 100 percent, and 100+ percent. Each additional level of programs is only implemented when the previous level is well established and meeting the needs of the community (Dropinski, 2007). Displaying cost recovery in this manner aids the community in understanding the need for fees as well as where tax dollars are spent. Although this specific example cannot be implemented in every organization, it is a sound model to use when pricing programs.

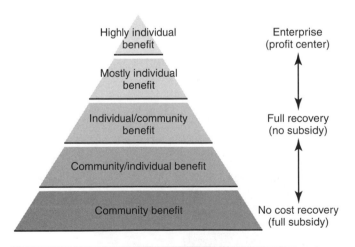

Figure 12.6 **This cost recovery model illustrates five levels of benefits from a community benefit up to a complete individual benefit. The more of a community benefit a service has, the more it will be subsidized with tax dollars.**

Adapted with permission from GreenPlay, LLC.

Differential Pricing

Differential pricing is charging a different price to different populations for the same service. Customer characteristics are one means for instituting differential pricing and include age, income, intensity of consumption, and so on. Age is arguably the most common way to differentiate prices. For example, the Chelsea Piers Sports and Entertainment Complex in Manhattan is home to a multiuse recreation area. The area includes a bowling alley, field house, golf driving range, roller rink and skate park, health club, and ice rink. The roller rink charges $7 for children and $8 for adults, and the ice rink at Chelsea Piers charges less expensive prices for children and seniors than adults. In addition, skaters can buy discounted tickets for 10 admissions to the rink, saving the skater $10.

Product level can also serve as a distinguishing variable for pricing. A rock-climbing class may be priced differently based on experience—beginning climbers would most likely pay the lowest fee whereas the advanced climbers would pay the most. The low fee for beginners is sometimes used as a promotional strategy with the idea that people are more inclined to try a new activity if the cost is lower. Once they begin to enjoy the activity and take more lessons, they're hooked and willing to pay more for it.

Distribution is also a common means of assigning differential pricing, including location of the program, seats in a venue, or time of day. At the Chelsea Piers bowling alley, it is least expensive to bowl Monday through Friday until 5:00 p.m., and it is most expensive to bowl Wednesday through Sunday evenings. Program location can have an impact on pricing, especially for the public sector. The location of a facility such as a pool may dictate the price of programs; an underused facility may charge less in order to stimulate use.

differential pricing—Pricing a service differently for different populations based on customer characteristics, product level, distribution, and so on.

Differential pricing can be seen as a marketing technique to attract youth to discounted programs or to entice people to use facilities during off-peak times.

Pricing programs is just one step in the financial management process. It is the impetus to budgeting and reaches to the core of recreation programming. It is far more complicated than simply pulling a price out of the air. It has marketing implications in terms of stimulating demand, and it has the ability to cross-subsidize worthy programs that would not otherwise be offered because of funding.

Creative Financing

Financial constraints often require organizations to be creative in their financing. Agencies do many things to bring in revenue, including the following:

▶ Reexamine the return on investment of monies invested.

▶ Use creative programming to attract a multitude of target markets. These programs are designed as cost centers to generate profits.

▶ Lease space for cell phone towers, which can generate anywhere from $12,000 to $22,000 per year.

▶ Corporate sponsorships and grants are on the rise. They often require the hiring of development staff to raise funds.

▶ Partnerships with local agencies enable the joint provision of services. These partnerships reduce the need to duplicate services in the community.

▶ Attracting national sporting and cultural events to communities brings in needed revenue through tourism dollars.

▶ Minor and major league sport teams often have variable pricing options where they charge higher prices for tickets to premier games such as opening day, rivalries, and weekend games.

▶ Eliminate inefficiencies in operations.

▶ Reexamine the core mission of the agency and eliminate services that do not meet the mission.

▶ Establish nonprofit foundations so that people may make tax-deductible donations to the organization.

Conclusion

▶ This chapter presented an overview of financial management in park and recreation services. Regardless of your job in the field, finance will be a major part of it. The foundation and most basic unit of finance is program pricing. Establishing prices means understanding revenue streams as well as expenditures since both influence the ultimate price. The steps outlined here move a manager from philosophical topics such as indirect cost allocations and whether to label services as public, merit, or private to more concrete elements such as fixed and variable costs, subsidy rates, and differential pricing.

▶ The pricing piece of the financial picture intimately involves programs, events, and services within the jurisdiction of each programmer. The next chapter looks at the big picture by bringing all of the pricing elements together to form the budget, and it is the budget that drives the entire organization.

REVIEW QUESTIONS

1. Define the five types of income. Indicate which sector is most likely and least likely to use each one.

2. Differentiate between real property taxes and personal property taxes.

3. Compare and contrast operating and capital expenditures.

4. Describe the four approaches to pricing.

5. Define the following terms: contingency costs, fixed and variable costs, and direct and indirect costs.

6. Explain subsidy rates and how private, merit, and public services affect subsidy rates.

7. Describe three ways to allocate indirect costs for leisure services agencies.

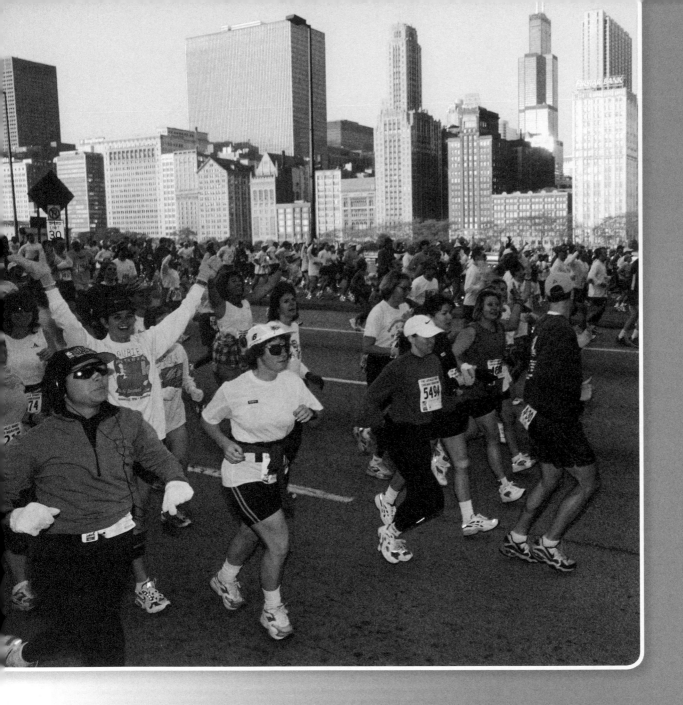

KEY WORDS

budgets, budget cycle, work plan, cutback management, capital budget, capital improvement plan (CIP), operating budget, allocated funds, petty cash, purchase requisition, purchase order, invoice, invitation for bid (IFB), request for proposal (RFP), request for quotation (RFQ), financial analysis, balance sheet

COMPETENCY CHECK

Take another look at table 1.3 (page 9) to see how you assessed these related competencies.

1. Understand financial processes (i.e., purchasing, budget).

2. Develop, monitor, and stay within a budget.

Budgets and Financial Cost Analysis

1. Demonstrate an understanding of the budget process.
2. Differentiate between capital and operating budgets.
3. Compare and contrast the most prevalent types of budgets used in leisure services.
4. Identify the most common financial analysis methods used in leisure services.

On this particular day I received two e-mails that indicate my day will not follow the schedule I had planned. Both situations require immediate attention so as not to ruin potential leads. Today I also have a staff meeting regarding the management of grants and the tiny details that have to be tracked and how we can best track those without getting in our cars and visiting the grantees personally. After that I have several big projects to attend to, including budget review for planning next year, starting and finishing a deck (organizational term used when presenting ideas/concepts to outside groups) for a meeting next week, writing a recommendation letter, and putting out a fire that has been caused by staff not following up. In general, management is all about flexibility!

Danielle Timmerman
Director of Program Relationships
KaBOOM!
Washington, DC

The previous chapter laid the groundwork for financial management. A thorough understanding of revenues, expenditures, pricing, and subsidy are the small pieces of the larger financial plan—the budget. This chapter focuses on the budget process from the development of the budget cycle and preparation to implementation, monitoring, and evaluation.

It is easy to think of the budget as a summary of the revenues and expenditures for a year, but it is much more than that. A budget has political, managerial, short- and long-term planning, communication, and financial implications (NACSLB, 1999). Financial management and budgeting serve several important functions in the organization, thus requiring extended discussion throughout this book.

Defining Budgets

budgets—Financial plans detailing revenues and expenditures of an organization for a fiscal year.

Budgets are the financial plan for the year. They outline revenues and expenditures, and this outline drives decision making for the organization. Any decision that has financial implications must be examined based on the financial resources available, thus allowing managers to make informed choices. For example, assume the Cincinnati Recreation Commission plans to change its registration system. This requires the purchase of new computers and software for the 31 recreation centers and 41 swimming pools in the city—a large expenditure that can either be phased in over several fiscal years or done within one. Analyzing the budget will determine what options are available and what the best financial decision is for the department.

Budgets also reflect the priorities of an agency. These priorities are a result of organizational goals, objectives, and strategic plans, and they are reinforced by the financial resources allocated to priority projects. For example, Camp Fire USA is a nonprofit program whose mission is youth development, including leadership, self-reliance, inclusion, and the reduction of sex-role, racial, and cultural stereotypes. The budget from the parent organization reflects this mission, with 79 percent allocated to programs for young people and to councils that provide these programs (Camp Fire USA, 2007).

In addition, budgets reflect the effectiveness and efficiency of resources, including how resources are spent and acquired. The effectiveness of resources demonstrates what programs and services achieve the goals and priorities of the organization, and efficiency relates to minimizing the waste of resources. In an ideal financial situation, programs are funded based on whether they are congruent with the mission of the organization and whether they meet its goals. Then these programs are operated so they are most efficient. This may mean that thorough planning is done so that the right number of staff members is hired, sufficient sponsors are sought, and participant demand is correctly projected.

As you will see, financial management is far more complex than a spreadsheet of expenditures and revenues—it guides processes and decision making throughout the entire organization. Without a solid understanding of budgeting, a manager can quickly face a multitude of problems because of poor decision making, inaccurate revenue or expenditure projections, or inefficient service provision. The following pages in this chapter build an understanding of the budgeting process, different types of budgets, and means of tracking and analyzing financial activities.

Budget Cycle

Developing a budget is a long process with several steps. These steps are called the **budget cycle** and are prevalent within all sectors of leisure services. Some organizations may modify the process or order of the steps, but the budget cycle remains relatively consistent throughout the profession.

budget cycle—Steps associated with the budgeting process, from preparation to approval to implementation to closing of the budget at the end of the fiscal year.

Step 1: Develop a Budget Calendar

A budget calendar is a time line of tasks to be completed, including when budget preparation begins, when the budget is due from each level of administration, when the budget is presented to and approved by a governing body, and when the fiscal year begins. A budget runs on a fiscal year and consists of the 12 months during which a financial cycle runs. A fiscal year does not have to start on January 1 and follow a calendar year. For example, the City of Columbia Parks and Recreation Department in Missouri has a fiscal year of October 1 to September 30, and the NRPA has a fiscal year of July 1 to June 30. The budget calendar is based on the start of the fiscal year, and all proposed budgets must be completed, approved, and ready for implementation before the new fiscal year starts.

A budget cycle can require working with the budget for more than one fiscal year. In the United States, the National Park Service (NPS) can be working in the 2009 budget, have a draft of the 2010 budget in the congressional review process, and begin formulating the 2011 budget. The budget process in the NPS is roughly 21 months, with that time frame expanding if a new presidential administration takes office (National Park Service, 2007).

Step 2: Develop a Departmental Work Plan

A **work plan** outlines what programs and services will be offered or what products will be produced. In essence, the work plan forecasts service volume. It also allows

work plan—Outline of what programs and services will be offered or what products will be produced.

for evaluation and opportunities to eliminate unsuccessful programs, services, and products, as well as add new ones. The work plan will drive the budgeting process since the budget should account for the products in the work plan.

Step 3: Develop an Expense Budget

Once the products, services, and programs are outlined in the work plan, it is time to develop the expenses to produce them. A major part of the expense budget is salaries and related employee expenses such as fringe benefits. Salaried employees receive a set annual wage that is broken evenly into the designated pay periods for the agency, and most agencies pay weekly, biweekly, or monthly. This salary, as well as any anticipated raises, should be included. An employee making $40,000 per year and anticipating a 3 percent raise at the beginning of the fiscal year would have $41,200 budgeted for salary.

Hourly employees are different in that there are more cost units to consider. Assume a facility supervisor is working 20 hours per week at $9 per hour. Wages would be calculated as

20 hours per week × 52 weeks a year × $9 per hour = $9,360.

In addition to wages and salaries, all other operating expenditures need to be accounted for including facility maintenance, equipment, and supplies. Managers have a tendency to overestimate expenditures in their budgets because spending less than projected is better than underestimating expenses and having to find additional revenue by eliminating some programs or other expenses.

Step 4: Develop a Revenue Budget

Sources of revenues for organizations in the public, nonprofit, and commercial sectors were discussed in chapter 12. It is during this step in the budgeting process that revenue is accounted for, whether it is fees and charges, taxes, or investment income. Many managers are conservative in their revenue projections. It is better to bring in more revenue than projected than to have a shortfall. If the projected revenues do not come in, then the expenses will need to be adjusted in the middle of the fiscal year to account for the miscalculation.

Step 5: Modify and Finalize the Budget

With the revenues and expenditures in place, it is necessary to analyze whether the budget meets the goals, objectives, and priorities of the organization. This includes ensuring that all subsidy projections are met and that products meant to be subsidized, break even, and turn a profit actually do. This step reviews whether the

This gift shop in the Starved Rock State Park Visitor's Center is managed and staffed completely by volunteers. Profits and donations from sales go to the Starved Rock Historical and Educational Foundation to support park activities.

expenditures are too high or revenues too low. In this step managers are sometimes asked to make budget cuts. They may be told to cut a percentage of money from the budget or given a flat amount to cut, either from reducing expenditures or increasing revenues. If revenues are increased, there should be a justification for doing so. Once revenues are projected, they are expected to actually materialize.

Step 6: Present, Defend, and Seek Approval for the Budget

The finalized budget will go through a review process with the administrative board for public and nonprofit agencies and larger commercial agencies. Small commercial agencies, such as partnerships and sole proprietorships, need only the approval of the owners. Budgets that are presented in front of a board will demonstrate the overall financial picture as well as explain any major increases or decreases in revenues and expenditures. The board usually asks numerous questions seeking justification for some areas. At this point in the process the board may approve the budget or ask for revisions. Once approved, the budget is set and ready to begin the fiscal year.

Summary of the Budget Cycle

Budget preparation requires involvement from all levels of the organization. Any staff members who are involved in spending money or bringing in revenues should be part of the process. This helps get commitment from staff who must work within the financial parameters set in the budget. In addition, these employees know the inner workings of their programs, services, and products. They will be well versed in what expenditures to expect as well as better able to project revenues than someone higher in the organization who does not work directly with the services, programs, or products.

Cutback Management

Developing a budget requires a great deal of time, fortitude, and foresight. However, sometimes it is necessary to cut budgets due to unforeseen circumstances such as a declining economy, as happened after the terrorist attacks of September 11, 2001, or unplanned expenses, such as a major facility falling short of revenues by thousands of dollars.

How Cuts Are Made

When such unforeseen events occur, it is necessary for the organization to implement **cutback management,** where the agency must cut projected expenses from the budget. Determining what to cut is a difficult task and can become political in nature. Cutback management has long-term effects and cannot be done quickly or without a plethora of information. Thus, cuts should be made with the involvement of stakeholders, as much information as possible, and the guidance of the strategic plan. When deciding what to cut, it is important to look at several aspects of the agency to see where cuts are possible. In terms of parks and recreation, managers should examine core values, vision, and mission; the vision for the future and how

cutback management—The process of determining what expenditures to reduce within a budget.

cuts will affect that vision; how well the organization is performing; what outcomes result from the programs and services; and what would happen if the programs and services were no longer offered (Thomas, 2002).

Cuts can be made in three areas: workforce reduction, where staff numbers are reduced; work redesign, where the work itself is the focus; and systematic change requiring a change in the culture, values, and tradition of the organization (Cameron, 1994). Workforce reduction means that staffing levels are reduced through such methods as attrition, where staff members who leave are not replaced; hiring freezes; elimination of positions currently held by employees; layoffs; and early retirements or buy-outs, where people are given a sum of money if they leave or retire from the company at a specified time. The workforce is often the first place managers look during cutbacks since staff is usually the single largest expenditure in the budget of a leisure services organization. The result of workforce reduction is often low morale. When staff is cut, it is logical to assume that the remaining employees will not trust the organization, they will be worried about their own job security, and they will be less committed to the organization (Thomas, 2002). It is a challenge for managers to clearly communicate why cutbacks were made and what it means for the rest of the organization. It is imperative to be honest with employees in order to aid morale.

Work redesign changes the products and services offered. Services may be eliminated altogether, phased out, or changed. At first glance, work redesign seems to be a negative concept. However, true work redesign requires the agency to look at what programs it is offering and determine which are the most important for meeting the needs of the constituency. It can identify labor-saving approaches to staffing and technology; eliminate duplication of services within the agency or with other agencies in the community; and eliminate organizational layers in staffing, giving the organization a larger span of control (see chapter 5) with fewer managers and layers of bureaucracy (Cameron, 1994).

Systematic changes in culture, values, and attitudes can be difficult. Such changes require the organization to operate more efficiently and effectively through streamlined processes, and they result in doing fewer things better. Streamlining processes requires reducing resource waste and hidden costs.

Politics of Cutback Management

Cutback management can result in agency politics, especially in the public sector. The political aspects of the budget process can include special interest groups, board or city council reelection, or city priorities. It is not uncommon for special interest groups to become involved and fight for their particular service if cuts are looming. These special interest groups may be very vocal, but that should not dictate whether their budget area is cut. Their programs must be evaluated just as those of less vocal interests are. With special interest groups, much information and misinformation will be presented. It is the job of the manager to acquire as much accurate information as possible and listen to these groups so their interests can be considered. It is not uncommon for special interest groups to present outcomes of programs and services that are unknown to the staff.

The election cycle also affects cutback management. If city council or board members are coming up for reelection, they may be more likely to make the popular decision for reelection purposes rather than making decisions in the best interest of the agency. Typically, politicians do not like to have bad publicity or controversies arise near a campaign season, and it is during this time that the special interest groups can become even more vocal.

Finally, understanding and negotiating the priorities of elected officials can be key to reducing cutbacks for specific departments. Let's use a midwestern city as an example. This city recently built a new coliseum despite the fact that the community voted in a nonbinding resolution not to build it. The city council made the decision to build the coliseum anyway and in its first year of business it lost over $2 million. Even though the city council members who voted to build the coliseum in the first place were not reelected, the current council has the task of covering the $2 million loss from the current year and in the future since upcoming fiscal years look only slightly better. This city council has decided that cutback management is needed rather than raised taxes. The council has also set as its priorities basic city services such as police and fire. However, it does not see parks and recreation as a basic service and is devaluing its effects on the community. This has caused the council to make major cuts to the park and recreation budget while leaving other city services intact. Now the challenge for the park and recreation department is to reposition itself as a vital service to the community in hopes of changing the priorities of the council (see chapter 9).

Cutback management is never easy. It is difficult to identify areas to cut and makes staff uneasy. It also brings out the political aspects of budgeting. However, it is something that managers face regardless of whether they are in the public, nonprofit, or commercial sectors. When it happens, the manager has many options, with the priority being to work with staff and other stakeholders to reach the best solution possible under difficult circumstances.

Types of Budgets

The previous steps outlined the process for developing the budget; now it's time to consider the types of budgets available to managers. Budgets typically come in two forms: capital budgets and operating budgets. Both types go through the same process but are considered separate budgets.

Capital Budgets

Capital budgets are developed for big projects such as land acquisition, facility development, or major equipment purchases. Expenditures included in capital budgets generally have a life expectancy of at least 10 years (Crompton, 1999). Capital budgets are a result of long-term planning and careful research—organizations do not just decide to build a new facility, put it in the budget, and open it the next year. Because of the cost and unique funding sources needed for these projects, much planning and research is required to make the right decisions and set project priorities that are in the best interest of the organization.

Capital improvement plans (CIPs) are established by organizations and their governing boards, and they can cover 2 to 5 years. Once the CIP is established, it

capital budget—Financial plan for large-scale purchases within an agency.

capital improvement plan (CIP)—Plan outlining capital projects to be completed; guides budget decisions related to the projects.

guides budgeting decisions and priorities. The CIP is reviewed annually and the order of projects can change over time. For example, Vancouver Parks and Recreation in British Columbia developed a $5.7 million CIP for 2006 through 2008 with their priorities being neighborhood park renewal, ice rinks, and an aquatics center. Some of these items became higher priorities than originally projected because Vancouver is hosting the 2010 Winter Olympic and Paralympic Games (Vancouver Parks and Recreation, 2007). CIPs are regularly evaluated and priorities adjusted as things such as the Olympic Games or changes in the economic climate arise.

An advantage of the long-term CIP is that many projects require phases of development that will not happen within a fiscal year. The CIP outlines the phases so that funds are available when needed for the project. For example, Illinois State University is in the process of building a new student recreation center. This multiyear project is budgeted in phases in different fiscal years:

▶ Phase 1: Feasibility study

▶ Phase 2: Planning meetings resulting in architectural drawings for the facility

▶ Phase 3: Razing of buildings in the future location of the building

▶ Phase 4: Building of the new recreation center

The capital budget is the financial plan for major resource investment, but the operating budget is also affected because daily operating costs such as staff, maintenance, and utilities are in the general operating budget and not the capital budget. So, although the two types of budgets are separate, they are very much intertwined in the management of the organization.

Operating Budgets

operating budget— Budget containing revenues and expenditures associated with day-to-day operations of the organization.

Operating budgets affect managers at all levels of an organization. Managers exercise most control with these budgets because they outline and implement the expenditures and revenues for their departments or areas within the fiscal year. Keep in mind that although a 12-month fiscal year is most common, some agencies operate on a 2- or 3-year budget cycle as well.

Operating budgets can come in several different formats. Each organization will differ, but a general understanding of the most common types will be beneficial to a manager new to the organization.

Line-Item and Object Classification Budgets

Line-item and object classification budgets are the most common budget formats in leisure services. They are similar in format and function. The line-item budget is a listing of expenditures, or items, and their dollar amounts. These expenditures are then placed in a line so they can all be viewed at once (table 13.1). This type of budget is best for small programs or agencies. With a line-item budget, it is easy to leave out expenditures since line items are not consistent from program to program. This also makes it difficult to compare budgets across programs if they do not have the same expenditures.

Table 13.1   Sample Line-Item Budget

Line items	Total
REVENUES	
Ticket sales	$1,875
Reserve (carryover from previous budget)	$36
Total revenue	$1,911
EXPENDITURES	
Meal	$900
Appetizers	$132
Damage deposit	$50
Facility rental fee	$75
DJ	$300
Mailings	$55
Printing—invitations	$15
Printing—information sheets	$60
Envelopes	$60
Total expenditures	$1,647

The object classification budget takes the line-item budget one step further in that it categorizes, or classifies, line items. There may be major classifications such as personnel services and contractual services (table 13.2), and within these categories there are often subcategories and objects. In table 13.2, personnel services does not have a subcategory but contractual services has numerous subcategories, such as communication and transportation and utilities. Personnel services moves directly to the objects with contractual employees and wages. The totals from each object line item are summarized in the subcategory totals, which are then totaled in the category column.

The predetermined categories are used by all managers within an organization, although not all managers will use all of the categories or line items. In order for these categories to be effective, each needs a standardized definition. For table 13.2, the definitions could be the following:

- ▶ Personnel services: Full- and part-time salaries and hourly wages paid to staff employed at the organization
- ▶ Contractual services: Products purchased on contract or services obtained through a contractual agreement between the agency and another party

Creating an object classification budget means assigning the appropriate monetary amounts to each object or line item. A manager is then allowed to spend the allocated amount in the budget. **Allocated funds** are those that are approved by

allocated funds— Money that has been approved by the authoritative body to be spent on specific line items within the budget.

Table 13.2 Sample Object Classification Categories

	Object total	Subcategory total	Category total
1000: Personnel services			$2,037,000
1100: Salaries, regular (full time)	$1,500,000		
1200: Salaries, temporary (part time)	$25,000		
1300: Wages, regular (hourly, full time)	$250,000		
1400: Wages, temporary (hourly, part time)	$175,000		
1500: Contractual employees	$75,000		
1600: Other compensations	$12,000		
2000: Contractual services			$641,252
2100: Communication and transportation		$183,252	
2110: Postage	$5,002		
2120: Telephone	$23,000		
2130: Freight and express	$10,000		
2140: Travel and lodging	$70,000		
2150: Vehicles	$32,000		
2160: Gasoline, oils, and lubricants	$43,250		
2300: Printing, binding, and advertising		$16,475	
2310: Printing and photocopying	$12,000		
2320: Typewriting and word processing	$500		
2330: Binding	$500		
2340: Photocopying and blueprinting	$250		
2350: Advertising and publication of notices	$3,225		
2400: Utilities		$396,375	
2410: Heating service	$54,500		
2420: Interior lighting service	$65,000		
2430: Street lighting service	$76,525		
2440: Power (electricity and gas)	$102,350		
2450: Water service	$98,000		
2500: Repairs		$17,700	
2510: Repairs to equipment	$2,350		
2520: Repairs to buildings and other structures	$15,350		
2600: Janitorial, cleaning, waste removal, and other services		$27,450	
2610: Park trash removal	$12,000		
2620: Outdoor facility cleaning	$15,450		
Totals			$2,678,252

the governing body to be spent on a specific line item. As money in this line item is spent, it needs to be tracked by the manager to ensure the money expended does not exceed the allocated amount and go over budget.

Object classification budgets are popular because of their ease and flexibility. The objects are predetermined so it is easy to see if any expenditures were omitted from the budget. The object classification budget also is relatively easy to learn and use by all levels of employees. It is flexible in that categories, subcategories, and objects can change as needed. However, for consistency purposes they remain relatively stable unless a major change occurs such as adding cemeteries or libraries to the local park and recreation agency. These units would need some of their own classifications since they most likely will not fit neatly into a park and recreation budget.

This budget format has some weaknesses as well. The most prevalent problem is that an object classification budget does not identify how budget figures were obtained, so a separate document outlining this information is needed. Second, with predetermined categories it is sometimes difficult to find an object for unusual expenditures. This means they get placed wherever seems the most logical to the manager. Object classification budgets have also been criticized for not being goal driven. They focus solely on how much the program costs and not how it fits with the goals of the organization. Finally, object classification perpetuates a status quo approach to budgeting. The manager continues to fund current programs and only adds programs when the budget allows. With this budget format, the benefits and costs of the services are not evaluated (Holdnak, Mahoney, & Garges, 2005). However, this weakness can be ameliorated by following the work plan that reviews programs and services.

Program Budgets

As mentioned, a weakness of object classification budgets is that they are driven more by expenditures and less by the value of the program to consumers. Program budgets focus more on results, benefits, beneficiaries of services, and how programs interconnect with the mission, goals, and objectives of the agency (Holdnak et al., 2005).

Program budgets are outcome driven. Outcomes are the benefits received from participation in the program, such as changes in behavior, skill, knowledge, attitudes, or fitness levels. These outcomes, discussed in detail in chapter 2, tie directly to the benefits discussed in chapter 8 and are often used to market the programs.

The format of the program budget requires program information be solidified before the budget process begins. Each program must have goals, objectives, a description, and a budget (figure 13.1). The goals and objectives demonstrate the value and results of the program rather than simply presenting budget figures. The emphasis is on effectiveness rather than efficiency. In program budgets, the programs are grouped together based on their outcomes or type. For example, program areas may include special events, aquatics, sports, and teens. The programs are then budgeted as a group with a manager overseeing and being accountable for the program area. These groupings of programs are called *cost centers*.

In addition to program budgets being outcome driven, they also account for all costs associated with a program, including indirect costs. This budget format provides a more realistic picture of what the program actually costs. A negative

Company: Backroads Bike Tours

Program budget: New York Wine Country Bike Tour

Program dates: October 2-7

Program length: 6 days

Number of participants: 20

Goals

1. Gain appreciation of the wine country in the Finger Lakes area.
2. Meet and interact with riders from all over the country.
3. Attract beginner, intermediate, and advanced riders.
4. Develop a program that will help fight obesity.

Objectives

1. Each rider will be given cue sheets describing the attractions and points of interest along the bike route each day.
2. The trip will be advertised nationally to attract a wide variety of riders.
3. Day riders will be given two or three distance options to choose from to meet the needs of all abilities.
4. Tour guides will emphasize the need for social interaction and support for beginning riders.
5. Riders will be given a training schedule to begin 6 months before the tour dates in order to achieve a needed level of physical fitness.

Description

This bike tour starts in Skaneateles, New York, and tours the wine country in the Finger Lake area. Riders stay at unique inns and bed-and-breakfasts along the 300-mile (483-kilometer) route. Trip fee includes 5 nights' lodging, 10 meals, beverages and snacks, van support, and 6 experienced guides.

Budget Summary

REVENUES		EXPENDITURES	
Tour charges	$27,000	Lodging	$9,750
Total revenues	**$27,000**	Meals	$4,316
		Supplies	$2,600
		Vehicles	$500
		Staff	$6,000
		Total expenditures	**$23,166**
Total profit = $3,834 (total revenues – total expenditures)			

Figure 13.1 Sample program budget.

aspect of program budgeting has to do with overemphasizing the outcomes of a program. Objectives that are inflated or overly lofty can be used to sell the value of the program to those who have final approval of the budget. Another weakness of this budget format is that it requires another system such as the object classification budget to present the data (Kelsey, Gray, & McLean, 1992). Many agencies that use program budgets combine them with the object classification budget to demonstrate revenues and expenditures. The combination of these two formats minimizes the identified weaknesses of both budgets.

Table 13.3 shows an object classification budget and program budget combined. The classifications, subclassifications, and objects are still present, but within each object is the program area or cost center (e.g., membership or marketing). This level of detail allows comparisons across program areas and within classifications.

Performance Budgets

Performance budgets present performance information alongside budget figures. This information comes in the form of outputs such as number of people served, efficiency of resource use, cost per acre (hectare), or cost per day. It is assumed that performance measures improve budget decisions and support requests for resources from the final approving body. This budget was first implemented by the U.S. government in 1997 in order to focus on results-oriented management, increase visibility of outputs to the public, improve decision making, offer effective programs, maximize performance, and achieve accountability. Performance budgets allow decision makers to more closely tie resource allocation to actual service provision (U.S. Department of Defense, 2007).

This budget format links funding and program results using inputs, activities, and outputs. Inputs are the resources dedicated to programs and services such as money, staff, time, equipment, and facility space. In terms of budgeting, activities include services and products. Outputs are the volume of work produced or the number of people served, such as the number of canoes sold or the number of people served in a soccer league. Outputs, or performance indicators, can be divided into three types: workload outputs, efficiency measures, and effectiveness measures.

> ▶ Workload outputs include number of parks managed, number of conferences held, number of worker hours, and so on.

> ▶ Efficiency measures include the cost per person served, hotel capacity rates, and so on.

> ▶ Effectiveness measures resemble outcomes in that they look at how satisfied people were with a program and how well it met its goals and objectives (Crompton, 1999).

Agencies such as the U.S. Fish and Wildlife Service use performance budgets that outline goals, objectives, and budget figures allocated to achieve goals and objectives (Tynan, 2005). Table 13.4 is an example of a performance-based budget that could be used in an outdoor agency.

Although budget formats will be unique to an organization, most will be some derivation of the object classification budget, program budget, or performance budget. Some agencies may even use a combination of one or more formats to outline their financial plan for the fiscal year.

Table 13.3   Combination of Program Budget and Object Classification Budget

	Object total	Subcategory total	Category total
1000: Personnel services			$802,100
1100: Salaries, regular (full time)		$600,000	
(12) Membership	$160,000		
(13) Marketing	$80,000		
(14) Meeting planning	$120,000		
(15) Special events	$240,000		
1200: Salaries, temporary (part time)		$190,300	
(12) Membership	$50,000		
(13) Marketing	$45,000		
(14) Meeting planning	$72,300		
(15) Special events	$23,000		
1300: Wages, regular (hourly, full time)		$11,800	
(12) Membership	$1,200		
(13) Marketing	$2,400		
(14) Meeting planning	$3,200		
(15) Special events	$5,000		
2000: Contractual services			$91,970
2100: Communication and transportation			
2110: Postage		$38,970	
(12) Membership	$10,000		
(13) Marketing	$9,000		
(14) Meeting planning	$9,870		
(15) Special events	$10,100		
2120: Telephone		$8,000	
(12) Membership	$2,000		
(13) Marketing	$2,000		
(14) Meeting planning	$2,000		
(15) Special events	$2,000		
2300: Printing, binding, and advertising		$45,000	
2350: Advertising and publication of notices			
(12) Membership	$5,000		
(13) Marketing	$25,000		
(14) Meeting planning	$6,000		
(15) Special events	$9,000		
Total budget			$894,070

Table 13.4 Sample Performance Budget

GOAL: EFFECTIVELY AND EFFICIENTLY MANAGE
NATURAL RESOURCES AREAS WITHIN THE PARK.

Objectives	Budget
1. Protect and maintain the raptor population by installing 250 perches for hawks and insulating electrical wires.	$72,508
2. Preserve 235 acres (96 hectares) of wetlands by stabilizing shoreline erosion.	$123,500
3. Institute a 7-bus transportation system within the park to minimize traffic congestion, danger to pedestrians, air pollution, and the need for parking lots.	$723,000

Approaches to Budgeting

There are many approaches to developing a budget regardless of the format used. Organizations may adopt zero-based budgeting, incremental budgeting, or activity-based costing. Each has its strengths and weaknesses.

Zero-Based Budgeting

With zero-based budgeting, managers are placed in decision units or cost centers, usually determined by program area or department. These units develop budgets for programs from scratch regardless of whether the program was offered in previous years. This requires managers to justify all programs and examine their effectiveness each fiscal year and the decision units to prepare decision packages. These packages are one-page summaries describing program objectives, outputs, outcomes, consequences of not funding the program, and money needed (Mayers, 2004). The decision packages (figure 13.2) are then ranked by decision unit and moved up the hierarchy of the budget process for review. A clear advantage of the decision unit is that it allows employees at all levels of the organization to get involved in the budget process and to establish their own priorities for programs rather than higher levels of management with less intimate knowledge of the programs establishing priorities.

Once the programs have been prioritized by units, all agency programs are prioritized, creating an overall ranking of programs. The available resources are determined and the programs are accepted in priority order as long as funds remain. For example, an organization has $5,000,000 for programs and services. This is enough money to fund 23 of the 37 programs on the list. Programs ranked 24 through 37 will not be funded because they were rated as less important.

An advantage of zero-based budgeting is that all programs are treated equally and expected to demonstrate how they meet the goals and objectives of the agencies and why they should be higher priorities. Programs that are stagnant will be replaced by more effective programs. However, zero-based budgeting is time consuming, especially for a large agency. In addition, the process lends itself to politicking, or trying to influence decision makers by overselling the outcomes of programs.

Priority Rank

3

Program

Friday Night Teen Dance

Objective

To provide structured and supervised activities for teens in the community to serve as alternatives to less positive behavior in the community

Outcomes

Reduced arrest rates of teens on Friday evenings in the area; reduced number of teens hanging out in local parks after closing hours; supervised place provided where teens feel comfortable

Consequences of Not Approving

Increased teen arrest rates for minor crimes; increased need for park police to patrol park areas to control behavior of teens

Workload

1. Number of teens served   500
2. Unit cost of service $5
3. Staff positions required   4
4. Personnel costs $2,000
5. Other expenses $500
6. Total income $0
   Total funding requested: $2,500

Figure 13.2 Zero-based budget decision package.

Incremental Budgeting

Unlike zero-based budgeting, incremental budgeting is based on past budgets. Proposed budgets are increased or decreased by a determined increment, usually a percentage each fiscal year. For example, a budget may increase by 3 percent for the next fiscal year, decrease by 2 percent, or see no increase or decrease.

Incremental budgeting is firmly entrenched in the history rather than the value of programs. Furthermore, program outcomes are not reviewed. They simply remain in the budget and are increased or decreased incrementally. With this philosophy it is difficult to incorporate new programs or large-scale change because previous budget decisions and priorities strongly affect current and future budgets.

Incremental budgeting is a fairly simple process to learn. A manager rarely makes adjustments line by line in a budget but usually by program or service. Incremental budgeting also makes defending and approving the budget simple. Programs that remain at the same funding level are approved without scrutiny and those that are increased are reviewed to ensure they were only increased by the designated increment (Crompton, 1999).

Activity-Based Costing

Activity-based costing (ABC) emerged in the commercial sector because of the difficulty in accounting for indirect costs, and it has since been adopted in the public and nonprofit sectors as well. This costing approach more accurately identifies the true costs of providing a service. It eliminates arbitrarily assigning indirect costs or leaving some indirect costs unaccounted for, and it identifies what a unit of production actually costs, taking into consideration administrative costs, facilities, technology, and so on. ABC links total production costs to outputs. It focuses on inputs and outputs and not so much on outcomes. However, the outputs must be measurable or quantifiable for this system to work effectively (OSD Comptroller iCenter, 2007). Because of this, commercial organizations that produce tangible products, sell memberships, or have other units of production may be more likely to use ABC than those that are service based since quantifying services is more challenging.

Multiyear Budgeting

Multiyear budgeting is becoming increasingly popular among state, provincial, and local entities. Multiyear budgets extend beyond the annual budget to 3 and even 5 years. The 2-year, or biennial, budget is the most common form of multiyear budgeting. The biennial budget is implemented one of three ways. First, the biennial financial plan uses an annual budget with an appended financial plan that serves as the tentative budget for the second year. Since the second part of the budget is a financial plan, it is not adopted by the governing body and is subject to change. A second form of biennial budgeting is the traditional biennial budget. This budget details revenues and expenditures for 2 years as one complete budget. Third is the rolling biennial budget. With this format, two annual budgets are created simultaneously but are adopted each year rather than as one budget covering 2 years (Jackson, 2002).

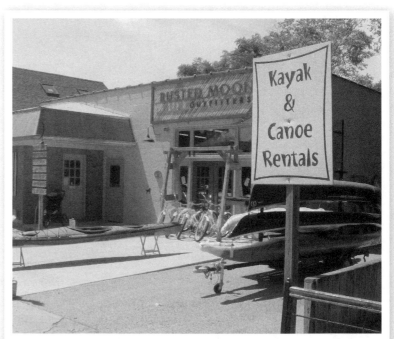

Located along a river, this business sells outdoor equipment and supplies as well as rents kayaks and canoes.

There are several advantages to the multiyear budget. First, there is a decrease in staff time dedicated to budgeting. Although this time is increased during the first year, the second year requires little time; the only task is to review and revise the second year of the budget. Second, multiyear budgeting integrates financial and strategic planning by requiring staff to think beyond a single year. They must focus on what is to be accomplished in the long term and build it into the budget. A third advantage is that multiyear budgeting requires the agency to reduce incrementalism where the annual budgets are simply increased a certain percentage each year. Instead, goals and objectives are linked with finance and planning (Blom & Guajardo, 2000; Jackson, 2002).

Multiyear budgeting also has disadvantages. First, it is difficult to project long-term expenditures and revenues. In particular it is difficult to project staff needs and current staff who will receive raises such as cost of living and merit pay. Since revenues are tightly tied to the economy in a given year, they can also be tricky to predict at times. A second disadvantage is that it is time consuming to put together a new budget for the upcoming fiscal years. Finally, multiyear budgeting lacks flexibility and the ability to respond to economic, political, and programmatic changes (Blom & Guajardo, 2000; Jackson, 2002). Regardless of its disadvantages, multiyear budgeting is increasingly popular in the public sector.

Budget Implementation

Once budgets are approved and the new fiscal year begins, they are implemented. This means that the revenue generated goes into the accounts represented in the budget and expended money goes out to pay bills.

The largest expenditure items in a budget are most often personnel, including salaries, hourly wages, and employee benefits. A payroll staff member within the accounting or bookkeeping department will have the responsibility of paying employees. Salaried employees are automatically paid the allotted amount whereas hourly employees submit time cards designating how many hours were worked and at what rate. The second largest expenditure items in a budget are regular operating expenditures such as equipment, supplies, and advertising. These items must be purchased by the manager in charge of each particular program or service.

All agencies have policies and procedures that guide purchasing. These guidelines vary too extensively to cover in depth here. However, purchasing can be categorized as petty cash purchasing, normal purchasing procedures, and the formal bidding process (Sellers, Gladwell, & Pope, 2005).

Petty Cash

petty cash—Cash on hand that is used for small purchases where it is inefficient to write a check.

Many organizations keep actual cash on hand for small purchases. This cash, generally $50 to $100, is called **petty cash.** This system allows managers to forgo normal purchasing procedures (described next), but it has its own processes, which usually require cash receipts for items purchased. Although petty cash is a faster means of purchasing small items, the downside for nonprofit and public agencies is that petty cash voids tax-exempt benefits on purchases. See figure 13.3 for a sample petty cash form from American University.

American University Club Sports
Petty Cash Form

Original receipts must be submitted taped to a sheet of paper within 14 days of trip/purchase.

Date: _____   Club: _____

Name: _____   AU ID #: _____

Phone: _____   E-mail: _____

Address: _____

City: _____   State: _____   Zip: _____

Signature: _____

Description	Price
Total	$

Reason for purchase or trip: _____

_____

_____

_____   _____   _____
Club treasurer signature   Name   Date

Contact #: _____

_____   _____
Director of club sports   Date

Budget account number: _____

Entered into tracking: _____

Figure 13.3 American University petty cash form.

American University Recreational Sports and Fitness.

Normal Purchasing Procedures

When purchasing equipment and supplies, each organization will follow its own process. However, most processes will include these basic steps.

Step 1: Complete a Purchase Requisition

A **purchase requisition** is a listing of the items to be purchased and a description of each item. The manager in charge of the program completes this requisition after reviewing the budget to ensure adequate funds exist.

Step 2: Request Quotations

Larger purchases require a manager to get quotes from vendors who sell the items. Purchasing policies and procedures will determine benchmarks for the minimum dollar amount that requires a quote. The same policies and procedures will identify the minimum number of quotes to be received. For example, an agency may require two quotes for purchases of $500 to $1,000 and three quotes for purchases of $1,000 to $2,500.

Step 3: Issue a Purchase Order

A **purchase order** is a purchase agreement from the agency with the specifics of the purchase. The vendor accepts this as an order for the products.

Step 4: Invoice When Products Are Received

Once products are received, they are accompanied by an **invoice** that serves as a receipt. The receipt is given to the accounts payable department so it may disperse funds to the vendors.

Formal Bidding Process

Many organizations have policies outlining the formal bidding process. Purchases over a predetermined amount require a formal bid. For example, the University of Miami (Florida) Department of Wellness and Recreation has a policy where goods and services costing more than $25,000 require a written quote from at least three vendors (University of Miami, 2007).

A formal bidding procedure is similar to receiving quotes but more structured. The bids are acquired either through an **invitation for bid (IFB), request for proposal (RFP),** or **request for quotation (RFQ)** (Business Owner's Toolkit, 2007).

Invitation for Bid

An IFB is an advertised contract, or sealed bid, where the specifications are detailed for the product or service. The bids are submitted by vendors in a sealed envelope to ensure the contents remain confidential until the predetermined opening. The low bidder is usually awarded the contract per the specifications in the bid.

Request for Proposal

An RFP is a negotiated contract. Specifications are outlined for the service or product and companies submit proposals detailing what they will do for what price.

---

purchase requisition— Form used to request and detail items to be purchased.

purchase order— Purchase agreement detailing the specifics of a purchase, including the brand, number, and what program the purchase is for.

invoice— Receipt of sale and delivery of products purchased; serves as a bill for the products.

invitation for bid (IFB)— Advertised contract, or sealed bid, where specifications are detailed for the product or service and bids are submitted by competing agencies.

request for proposal (RFP)— Binding, negotiated contract for services where both parties determine what work will be done for what price.

request for quotation (RFQ)— Nonbinding, negotiated contract for services where both parties determine what work will be done for what price.

Proposals are discussed and the bidder may have the opportunity to change bid pricing, procedures, and so on. Pricing and other factors such as work to be done will determine the winner of the contract. The contract is binding once both parties reach a signed agreement.

Request for Quotation

An RFQ is similar to an RFP except it is not a binding contract. An RFQ seeks information and prices and is negotiable after discussion of the details obtained from the quotations.

Financial Analysis and Reporting

Once the budget is complete, approved, and implemented, the financial analysis phase of the process begins. **Financial analysis** is done through records of revenues, expenditures, and other financial activity over a given time frame, usually monthly, quarterly, or annually depending on the analysis or report used. It monitors activity through several methods including a break-even analysis, balance sheets, income statements, cash-flow statements, and budget statements. Although some of these reports are most likely prepared by accountants, it is important to understand what they are and what they mean for the organization.

> **financial analysis—** Methods to monitor the fiscal status of the organization over a period of time.

Break-Even Analysis

Break-even analysis determines how many units of a product must be sold in order to cover all costs of producing that unit. This analysis uses fixed and variable costs to determine profit levels; profit occurs after enough units are sold to cover all of the fixed and variable costs. Managers calculate the break-even point using the following formula:

> $BE = F / (P - V)$, where
> BE = break-even point,
> F = fixed costs,
> P = selling price per unit, and
> V = variable costs per unit.

For example, a bike rental shop is located in a tourism town on a boardwalk, and they rent bikes for $50 per day. Fixed costs for the month total $8,000, and variable costs are $10 per bike. This company needs to rent 200 bikes per month to break even:

> $BE = \$8,000 / (\$50 - \$10)$
> $BE = 200$ **bikes per month.**

Notice in figure 13.4 that each rental above the break-even point is considered profit. The total costs keep going up in $10-per-bike increments because of the variable costs, so for every bike rented above 200, the company sees a $40 profit. If 350 bikes were rented for the month, the company would realize a $6,000 profit.

Figure 13.4 **Break-even analysis.**

balance sheet—
Accounting report demonstrating the financial condition of an organization, including assets, liabilities, and equity.

Balance Sheets

The **balance sheet,** sometimes called the *statement of financial position,* is a record of the accounting equation:

$$\text{Assets} = \text{liabilities} + \text{equity.}$$

The balance statement is divided in half with assets on the left and liabilities and equity on the right (table 13.5). It depicts the financial position of an organization at a given point in time (Fried, Shapiro, & DeSchriver, 2003).

Assets are the things owned by the organization such as cash, land, and equipment. The assets can be divided into current and fixed assets. Current assets can be converted into cash within a year whereas fixed assets cannot be quickly converted to cash (Brayley & McLean, 2001).

On the liabilities side of the balance sheet, the different types of liabilities are listed according to when they must be paid. Current liabilities must be paid within a year whereas long-term liabilities will not be paid within this time. Equity, also on the right side of the balance sheet, is the money invested in the organization by the owners in a commercial organization or the balance in specific funds for public and nonprofit organizations. The bottom line in each column must balance with total assets equal to total liabilities and equity.

Income Statements

Income statements reflect the profitability of the organization during a certain length of time such as a month, quarter, or fiscal year. It includes revenues, expenses, and net income (table 13.6). The income statement shows whether the organization is making a profit (running in the black) or losing money (running in the red).

In table 13.6, revenues exceed expenditures, so the organization showed a $3,914 profit for the month of July.

Cash-Flow Statements

A cash-flow statement depicts revenues versus expenditures (table 13.7). The statement shows positive and negative cash flow and determines if cash should be borrowed to remain solvent or if excess cash should be invested (Crossley, Jamieson, & Brayley, 2001).

In table 13.7, although expenses are greater than revenues for February and March, the $12,000 at the beginning of February helps carry this seasonal business through the off-peak season.

Budget Statements

A budget statement reports how much money has been received and spent in comparison to what was allocated in the budget (table 13.8). Revenues and expenses are listed as well as the amount of money that has been committed, the amount of money budgeted, and the amount remaining to be spent.

A manager would be responsible for analyzing the budget to ascertain if it is on track with projected revenues and expenditures for the first quarter of the fiscal

Table 13.5 Sample Balance Sheet

CLEAR WATER RAFTING COMPANY
BALANCE SHEET AS OF DECEMBER 31, 2007

ASSETS		LIABILITIES	
Current assets		*Current liabilities*	
Cash and investments	$3,546,975	Accounts payable	$25,729
Accounts receivable	$1,243,785	*Long-term debt*	
Total current assets	$4,790,760	Mortgage	$376,971
Fixed assets		Total liabilities	$402,700
Store fixtures	$243,876		
Office equipment	$7,659	Equity	$5,175,923
Rafting inventory	$543,987		
Total fixed assets	$787,863		
Total assets	$5,578,623	**Total liabilities and equities**	$5,578,623

Table 13.6 Sample Income Statement

CLEAR WATER RAFTING COMPANY
INCOME STATEMENT AS OF JULY 31, 2007

REVENUES	
Trips	$12,320
Concessions	$2,486
Store receipts	$3,345
Total revenues	$18,151
EXPENDITURES	
Staff	$9,562
Supplies	$527
Utilities	$452
Mortgage	$2,342
Marketing	$732
Maintenance	$622
Total expenditures	$14,237
Net revenue	$3,914

year. In table 13.8, 67.7 percent of the projected expenditures have been realized and 58.2 percent of the projected revenues have been received. The manager will need to monitor expenses for the remaining year so as to stay within the budget. However, since this is a seasonal business, it is not unusual to spend a larger portion of the budget during the peak season.

The reports are a means of analyzing data from several different perspectives, including revenues, expenditures, assets, and equity. Each report provides a different view of financial activity and requires constant management in order to stay within the financial parameters set in the budget. Reports track and monitor revenues and expenditures for analysis, but several other financial analysis indicators are also used in leisure services to determine efficiency of an organization, particularly in the commercial sector. Most of the data needed for the ratio analyses are available from income statements, balance sheets, and other financial reports. See page 340 for a brief description of the more common financial indicators used in the field.

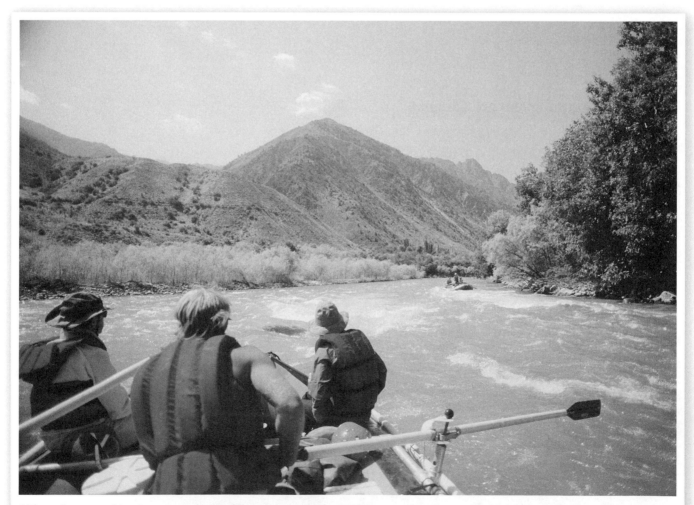

Although seasonal businesses such as rafting companies do not have consistent monthly revenues and expenditures, monitoring and analyzing financial aspects of the business remain important responsibilities for a manager.

Table 13.7   Sample Cash-Flow Statement

CLEAR WATER RAFTING COMPANY
CASH-FLOW STATEMENT, 1ST AND 2ND QUARTERS

	February	March	April	May	June	July	Total
Net revenues	$1,276	$4,985	$8,076	$12,486	$16,958	$18,151	$61,932
Expenses	$4,978	$6,890	$7,013	$9,213	$11,345	$14,237	$53,676
Monthly cash flow	$(3,702)	$(1,905)	$1,063	$3,273	$5,613	$3,914	
Cumulative cash flow	$(3,702)	$(5,607)	$(4,544)	$(1,271)	$4,342	$8,256	
Cash position at beginning of month	$12,000	$8,298	$6,393	$7,456	$10,729	$16,342	
Cash position at end of month	$8,298	$6,393	$7,456	$10,729	$16,342	$20,256	

Numbers in parentheses indicate a negative balance.

Table 13.8   Sample Budget Statement

CLEAR WATER RAFTING COMPANY
BUDGET STATEMENT, 1ST AND 2ND QUARTERS

	Actual	Budget	Committed	%	Balance
REVENUES					
Trips	$42,113	$72,500	$0	58.1%	$30,387
Concessions	$8,671	$14,000	$0	61.9%	$5,329
Store receipts	$11,148	$20,000	$0	55.7%	$8,852
Total revenues	$61,932	$106,500	$0	58.2%	$44,568
EXPENDITURES					
Staff	$35,963	$52,100	$1,500	71.9%	$14,637
Supplies	$2,147	$3,100	$0	69.3%	$953
Utilities	$1,610	$2,430	$0	66.3%	$820
Mortgage	$8,051	$16,000	$0	50.3%	$7,949
Marketing	$2,684	$4,300	$500	74.0%	$1,116
Maintenance	$3,221	$4,300	$0	74.9%	$1,079
Total expenditures	$53,676	$82,230	$2,000	67.7%	$26,554

Financial Indicators

Following is a brief description of the more common indicators used in the field (Fried, Shapiro, & DeSchriver, 2003). Financial indicators are typically classified as liquidity ratios, activity ratios, and profitability ratios. Each has a different purpose in the financial management of the organization. Listed here are just a sample of those that can be used. Some of them are more applicable to the commercial sector where sales of inventory are more prominent. While it will be typical for the accountant in the organization to prepare the financial indicators, it will be the manager's responsibility to know what they actually mean.

Liquidity Ratios

Liquidity ratios reflect the ability of the organization to meet its short-term financial obligations. They include the following ratios.

▶ A current ratio above 1.0 indicates that the company can use its current assets to cover current liabilities.

Current ratio = total current assets / total current liabilities.

▶ A quick ratio indicates whether the organization can meet its short-term liabilities without selling inventory to meet them.

Quick ratio = (total current assets – inventories) / current liabilities.

Activity Ratios

Activity ratios, sometimes called *efficiency ratios*, determine the ability of an organization to efficiently manage its resources.

▶ Inventory turnover ratio indicates how many times during the year the inventory is purchased and sold. Companies want a high ratio because this indicates the inventory is turned over efficiently.

Inventory turnover ratio = cost of goods sold / average inventory.

▶ Assets-to-sales ratio determines how efficiently assets are being used.

Assets to sales = total assets / total sales.

▶ Average collection period is the average time it takes to convert sales to cash. The average collection period is measured in days and is not an actual ratio.

Average collection period = (accounts receivable / sales) × 365 days.

Profitability Ratios

Profitability ratios show how successful a business has been over a certain time frame.

▶ Net profit margin and gross profit margin demonstrate the ability to turn a profit on sales.

Net profit margin = return on sales = net income / revenues.

Gross profit margin = earnings before interest and taxes / revenues.

▶ Return on assets depicts the effectiveness of investment in assets.

Return on assets = net profit after taxes / total assets.

Conclusion

▶ Sound financial management is required by professionals at all levels of organizations in all three sectors. Revenues and expenditures are a daily part of doing business. Agency budgets are as unique as the agencies themselves, but a clear understanding of the different types of budgets is important. A strong grasp of basic budgeting principles helps lessen the learning curve in terms of financial management for anyone entering a new agency.

▶ In addition to preparing a budget, a manager with strong financial skills will closely monitor and analyze the activity within it. In order to stay within the budget, managers need an understanding of financial reports. Although most organizations will have an accountant to prepare the statements, the manager must interpret the statements and handle problems involving cash flow or liabilities.

REVIEW QUESTIONS

1. Describe the budget process and the steps taken to develop a budget.

2. Differentiate between pricing and budgeting.

3. Discuss how capital and operating budgets interrelate.

4. Compare and contrast object classification budgeting, program budgets, and performance budgets.

5. Explain zero-based budgeting, incremental budgeting, and activity-based costing.

6. Describe the three ways bids are acquired.

7. There are several ways to track budgets, revenues, and expenditures. Discuss how each method works.

Check out the online student resource at www.HumanKinetics.com/LeisureServicesManagement for additional material, including sample documents, case studies, Web links, and more.

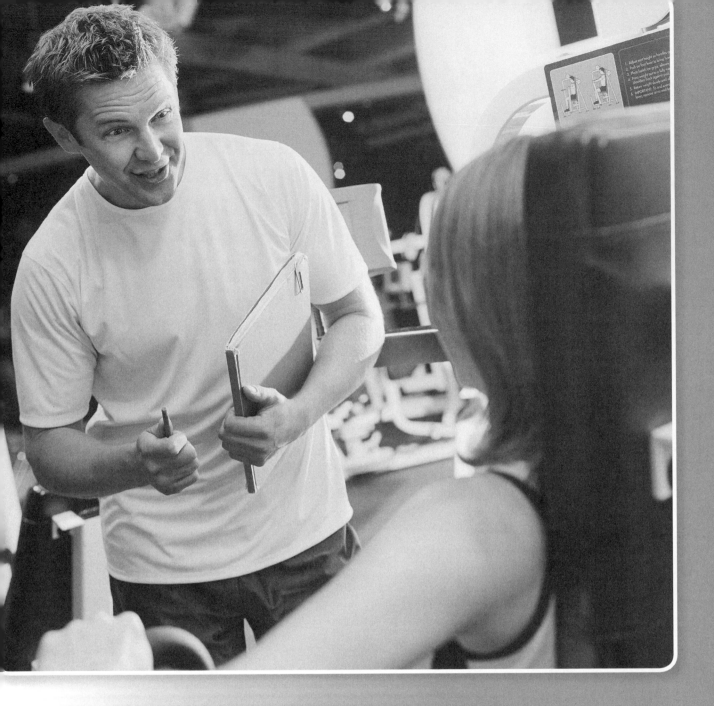

KEY WORDS

process evaluation, outcome evaluation, formative evaluation, summative evaluation, evaluation process, quantitative research, qualitative research, questionnaire, attitude scale, raters, secondary data, case study, sampling, best practices, benchmarking

COMPETENCY CHECK

Take another look at table 1.3 (page 9) to see how you assessed these related competencies.

11. Know the community and its needs.

34. Conduct program evaluations.

39. Conduct research and evaluation.

40. Conduct needs assessments.

CHAPTER 14

Evaluation

1. Understand the rationale for evaluation in leisure services organizations.
2. Identify and explain the types of tools for evaluation.
3. Become familiar with the five-step evaluation process.
4. Differentiate between formative and summative evaluation.
5. Explain the difference between probability and nonprobability sampling.

My position is a new one, created at a time when the campus recreation department was taking over the management of our university's 6,000+ seat arena from a private management company. When I began my job, I was given a full plate of potential ideas and an empty slate to work with. This has created an opportunity to leave my own mark on the organization. Since starting, my main focus has been on unifying the campus recreation department and the arena through the creation of a new logo and print template. I am also working on a student benchmarking survey, focused on our facilities and programs, for our department and the National Intramural-Recreational Sports Association. Other projects include the creation of a graduate assistantship informational packet for the University of New Hampshire; a promotional video of our sport clubs, recreation programs, and facilities geared toward incoming freshmen and prospective students; and the everyday task of being an intermediary between our arena and recreation center programs and staff. It's a great deal of responsibility, but a fantastic learning experience!

Gabby Schiavone
Campus Recreation Marketing Coordinator
Durham, New Hampshire

Managers evaluate many things, from people, programs, and facilities to organizational direction, goals, risk profiles, and fiscal situations. Without evaluation, it is difficult to know how well the organization is performing or if goals are being met. This chapter explains the importance of evaluation, describes types of evaluation, and provides practical information on conducting evaluations in leisure services organizations. In simple terms, evaluation is making a judgment about the value of something (Henderson & Bialeschki, 2002). Evaluation can range from formal, such as a survey or focus group, to less formal, such as simply walking around and talking with people. This chapter will focus less on informal forms of evaluation and more on the process of systematically collecting data for evaluation by leisure services organizations and related stakeholders.

Why Evaluate?

The reasons for evaluation differ depending on who the user of the information is. For example, a recreation programmer may use evaluation information to guide future programming decisions, an elected official may use evaluation information to demonstrate that a program is serving constituents, and a researcher may use evaluation information to recommend policy change, build on current understanding of leisure behavior, or discover best practices in an area. Understanding the purpose of the information is critical before any other evaluation decisions are made. However, regardless of the purpose, the goals of evaluation are to provide information; to help make decisions for continuing, improving, or discontinuing activities; and to simply learn more about the desires of the people an organization serves or employs.

One of the fundamental reasons for evaluation is to determine if what is being evaluated is doing what it is intended to do. Earlier in the text the notion of goal setting was discussed. Goals provide a basis for evaluation—is the organization actually achieving what it set out to achieve? For example, are swimming lessons actually teaching children the skills needed to swim? Goals may have included certain strokes children need to learn at a particular level, and in order to see if they have learned those skills, some form of evaluation must occur.

Evaluation can also aid in understanding whether the objectives and goals are appropriate in the first place. To continue with the swimming example, perhaps the children could already swim and what they really desired was training for the next IronKids triathlon. In addition, evaluation can help managers learn more about the clients they serve. For instance, you may find that participants in the swim class are also seeking social benefits from their leisure pursuits. The evaluation would lead to altering goals and revising them for the next program to better meet client desires. The programmer might choose to set up a kids' triathlon club with group runs and bike rides and perhaps even informal social get-togethers such as a pasta party before big events.

Evaluation can also tell managers about the appropriateness of program scheduling times, frequencies, and locations. A common use for evaluation in leisure services organizations is the evaluation of community needs through a needs assessment. A needs assessment can look at facility needs, staffing needs, community needs, or any concerns an organization may have related to the effective delivery of leisure services. Application of the concepts in this chapter will provide a strong foundation to develop effective needs assessments.

In addition, evaluation can help managers learn about their facilities and assess whether they meet clients' needs and expectations. This information may help in future planning or justify facility changes to a recreation commission. The things that can be measured are nearly infinite. Often this can be overwhelming for managers, and in turn they measure nothing or simply do a token evaluation that serves little use in future decision making. However, by no means does this suggest that everything must be measured or that managers must be expert researchers to successfully conduct evaluations in leisure services organizations.

As you have learned throughout this text, information is the key to helping managers make decisions about the things that are important to their organization. The manager should already understand what those priorities are and then go about collecting information on them. For example, if the main concerns are employee satisfaction, client satisfaction, and facility safety, then develop systematic ways to collect information on those areas. The following section briefly discusses some of the common areas that are evaluated in leisure services organizations, but each situation is unique and, as the manager, you will be in the best position to determine what to actually measure.

Types of Evaluation

Evaluation can focus on what is being done (the process) as well as the results (the outcomes) of what is being done. For example, a recreation programmer may care about how many people use the tennis courts (a process evaluation) as well as what benefits people seek or receive from using the facility (an outcome evaluation). Both types of evaluation provide essential information and are important for managers to understand. However, they address different questions, so managers must understand what they hope to achieve for each evaluation they conduct (Patton, 2001).

Process Evaluation

It is possible to measure both the means and the ends of what we do in leisure services organizations. The means are those factors required for an activity, often called *process factors,* including people, programs, and physical resources. **Process evaluation** is often referred to as *first-level evaluation,* an evaluation of how we are doing things. It can keep track of attendance, how many people register for a particular program, and the number of courts used at a particular time at a tennis facility. This information is usually easy to collect and has been the most frequent form of evaluation in many sport, leisure, and recreation settings. The downside is that although managers may know what the organization is doing, they don't gain any information on the outcomes of its processes.

Outcome Evaluation

As a result of outcomes-based management, recently a move has been made to also collect information on outcomes in leisure services organizations. **Outcome evaluation** is an evaluation of what we are doing—the results or outcomes of the evaluation target. Outcomes can be physical, social, psychological, environmental, or economic and can accrue to people, the organization, or the community as a whole. The term *outcome* is used instead of *benefits* because results may not always be perceived as beneficial. Outcomes constitute positive, negative, and neutral impressions of organizations. Although we all hope to do good, it is equally if not more important to also learn about the negatives since those messages become the impetus for change in programs, processes, and facilities. This form of evaluation stems from outcomes-based management (see chapter 2).

As an example of measuring outcomes, take a campus recreation course that teaches participants how to commute by bicycle. Table 14.1 indicates the outcomes and the group benefiting. For example, participants can receive physical benefits from increasing their exercise time by bike commuting, and employees conducting the course may also receive physical benefits from being active during work. Similarly, the program may also provide social and psychological benefits through the interaction between staff and participants and the stress reduction offered by riding a bicycle. Environmental benefits may accrue to participants who begin to use their bikes to accomplish more of their daily tasks, and a similar sentiment may be reinforced in staff conducting the course. The community and society at large may also receive environmental benefits through decreased car usage and fewer emissions. Finally, all the groups may receive economic benefits. Participants may be better off financially using their bike, employees are paid to conduct the course, the organization receives money from the course, and the community and society may in the long term see lower road maintenance costs and even health care costs if more people bike commute.

In this example, it is assumed that all outcomes are positive, but that is not always the case. For example, an instructor conducting a number of commuting courses may see negative physical outcomes through repetitive-use injuries or may feel stressed being responsible for new cyclists in busy traffic.

Table 14.1 Benefits of Bicycle Commuting Course

	Physical	Social	Psychological	Environmental	Economic
Participants	✔	✔	✔	✔	✔
Employees	✔	✔	✔	✔	✔
Organization					✔
Community				✔	✔
Society				✔	✔

This simplified example is intended to show the breadth and depth of outcome evaluations. It is important to consider the purpose of the evaluation and ask the questions and measure the things that are most important to the audience for whom the evaluation is intended.

Formative and Summative Evaluation

Formative evaluations and *summative evaluations* are two terms that often come up when dealing with evaluation. Formative evaluation focuses on the early stages of evaluation whereas summative evaluation relates to the effectiveness of a program. The following sections explain these forms of evaluation and provide some examples in leisure services.

Formative Evaluation

As the name implies, a **formative evaluation** is a way of judging the value of a program as it is happening. For example, when designing a new recreation facility, getting user, community, and staff feedback on architectural plans would be a type of formative evaluation; you are assessing the fit of the building before spending large sums of money on it. Creating a prototype of a product would also be considered formative evaluation, such as if a baseball team invites a group of season-ticket holders to give their perceptions of potential new uniforms. Formative evaluation can include continual feedback from participants throughout a program that is used to make changes as the program continues, such as when a tennis instructor asks participants what they enjoyed most from a lesson and what they would like to do more of. This is an informal yet effective formative evaluation. The instructor can come back to the next lesson with a plan that is even better suited to the students' needs.

formative evaluation—Evaluation conducted during an event or to pretest a product or program before implementation.

Summative Evaluation

Summative evaluation concerns the sum total of activities in a program. It is a way of judging the worth of a program at its conclusion. Using the facility example, a summative evaluation of a recreation facility could assess its impact on the community after it has been built, including economic impact and impact on participation rates in physical activity. A summative evaluation could also look at the results of a program that has been operating in a community for a long time, such as the

summative evaluation—Evaluation of the sum total of a program and its activities.

impact of an ongoing youth club on crime in a community or how the fitness level of participants in a fitness program has changed since they joined.

Understanding that different types of evaluation provide answers to different questions will help ensure that the right information to answer the questions important to the organization and its key stakeholders is collected. Regardless of evaluation type, the five-step evaluation process that follows can be insightful (Henderson & Bialeschki, 2002).

Five-Step Evaluation Process

evaluation process—
The collection and analysis of information in systematic ways to make better decisions or to improve programs, products, or policies.

The **evaluation process** follows five steps (figure 14.1). The process starts by determining what needs to be evaluated and then choosing how to approach that evaluation (what research methods and instrument to use). Next, data are collected, data analysis methods are determined, the report is developed, and findings are implemented. The following sections explain each step. Working through this evaluation process is a science; it is systematic and requires rational decisions throughout. However, it is also an art. As more evaluation experience is gained, it will become easier to choose evaluative methods and tools that best fit the organization.

Step 1: Decide What to Evaluate

We have already discussed in the previous section what managers might want to evaluate. However, how do we decide what to measure when resources are limited and everything seems important? At this point, managers must step back and look at what the organization is there to do. Managers should measure those things that best fit with the vision, mission, goals, and objectives of the organization, and then they should measure what is most important for delivering on them. If it is important and it needs to be accomplished, it should be evaluated.

For example, a national sport organization may want to measure the performance of elite athletes, the growth or decline in participation rates in that sport across the country, and what outcomes participants receive. This could be helpful in planning

Figure 14.1 The evaluation process.

marketing campaigns, seeking funding from public and private sources, and designing programs to address these needs. Again, the rule is simple, but it is not necessarily easy! Measure the things that are important and that need to get accomplished in the organization. These may change over time, and that's okay. Anticipating and adapting to changing circumstances is a big part of a manager's job and one you will become increasingly proficient at as you gain more experience.

Step 2: Decide How to Approach the Evaluation

Once you have determined what needs to be evaluated, the next decision is how to approach that evaluation. Two broad research methods are used: quantitative and qualitative. **Quantitative research** is what many people associate with evaluation because it involves numbers; it includes counts of program participants, program satisfaction, number of injuries per facility hour, or other such indicators. **Qualitative research** uses information in the form of words, pictures, objects, or other visual images. For example, participants' descriptions of how they felt about a program or an instructor would be qualitative impressions.

There is much debate over the appropriateness of these approaches in various situations; however, for managers, one approach is not better than the other. Rather, the question being asked should dictate the approach. If you are looking at questions of how many participants reached a certain standard or the cost–benefit ratio of a particular program or facility, for example, then a quantitative approach may be the way to go. As a general guideline, many process-oriented evaluations can be addressed with quantitative approaches. Conversely, qualitative approaches tend to be well suited to examining many outcomes, particularly questions about attitudes or impressions, such as asking participants what they liked about a program or what features of a facility need improvement. These kinds of questions lend themselves to a more qualitative approach. You may also end up combining approaches, often starting with a quantitative approach to understand a particular situation, then examining it in detail using a qualitative approach to get a deeper understanding of the situation.

Experience will help you adapt methods to get the information necessary to make quality decisions. Within these approaches there are many tools to choose from. Some of the most common tools include questionnaires, observation, interviews, focus groups, secondary data, and case studies.

Questionnaires

Questionnaires, or surveys, may be one of the first things that come to mind when thinking of evaluation. Questionnaires are effective at soliciting opinions, attitudes, and demographic information or providing information about participant or employee behavior. A questionnaire can collect quantitative data through yes-or-no questions or through scales that rate some attitude or element of the evaluation target, or it can collect qualitative data through open-ended questions.

In figure 14.2, questions 1 and 2 are two ways of collecting data on participants' thoughts about a program. Question 1 is a quantitative approach and a simple question that does not provide much detail. An improved quantitative approach to this question could be to use a rating or Likert scale, discussed in the section

quantitative research— Number-based approaches to evaluation.

qualitative research— Data collection based on words, pictures, or objects.

questionnaire—Form containing a set of questions that is submitted to people to gain insight into issues of interest or concern.

on attitude scales. Question 2 is an open-ended qualitative approach whereby participants supply a response under their own terms. This can result in richer data and a deeper understanding of what is being investigated. For example, consider evaluating someone's satisfaction with an outdoor experience. Rather than a score of very satisfied or unsatisfied, a qualitative question may elicit much more detail on what the participant liked or didn't like about the experience. This type of question can provide a lot of information but in doing so it allows participants to choose what they divulge, so responses may have little consistency. Additionally, in some cases input may be limited because the question requires more effort to answer (Babbie, 2004).

Rating Scales   In figure 14.2, question 3 uses a rating scale to assess participants' impression of an instructor. Rating scales commonly use wording such as *strongly agree, agree, neutral, disagree,* or *strongly agree.* Other terms might include *excellent, good, fair, poor,* or *very poor,* or *always, sometimes,* or *never.* It is important to have balanced rating scales. For example, a form asking customers to rate a restaurant where the rating options are outstanding, excellent, very good, good, and fair is not balanced. Although the owners may be happy that 75 percent of customers see the service as good, the scale biases the results because no negative options are available. A balanced rating scale has an equal number of positive and negative choices.

Another problem with rating scales is that different people may view excellence in different ways. Rating scales can also bias future answers. Once you circle *very good,* you might continue with similar responses throughout rather than carefully reading and responding to each individual question (Babbie, 2004).

Checklists   In figure 14.2, question 4 is an example of a checklist. This type of question works best to obtain the frequency of an occurrence compared with some standard. It can also be used to better understand customers or employees such as what activities they take part in or what services they would like to see in a new facility. A checklist often includes a line for *other* to give respondents the opportunity to add something that the organization may not have thought of.

attitude scale— Numeric representation of a person's agreement or disagreement with a statement, often reflected in a Likert scale.

Attitude Scales   An **attitude scale** uses a rating scale to examine a person's opinion or attitude on a topic of interest. Likert scales are the most frequently used attitude scale. Similar to a rating scale, the Likert scale offers options for a person to respond to some statement. For example, for the evaluation of a dance instructor for a salsa class, a statement may be given such as "The instructor is prepared for each session." Respondents would then answer on a scale of 1 to 5 where 1 is equal to *strongly disagree* and 5 is equal to *strongly agree.* More moderate options include 2 and 4, *disagree* and *agree,* and 3 is neutral, often labeled *undecided* (figure 14.3). Likert scales provide more detail than yes-or-no questions but have more consistent responses than open-ended qualitative questions. As the name implies, these scales are great at assessing perceptions and attitudes about some statement provided by the researcher (Babbie, 2004).

Observation

Observation is watching someone or something and recording observations in a systematic way. A simple example would be an aquatics director taking a daily walk

CLIENT SATISFACTION QUESTIONNAIRE

Q1: Sample Quantitative Question

Overall I was satisfied with the program. (Please circle the best response.)

Yes   No   No opinion

Q2: Sample Qualitative Question

Please describe your satisfaction level with the program. Tell us what we could improve upon and what you liked about the program.

_____

_____

_____

_____

_____

Q3: Sample Rating Scale

The instructor was well prepared for classes. (Please circle the best response.)

Always   Sometimes   Never

Q4: Sample Checklist

How did you learn about our program? (Please check all that apply.)

_____ Local newspaper

_____ TV ad

_____ Leisure magazine

_____ Radio ad

_____ From a friend

_____ Poster in the facility

_____ Other (please list) _____

Q5: Sample Likert Attitude Scale

The program was appropriate for my skill level. (Please circle the best response.)

1	2	3	4	5
Strongly disagree	Disagree	Neutral	Agree	Strongly agree

Figure 14.2 Sample client satisfaction questionnaire.

SAMPLE QUESTION

Circle the number following each statement that best fits your opinion about that statement, where 1 means you strongly disagree with the statement and 5 means you strongly agree with the statement.

Q1: The instructor for the Saturday evening salsa class comes prepared for each class.

1	2	3	4	5
Strongly disagree	Somewhat disagree	Neutral	Somewhat agree	Strongly agree

Figure 14.3 **Sample Likert scale questionnaire.**

around the pool to check for safety, risk management, and maintenance concerns. A predetermined list could be used to check off concerns or the manager could simply take a note of anything that needs attention. This can also be done with employees or clients. A formal example may be an evaluation of the employee's customer service where you watch or hire someone to watch how the employee interacts with clients. A checklist could be used to check for required behaviors such as whether the employee greeted the client within a predetermined time frame or provided information on some upcoming event.

A qualitative approach could also be used for noting negative and positive service behaviors. The effectiveness of this approach often lies in consistency among raters and even consistency of the same rater from one time to the next. **Raters** are simply the people collecting the information; consistency refers to different people rating the same thing similarly. For example, if two raters said a trail was busy, there should be similar numbers of people on that trail during both their observations. Careful definition of terms and training of raters goes a long way toward increasing consistency.

raters—People who judge or evaluate performance against some set of criteria.

As a manager, informal behavior observations can be effective if conducted in a thoughtful manner. The idea of management by walking around helps managers stay connected to issues in their organization and may help in developing more formal evaluation methods based on informal observations (Patton, 2001).

Interviews

Interviews are a common way to evaluate areas such as employee performance. An interview can range from structured to informal. With a structured approach, the interviewer asks predetermined questions and records the responses, much like a verbal questionnaire. A more informal approach is similar to an open conversation where some topics may be predetermined by the interviewer, who can probe for deeper answers or to clarify responses, but each interview has its own unique direction. This approach also lends itself to discovering information managers may not have known or considered important. The disadvantage of the less structured approach is that it often does not provide consistency between interviews and makes the data analysis more difficult. For example, an informal interview may help the manager learn about an employee's satisfaction level or needs in the workplace, but it may not work as well for assessing the performance of employees compared against a standard or each other (Patton, 2001).

Focus Groups

Focus groups can be thought of as group interviews. They are usually conducted with groups of 8 to 12 people who have been screened in some way before the meeting so that the group is of interest to the evaluator. For example, a group may include people who have attended a Vancouver Canucks hockey game in the past year in order to discuss their thoughts on client service at the event. Focus groups are an excellent way to get an impression of a new program or initiative such as changes to a facility. A professional sport organization, for example, may use a focus group to get fans' impressions of a uniform change.

Focus groups can be hard to handle if the moderator is inexperienced, and organizations might also call for outside assistance to get unbiased participant responses. Moderators may encounter one person dominating the group or people who don't want to speak. In addition, some people may modify their opinions to avoid conflict in the group, and thus focus groups may not be as well suited to highly personal topics where politically correct answers are the norm. However, focus groups can help bring out new ideas or raise issues that the manager may not have thought of, and the group dynamics can enhance creativity and help people think more broadly than they might in a more individual setting.

Following is a simple example of how a focus group could be used in a university athletic department. The athletic director wants to know how season-ticket holders for women's basketball feel about the game-day service, particularly concerning the concessions. He sends a letter out to all season-ticket holders and plans to conduct three focus groups of 10 people each. He feels that community ticket holders, faculty and staff ticket holders, and student ticket holders may have different needs, so he randomly picks 10 people from each type of ticket holder. He brings in a person to facilitate the session so as not to bias the answers. The groups are recorded with their consent.

The focus groups are held before a game and food is provided as an incentive for the participants. The participants introduce themselves and the facilitator makes them feel comfortable with some chat about basketball. The facilitator then asks the group what they currently like about the concessions, followed by what they would improve. Group discussion ensues. Food is then provided and the facilitator mentions that some of this food could be in the concessions. She asks if they would be interested in purchasing it, what they might pay, and what they might change about it. The discussion continues for an hour or so and is repeated three times with the different groups. The value of the focus group is that it provides detailed comments from key customers about current service (summative evaluation) as well as some formative evaluation on future items that might be offered in the concession (Patton, 2001).

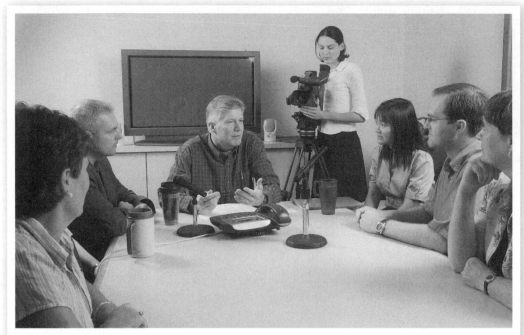

Focus groups can be an effective technique to learn more about how to improve programs and services.

Secondary Data

secondary data—Data collected by another person or for another purpose that is used to gain understanding of a topic.

Secondary data is information already available that can be used in an evaluation. It may include census data for understanding changing patterns in a community, as well as program records, employee records, and operational records. Program records may document equipment use, participation numbers in various programs, and so on. Employee records might track attendance and absenteeism, employee turnover, disciplinary notes, client complaints, and compliments directed to specific employees. Operational records may document safety inspections, accident reports from staff and clients, and revenue and expense information, as well as problems with equipment or facilities. Secondary data might also come from previous participant registrations stored in a database. This information can be valuable for learning about registration trends and participant demographics of various programs (Patton, 2001). Many process-oriented evaluations can use this type of information.

Case Studies

case study—Research method that involves an in-depth examination of a single instance or case.

Case studies are similar to observation but much more involved. A **case study** is an in-depth longitudinal look at a single instance or case. Case studies can combine many of the elements discussed previously. Let's say an evaluation of client service ratings has noted a consistent decrease over the past 6 months. You know things aren't going well, but you don't know why. A case study would use a variety of tools to take an in-depth look at how the organization provides client service. During some informal evaluations of staff–client interactions, interviews with a few staff members, and focus groups with long-term clients, a generally less-happy mood around the facility is discovered due to the desire for an increase in staff sick days.

As you gradually piece together the puzzle, you realize that your success is actually your downfall. Client numbers are up and, correspondingly, staff workloads are also way up. The staff is committed to getting the work done, but it is taking a toll. The fatigue is now resulting in less friendly and attentive client service, something that is essential to the business, so you adjust the staff scheduling to accommodate the new busy times at the facility. Obviously the case study approach is resource intensive and not for all situations. However, when faced with complex problems that are essential to success, it may well prove to be an effective management tool (Patton, 2001).

Step 3: Analyze the Data

Step 3 involves analysis of the data collected through one or more of the previous methods. Data analysis is part art and part science. The data simply provide information that managers must apply to their particular context. Often, analysis may be a regular monitoring of trends. In the previous example, when the monitoring of client satisfaction ratings noted a decline, the manager was able to react. If the manager had waited until complaints increased or clients began to leave the facility, it may have been too late to correct the problem. Monitoring important aspects of an agency helps managers be proactive concerning challenges and opportunities rather than reactive.

Analysis of quantitative data may be more straightforward than qualitative analysis. The use of simple spreadsheet programs such as Microsoft Excel often allows managers to conduct the necessary analysis through simple statistics such as averages or the most frequent response to a question. Qualitative data, on the other hand, are often more obscure but may be richer in information. They may require a manager to look for patterns or trends over time or between respondents. It is important not to overgeneralize any findings, particularly an individual respondent's comments.

Step 4: Prepare the Report

Evaluation can have many uses and audiences, and the evaluation report must be tailored to each of these constituencies. The challenge managers often face is dealing with more information than they can handle. The key to preparing an evaluation report is making sure it answers the questions that are important to the audience. Putting everything in the report may make it cumbersome and not useful to the target audience. Two key considerations are the size of the report and the choice of medium. The latter can be as simple as a verbal report to instructors on how their clients felt they did this session or a sit-down meeting with employees to discuss their performance. If the material is confidential or of a personal nature, a verbal report may well be a good route to take. In some circumstances, findings may be presented to a board, commission, or council. This may require a comprehensive written report as well as a verbal presentation. Under these circumstances, it is essential to focus on the questions that are important to the audience.

For example, a local council may be concerned with the effects of certain programs in the community, so highlighting related findings would be critical. Similarly, at a community meeting people may be interested in access to services, quality ratings, and other concerns that directly affect them. Visual tools such as PowerPoint slides can help present findings. Avoid excessive use of text in such presentations; as the saying goes, a picture is worth a thousand words. Easy-to-understand charts, relevant pictures, or even video and audio clips of actual staff or participant comments can be powerful ways to deliver the message. Just be careful not to let the technology make or break the report. Well-thought-out evaluations, a solid collection strategy, and thoughtfully analyzed data should take center stage. One final caution is to keep the language appropriate to the audience. An academic setting may want to hear about the evaluation methods, but a council might want to know about results and what the staff plans to do with them.

Step 5: Implement Recommendations

Implementation may seem obvious, but for busy managers it is an important step to keep in mind. Evaluations are done for a reason: to address important areas of operation. Managers must track the implementation of recommendations for change. As we have learned elsewhere in the text, change is often met with resistance, so it is important to continue to monitor the implementation. Finally, remember that evaluation is an ongoing effort, including reassessing the program, improving areas viewed as weak, and reevaluating the program.

Selecting Evaluation Participants

Even if all five steps of the evaluation process are successfully completed, the end result may still be evaluation information that does not represent the people you want it to represent. How to choose who to observe, give questionnaires to, interview, or invite to join focus groups is essential to successful evaluation. In research terms this is often referred to as *sampling*. The following section provides a brief overview of sampling for both qualitative and quantitative evaluation.

Sampling

sampling—Selecting a certain number of cases from a larger set of data that you believe is similar to or representative of the larger group.

Sampling is selecting a certain number of cases from a larger set of data that is representative of the larger group. In some cases, managers may collect data from all the people they are interested in evaluating; this is called the *population*. For example, if all employees filled out a questionnaire on job satisfaction, that would not be a sample but rather a survey of the entire population. In many cases, though, surveying an entire population is not feasible. Take a university athletic department that wants to know how its football fans feel about the food service at the game. Several hundred thousand people may attend games over the course of a season, so asking them all, let alone dealing with that amount of data, is impractical. Sampling is simply taking a smaller number of cases from a larger pool and then generalizing that sample to the population (Babbie, 2004).

Sampling is done to save time and cost. There are two forms of samples: probability and nonprobability samples. A probability sample consists of random selection procedures to make sure that each unit of the sample is chosen by chance.

All units of the evaluation should have an equal chance (or at least a known chance) of being selected for the sample. For example, if you want a probability sample of participants in fitness classes during the past year, you would need to create a sampling frame that contains the entire population. A sampling frame is simply the list of all the people or cases that could be selected for the evaluation. Most likely the participants can be found through registration data, so such a list could easily be created. Then assign a number or some identifier to each person on that list and put the numbers in a hat or use a random-number generator to select the participants. If at all possible, a random sampling method should be used because it will result in the most accurate data.

Choosing a representative sample is an important consideration when conducting evaluations.

A probability sample using a stratified random sample or a systematic sample can also be conducted.

Stratified Sampling

A stratified random sample involves creating a sampling list for each of several categories of interest and then drawing a random sample from those categories. For example, you might want to sample program participants from the key program areas in an organization, such as fitness, sport, arts, and aquatics. To do so, create four separate sampling frames (one for each area) and then draw a random sample from each (Babbie, 2004).

Systematic Sampling

Systematic sampling is when every *n*th person on a list is selected. To create a sampling frame, randomly choose a starting place and select every seventh person on the list. (Choosing the seventh person is an example; you could choose every third person, every ninth person, or whatever you wish.) Continue to select every seventh person on the list until reaching the appropriate number of people for the evaluation. This may mean going through the list numerous times.

Sample Size

A common question in creating a probability sample is how large the sample should be. Unfortunately, the best answer is that it depends on the situation. Statistical equations can be used to understand the size of the sample, but they require a statistical discussion that is beyond the focus of this chapter. With statistical equations, researchers make assumptions about the sampling errors and degree of difference or variation in the population. But don't despair—two rules of thumb are helpful in the vast majority of cases, especially in the context of evaluation.

First, the smaller the population is, the larger the sample should be. If you have a relatively small population, you will need to use a larger percentage of that population; however, small increases in sample size produce big gains for all samples. Determine sample size based on

- ▶ the accuracy required,
- ▶ how diverse or variable the population is, and
- ▶ the number of things being evaluated.

Evaluators can get by with a smaller sample when less accuracy is needed, the population is relatively homogenous, or only a few variables are being measured.

Second, methods used to analyze the data also influence the sample size. Generally speaking, you would ideally want at least 50 people for each group to be investigated. For example, to compare males with females, a sample of at least 100 (50 for each group) would be needed. Ultimately the accuracy of the numbers, the resources available (money, time, and people), and the size of the population will determine the best sample size. Links to sample size charts are included in the Online Student Resource. As with management, evaluation research is part art, part science, so your understanding of the stakeholder population will be the best guide in ensuring that you select appropriate samples (Henderson & Bialeschki, 2002).

Nonprobability Sampling

In many cases it may be impossible to have a complete sampling frame, or a qualitative approach may be desired. Under these conditions, a nonprobability sampling method would be used. This form of sampling often focuses on the relevance to the evaluation topic as opposed to accurately representing the population. Nonprobability sampling is a selection of cases or people based on some factor of importance to the evaluator instead of by random chance.

For example, let's look at how you might create a sample to understand client intentions to renew a fitness club membership. You could select a group of people who have not renewed their membership and invite them to discuss their reasons with you. Rather than randomly selecting from the membership list, you purposely select people who have chosen not to renew their membership. This is nonprobability sampling in action. You could choose from a variety of nonprobability sampling methods when selecting which people to invite, including convenience, quota, purposive, snowball, and deviant-case samples (Patton, 2001).

Convenience Sample

A convenience sample involves selecting cases that are convenient, such as talking to participants who happen to be at a facility that day. These samples are easy and cheap, but they can produce ineffective, unrepresentative samples or even misleading information. Selecting a readily available case may create some kind of bias in the response. For example, if the athletics department wanted to know how the students at a university felt about university sports, the staff could talk to groups of students who were tailgating before a big game. These students would be easy to find and the data could be quickly collected with little expense, but it is likely to result in a positive response to university athletics. This sample of convenience could be unrepresentative of all students since students who don't like university athletics are not likely to attend games.

Quota Sample

Quota sampling attempts to get a preset number of cases in each of several preselected categories. For example, if campus recreation is looking at client satisfaction in a campus recreation facility, the staff may want to have a certain number of students, a certain number of faculty and staff members, and a certain number of community members. It may also be beneficial for each group to represent gender and age in those groups. Table 14.2 shows a sample size chart to use for quota sampling in this situation. The numbers in this table are examples; actual numbers would be determined by the specific situation.

Table 14.2   Sample Size Chart for Quota Sampling

Gender or role	Faculty members or staff	Students	Community members
Male	20	50	45
Female	20	50	45

Purposive Sample

A purposive sample (sometimes called a *judgmental sample*) uses an expert to select cases with a particular purpose in mind. For example, you might want to conduct a focus group with participants who have complained during the year, or you might want to speak with those employees who are deemed the most effective at their jobs in order to gather ideas for improving services. Purposive sampling is ideal for many evaluation efforts, particularly if they are exploratory, meaning you are in the initial stages of understanding what you are evaluating (Patton, 2001).

Snowball Sample

A snowball sample helps in understanding interconnected groups of people or even organizations. Essentially, one person recommends the next as a possible participant in the evaluation. For example, this approach might be helpful in trying to develop a new club for rock climbing and to understand the needs and desires of climbers. You likely would have no data or contact information for creating a list of climbers, but you may know one or two climbers who have been eager to get something started. You can ask those people if they know others who may be interested in speaking with you. Through these connections you can learn more about the local climbing community so you can design a program that will better fit their needs and desires (Patton, 2001).

Deviant-Case Sample

A deviant-case sample is a look at extreme cases. When looking at client satisfaction at an aquatics center, staff would want to sample both those who are enthusiastic supporters of the center and those who think the center is the worst facility on the planet. Managers could also look at employees who are extremely satisfied on the job and those who are not to get a better understanding of the workplace dynamics. Caution must be taken, though, not to assume that all clients or employees hold these extreme values.

Best Practices and Benchmarking

Another purpose of evaluation is providing information that can help benchmark best practices and provide information to others in similar organizations in order to enhance the quality of programs, facilities, or personnel practices. Evaluation research of this type can also help develop policies or assess their effectiveness. Often this research is conducted by researchers or people in an academic setting such as a university. Although managers might not conduct this research themselves, the information gained may be helpful in understanding industry trends and best practices. Best practices and benchmarking can be useful tools in many organizations; however, they must be pursued with caution and not seen as a quick fix to problems an organization might be facing.

Best Practices

best practices—A part of a business, process, procedure, or system that is considered the best or superior to other ways of doing something.

A best practice is some aspect of a business, process, or system that is considered superior. **Best practices** have been used extensively in the commercial sector and have more recently been adopted by public and nonprofit organizations. An example of a best practice might be the current standard for software used to register people in leisure programs or a training plan for the best customer service. Because best practices are constantly evolving, staying on top of current industry standards is an important task for managers. This can be done informally by keeping up with journals and professional magazines in the industry and attending seminars or conferences as part of a commitment to lifelong education.

More formal research on best practices would involve researchers studying organizations that are leaders in an area. Often a case study (see page 354) will aid in understanding why an organization is so good at what it does. Industry groups may also conduct this research, which is often provided to their members as part of membership or at a cost. For example, the Tennis Industry Association conducts research on trends in the sport and consumer behavior that would help those in the industry identify best practices in running a tennis facility or retail outlet.

Benchmarking

Benchmarking is a way to identify best practices. A benchmark is a standard of performance that allows an organization to compare its performance with others or an industry average. Internal benchmarking studies the practices and performance within a particular organization whereas external benchmarking examines an outside organization. Benchmarking may sound like a quick and easy way to poach the best ideas from other companies, but seldom is that the case. Effective benchmarking is holistic—it involves understanding how a best practice fits into a particular organization. Each organization is unique and thus implementing a best practice in each organization is also unique. It is important to understand how making a change will affect not only the process being studied but also the organization as a whole.

For example, if an agency was to change from in-person registration to an online registration standard seen as a best practice, staff would want to look at a variety of its effects. What will it cost and how will it affect clients who do not have Internet access? Are the agency's programs similar to those where the best practice originated, or are they more complex and require human interaction to help clients? Does the agency have the technology support and infrastructure to use such a system? Is current staff trained or willing to be trained to use the new system? Because of these questions and the varying answers, benchmarking is often used with caution.

> **benchmarking**—A standard of performance that allows an organization to compare its performance to others or to an industry average.

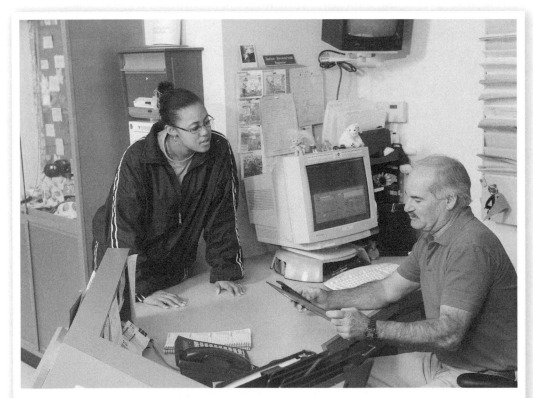

Benchmarking can help an organization assess the effectiveness of its registration process.

Conclusion

▶ Understanding how to conduct systematic evaluation is an integral part of a manager's job. This involves collecting information on what matters—the things that lead to effectiveness and success. The more effective managers are at collecting and using this information, the more likely they will be to accomplish organizational goals, provide the programs and services that clients desire, and create an environment where employees can help move an organization forward.

REVIEW QUESTIONS

1. Differentiate between process-based and outcome-based evaluation. How would you decide which approach to choose when beginning an evaluation?

2. Why is evaluation important?

3. Describe the steps in the evaluation process.

4. Compare and contrast probability sampling and nonprobability sampling.

5. How would you answer the question, "How many people do I need to sample?"

6. What is a sampling frame and how would you go about developing one?

7. What kinds of things might you evaluate as a director of aquatics at a municipal pool? As the general manager of a minor league baseball team? As the executive director of a local nonprofit organization such as the United Way?

Appendix A: Standards Established by the NRPA Council on Accreditation for Recreation, Park Resources, and Leisure Services Education

The NRPA Council on Accreditation for Recreation, Park Resources, and Leisure Services Education is sponsored by the National Recreation and Park Association (NRPA). The NRPA Council on Accreditation has established professional competencies for all students. Universities implement these standards within their curricula so that students gain competence in these areas. The standards listed are ones the authors believe they have addressed in part in their chapters. The chapter numbers for each standard are in parentheses.

8.07 Understanding of ethical principles and professionalism (chapter 5)

8.08 Understanding of the importance of maintaining professional competence and the available resources for professional development (chapters 1 and 3)

8.09 Understanding of the roles, interrelationships, and use of diverse delivery systems addressing recreation, park resources, and leisure (chapter 5)

8.14:01 Assessment of needs (chapter 14)

8.14:02 Development of outcome-oriented goals and objectives (chapter 3)

8.14:03 Selection and coordination of programs, events, and resources (chapter 6)

8.14:04 Marketing of programs and events (chapter 8)

8.14:07 Evaluation of programs and events (chapter 14)

8.15 Understanding of group dynamics and processes (chapter 6)

8.16 Ability to use various leadership techniques to enhance individual, group, and community experiences (chapter 2)

8.17 Ability to apply basic principles of research and data analysis related to recreation, park resources, and leisure services (chapter 14)

8.18 Understanding of the fundamental principles and procedures of management (chapters 3 and 5)

8.19 Understanding of the principles and procedures of human resource management (chapters 10 and 11)

8.20 Understanding of the principles and procedures of supervisory leadership (chapter 2)

8.21 Understanding of the principles and procedures of budgeting and financial management (chapters 12 and 13)

8.22 Understanding of the principles and procedures related to agency marketing techniques and strategies (chapter 8)

8.23 Ability to utilize the tools of professional communication (chapter 9)

8.25:01 Knowledge of assessment (chapter 7)

8.25:02 Knowledge of planning (chapter 7)

8.25:04 Knowledge of evaluation (chapter 14)

8.26:01 Understanding of the legal foundations and the legislative process (chapter 4)

8.26:02 Understanding of the contracts and tort law (chapter 4)

8.26:03 Understanding of the regulatory agents and methods of compliance (chapter 4)

8.27 Understanding of the principles and practices of safety, emergency, and risk management related to recreation, park resources, and leisure services (chapter 4)

7A.01 Understanding of and ability to apply both traditional and innovative techniques of financial management, including development of budgets for operating and capital budgets, revenue generation and accountability, pricing of services, cost analysis, and financial forecasting (chapter 13)

7A.02 Understanding of the management role, including organizational behavior and relationships, politics of organizations, strategic planning, policy development and implementation, decision making, cooperative problem solving, and managing conflict (chapters 5, 6, and 7)

7A.03 Understanding of the relationship of business, society, and the economy, including the role of the entrepreneur (chapter 5)

9A.01 Understanding of and ability to apply organizational and political techniques to foster meaningful and principled relationships with boards, commissioners, and staff; governmental, nonprofit, and private organizations; and the public to enhance leisure services opportunities (chapter 5)

9A.03 Understanding of the use of the law in management of leisure services, including land management, personnel, human rights, financing, and risk management (chapter 4)

9A.05 Understanding of and ability to apply techniques of program evaluation and policy analysis that measure service effectiveness and the extent to which programmatic and organizational goals and objectives have been achieved (chapter 14)

Adapted from *Standards and Evaluative Criteria for Baccalaureate Programs in Recreation, Park Resources and Leisure Services*, 2004 ed., pp. 8–18, National Recreation and Park Association.

Appendix B: Accreditation Standards for the Commission for Accreditation of Park and Recreation Agencies

Charged with providing high-quality recreation services and experiences, an increasing number of park and recreation agencies across the country are applying for the Agency Accreditation Program through the Commission for Accreditation of Park and Recreation Agencies (CAPRA).

CAPRA administers a rigorous program based on self-assessment and peer review using national standards of best practice to better promote the quality of agency services and delivery systems.

Agency accreditation is available to all entities administering park and recreation systems, including municipalities, townships, counties, special districts and regional authorities, councils of government, and schools.

Agency accreditation is voluntary but an essential part of producing quality environments for communities to play, live, and grow. The following standards are addressed in this text.

1.0 Agency Authority, Role, and Responsibility

1.1 Legal Authority and Jurisdiction (chapter 5)

1.2 Mission (chapter 3)

1.3 Goals and Objectives (chapter 3)

1.4 Policy Formulation and Review (chapter 6)

2.0 Planning

2.2 Community Planning (chapter 7)

2.3 Strategic Planning (chapter 7)

2.4 Comprehensive Planning (chapter 7)

2.4.1 Recreation Programming Plan (chapter 7)

2.4.2 Resource Management and Land Use Planning (chapter 7)

3.0 Organization and Administration

3.1 Organization (chapter 5)

3.3 Public Information, Community Relations, and Marketing (chapter 8)

4.0 Human Resources

4.1 Employees (chapter 10)

4.1.2 Staffing (chapter 10)

4.1.3 Recruitment and Selection (chapter 10)

4.1.4 Management Policies and Procedures (chapter 6)

4.1.4.3 Compensation, benefits, conditions of work (chapter 11)

4.1.4.4 Training, career development (chapter 10)

4.1.4.5 Performance evaluation (chapter 10)

4.1.4.6 Promotion (chapter 10)

4.1.4.7 Disciplinary action, appeals and grievances (chapter 11)

4.1.4.8 Termination of employment (chapter 11)

4.2 Volunteers (chapter 10)

5.0 Finance (Fiscal Policy and Management)

5.1 Fiscal Policy (chapters 12 and 13)

5.2 Fiscal Management (chapters 12 and 13)

5.3 Auditing/Accountability (chapters 12 and 13)

5.4 Budgeting Procedures (chapters 12 and 13)

10.0 Evaluation and Research (Evaluative Research)

10.1 Systematic Evaluation Program (chapter 14)

10.3 Evaluation Personnel (chapter 10)

Adapted from *The Self-Assessment Manual for Quality Operation of Park and Recreation Agencies,* 3rd ed., National Recreation and Park Association, 2001.

Appendix C: Certified Park and Recreation Professional Study Guide Criteria

An examination is one of the principal requirements for certification as a Certified Park and Recreation Professional (CPRP). It is designed to assess the base knowledge of job-related tasks common to entry-level professionals. The examination is administered under the auspices of the National Recreation and Park Association (NRPA) and the National Certification Board (NCB). A national job analysis was conducted in 1989 and again in 1999 and 2006 to identify the important core components of the leisure services profession. The NCB-appointed Job Analysis Advisory Committee conducted the study, which culminated in the test specifications. The test content outline serves as the blueprint for constructing the examination. There are three core components of the examination: general administration, programming, and operations management. The detailed test specifications are included in this appendix. For the most recent criteria in the other two areas, please visit www.nrpa.org. For more information about becoming certified or to obtain a copy of the latest exam study guide, please contact the NRPA at 1-800-626-6772 or www.nrpa.org.

1.A.1. Provide input for the organization's comprehensive strategic plan (includes plans for operations, program, marketing, facility, and natural resources) (tasks) (chapter 7)

1.A.2. Implement a comprehensive strategic plan (chapter 7)

1.A.3. Develop partnerships with other organizations (chapter 6)

1.A.4. Conduct research (e.g., program delivery, facility operations, natural resource development, participant outcomes) (chapter 14)

1.B.1. Prepare budget for areas of responsibility (chapter 13)

1.B.2. Provide input regarding decisions concerning fees and charges (chapter 12)

1.B.3. Determine actual fees and charges (chapter 12)

1.B.4. Forecast revenue/expenses for area of responsibility (chapter 13)

1.B.5. Provide input concerning capital improvements (chapter 13)

1.B.6. Pursue alternative sources of funding (e.g., grants, reimbursements, foundations, commercial sponsorships) (chapter 12)

1.B.7. Implement cash-handling practices (e.g., fee collection, deposits, petty cash) (chapter 13)

1.B.8. Obtain bids and price quotes (e.g., equipment, commodities, services) (chapter 13)

1.B.9. Originate purchase requisition/order (chapter 13)

1.B.12. Collect financial and/or operating data (e.g., attendance, revenue, expenditures, maintenance) (chapter 13)

1.B.13. Analyze financial and/or operating data (e.g., profit margins, cost per participant, cost–benefit analysis) (chapter 13)

1.B.14. Prepare financial reports (chapter 13)

1.C.1. Provide input to job descriptions (chapter 10)

1.C.2. Determine pay levels for subordinate staff within organization guidelines (chapter 5)

1.C.3. Recruit personnel (chapter 10)

1.C.4. Hire personnel (chapter 10)

1.C.5. Dismiss personnel (chapter 11)

1.C.6. Conduct employee performance appraisals (chapter 10)

1.C.7. Administer employee disciplinary action (chapter 11)

1.C.11. Conduct orientation for new staff (chapter 10)

1.C.16. Establish volunteer recognition programs (chapter 11)

1.C.19. Design in-service training programs (chapter 10)

1.C.20. Conduct in-service training programs (chapter 10)

1.C.21. Conduct staff motivation activities (chapter 11)

1.C.22. Establish staff recognition programs (chapter 11)

1.D.2. Recommend risk management policies and procedures (chapter 4)

1.D.3. Collect public input regarding policies (e.g., public hearings, focus groups, surveys) (chapter 14)

1.D.4. Provide recommendations to policy-making bodies (e.g., boards and commissions) (chapter 6)

1.D.6. Participate in policy evaluation and revision (chapter 7)

1.D.10. Encourage public advocacy for support of parks and recreation (chapter 9)

1.E.1. Network with related organizations (chapter 9)

1.E.2. Communicate organization's vision and mission (chapter 3)

1.E.3. Develop promotional pieces (e.g., news releases, newsletters, brochures, spot announcements, features, Web sites) (chapter 8)

1.E.5. Communicate to participants through appropriate techniques (chapters 8 and 9)

1.E.7. Respond to requests for information from the public (chapter 9)

1.E.10. Implement marketing plan (chapter 8)

1.E.11. Evaluate marketing effectiveness (chapter 8)

2.A.1. Assess target population program needs (e.g., community surveys, focus groups) (chapter 14)

2.A.2. Assess individual participant needs (chapter 14)

2.A.3. Assess resources (e.g., areas, facilities, supplies, equipment fiscal) (chapters 3 and 7)

2.B.1. Write program purpose and goal statements (chapter 3)

2.B.2. Develop participant objectives (chapter 3)

2.B.7. Coordinate activities and services with other organizations (chapter 3)

2.B.10. Develop management plan for program/special event delivery (chapter 2)

2.B.11. Develop risk management plan related to programs (chapter 4)

2.C.2. Provide direct leadership of recreation activities (chapter 2)

2.C.3. Supervise recreation programs (chapter 2)

2.C.4. Supervise special events (chapter 2)

2.D.1. Develop program evaluation tools (chapter 14)

2.D.2. Conduct program evaluation (e.g., formative and summative research) (chapter 14)

2.D.3. Conduct individual participant evaluation (chapter 14)

3.A.1. Conduct needs assessment for resource development (chapter 14)

3.A.3. Provide input for capital improvements programs (chapter 13)

Adapted from *National Recreation and Park Association Certified Park and Recreation Professional Examination Candidate Handbook,* pp. 9-10, National Recreation and Park Association, 2007.

References
and Resources

Adams, J.H. (2008). *Creating community: An action plan for parks and recreation.* Champaign, IL: Human Kinetics.

Adams, J.S. (1965). Inequity in social exchange. In L. Berkowitz (Ed.), *Advances in experimental social psychology* (pp. 267-299). New York: Academic Press.

Alaska State SCORP. (2007). Alaska's outdoor legacy. www.dnr.state.ak.us/parks/plans/scorp/2004scorpweb.pdf.

Alberta Lottery Fund. (2007). http://albertalotteryfund.ca/aboutthealf/wherethemoneygoes.asp.

Alliance for Nonprofit Management. (2007). What is strategic planning? www.allianceonline.org/FAQ/strategic_planning/what_is_strategic_planning.faq.

American Hospitality Academy. (2007). Training locations. www.americanhospitalityacademy.com/training_locations.php.

Americans with Disabilities Act (ADA). (1990). Sec. 511(b)(1), 42 U.S.C.A. sec. 12211(b)(1).

Andereck, K.L. (1997). Case study of a multiagency partnership: Effectiveness and constraints. *Journal of Park and Recreation Administration, 15*(2), 44-60.

Andreasen, A., & Kotler, P. (2003). *Strategic marketing for nonprofit organizations* (6th ed.). Upper Saddle River, NJ: Prentice Hall.

Argyris, C. (1990). *Overcoming organizational defenses.* New York: Prentice Hall.

Arnold, M.L., Heyne, L.A., & Busser, J.A. (2005). *Problem solving: Tools and techniques for the park and recreation administrator.* Champaign, IL: Sagamore.

Austin Parks and Recreation Department. (2007). Annual concession report, 2004-05. www.ci.austin.tx.us/parks/downloads/concessionreport05.doc.

Babbie, E. (2004). *The practice of social research* (10th ed.). Belmont, CA: Wadsworth.

Barcelona, B., & Ross, C.M. (2004). An analysis of perceived competencies recreational sports administrators. *Journal of Park and Recreation Administration, 22,* 25-42.

Barcelona, R.J., & Carroll, J. (2007). *NH recreation and conservation needs assessment.* Concord, NH: New Hampshire Office of Energy and Planning.

Ben and Jerry's Homemade Ice Cream. (2007). www.benjerry.com.

Bennis, W.G. (1989). *On becoming a leader.* Reading, MA: Addison-Wesley.

Bike Chicago Rentals and Tours. (2007). www.bikechicago.com.

Blake, R.R., & McCanse, A. (1991). *Leadership dilemmas: Grid solutions.* Houston, TX: Gulf.

Blake, R.R., & Mouton, J.S. (1964). *The managerial grid.* Houston, TX: Gulf.

Block, P. (1996). *Stewardship: Choosing service over self-interest.* San Francisco: Berrett-Koehler.

Blom, B., & Guajardo, S. (2000). Multiyear budgeting: A primer for finance officers. *Government Finance Review, 16,* 39-43.

Board Source. (2005). Nonprofit governance index 2004. www.boardsource.org/dl.asp?document_id=424.

Bocarro, J.N., & Barcelona, R.J. (2003, October). University and community park and recreation department partnerships: Tips for unlocking the potential of collaboration. *Parks and Recreation, 38*(10), 50-55.

Boise State University Campus Recreation. (2007). http://rec.boisestate.edu/mission.

Bolman, L.G., & Deal, T.E. (2003). *Reframing organizations: Artistry, choice, and leadership.* San Francisco: Jossey-Bass.

Borrie, W.T., & Roggenbuck, J.T. (1995). Community-based research for an urban recreation application of benefits-based management. In D.J. Chavez (Ed.), *Proceedings of the Second Symposium on Social Aspects and Recreation Research,* February 23-25, 1994, San Diego (pp. 159-163).

Boyatzis, R.E. (1982). *The competent manager: A model for effective performance.* New York: Wiley.

Brayley, R.E., & McLean, D.D. (2001). *Managing financial resources in sport and leisure service organizations.* Champaign, IL: Sagamore.

Bryson, J.M. (1994). Strategic planning and action planning for nonprofit organizations. In R.D. Herman (Ed.), *The Jossey-Bass handbook of nonprofit leadership and management* (pp. 154-183). San Francisco: Jossey-Bass.

Bureau of Land Management. (2007). www.blm.gov/wo/st/en/info/regulations/Instruction_Memos_and_Bulletins/national_instruction/2006/im_2006-060__.html

Business Owner's Toolkit. (2007). Types of bids/solicitations. www.toolkit.cch.com/text/P09_2610.asp.

Byrnes, N. (2007). Toys "R" Us: Beaten at its own game. www.businessweek.com/magazine/content/04_13/b3876105_mz017.htm.

California Park and Recreation Society (CPRS). (n.d.). *Creating community in the 21st century: Executive Summary VIP Action Plan.* Sacramento, CA: CPRS.

California State Parks. (2002). *Department of parks and recreation operations manual.* Sacramento, CA: Author.

Cameron, K.S. (1994, Summer). Strategies for successful organizational downsizing. *Human Resource Management Journal, 33,* 89-112.

Camp Fire USA. (2007). *2004-2005 annual report.* www.campfireusa.org/all_about_us/2004-2005AnnualReport.pdf.

Canada Revenue Agency. (2007). How GST/HST works. www.cra-arc.gc.ca/tax/business/topics/gst/individual/how/menu-e.html.

Center for Digital Government. (2004). Governing faster, smarter: The promise of useful data close at hand. www.centerdigitalgov.com/story.php?id=103491.

Certo, S.C. (2003). *Modern management* (9th ed.). Upper Saddle River, NJ: Prentice Hall.

Chelladurai, P. (2001). *Managing organizations for sport and physical activity: A systems perspective.* Scottsdale, AZ: Holcomb Hathaway.

Chelladurai, P. (2006). *Human resource management in sport and recreation* (2nd ed.). Champaign, IL: Human Kinetics.

Ciconte, B.L., & Jacobs, J.C. (2001). *Fundraising basics: A complete guide* (2nd ed.). Gaithersburg, MD: Aspen.

City of Albuquerque. (2007). www.cabq.gov/cip/questions.html.

City of Arlington, Texas, Convention and Visitors Bureau. (2007). www.arlington.org/cvb.php.

City of Dubuque. (2007). www.cityofdubuque.org/index.cfm?pageid=673.

City of Kirkwood. (2007). www.ci.kirkwood.mo.us/finance/0708budget%20info.htm#Sales%20Tax.

City of Madison Parks. (2007). www.ci.madison.wi.us/parks/aboutPark.html.

City of Norman. (2007). University North Park TIF project. www.ci.norman.ok.us/pdf_files/UnivNorthParkTIF.pdf.

Clawson Freeo, S.K. (2007). Crisis communication plan: A PR blueprint. http://newsplace.org/crisis.html.

Clear Creek Rafting Company. (2007). www.clearcreekrafting.com/trips.html.

Cohen, A. (2000). Torn apart: The rift widens between for-profit clubs and nonprofit centers. *Athletic Business, 10,* 51-56.

Collins, J. (2001). *Good to great.* New York: HarperCollins.

Conger, J.A., & Kanungo, R.N. (1998). *Charismatic leadership in organizations.* Thousand Oaks, CA: Sage.

Connecticut Department of Environmental Protection. (2007). http://dep.state.ct.us/rec/mission.htm.

Crainer, S. (2000). *The management century.* San Francisco: Jossey-Bass.

Craumer, M. (2001, March). The effective meeting: A checklist for success. *Harvard Management Communication Letter, 4*(3), 3-5.

Crompton, J.L. (1999). *Financing and acquiring park and recreation resources.* Champaign, IL: Human Kinetics.

Crompton, J.L., & Lamb, Jr., C.W. (1986). *Marketing government and social services.* New York: Wiley.

Crossley, J.C., Jamieson, L.M., & Brayley, R.E. (2001). *Introduction to commercial recreation and tourism: An entrepreneurial approach* (4th ed.). Champaign, IL: Sagamore.

Dagger Kayaks. (2007). www.dagger.com.

Dallas Parks and Recreation. (2007). www.dallasparks.org/facilities/facilitiesmain.aspx.

Dessler, G., Starke, F., and Cyr, D. (2001). *Management: Leading people and organizations in the 21st century.* Toronto: Prentice Hall.

DiGrino N., & Whitmore, S. (2005). Recreation program planning. In B. van der Smissen, M. Moiseichik, & V.J. Hartenburg (Eds.), *Management of park and recreation agencies* (pp. 127-157). Arlington, VA: National Recreation and Park Association.

Dropinski, C. (2007). Cost recovery in parks and recreation. *Illinois Parks and Recreation, 38*(5), 12-17.

Drucker, P.F. (1954). *The practice of management.* New York: Harper.

Drucker, P.F. (2001). *The essential Drucker: Selections from the management works of Peter F. Drucker.* New York: HarperBusiness.

Drucker, P.F. (2002). *The essential Drucker.* New York: HarperBusiness.

Dumler, M.P., & Skinner, S.J. (2005). *A primer for management.* Mason, OH: Southwestern.

Edginton, C.R., Hudson, S.D., & Lankford, S.V. (2001). *Managing recreation, parks, and leisure services: An introduction* (2nd ed.). Champaign, IL: Sagamore.

Ellard, A., Geisthardt, C., & Schilling, M. (2004). Child abuse prevention strategies in public recreation agencies in Michigan. *Journal of Park and Recreation Administration, 22*(1), 23-36.

Ewing, M.E., Gano-Overway, L.A., Branta, C.F., & Seefeldt, V.D. (2002). The role of sports in youth development. In M. Gatz, M.A. Messner, & S. Ball-Rokeach (Eds.), *Paradoxes of youth and sport* (pp. 31-48). Albany, NY: SUNY Press.

Farris, S. (2006, May). Ushering in the future: Advice on strategic medical technology planning. *Health Facilities Management Magazine,* 23-26.

Fayol, H. (1949). *General and industrial management.* London: Pitman Publishing Company.

Federal Tort Claims Act. (1946). 28 U.S.C. § 1346(b) and 28 U.S.C. § 2671-2680.

Ferguson, R.F., & Stoutland, S.E. (1999). Reconceiving the community development field. In R. Ferguson & W. Dickens (Eds.), *Urban problems and community development* (pp. 33-75). Washington, DC: Brookings Press.

Fiedler, F.E. (1971) *Leadership.* New York: General Learning Press.

Forest, K.K. (1999). Benefits-based management. www.lib.niu.edu/ipo/1999/ip990741.html.

Form 1023 Help. (2007). Comparison of 501(c) status. http://members.aol.com/irsform1023/misc/comp501s.html.

Fried, G., Shapiro, S., & DeSchriver, T.D. (2003). *Sport finance.* Champaign, IL: Human Kinetics.

Fullerton, H.N., & Toosi, M. (2001, November). Labor force protections to 2010: Steady growth and changing composition. *Monthly Labor Review,* 21-38.

Gardner, J.W. (1993). *On leadership.* New York: Free Press.

Gatta, J.L. (2003). *Mixed methodological survey research: A nested paradigm approach.* Unpublished doctoral dissertation, Loyola University, Chicago.

George, J.M., & Jones, G.R. (2002). *Organizational behavior* (3rd ed.). Upper Saddle River, NJ: Prentice Hall.

Gilbreth, F.B., & Gilbreth, L.M. (1916). *Fatigue study, the elimination of humanity's greatest unnecessary waste.* New York: Sturgis & Walton.

Gittell, J.H. (2000). Paradox of coordination and control. *California Management Review, 42*(3), 177-183.

Gladwell, N.J., Anderson, D.M., & Sellers, J.R. (2003). An examination of fiscal trends in public parks and recreation from 1986 to 2001: A case study of North Carolina. *Journal of Park and Recreation Administration, 21,* 104-116.

Glover, T.D. (1999). Municipal park and recreation agencies unite! A single case analysis of an intermunicipal partnership. *Journal of Park and Recreation Administration, 17*(1), 73-91.

Gonring, M.P. (1997). Global and local media relations. In C.L. Caywood, *The handbook of strategic public relations* (pp. 63-76). New York: McGraw-Hill.

Gray, D.P., & McEvoy, C.D. (2005). Sport marketing: Strategies and tactics. In B.L. Parkhouse (Ed.), *The management of sport: Its foundation and application* (4th ed., pp. 228-255). New York: McGraw-Hill.

Guba, E.G., & Lincoln, Y.S. (1989). *Fourth generation evaluation.* Newbury Park, CA: Sage.

Hall, M., Knighton, T., Reed, P., Bussiere, P., McRae, D., & Bowen, P. (1998). *Caring Canadians, involved Canadians: Highlights from the 1997 National Survey of Giving, Volunteering, and Participating.* Ottawa: Minister of Industry (Statistics Catalogue No. 71-542-XIE).

Hammersley, C.H., & Tynon, J.F. (1998). Job competencies of entry-level resort and commercial recreation professionals. *Journal of Applied Recreation Research, 23*(3), 225-241.

Harrah's Entertainment. (2007). www.harrahs.com/harrahs-corporate/careers-mission-vision.html.

Havitz, M.E., & Glover, T.D. (2001). *Financing and acquiring park and recreation resources: A Canadian supplement.* Champaign, IL: Human Kinetics.

Henderson, K.A., & Bialeschki, M.D. (2002). *Evaluating leisure services: Making enlightened decisions* (2nd ed.). State College, PA: Venture.

Hensley, S., Markham-Starr, S., Montague, E., & Hodgkinson, J. (2006). Public recreation. In Human Kinetics (Ed.), *Introduction to recreation and leisure* (pp. 109-142). Champaign, IL: Human Kinetics.

Herscovitch, L., & Meyer, J.P. (2002). Commitment to organizational change: Extension of a three-component model. *Journal of Applied Psychology 87*(3), 474.

Hersey, P., Blanchard, K.H., & Johnson, D.E. (2001). *Management of organizational behavior: Leading human resources* (8th ed.). Upper Saddle River, NJ: Prentice Hall.

Herzberg, F. (1966). *Work and the nature of man.* Oxford: World.

Herzberg, F., Mausner, B., & Snyderman, B.B. (1959). *The motivation to work.* New York: Wiley.

Holdnak, II, A., Mahoney, E.M., & Garges, J.R. (2005). Budgeting. In B. van der Smissen, M. Moiseichik, & V.J. Hartenburg (Eds.), *Management of park and recreation agencies* (2nd ed., pp. 537-591). Ashburn, VA: National Recreation and Park Association.

Howard County Museum. (2007). www.howardcountymuseum.org/museum/index.htm.

Howard, D.R., & Crompton, J.L. (1980). *Financing, managing, and marketing recreation and park resources.* Dubuque, IA: Wm. C. Brown.

Howard, D.R., & Crompton, J.L. (2005). *Financing sport* (2nd ed.). Morgantown, WV: Fitness Information Technology.

Hronek, B., & Spengler, J.O. (2007). *Legal liability in recreation, sports and tourism* (3rd ed.). Champaign, IL: Sagamore.

Hsu, C.H.C., & Powers, T. (2002). *Marketing hospitality* (3rd ed.). New York: Wiley.

Huebner, A.J., Walker, J.A., & McFarland, M. (2003). Staff development for the youth development professional: A critical framework for understanding the work. *Youth and Society, 35*(2), 204-225.

Humphreys, J.M. (2004). The multicultural economy 2004: America's minority buying power. *Georgia Business and Economic Conditions, 64*(3), 1-28.

Hurd, A.R. (2004). Competency development for board members in public parks and recreation agencies. *Journal of Park and Recreation Administration, 22,* 43-61.

Hurd, A.R. (2005). Competency development for entry-level public park and recreation professionals. *Journal of Park and Recreation Administration, 23,* 45-62.

Hurd, A.R., & McLean, D.D. (2004). An analysis of perceived competencies of CEOs in public parks and recreation agencies. *Managing Leisure, 9,* 96-110.

Indiana Fever. (2007). 2006 Indiana Fever ticket packages.

www.wnba.com/fever/tickets/2006_Fever_Ticket_Packages.html#Half%20Season%20Ticket.

Jackson, A. (2002, August). Taking the plunge: The conversion to multi-year budgeting. *Government Finance Review*, 24-27.

Jarvis, C. (2007). Fayol's functions and principles of management. www.bola.biz/competence/fayol.html.

Jensen, C.R., & Guthrie, S.P. (2006). *Outdoor recreation in America* (6th ed.). Champaign, IL: Human Kinetics.

Jones, C., & Hellmich, N. (2006, December 6). NYC bans trans fats in restaurants. *USA Today*. www.usatoday.com/news/health/2006-12-04-trans-fat-ban_x.htm.

Jones, G.R. (2004). *Organizational theory, design, and change* (4th ed.). Upper Saddle River, NJ: Prentice Hall.

Jordan, D.J. (2001). *Leadership in leisure services: Making a difference* (2nd ed.). State College, PA: Venture.

KaBOOM. (2007). www.kaboom.org/AboutUs/WhatIsKaBOOM/OurVisionandMission/tabid/108/Default.aspx.

Kaczynski, A.T., & Crompton, J.L. (2004). Development of a multidimensional scale for implementing positioning in public park and recreation agencies. *Journal of Park and Recreation Administration, 22*(2), 1-27.

Kaczynski, A.T., & Crompton, J.L. (2006). Financing priorities in local governments: Where do park and recreation services rank? *Journal of Park and Recreation Administration, 24*(1), 84-103.

Kaiser, R. (1986). *Liability and law in recreation, parks and sports*. Englewood Cliffs, NJ: Prentice Hall.

Keeton, W.P. (1984). *Prosser and Keeton on the law of torts* (5th ed.). St. Paul, MN: West.

Kelsey, C.W., Gray, H.R., & McLean, D.D. (1992). *The budget process in parks and recreation: A case study manual*. Reston, VA: American Alliance for Health, Physical Education, Recreation and Dance.

Knapp, J., & McLean, D. (2002). Help employees move to the top of your organization. *Parks and Recreation (Ashburn), 37*(8), 20-27.

Kohm, A., La Piana, D., & Gowdy, H. (2000). *Strategic restructuring: Findings from a study of integrations and alliances among non-profit social services and cultural organizations in the United States*. Chicago: Chapin Hall Center for Children, University of Chicago.

Kotler, P., Bowen, J., & Makens, J. (2006). *Marketing for hospitality and tourism* (4th ed.). Upper Saddle River, NJ: Prentice Hall.

Kouzes, J.M., & Posner, B.Z. (1987). *The leadership challenge: How to get extraordinary things done in organizations*. San Francisco: Jossey-Bass.

Kouzes, J.M., & Posner, B.Z. (1995). *The leadership challenge: How to keep getting extraordinary things done in organizations* (2nd ed). San Francisco: Jossey-Bass.

Kouzes, J.M., & Posner, B.Z. (2002). *The leadership challenge* (3rd ed.). San Francisco: Jossey-Bass.

Krattenmaker, T. (2003, May). How to make every meeting matter. *Harvard Management Communication Letter, 6*(5), 3-5.

Krause, R.G., & Curtis, J.E. (2000). *Creative management in recreation, parks, and leisure services* (6th ed.). Boston: McGraw-Hill.

Lee, M.E., & Driver, B.L. (1992). Benefits-based management: A new paradigm for managing amenity resources. Paper presented at the Second Canada/U.S. Workshop on Visitor Management in Parks, Forests, and Protected Areas, May 13-15, 1992, University of Wisconsin at Madison.

Lipton, P. (1993). *Inference to the best explanation*. New York: Routledge.

Locke, E.A. (1968). Toward a theory of task motivation and incentives. *Organizational Behavior and Human Performance, 3*(2), 157-189.

Loehr, J.E., & Schwartz, T. (2001, October 1). The making of a corporate athlete. *Harvard Business Review*.

Lovelock, C. (2001). *Services marketing* (4th ed.). Upper Saddle River, NJ: Prentice Hall.

March of Dimes. (2007). "SMART" objectives. www.marchofdimes.com/files/SMART_objectives.pdf.

Maslow, A.H. (1954). *Motivation and personality*. New York: Harper & Row.

Mayers, R.S. (2004). *Financial management for nonprofit human service organizations* (2nd ed.). Springfield, IL: Charles C. Thomas.

Mayo, E. (1933). *The human problems of industrial civilization*. New York: Macmillan.

McCarville, R.E. (2002). *Improving leisure services through marketing action*. Champaign, IL: Sagamore.

McClelland, D.C. (1961). *The achieving society*. Princeton, NJ: Van Nostrand.

McGregor, D. (1960). *The human side of enterprise*. New York: McGraw-Hill.

McLean, D.D. (2006). *2005 annual information exchange*. Terre Haute, IN: Center for State Park Research at Indiana State University.

McLean, D.D., Bannon, J.J., & Gray, H.R. (1999). *Leisure resources: Its comprehensive planning* (2nd ed.). Champaign, IL: Sagamore.

McLean, D.D., Hurd, A., & Brattain Rogers, N. (2008). *Krause's leisure in modern society* (8th ed.). Boston: Jones and Bartlett.

McLean, D.D., Hurd, A.R., & Jensen, R.R. (2005). Using Q-methodology in competency development for CEOs in public parks and recreation. *Managing Leisure, 10,* 156-165.

Meyer, J.P., & Allen, N.J. (1997). *Commitment in the workplace: Theory, research and application*. Thousand Oaks, CA: Sage.

Meyer, J.P., Becker, T.E., & Vandenberghe, C. (2004). Employee commitment and motivation: A conceptual analysis and integrative model. *Journal of Applied Psychology, 89*(6), 991.

Miller, D.C. (1991). *Handbook of research design and social measurement* (5th ed.). Newbury Park, CA: Sage.

Mintzberg, H. (1979). *The structuring of organizations.* Upper Saddle River, NJ: Prentice Hall.

Moiseichik, M., & Bodey, K. (2005). Legal authority and jurisdiction. In B. van der Smissen, M. Moiseichik, & V.J. Hartenburg (Eds.), *Management of park and recreation agencies* (2nd ed., pp. 25-60). Ashburn, VA: National Recreation and Park Association.

Montgomery County Friends of Recreation. (2007). www.montgomerycountymd.gov/rectmpl.asp?url=/content/rec/for.asp.

Mull, R., Bayless, K., & Jamieson, L. (2005). *Recreational sport management.* Champaign, IL: Human Kinetics.

Mullins, B.J., Hardy, S., & Sutton, W.A. (2000). *Sport marketing* (2nd ed.). Champaign, IL: Human Kinetics.

National Advisory Council on State and Local Budgeting (NACSLB). (1999). *Recommended budget practices: A framework for improved state and local government budgeting.* Chicago: Government Finance Officers Association.

National Environmental Policy Act. (1969). 42 U.S.C. 4321-4370.

National Park Service (NPS). (2007). Federal budget process. www.nps.gov/applications/budget2/fedbud.htm.

National Park Service Organic Act. (1916). 16 USC 1 et seq. (1988), August 25, 1916.

National Recreation and Park Association (NRPA). (2006). Recommended guidelines for credentialing volunteers. www.nrpa.org/content/default.aspx?documentId=4458.

National Recreation and Park Association (NRPA). (2007a). *2007 annual check-up.* Arlington, VA: Author.

National Recreation and Park Association (NRPA). (2007b). *Playground safety certification.* Retrieved Dec. 12, 2007, from www.nrpa.org/content/default.aspx?documentId=5129.

NetMBA. (2007). Frederick Taylor and scientific management. www.netmba.com/mgmt/scientific/.

Newfoundland and Labrador Tourism Marketing Council. (2007). Strategic marketing plan, 2004-2008. www.tcr.gov.nl.ca/tcr/nltmc/strtmarketingplan20042008.pdf.

North Carolina Department of Transportation. (2007). https://edmv-sp.dot.state.nc.us/sp/demo/special_viewer_specialinterest.htm.

Northstar-at-Tahoe Resort. (2007). Northstar-at-Tahoe golf tee times. www.northstarattahoe.com/info/summer/golf_tee_times.asp.

Occupational Health and Safety Act. (1970). OSHA, 29 U.S.C. chap 15.

Oklahoma City Zoological Park and Botanical Garden. (2007). www.okczoo.com/abou.htm.

Ontario Ministry of Tourism. (2007). www.tourism.gov.on.ca.

OSD Comptroller iCenter. (2007). Activity-based costing: Accounting for operational readiness. www.dod.mil/comptroller/icenter/learn/abconcept.pdf.

Oss, M.E. (2004). Eight strategies for human resources development. *Behavioral Health Management, 2,* 22-26.

Ostergren, D., Solop, F.I., & Hagen, K.K. (2005). National Park Service fees: Value for the money or a barrier to visitation? *Journal of Park and Recreation Administration, 23*(1), 18-36.

O'Sullivan, E.L. (1991). *Marketing for parks, recreation and leisure.* State College, PA: Venture.

Pascale, R.T., & Athos, A.G. (1981). *The art of Japanese management: Applications for American executives.* New York: Simon & Schuster.

Patagonia. (2007a). Company information: Our reason for being. www.patagonia.com/web/us/contribution/patagonia.go?assetid=2047.

Patagonia. (2007b). Environmentalism: What we do. www.patagonia.com/web/us/patagonia.go?assetid=2329.

Patton, M.Q. (2001). *Qualitative research and evaluation methods.* Newbury Park, CA: Sage.

Paul, J.P., Robertson, K.B., & Herzberg, F. (1969). Job enrichment pays off. *Harvard Business Review, 47*(2), 61-78.

PeyBack Foundation. (2007). www.peytonmanning.com/peyback/grantguidelines.html.

Pfeffer, J. (2004). Managers, not MBAs: A hard look at the soft practice of managing and management development. *Administrative Science Quarterly, 49*(3), 476.

Pfeffer, J., & Veiga, J.F. (1999). Putting people first for organizational success. *Academy of Management Executive, 13*(2), 37.

Pointer, D.D., & Orlikoff, J.E. (2002). *The higher performance board: Principles of nonprofit organization governance.* New York: Jossey-Bass.

Poznak Law Firm, Ltd. (2007). Approaches to ethical decision making. www.poznaklaw.com/articles/bizethics.htm.

Prahalad, C.K., & Hamel, G. (1990, May/June). The core competence of the corporation. *Harvard Business Review, 68*(3), 79-91.

Rallis, S.F., & Rossman, G.B. (2003). Mixed methods in evaluation contexts: A pragmatic framework. In A. Tashakkori & C. Teddlie (Eds.), *Handbook of mixed methods in social and behavioral research* (pp. 491-512). Thousand Oaks, CA: Sage.

REI Community Grants. (2007). www.rei.com/email/articles/gm0331_parks.html?cm_re=b*b*grants&vcat=REI_HP_L4.

Restatement of the Law of Torts, 2d. (1965). Sec. 329-332. Washington, DC: American Law Institute.

Reynoso, J., & Moores, B. (1995). Towards the measurement of internal service quality. *International Journal of Service Industry Management, 6*(3), 64.

Robbins, S.P. (1997). *Managing today.* Upper Saddle River, NJ: Prentice Hall.

Rossman, J.R., & Schlatter, B.E. (2003). *Recreation programming: Designing leisure experiences* (4th ed.). Champaign, IL: Sagamore.

Rowntree, D. (2004). *Statistics without tears: A primer for non-mathematicians.* Toronto: Pearson/Allyn & Bacon.

Rubin, D.B. (1987). *Multiple imputation for nonresponse in survey.* New York: John Wiley.

Saint Paul Parks and Recreation. (2007). Saint Paul Parks and Recreation plan and five-year strategic action plan. www.stpaul.gov/depts/parks/administration/comp-plan.html.

San Francisco Parks Trust. (2007). www.sfpt.org.

Saskatchewan Tourism, Parks, Culture, and Sport. (2007). www.cyr.gov.sk.ca.

Sawyer, T.H., Hypes, M., & Hypes, J. (2004). *Financing the sport enterprise.* Champaign, IL: Sagamore.

Schein, E.H. (2004). *Organizational culture and leadership* (3rd ed.). New York: Jossey-Bass.

Schmitt, F.F. (1995). *Truth: A primer.* Boulder, CO: Westview.

SCORE. (2007a). Business plan for a start-up business. www.score.org/downloads/Business%20Plan%20for%20a%20Startup%20Business_July.doc.

SCORE. (2007b). www.score.org/explore_score.html.

Searle, M.S., & Brayley, R.E. (2000). *Leisure services in Canada: An introduction* (2nd ed.). State College, PA: Venture.

Seattle Parks and Recreation. (2007). *Annual report: 2005.* www.seattle.gov/parks/Publications/2005AnnualReport.pdf.

Sellers, J.R., Gladwell, N.J., & Pope, M.S. (2005). Financial management. In B. van der Smissen, M. Moiseichik, & V.J. Hartenburg (Eds.), *Management of park and recreation agencies* (2nd ed., pp. 493-536). Ashburn, VA: National Recreation and Park Association.

Senge, P.M. (1994). *The fifth discipline: The art and practices of the learning organization.* New York: Currency Doubleday.

Senge, P.M. (2006). *The fifth discipline: The art and practice of the learning organization* (2nd ed.). New York: Currency Doubleday.

Silverberg, K.E., Marshall, E.K., & Ellis, G.D. (2001). Measuring job satisfaction of volunteers in public parks and recreation. *Journal of Park and Recreation Administration, 19*(1), 79-92.

Smale, B.J.A., & Frisby, W. (1992). Managerial work activities and perceived competencies of municipal recreation managers. *Journal of Park and Recreation Administration, 10*(4), 81-108.

Small Business BC. (2008). www.smallbusinessbc.ca.

South Carolina Department of Parks, Recreation and Tourism. (2007). SCPRT marketing plan, FY 2005-06. www.scprt.com/files/Marketing%20Partners/Marketing%20Plan%20FY%2005-06%20no%20budget2.doc.

Spengler, J.O., Connaughton, D.P., & Pittman, A. (2006). *Risk management in sport and recreation.* Champaign, IL: Human Kinetics.

Spengler, J.O., & Siehl, G. (1988). *Manassas National Battlefield Park: The battle continues.* Congressional Research Service, Report for Congress.

Stadiums of the NFL. (2007). Lucas Oil Stadium. www.stadiumsofnfl.com/future/LucasOilStadium.htm.

Statistics Canada. (2006). Caring Canadians, involved Canadians: Highlights from the 2004 Canadian survey of giving, volunteering and participating. www.givingandvolunteering.ca/pdf/CSGVP_Highlights_2004_en.pdf.

Statistics Canada. (2007a). Canada e-book. www43.statcan.ca/02/02_000_e.htm.

Statistics Canada. (2007b). Visible minority. www.statcan.ca/english/concepts/definitions/vis-minorit.htm.

Steve Nash Foundation. (2007). www.stevenash.org.

Stogdill, R.M. (1974). *Handbook of leadership: A survey of the literature.* New York: Free Press.

Strigas, A. (2006, April). Making the most of volunteers. *Parks and Recreation,* 26-29.

Tashakkori, A., & Teddlie, C. (Eds.). (2003). *Handbook of mixed methods in social and behavioral research.* Thousand Oaks, CA: Sage.

Taylor, F.W. (1911). *The principles of scientific management.* New York: Harper.

Tew, P.F, Havitz, M.E., & McCarville, R.E. (1999). The role of marketing in municipal recreation programming decisions: A challenge to conventional wisdom. *Journal of Park and Recreation Administration, 17*(1), 1-20.

Thomas, E.C. (2002, January-March). The challenge of cutback management. *Public Policy and Practice, 1*(2), 5-8.

Toronto. (2007). Toronto's racial diversity. www.toronto.ca/toronto_facts/diversity.htm.

Toronto Parks, Forestry, and Recreation. (2007). www.toronto.ca/parks.

Town of Bedford. (2007). www.town.bedford.ma.us/conservation/open_space.html#anchor.osrp.goals.

Tynan, K. (2005). Budget and performance integration innovation at Fish and Wildlife Service (FWS): FY 2007 budget planning exercise for FWS senior managers. Washington, DC: U.S. Fish and Wildlife Service. www.fws.gov/planning/Documents/FY07%20Budget%20Exercise.pdf.

United Way of America. (1996). *Measuring program outcomes: A practical approach.* Alexandria, VA: United Way of America.

University of Miami. (2007). Business services—policies and procedures. www.miami.edu/policies_procedures/Purchasing/PDF-Version/BSJ-015.pdf.

U.S. Army Garrison–Detroit Aresenal Selfridge. (2007). www.selfridgemwr.com/home/mission.htm.

U.S. Bureau of Labor Statistics. (2006). *Volunteering in the United States, 2006*. Washington, DC: U.S. Government Printing Office.

U.S. Bureau of the Census. (1997). 1992 census of governments (vol. 4, no. 2). www.census.gov/prod/3/98pubs/gc924-2.pdf.

U.S. Census Bureau. (2005a). *1992 Government finance and employment classification manual*. www.census.gov/govs/www/class.html.

U.S. Census Bureau. (2005b). Computer and Internet use in the United States: 2003. www.census.gov/prod/2005pubs/p23-208.pdf.

U.S. Census Bureau. (2006). State and county quick facts. http://quickfacts.census.gov/qfd/.

U.S. Department of Defense. (2007). Performance budgeting. www.dod.mil/comptroller/icenter/budget/perfbudg.htm.

U.S. Department of Education. (2006). Toward a new golden age in American education—How the internet, the law and today's students are revolutionizing expectations. www.ed.gov/about/offices/list/os/technology/plan/2004/edlite-xplan-sdm.html.

U.S. Office of Personnel Management. (2007). Qualification standards for general schedule positions. www.opm.gov/qualifications/SEC-II/s2-c-d.asp.

Vancouver Parks and Recreation. (2007). http://vancouver.ca/Parks/board/2006/060116/advanceapproval20061.pdf.

Ventana Inn. (2007). www.ventanainn.com.

Virginia Beach Parks and Recreation Department. (2007). *2006-2007 annual report*. Virginia Beach, VA: City of Virginia Beach. www.vbgov.com/file_source/dept/parks/Document/ADM_Annual_Report.pdf.

Volunteer Protection Act. (1997). Public Law No: 105-19.

Vroom, V.H. (1964). *Work and motivation*. New York: Wiley.

Ward, R.D. (2000). *Improving corporate boards: The boardroom insider guidebook*. New York: Wiley.

Wayne County, PA. (2007). www.co.wayne.pa.us/?pageid=13.

Wedel, M. (2001, Winter). Is segmentation history? *Marketing Research, 27-29.*

White Hutchison Leisure Learning Group. (2005). Reinventing bowling. www.whitehutchinson.com/news/lenews/2005_05.shtml#4.

Wilderness Act. (1964). Public Law 88-577, 78 Stat. 890, 16 U.S.C. 1131-1136.

Wolter, S.A. (1999). Master planning leisure resources. In D.D. McLean, J.J. Brannon, & H.R. Gray (Eds.), *Leisure resources: Its comprehensive planning* (2nd ed., pp. 153-209). Champaign, IL: Sagamore.

YMCA of Metropolitan Dallas. (2007). Healthy choices healthy futures: YMCA of Metropolitan Dallas 2006 annual report. Dallas, TX: YMCA of Metropolitan Dallas. www.ymcadallas.org/images/upload/YMCA%20Annual%20Report%2006.pdf.pdf.

Yoder, D.G., & Ham, L.L. (2004). Partnerships. In B. van der Smissen, M. Moiseichik, & V.J. Hartenburg (Eds.), *Management of park and recreation agencies* (pp. 85-101). Reston, VA: National Recreation and Park Association.

Index

Note: The italicized *f* and *t* following page numbers refer to figures and tables, respectively.

About the Authors

Amy R. Hurd, PhD, is an associate professor in the School of Kinesiology and Recreation at Illinois State University in Normal, where she teaches graduate and undergraduate courses in recreation management, leadership, and marketing. Hurd received her PhD in leisure behavior from Indiana University in 2001.

Hurd has worked in public-sector parks and recreation as a marketing director for the Champaign Park District in Champaign, Illinois. She has also served on the National Recreation and Park Association's American Park and Recreation Society board. She has coauthored *Kraus' Recreation and Leisure in Modern Society* and the *Official Study Guide for the Certified Park and Recreation Professional Examination*.

In her free time, Hurd enjoys biking, kayaking, and hiking. She lives in Normal, Illinois.

Robert J. Barcelona, PhD, is an assistant professor in the department of parks, recreation, and tourism management at Clemson University and teaches courses in the youth development leadership program. Barcelona received his doctorate from Indiana University after working professionally in the field of campus recreation, specifically in intramural sports and sport club administration. He has also worked with numerous recreation and sport organizations in both programming and research efforts. His research has been published in several refereed, professional journals, and he is the author of several book chapters related to recreation and sport management.

Barcelona has presented locally, regionally, and nationally for associations such as the National Intramural-Recreational Sports Association, the NOrth American Society for Sport Management, the Sport Marketing Association, and the National Recreation and Parks Association.

John T. Meldrum, PhD, is an assistant professor in the School of Exercise Science, Physical and Health Education at the University of Victoria in British Columbia, Canada. Meldrum received his MBA in management (1995) from the University of Manitoba in Winnipeg, Canada, and his doctoral degree in recreation and leisure studies (2007) from the University of Waterloo in Ontario, Canada.

Meldrum has worked in sport and recreation settings for over a decade. Before beginning his career in academia, he was the CEO of a nonprofit organization and a consultant to recreation agencies. He is a member of the National Park and Recreation Association and the Canadian Park and Recreation Association.

Meldrum and his wife, Mary, live in Victoria. In his free time, Meldrum enjoys cycling, playing tennis, and visiting local markets.